DATE DUE

FEB 1 0 2002			

DEMCO 38-297

FUNDAMENTALS OF
VOICE & DICTION

EIGHTH EDITION

FUNDAMENTALS OF
VOICE & DICTION

LYLE V. MAYER
Incarnate Word College
San Antonio, Texas

wcb
Wm. C. Brown Publishers
Dubuque, Iowa

Book Team

Editor *Stan Stoga*
Developmental Editor *Michael Lange*
Designer *K. Wayne Harms*
Production Editor *Harry Halloran*
Visuals Processor *Renée Pins*
Marketing Manager *Kathy Law Laube*

wcb group

Chairman of the Board *Wm. C. Brown*
President and Chief Executive Officer *Mark C. Falb*

wcb

Wm. C. Brown Publishers, College Division

President *G. Franklin Lewis*
Vice President, Editor-in-Chief *George Wm. Bergquist*
Vice President, Director of Production *Beverly Kolz*
National Sales Manager *Bob McLaughlin*
Director of Marketing *Thomas E. Doran*
Marketing Information Systems Manager *Craig S. Marty*
Executive Editor *John Woods*
Manager of Design *Marilyn A. Phelps*
Production Editorial Manager *Colleen A. Yonda*
Photo Research Manager *Faye M. Schilling*

Cover illustration by ArtNET

The credits section for this book begins on page 263, and is considered an extension of the copyright page.

Library of Congress Catalog Card Number: 87–70744

ISBN 0–697–04283–9

Printed in the United States of America by Wm. C. Brown Publishers
2460 Kerper Boulevard, Dubuque, IA 52001

10 9 8 7 6 5 4

BRIEF CONTENTS

CONTENTS

PREFACE

A text should be judged by the results it gets, and *Fundamentals of Voice and Diction,* in the thirty-five years since the first edition, has worked successfully for an astonishing number of students and teachers.

The book is still aimed primarily at students who want to improve their speaking voices. It's a basic book, ideally suited to a one-semester course. It can be used by the nonspecialist for whom a voice and diction course might be the only contact with the speech communication area. It can be used as readily by the specialist—by the communication arts or drama major. Whatever the background of the student, the book's practical, nontechnical approach sets specific goals and targets for anyone interested in skills improvement—in developing effective voice and speech. The student and the instructor are told succinctly and in comprehensible language how to reach those goals and hit the targets.

THE EIGHTH EDITION

Chapter 1, "A Preview," addresses the not infrequently asked questions, "Why should *I* take a course in voice and diction? What's in it for me? What's the payoff?" It also analyzes the ingredients of effective voice and speech.

Chapter 2, "Sound Off! The Beginnings of Voice," discusses good breathing habits and the mechanics and production of sound.

Chapter 3, "Put Your Best Voice Forward!—Quality," details how a pleasant quality is developed, and it takes a head-on approach toward such problems as breathiness, harshness, nasality, throatiness, and hoarseness.

Chapter 4, "Conserve Your Consonants—Articulation," describes the correct manner of producing all English consonants, and achieving clear, distinct and intelligible speech.

Chapter 5, "Varnish Your Vowels—Discipline Your Diphthongs—Articulation," concentrates on the correct production of all English vowels and diphthongs.

Chapter 6, "Speak Up! Loudness," focuses on "getting the voice across" with energetic projection while avoiding vocal abuse.

Chapter 7, "Be Varied and Vivid—Expressiveness," emphasizes acquiring a well-pitched and varied voice and speaking with animation and spontaneity.

Appendix A looks at pronunciation (including three hundred commonly mispronounced words), sound symbols, and correct use of the dictionary.

Appendix B contains voice and speech analysis charts. The instructor may use them to evaluate students; students may appraise themselves or outside speakers.

WHAT'S MENDED OR IMPROVED?

Drill material and exercises, as always, have been updated, augmented, and enlivened. There are numerous colorful and relevant quotations from contemporary celebrities, ranging from Olympic champions to rock stars and from movie and TV personalities to politicians.

Drill material has been kept lively—even fun. In my thirty-five plus years of teaching I've rarely found a student who resisted humor in drill material, but I've known many who dislike intensely the dull and unimaginative material found in too many voice and diction textbooks.

Many of the exercises have been recycled, and there are new approaches to old material or exercises. Every exercise in the book, in one form or another, has been tested for more than a third of a century. They've been successful with more than five thousand human beings—a majority of them college students—but also including major generals, grandmothers, yuppies and groupies.

The lengthy *Articulation* chapter of the seventh edition has been divided into two chapters—one dealing with consonants, the other with vowels and diphthongs.

Suggested Checklists for specific assignments and the Voice and Speech Analysis charts have been condensed, and made more viable and accessible.

Theoretical material is presented in a more concise and less verbose manner, technical jargon has been toned down, and the discussions made more readable. All in all, the entire book has been "tightened." Repetitiousness and gristle have been eliminated. The book has, I hope, a leaner look.

The pronunciation lists in Appendix A have been revised; new words are included among the three hundred commonly mispronounced words. For those preferring shorter lists, the one hundred and fifty most commonly mispronounced words are marked with asterisks.

WHAT'S BEEN ADDED?

- New exercises and material for quality, articulation, relaxation, loudness, and expressiveness.
- A brief discussion of the nonvocal aspects of delivery: posture, eye contact, and bodily activity.

TO THE INSTRUCTOR

There is much more in this book than any class will be able to use. I've never covered all twenty-one assignments, nor have I ever had enough time to drill students in all 257 exercises. The instructor should take advantage of the flexibility of the book and *assign material on the basis of individual needs and differences.*

I've used every possible combination of assignments. Here is a basic, suggested outline, and it contains the most essential of the twenty-one assignments.

A. Choose one or more, as needed, from the following assignments: 2, 3, 4, 5, or 6.
B. Assignment 7.
C. Choose one or more, as needed, from the following assignments: 8, 9, 10, 11, 12, or 13.
D. Assignment 14 or 15.
E. Choose one or more, as needed, from the following assignments: 16, 17, 18, 19, or 20.
F. Assignment 21.

ACKNOWLEDGMENTS

Grateful acknowledgment is due to those anonymous authors whose works have been quoted. In a majority of cases, unsuccessful attempts have been made to trace the holder of the copyright.

Above all, a hearty "thank you" is extended to the dozens of students who, over the years, have brought into class for their oral assignments unusually interesting and colorful material. Some of this is original; some of it will have a familiar ring: old proverbs, axioms, and famous quotes from dead but not forgotten authors. I have made use of this material extensively.

I'll conclude by stealing from myself. There is a paragraph from the preface of several earlier editions that I wish to repeat.

Some time ago, a distinguished professor addressed a conference of educators. He caused some academic eyebrows to vault upward when he commented, "It's about time that writers of textbooks write for their students and stop writing to impress their colleagues."

That statement has also guided me in writing the eighth edition of my book.

FRIEND AND FOE:
Like to make some comments or suggestions—friendly or otherwise? Do you have some tips for me? Why not share them? (Already I'm thinking of the ninth edition . . . and the tenth!)
Write to me. I answer all letters.

Lyle V. Mayer
8800 Starcrest Drive; #206
San Antonio, TX 78217

A PREVIEW

WOULD YOU BELIEVE THAT

. . . People who have poor speaking voices—the kind that set your teeth on edge—are almost always unaware of this? We are our most enchanted listeners, and it's human nature for each of us to believe that nobody speaks as well as we do.

. . . You don't have to yell to lose your voice? If you're a telephone addict and have a tendency to cradle the phone between your shoulder and neck as you're talking, you can easily strain your voice.

. . . Tongue twisters, once regarded as children's games, are making a comeback? Christopher Reeves, who prefers acting in plays to films, always warms up before going on stage with: "Twixt Trent and Tweed. Gig-whip. Gig-whip. Gig-whip." Simple? Try them.

. . . Being tall, strong, and well-proportioned doesn't necessarily guarantee you a deep, rich, or booming voice? Tom Selleck, popular television star, confesses: "I don't have a six-foot-four voice."

THE COURSE

If you decide to buy a new car, you must be prepared to invest quite a bit of money. Generally, before you close the deal, you listen to the salesperson at some length. This individual gives you a sales talk and spends quite a bit of time not only telling you about the outstanding features of the product, but also telling you why you should own it. If you're a good buyer, you'll ask questions. If the salesperson is good at his job, he'll expect you to ask questions. You're tying up a substantial amount of money, and you have a right to know all about the product.

If you're reading this page, it probably means just one thing: you're enrolled in some kind of a course in voice and speech improvement. Perhaps you've elected the course; perhaps you're required to take it. In either case, this course—like a new car—represents a substantial investment on your part of not only money, but also of time. Your very first question might well be, "What am I getting into?" or "What can I expect to get out of a course such as this?" I've jumped the gun in anticipating a few of your questions and have tried to provide a few answers.

What is a course in voice and diction?

A course in voice and diction deals with talking. It doesn't concern itself so much with *what* you talk about, but *how* you talk. Do you realize how much talking you do? About 30,000 words a day! That's equivalent to half a dozen books a week. In general, do the people you talk to daily react favorably to your voice? Can they understand you easily? Can they hear you? Do they find the sound of your voice pleasant and agreeable? Do they find you animated and interesting to listen to?

Another way of answering the main question is by telling you what this kind of course is *not*. It isn't an arty course. It isn't going to make you so different that you'll stand out like a sore thumb. It won't make your speech elegant. It isn't a course in how to read poetry, how to be an actor, or how to be an announcer.

Do I really need a course in voice and diction?

The chances are that you'll profit from such a course. Most people will. Here are some interesting but alarming examples that'll explain why.

Every spring, many companies and industries send representatives to college campuses to interview prospective employees. Five large state universities and ten smaller private colleges recently asked various firms to state their reasons for not hiring the students they had rejected. In approximately two-thirds of the cases, the reason given was that the job seeker did not speak effectively during the interview. A General Motors vice president stated in a letter to me:

> I hire, fire, and promote people, and I find it quite appalling that the reasons I don't hire too many of them in the first place is not so much *what* they say during the interview as *how* they say it. I have very little time for mumblers—those with a mouthful of mush and a dumpling in the throat. And then there are the ones who come in with the Minnie or Mickey Mouse voices—so weak and thin that, even though I sit about 4 feet from them, I can't hear half of what they say (and my doctor tells me I have 20–20 hearing). Maybe worst of all is the hopeful young person with the harsh, raw, and grating voice. It is like running your fingernails up and down the blackboard; it sets your teeth on edge.

Speech communication instructors contact and listen to many students each year. Over a period of years, the total figure may run into the hundreds. Most speech teachers agree that at least two-thirds of their students have faults of voice or diction and that these students could benefit from a course in voice and speech improvement.

What about the postcollege years? You may spend approximately 5 percent or less of your life in college before you enter the professional world. Poor speech habits will definitely not increase your chances for success and advancement in your chosen occupation.

Listen to Dr. Arnold Aronson, head speech pathologist at the Mayo Clinic: "The higher one ascends the socioeconomic scale, the greater the emphasis placed on pleasant, effective voices. With few exceptions, the greater the dependence on voice for occupational and social gratification, the more devastating the effects of a voice (or speech) disorder in a person."

I taught in a midwestern college for twenty-five years. We kept careful track of dozens of job hunting graduates. This we learned: students who had participated in dramatics and debate and who had taken one or more public speaking or voice and diction courses land jobs much faster than did other students. Many colleges have done follow-up surveys and have found the same results.

The U.S. Department of Labor, Washington, D.C., says bluntly that for eight out of ten jobs, you have to be able to talk. Carhop or carpenter, data processor or doctor, nurse or nuclear physicist, lawyer or librarian, teacher or tambourine player, actor or archbishop, you had better plan to do a lot of talking—more than eleven million words a year!

Recently, a woman was hired by an employment agency in a large western city. Every day she called as many as 150 corporations, firms, or small businesses to seek job listings. She discovered that approximately one-third of the receptionists or switchboard operators—those who provide the first business contact with a company—had unpleasant vocal traits or were totally unintelligible and mangled the names of the companies who paid their salaries. *Gunnery War Ickle Armen,* she learned, was *Montgomery Ward Optical Department.* The *Oh Noy Lassner Vision* was discovered to be *Owens-Illinois Glass Container Division.* These same Sloppy Joes and Josephines pepper their business dialogue with such gems as, "Gimme yer name agin." and "Woncha hang on a mint?"

It makes no difference whether one is executive vice president, personnel director, or custodian of a company. Sloppy speech or an unattractive voice, heard via telephone or face-to-face, turns off potential customers.

How a person says something rather than *what* the person says forms a lasting and almost permanent impression. Your voice is the sharp cutting edge of your personality. First impressions, not to mention second and third, *do* count! And have you noticed something? Even though you may be wrong, it's difficult to change your opinion.

Careless, mush-mouthed speech and unpleasant voices are bad enough, but they don't give the whole picture. More and more citizens—and this certainly includes college students—take an active part in campus or local politics or other community affairs. There are altogether too many of these individuals who insist on making public comments or speeches and who simply can't be heard. Microphones and P.A. systems aren't always available. Now and then a few individuals turn out to be mike-shy and are greeted with a chorus of "Louder! Louder! We can't hear you!" from their would-be listeners. Many individuals with vocal mufflers show up in classrooms, too.

We all want friends. We all want to be liked. We all want social approval. But many people persist in thinking that an unpleasant speaking voice always signifies a disagreeable personality. A shrill, strident, grating voice, for example, is supposed to belong to an individual who is tense or neurotic—a person to be avoided. A weak or too-soft speaking voice suggests that its owner has a cotton candy personality and is completely lacking in strength of character and guts. Such stereotypes are not always fair, of course, but nevertheless our listeners often jump to hasty conclusions about our personalities on the basis of listening to our speech for only a few minutes. Agreeable speech habits obviously increase our chances of social and professional success.

The popular newspaper column *Miss Manners* is the work of Judith Martin, a funny and charming lady who has much to say about correct etiquette and behavior. Says she: "If you are single, your speech may decide whether you will ever marry. If you are married, your speech may decide whether you stay that way." Miss Manners may be putting us on a bit, but her statement is worth pondering.

A prominent Beverly Hills, California, speech and communication specialist has decided that the way we talk is actually of far greater importance than the way we look. Dr. Lillian Glass conducted an interesting study. The results are startling.

She selected two groups of people, ten people to a group. Each of the groups was to be judged, although the individuals being judged were not told how and why they were being judged. One group consisted of people who were considered to be relatively good-looking but who had poor speaking voices—abrasive or nasal. This group was also guilty of sloppy articulation. The jury, a group of volunteers, rated the group unattractive.

The same jury rated the other group, consisting of people who were average looking but who had melodious voices and clean-as-a-whistle articulation as relatively attractive. Beauty, it seems, is not necessarily in the eye of the onlooker. Most of it is in the ear of the listener.

After all, I've been talking for eighteen years, more or less. If there's something wrong with the way I talk, why haven't I found out about it before now?

The truth of the matter is that you've been told quite a few things about your talking. Your parents started giving you advice when you were a year old: "Speak up!" "Don't mumble!" "Don't talk so fast." "Sh-h-h-h!" "Don't talk with your mouth full!" Like a lot of other parental advice, it may have gone quite unheeded, maybe because you heard it so often. And you probably reacted the same way toward the advice of your teachers.

You should also remember that your parents, siblings, friends, or spouses hear you a great deal. They become accustomed to the way you speak. You may be a terrible mumbler. You may have clogged speech, a galling, whiny or one-half decibel voice. The people closest to you, however, like you in spite of these faults. As far as your friends are concerned, they wouldn't be your friends if they continually harped at you about your faults.

Popular magazines bulge with advertisements that warn us about body odor, morning-after breath, gray teeth, zits, and dandruff. But bad speech habits? As the old advertisement says, "Even your best friend won't tell you."

Maybe my voice isn't as good as it should be, but I've been communicating successfully with other people for quite a few years. What's also important: I can certainly hear myself when I talk. Doesn't that count for something?

Robert Burns in his wise little poem "To a Louse" wrote this:

Oh, would some power the gift give us,
To see ourselves as others see us!

Have you seen yourself in home movies? Were you startled or embarrassed? You didn't realize that you walked, gestured, postured, or arched your eyebrows in quite the way the screen so realistically insists.

The first time you hear a recording of your voice may be almost as great a shock. "That can't be me!" you say. "Do I really sound like an eighth grader?" "I don't sound like *that!*" Indeed, you don't sound like *that*—at least, not to yourself. When you're speaking in a conversational situation, or even when you're speaking in front of the class, how *do* you hear yourself? Other people can hear you only via sound waves that reach their outer ears. To them, your voice is entirely airborne. You hear yourself partly by the same waves, but don't forget that your voice is also amplified by the bones in your skull. And you are, of course, much closer to the sound of your own voice than anyone else. Furthermore, not only are you used to the sound of your voice, you're fully aware of what you're thinking, so that as a rule you give little thought to how you sound as you speak.

The sad fact remains: you *do* sound like that!

This course will help you to cultivate an educated ear, an ear that not only listens to, but hears critically, the world of sounds—speech or otherwise—around you. In the process of accomplishing this, you will become a far better critic of your own voice.

Why is it that some people are born with good voices?

Michelangelo wasn't born a great sculptor, Beethoven wasn't born a great composer, Meryl Streep wasn't born a fine actress, Boris Becker wasn't born a remarkable tennis player, and Linda Ronstadt wasn't born a delightful song stylist. These people plodded and struggled for some years before they hit the jackpot. As the wheezy old saying goes, "Genius is 99 percent perspiration and 1 percent inspiration." The percentage is probably exaggerated, but it's safe to say that very few people are born with great speaking voices. Even these people, however, can improve their natural gifts with proper training. Nobody ever does his best. That's why we all have an excellent chance to do better.

To be born with a great voice is certainly an advantage, but you don't have to have a golden voice to make a success of your life. Abraham Lincoln, for all of his backwoods ruggedness, had a rather high-pitched and reedy voice. Winston Churchill had a slight lisp. Julia Childs sounds as if she's gargling ground glass. Tradition has it that Moses was a stutterer.

Speech is a learned skill. You learned to speak when you were a small child, just as you learned to walk. You imitated your parents, brothers, sisters, friends, and later, your teachers. The good voices you occasionally hear in TV, radio, movies, or plays were generally acquired by their owners only as the result of extensive work and training. Good voices are rarely acquired accidentally.

Can I actually change my voice?

Definitely yes! Perhaps *improve* is a better word. Your Adam's apple won't suddenly get bigger or disappear. You can discover, however, ways and means of taking the basic equipment you already have and using it with greater efficiency. Golfers can better their strokes, sopranos can learn to hit high notes without screeching, and sprinters can shorten their running time. When you've finished this course, you'll have acquired the charisma of a new voice, one that is more likeable and appealing than your present speaking voice.

How do I go about improving my voice and diction?

> We ain't as good as we should be;
> And we ain't as good as we're going to be;
> But we're better than we was!

The largest room in the world is the room for improvement! The most important thing is practice, practice, and then more practice!

The eye-popping performances of the Miami Dolphins, the Edmonton Oilers, or the Los Angeles Lakers are not spur of the moment inspirations. They're the result of endless, grueling hours of practice long before the season starts.

Olympic gold medal winner Carl Lewis was asked how many years he'd spent developing his tremendous athletic skills. He replied, "The day I stopped crawling, I took up running."

You won't have time to do all of the assignments in this textbook, nor will you need to. Your instructor will help you select the ones most beneficial for you. You'll note that most of the assignments ask you to concentrate on one particular aspect of voice or speech at a time. This is by far the best way to proceed. You can't rid yourself of every vocal fault overnight or by doing only one or two assignments. Experience has taught that few of us can make substantial progress or improvement with less than thirty minutes of daily practice. In many cases, forty-five minutes would be better.

Take your time, don't become impatient, and concentrate. Learn how to listen critically and objectively to yourself.

PLEASANT QUALITY

A top-notch speaking voice has a pleasing quality

Quality *is the timbre, tone color, or texture of a voice.* If a clarinetist, a trumpet player, and a violinist stand behind a screen and play "Dixie" in the key of C at the same rate of speed and the same degree of loudness, you'll have no problem recognizing which is which. Each instrument has its own personality or timbre. Similarly, if we overhear two friends talking in an adjoining room, we can invariably tell who is who.

You already know a great deal about yourself, but primarily from the inside out. It may come as a bit of a shock to you to be told that you come across to others as arrogant, cranky, sarcastic, or bitchy when you really don't have the slightest desire to create that kind of an impression. "There is no index of character so sure as the human voice," once remarked British Prime Minister Benjamin Disraeli.

Here's a list of undesirable vocal qualities:

Breathy   Feathery, fuzzy, and whispery. Breath seems to be escaping noticeably. The voice is generally too soft and doesn't carry well. The late Marilyn Monroe had a downy, wafer-thin little voice.

Strident   Hard, tense, brassy, and sometimes relatively high-pitched. The voice seems tight, as if it were produced by a pressure cooker. Joan Rivers, to some, is strident.

Harsh   Rough, raspy, gravelly, and sometimes relatively low-pitched, reminding you of rusty hinges and creaky doors in slasher movies. George C. Scott used this growly quality to great effect in his Oscar-winning movie, *Patton.*

Nasal   Talking through the nose—a nasal twang. The voice has a foghorn and sometimes a wailing quality. Singers of country music frequently use it.

Denasal   A cold-in-the-nose, stuffy quality. The voice sounds bottled up. Actors like to use this one to play the boxer with the once-too-often broken nose.

Throaty   Hollow, muffled, dullish. A voice-from-the-tomb quality. Walt Disney's Goofy and other cartoon characters use it. (Which way did he go, George?)

Hoarse   Noisy, scratchy, raw, strained. The voice suggests that its user either has laryngitis or needs to clear his throat. Those two feisty old gentlemen in "The Muppets," Statler and Waldorf, are colorful examples.

CLEAR ARTICULATION

A first-rate voice is distinct, intelligible and easy to understand

Articulation *involves movements of the lips, jaw, tongue and velum (soft palate) to form, separate and join individual speech sounds.*

Articulation must be as sharp and incisive as a laser beam. (Articulation, enunciation, and diction, for all practical purposes, mean the same thing.)

Feeble articulation is our *numero uno* problem as far as voice and speech are concerned. LAZY LIPS! The word *mumbling* is often used to describe careless, sluggish articulation. The more you gobble your words, the more indistinct you become. Mumblers don't open their mouths. Their lips, which have as much spring and bounce as two pieces of stale liver, never move. These word-wreckers drop or omit sounds:

give me is heard as *gimme*
thinking becomes *thinkin'*
going to changes to *gunna*
understand turns to *unerstan*

Garblers are first cousins of mumblers. They mangle sounds or add extra, unwanted sounds.

These, them, with are heard as *deze, dem, wit.*
Length, strength alter to *lenth, strenth.*
Athlete, across become *ath-a-lete, acrosst.*

A popular movie star—his pictures break box office records—loves to play the underdog who battles his way to the top. Mr. Macho deserves a double Oscar. A representative of the shoot-now-mumble-later school of acting, he's the only performer who can mumble and garble simultaneously. A TV movie critic remarked about one of the star's recent, sizzling hits:

> The problem with [him], said the critic, is not that he can't act. It's that he can't speak! Most of the time he sounds as if he has a mouth full of wet . . . tissue. In his most recent film epic, he emits Tarzan-like grunts and yowls through most of the movie. This is OK with audiences, because they do not expect grunts and yowls to be intelligible. But then at the very end of the picture, [this actor] delivers a message to give the film social significance, and at this point the movie stumbles and falls flat on its face, along with anybody in the audience who tries to figure out what the man is saying.

APPROPRIATE LOUDNESS

An outstanding speaking voice is easily heard

Loudness refers to intensity (sound level), volume, or projection.

"What did you say?" Do your friends often ask you that? Maybe you're muttering. It's more likely that you're not talking loudly enough.

You might have beautiful enunciation and still be unable to reach your listeners. A voice that is excessively faint or frail annoys most people. It also labels you as timid and weak-kneed.

Too loud is as hard on your listeners as too soft. Have you ever run into the Boomer? This one could easily make a speech in the Houston Astrodome without a mike, and nobody would miss a word.

EXPRESSIVENESS

A superfine voice is animated, expressive, and well-pitched

Expressiveness means vocal variety: the pitch level at which we speak, our vocal movements from pitch to pitch, our rate of speaking, phrasing, emphasis, and contrast.

An excessively high-pitched voice can earn you the wrong kind of attention. A voice of lower pitch is an advantage for both a man and a woman. According to Dr. Joyce Brothers, popular psychologist, "While pitch is probably more important in a woman's rise up the ladder of success, a male with a very high voice is going to have trouble being taken seriously. A high, thin voice is a distinct disadvantage to a man."

Michael Jackson is great as long as he just sings.

An extremely low pitch can make your listeners edgy. Are you a one-note speaker with little pitch variation? You can put your listeners to sleep. If you have no fire in yourself, you can't warm others. A too-fast speaking rate may prevent your message from being understood, and a consistently slow and draggy rate is dull. Without phrasing, emphasis and contrast, your conversation or speeches will sound stuffy and pointless.

UNOBTRUSIVE PRONUNCIATION

A good voice doesn't attract undue attention to itself

Good pronunciation should be appropriate to the speaker, to the area in which the speaker lives, and to the speaker's audience. Are you being arty if you talk about your *Awnt* Jane instead of your *Ant* Jane? Do you start out with *to-may-toes* in your garden and wind up with cream of *to-maw-toe* soup in your dining room? You may possibly be attracting undue attention to your manner of speaking.

Perhaps in the twilight zone of what is conspicuous or what is inconspicuous are the words *either* and *neither* pronounced as *eye-ther* and *neye-ther*. Most Americans seem to lean toward an *ee* pronunciation: *ee-ther* and *nee-ther*. *Eye-ther* and *neye-ther* are commonly heard in Canada and Great Britain. Yet several prominent American newscasters and the actors in at least six soap operas consistently use *eye-ther* and *neye-ther*. Which are correct? *Ee-ther* is used more frequently than *eye-ther*, but *eye-ther* seems to be coming up fast. In other words, both pronunciations are standard.

DIALECT

Accent? Who, me?

You probably have one. Actually, a better word is dialect.

If you send a greeting card to your *mudda* on *Mudda's* Day, or if you spent your weekend in *Lon Guyland*—you're from New York.

If you sit on a *sofar* instead of a *sofa*—you're from Massachusetts.

If you're a *boid-watcher* instead of a *bird-watcher*—you're from New Jersey (Joisey?)

If you say to your host, "*Ah* never drink *bear*"—you're from Alabama or Texas.

If you add a drop of mountain color to *right here* and come up with *ri-cheer*—you're from West Virginia or Kentucky.

If you meow when you say *how now, brown cow?* so that it sounds like *heow neow, breown ceow?*—you're from Maryland, Delaware or eastern Pennsylvania.

If you go *afishin'* instead of *fishing*—you're from practically anywhere.

***Dialect** is a variety of language that is distinguished from other varieties of the same language. It is used by a group of speakers in a certain area who are set off from others geographically and socially.* There are three major regional dialects in the United States.

General or standard American is spoken by the greatest number of people in America. Boundary lines between various dialects are not sharp and rigid. In general, however, this dialect is most commonly spoken in the Midwest (as far south as the Mason-Dixon line), in the West and in parts of the Southwest.

Prominent network newscasters such as Jane Pauley, Tom Brokaw, Dan Rather, and David Hartman use the general American dialect, which is the nationally preferred pronunciation for television and radio speech.

Eastern includes the New England and Middle Atlantic states, although the dialects of New York City, Boston and Baltimore are touch-and-go and not easy to locate specifically. Compare the speech of certain well-known political leaders from Massachusetts with that of their New York counterparts, and you'll hear vast differences.

Southern is used in the region that is roughly equivalent to the states of the old Confederacy. It extends as far west as Arkansas and into parts of Texas.

Is one of the dialects better than the other two? Definitely not. The educated, cultivated New Yorker can be understood in Nashville just as easily as the cultured Bostonian can be understood in Butte, Montana.

Each of the major dialects has several dozen subdialects. I've personally heard such a simple word as *right* pronounced ten different ways in Dallas—*rot* and *riot* representing two of the extremes. A New York cabbie once told me about a friend who had been killed by a "shock ina waduh." Electrical shock? No. A *shark*. The cabbie was using a subdialect.

We have tapes to prove that former Governor George Wallace of Alabama used standard Southern dialect when talking to business people and college graduates, but with laborers, farmers, and the Ku Klux Klan, he slipped into a folksy subdialect.

No section of the United States has a monopoly on good or correct speech. Nor is there any reason why we should all sound alike any more than we should all look or dress alike. An interesting feature story in a late summer issue of a Forth Worth, Texas newspaper gave advice to Texas preppies getting ready to go to exclusive colleges back east. "Worried about your Texas accent?" asked the writer. "Do not—we repeat—*do not* attempt to get rid of it. They'll absolutely adore it back east."

Where does all of this put you? You've heard the old saw, "When in Rome, do as the Romans do."

Let's amend that one: "When in Rome, do as the Romans do, that is, *if the Romans do as they're supposed to do.*"

If you've been told that your dialect is peculiar or quaint or if people complain that it's hard to understand you, you don't need to get rid of the accent. Put it on a sliding scale and renovate it.

It's essential that you try to sound like the enlightened and educated people in *your own area*. Emulate them! After all, imitation is the sincerest form of flattery.

LISTENING OBJECTIVELY

Prick up your ears: listen!

There's a big difference between hearing and listening. Even a duck can hear, but a duck doesn't listen.

In spite of the fact that we spend 30 percent of each day talking and 45 percent listening, most of us don't listen too well. People love to talk but hate to listen.

You're now embarking on a voice improvement program. *An important part of this is learning how to listen carefully and critically to the voices around you.* (You can't improve if you have no model to copy but yourself.) Note their bad as well as their good points. You won't be too surprised to discover that you share some of their vocal weaknesses, as well as their virtues. You'll soon become more sensitive to your own voice personality. *The first step toward improvement is self-awareness.*

You'll enjoy the following exercises, but they're tricky. Don't concentrate on WHAT your subject is saying. Concentrate on HOW the subject is saying it. Become a human sponge. Absorb and size up every sound you hear.

1. Listen to a radio drama or try this interesting experiment. Listen to a TV soap opera, preferably one with which you're not familiar—*by closing your eyes or keeping the picture off the screen.* Concentrate intensely on the sounds of the voices rather than the dialogue. Most soaps have stereotypes: the heavy, the Good Samaritan, the other woman, the decent and long-suffering spouse. Can you identify them by their vocal traits? Do you like or dislike them? Why?

2. *Listen to rather than watch* other programs such as talk shows, "60 Minutes," interviews and newscasts. Don't prejudge the speakers. Empty your mind of physical images or preconceptions. Rate and compare their voices. Why do you react favorably to some and unfavorably to others?

3. Your library probably has recordings of prominent personalities reading poetry, prose, plays or giving speeches.

   Robert Frost and Sylvia Plath have recorded some of their own poetry. Laurence Olivier, Richard Burton, and Meryl Streep have done scenes from plays. Rock star David Bowie's narration of Prokofiev's *Peter and the Wolf* is delightful. The voices of John Kennedy, Richard Nixon, Martin Luther King, Coretta King, Jimmy Carter, and Ronald Reagan are also available. Select a few voices that particularly interest you, and using Analysis Charts 1 through 3, Appendix B, evaluate them.

4. Listen to and appraise the voices of one or two of these individuals:

   a. a favorite professor
   b. a professor you dislike
   c. a close friend
   d. an acquaintance you dislike
   e. a clergyperson or a salesperson
   f. someone you know who has an unusual voice

5. HEAR YOURSELF AS OTHERS HEAR YOU!

Recording Your Voice

Record your own voice. If time permits three recordings, the first one should be made at the beginning of the course, the second—midterm, and the final one—at the end of the course. By doing this you'll be able to monitor your own progress. Analysis Charts 4 through 6, Appendix B, are convenient ways of evaluating recorded performances.

Be sure that part of each recording is devoted to informal, conversational, and unrehearsed material. An interview with a classmate or the instructor or a brief impromptu chat are suggested.

An unrehearsed reading should be included in the material that you record. Selections a. through c. that follow are examples of effective recording material. They contain all of the sounds of the English language commonly found to be troublesome or temperamental.

It's advisable to begin each recording with a sentence or two of identification:

My name is _____ . This is a sample of my speaking voice as recorded during the course in ___(Voice and Diction)___ at ___(Smith College)___ , ___(September, 19)___ .

a. I heard someone say, "Pop music is the hamburger of the day." For me, it's a lot more. Music is the commonest vibration, the people's news broadcast. I would like to study music and find out how we could use it to heal. Half the battle is selling music, not singing it. It's the image, not what you sing. Anyway, the softer you sing, the louder you're heard. Music does things to you whether you like it or not. Fast tempos raise your pulse and blood pressure. Slow music lowers them. You know yourself, music can calm the savage beast. A person can charm a snake with a flute. You place speakers in a jungle with wild animals and play Beethoven, and the animals will come into your camp. In music you have to think with the heart and feel with the brain. On stage I make love to twenty-five thousand people; then I go home alone. Not even boot camp could be as tough as being in rock and roll. The truth is where the truth is, and sometimes it's in the candy store. [Janis Joplin]

b. When you get a hundred-million people watching a single pro football game on television, it shows you that people need to identify with something. Pro football is like atomic warfare. There are no winners, only survivors. The football season is like pain. You forget how terrible it is until it seizes you again. Is it normal to wake up in the morning in a sweat because you can't wait to beat another human's guts out? Every time you win, you're reborn. When you win, nothing hurts. When you lose, you die a little. No one knows what to say in the loser's room. How you play the game is for college boys. When you're playing for money, winning is the only thing that matters. Fewer than three touchdowns is not enough, and more than five is rubbing it in. You're a hero when you win and a bum when you lose. That's the game. They pay their money, and they can boo if they feel like it. Hell, if football was half as complicated as some sportswriters make out it is, quite a few of us would never have been able to make a living at it.

c. Once there was a prince, and he wanted to marry a real princess. He traveled all around the world to find one, but always there was something wrong. There were princesses enough, but he found it difficult to make out whether they were real ones. One evening a terrible storm came along. Suddenly a knocking was heard at the gate. It was a princess. But what a sight she was after all the dreadful weather. The water ran down her hair and clothes. And yet she said she was a real princess.

"We'll soon find out," thought the old queen. She went into the bedroom, took all the bedding off the bedstead, and laid a pea at the bottom. Then she took twenty mattresses and laid them on the pea. On this the princess slept all night. In the morning she was asked how she had slept.

"Terribly!" said the princess. "Heaven only knows what was in the bed. It felt as though a huge rock was under that mattress. I am black and blue all over."

Nobody but a real princess could be as sensitive as that. So the prince married her, for now he knew that he had a real princess. [Fairy Tale]

A SUGGESTION OR TWO

If you have access to a tape recorder, use it. The market is flooded with small, inexpensive recorders, and a good one is worth its weight in gold. You can tape and listen to a lot of your assignments before you give them in class. Check your progress as you go through the course.

Want to have some fun? Try the Buddy System. Choose a partner, preferably a classmate who's interested in improving his or her own speaking voice. Not only can you monitor each other, but this also gives you a chance to retaliate. Word of caution: Select somebody who's honest and brutally candid—who'll tell you what you *need* to hear and not what you *want* to hear. You're asking the person to be a referee or a connoisseur, not a sympathetic witness.

TOPOPHOBIA (STAGE FRIGHT)

In half a dozen recent speech communication textbooks, the words *stage fright* never appear. Instead several recently coined substitutes are used: *speech anxiety, communication apprehension, speech fright,* and believe it or not, *speech trepidation!*

Call it whatever you wish, but when you get up for the first time in front of this class or any other kind of audience, most of you will be scared spitless.

There is bad news and there is good news.

The bad: you may never get rid of your stage fright entirely.

The good: stage fright has never been listed as a cause of death.

Here is another consolation: almost everybody, even professionals, suffers from it. Join the crowd.

Olivia Newton-John: "For half an hour before I go out there on that stage, I cry and I'm a miserable coward. It's like sitting and waiting in death row. Once I get started, though, the fear quickly evaporates."

Enrico Caruso, perhaps the world's greatest tenor, sang 607 performances at the Metropolitan Opera in New York: "I've never done a stage performance in my life without being knock-kneed with terror."

Richard Pryor: "That first day on the set for a new movie, I'm as nervous as a tree on the Lassie program."

And speaking of being scared, I am scared every time I face a new class. What about your instructor? Ask him or her.

What are the physical causes of stage fright? Adrenalin, released into your blood stream, speeds up your heart beat and raises your blood pressure. Your breathing rate increases. You get bats, butterflies, and ice cubes in your stomach. Your hair stands on end, and you get goose pimples. (No, the goose pimples do *not* cause your hair to stand on end.)

Your pounding heart sounds like the cannon they use in Tchaikovsky's *1812 Overture.* (Your classmates in the first row can't hear it, however.) All in all, it's like being strapped in the electric chair and given your choice of AC or DC.

All these phenomena—the increased flow of adrenalin, the increased heart rate, and the raised blood pressure—simply serve to make you think and react more rapidly and make you far more energetic and alert. You've shifted into high gear. You're psyched up! It's nature's way of preparing you to act in case of emergency. As far as performing in front of this class is concerned, there isn't one chance in a million that you'll ever come face to face with a genuine emergency, so don't worry about it.

"The only thing we have to fear is fear itself." Franklin Roosevelt didn't have stage fright in mind, but what he said applies. You can put your fear-energy to work for you.

Carol Channing, who has appeared more than a thousand times in the musical *Hello, Dolly!* was asked before her first performance if she suffered from stage fright. "No," she replied. "What is there to be nervous about? I know my lines." There is a little hint for you. Be prepared!

Count your blessings. In most so-called public speaking courses, a certain amount of memorization is necessary. Even if you use notes, your instructor will harangue you not to read your speech word for word and to look at your audience 95 percent of the time. In this course, you will rarely if ever be asked to memorize anything. You will probably be reading most of your material. Nevertheless, be prepared!

Practice, rehearse, practice, rehearse! The more you practice your material outside the classroom, the sooner you will get stage fright under control. The more you rehearse, the sooner you will force excessive fear-energy to work *for* you rather than *against* you.

DELIVERY

And now that you're up front . . .

You'll spend some time behind that lectern up front. Good posture makes you look *and* sound better! Don't lean on the speaker's stand or drape yourself around it. Stand comfortably erect, but not rigid. Rock and roll is great for concerts, but not in the classroom. Stand still and don't be a weight shifter. And don't fidget with notes, hair, beard, clothing, or your car keys.

What are you supposed to do with your hands? It's only when you face an audience that you discover that each hand weighs 150 pounds. The best thing to do with them: leave them right where they are at the ends of your arms, relaxed at your sides.

Look at your audience!

Be so familiar with your material that you don't have to read it word for word. Eyeballing your audience is also a marvelous antidote for stage fright. You'll be amazed to see that there are twenty or more friendly faces beaming in your direction. Not a hostile face among them. When you've finished, everybody in the class ought to feel that you've read or talked to him or her personally for at least half of your presentation.

WRAP-UP

1. Many authorities feel that the way we talk is actually far more important than the way we look.

2. A course in voice and diction is concerned with how you sound when you talk, rather than what you talk about.

3. Almost everybody can profit from a course in voice and diction since talking effectively is vital to success in life.

4. People are seldom aware of their own vocal faults and almost never aware of how their voices sound to others.

5. Practice is the single most important factor in voice improvement.

6. *Quality* refers to the timbre, tone, or texture of the voice. Voices are usually described as breathy, strident, harsh, nasal, denasal, throaty, or hoarse.

7. *Articulation* involves the movements of the lips, tongue, jaw and velum to form, separate, and to join individual speech sounds. Poor articulation is the most common speech fault.

8. *Loudness* refers to the intensity (sound level), volume, or projection of the voice.

9. *Expressiveness* refers to vocal variety: pitch level, vocal movement, rate of speaking, phrasing, emphasis and contrast.

10. *Good pronunciation* is unobtrusive and appropriate to the speaker, the area in which the speaker lives, and the speaker's audience.

11. *Dialect* refers to one of the regional or social varieties of the same language. The United States has three main dialects: general American, eastern and southern.

12. Objective listening, which is another way of defining critical listening, is essential if you are to learn to judge your own speech habits accurately.

13. A series of physical phenomena—increased flow of adrenalin, increased heart rate, and raised blood pressure—are responsible for the stage fright that most speakers and performers experience. Much practice will help you to get stage fright under control.

14. Good posture and eye contact have a positive effect on the way you sound.

SOUND OFF!
THE BEGINNINGS OF VOICE

WOULD YOU BELIEVE THAT

. . . The loud sounds that accompany enthusiastic kissing are made as you inhale? You also inhale as you sob. You exhale, however, as you laugh.

. . . The Adam's apple is so called because according to folklore a piece of the apple that Adam ate in the Garden of Eden allegedly got stuck in his throat?

. . . Lungs are not hollow sacks or bags? They more closely resemble sponges. The surface area within one of your lungs is twenty times greater than the surface area of your skin.

. . . Before puberty, the male larynx differs little from the female larynx? After puberty, the male larynx almost doubles in size.

. . . The primary purpose of breathing is to maintain life, not to enable us to speak?

. . . When you are silent, you do about twelve to sixteen inhale–exhale cycles per minute? By practicing Yoga, a Hindu philosophy, you can train yourself to breathe only twice a minute. A brand new baby breathes thirty-five to forty times a minute.

. . . When jogging, you take in about 125 quarts of air a minute?

THE PRODUCTION OF SOUND

If you've taken a course in physics, you may have been intrigued with the section of the course that dealt with sound. But despite this interest, you probably don't sit through a performance of *Cats* or Beethoven's Fifth Symphony analyzing what you hear in terms of sound waves and vibrations. You're certainly aware, however, that the pleasant sounds come from a group of skilled musicians seated in the orchestra pit or on the stage, who bow, pluck, strike their instruments, or blow air into them. All of this might remind you of a simple law of physics: sound has as its source an object that vibrates.

What makes such an object vibrate? The violinist runs a bow across the strings of a Stradivarius. The harpist plucks the strings of the instrument. The xylophonist strikes graduated wooden bars, and the French-horn player, by blowing into a mouthpiece, sets into motion a column of air in about twelve to sixteen feet of coiled metal tubing. But what about the speaker, actor, or singer who must produce sound without the aid of strings, bars, or metal tubing? Such an individual has, of course, in his or her throat, the most remarkable instrument of all—the larynx, or voice box.

The larynx houses the vocal folds, or bands, and a flow of air sets them into vibration. To produce sounds successfully, you have to regulate and control this flow of air, which brings up the interesting subject of breathing.

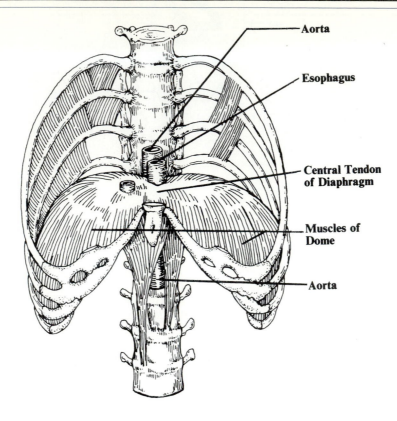

Aorta

Esophagus

Central Tendon
of Diaphragm

Muscles of
Dome

Aorta

Figure 2.1   The diaphragm.

THE NATURE OF BREATHING

Take a deep breath.

You'll notice that your chest expands and lifts. What are you doing? You're making your body (and lungs) bigger. Air flows in. Inhalation, in other words. But when you exhale, you make your body smaller in volume. Air flows out.

The thorax, or chest, is a large, almost barrel-shaped container. At the rear is the spinal column (backbone). Attached to the backbone are twelve pairs of ribs. The ten upper pairs are connected, directly or indirectly, by means of cartilage to the sternum (breastbone). The two lowest pairs, because they are not directly attached in front, are called free, or floating, ribs. It's obvious that the rib cage isn't a rigid structure and that the lower part is more flexible in outward movement. The whole thorax can be lifted and enlarged from front to back as well as from side to side.

Within the thorax are two large, cone-shaped lungs. They're not hollow sacs but spongy, porous organs that, except for the heart and esophagus, almost completely fill the cavity. The base of each lung is in contact with the upper surface of the diaphragm.

Breathing doesn't consist of sucking in or pushing out air. The lung tissues are passive. Actually, the lungs serve as reservoirs for air.

The diaphragm, which is a tough, double-domed muscle, plays an active and important part in inhalation. This muscular partition, which separates the chest and abdominal cavities, isn't a solid, unbroken sheet. Openings in it permit the esophagus, various nerves, and an important blood vessel (the aorta) to pass through it (figure 2.1).

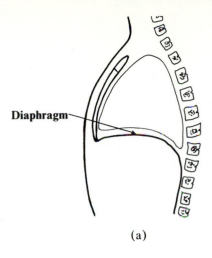 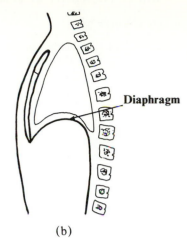

Figure 2.2 Changes in thoracic cavity and positions during (a) inhalation and (b) exhalation.

INHALATION

When you inhale, this is what happens.

- As the muscles of your diaphragm tense and contract, the diaphragm moves downward and flattens slightly. (In normal respiration, the movement is less than an inch.)
- This downward movement pushes the organs of the abdomen against your relaxed abdominal wall, causing a slight outward bulge.
- Your ribs are raised upward and outward.

Your chest capacity is now increased in three directions: top to bottom, side to side, and front to back. Because of this increase in capacity, the air pressure within your lungs is decreased (a partial vacuum also is created in your chest), and air from the outside rushes in to equalize the pressure.

EXHALATION

This is what happens when you exhale, if you're not talking but are only breathing quietly.

- The various muscles of your diaphragm relax, permitting the diaphragm to return to its arched position.
- Your abdominal organs, which have been under slight pressure, return to their relaxed, uncompressed position.
- As the muscles relax, your ribs move downward and inward because of the pull of gravity.

These movements decrease the size of your chest cavity and compress the air in your lungs. The internal air pressure is now greater than that outside your body, and the air is expelled through your mouth and nose. This kind of exhalation requires no conscious control or awareness. It's basically a process of muscular relaxation rather than of tension.

When you're talking, however, exhalation must be consciously controlled. Greater pressure and push are involved.

- Four powerful sheaths of muscle that form the front wall of your abdomen contract and push in on the abdominal organs.
- In turn, the abdominal organs push up against your diaphragm.
- Your diaphragm then returns to its arched position.

These movements decrease the size of your chest cavity and, consequently, increase the pressure on the air within your lungs (figure 2.2).

Table 2.1   Differences between Breathing to Live and Breathing to Speak

Breathing to Live (Nonspeech)	Breathing to Speak
Inhalation is active. The diaphragm plays an active role, which means that the diaphragm does most of the work.	Inhalation is active.
Exhalation is passive. The diaphragm plays a passive role.	Exhalation is active.
Breathing is comparatively shallow. Approximately one pint of air is involved.	Breathing is somewhat fuller and deeper, depending upon the needs of the speaker (length of sentences to be spoken, increase in loudness). Approximately one to two quarts of air are involved.
Inhalation occurs at about the same rate as exhalation. Inhalation and exhalation occur smoothly and rhythmically, about twelve times per minute.	Inhalation occurs quickly between phrases. About one-sixth of speaking time is spent taking in air. Exhalation is generally slow and irregular. About five-sixths of speaking time is spent in letting air out as sounds are produced.

BREATHING TO SPEAK

Breathing to sustain life is primary and automatic—we're not always conscious of breathing. Only secondarily do we breathe to speak. In breathing for speech, we form intelligible vocal sounds (phonation) during the process of exhalation (try to speak intelligibly while inhaling and see what happens). When we breathe to speak, we control the process of exhalation (table 2.1).

BREATH CONTROL

In breathing to speak, then, an easy, natural, and flexible control of your exhalation will help you achieve effective vocal production.

Is there any method of breathing that will give you the right kind of control? A lot of gibberish has been written about so-called diaphragmatic breathing. It would be impossible to breathe normally without the diaphragm! Actually, it makes more sense to talk about *central* or *deep* breathing. Probably 95 percent of you breathe this way.

Central-Deep Breathing

Most of the expansion-contraction activities occur in the abdominal area. A majority of people with good speaking voices, as well as numerous fine singers, actors, speakers, and athletes use this kind of breathing because it promotes sensitivity, flexibility, ease, and comfortableness in the control of breathing.

How about the other 5 percent?

Clavicular-Shoulder Breathing

Most of the movement involves the extreme upper chest and consists of raising and lowering the clavicles (collarbones) and shoulders while breathing. Superior voices are found infrequently among individuals using this type of breathing, because it doesn't allow for sensitivity or flexibility of control. In certain extreme activities—the 100-yard dash and the Olympic swimming races—this method may, as a breathing supplement, enable an individual to take in additional oxygen. Under most circumstances, however, clavicular-shoulder breathing may hinder the development of good voice.

Table 2.2   An Evaluation of Breath Control Methods

Clavicular-Shoulder	Central-Deep
Breathing is shallow rather than deep. The movements of the upper chest are too meager to provide an adequate amount of air.	The *control* of the breath stream rather than the amount of air inhaled is of primary importance. Expansions and contractions in these areas are natural movements and unlabored. A greater ease of control is possible.
Inhalation may become too frequent. Speaking rhythm is apt to be jerky. The individual is forced to pause for breath too often and at places that chop phrases into awkward, meaningless chunks.	Inhalations will generally be less frequent. The speaker doesn't have to gasp for breath. Longer phrases can be used and jerky rhythms can be avoided.
Excessive tension is created in the upper chest, straining the vocal machinery. A grating, strident voice results.	If most of the expansion and contraction movements are in or near the midregion of the body, the throat and larynx are likely to remain free of unnecessary tensions. Experience has shown that if an individual who has an unpleasant voice quality changes breathing habits by eliminating clavicular-shoulder breathing and adopting central-deep breathing, voice improvement generally results.

EFFICIENT BREATHING

The following exercises will make you aware of the differences between efficient and inefficient breathing, and they'll help you acquire efficient habits in breathing to speak.

1. Stand comfortably erect and try each of the two methods of breathing. Deliberately exaggerate the movements involved. Which method of breathing seems the most natural and comfortable to you?

    a. Clavicular-Shoulder: Get the feel of raising and lowering your collarbones and shoulders.
    b. Central-Deep: Place your hand below and in front of your lower ribs. Inhale. Exhale.

    If you seem to be using only central-deep breathing, your breathing habits are probably efficient. If you're using clavicular-shoulder breathing, however, try to eliminate it. Exercises 2–5 will help you get rid of extreme upper-chest breathing.

2. Place your hands on your upper chest with the thumbs aimed at your collarbone. Take a deep breath, and then count from one to ten. If you are aware of any pronounced movement of your shoulders, repeat the exercise and deliberately use the pressure of your hands to prevent this kind of movement. Repeat this procedure saying the months of the year: January through June, and then July through December.
3. Sit comfortably erect in an armless chair. Grab the bottom of the chair seat firmly. Your shoulders should not be able to rise. Inhale and exhale, concentrating on movements in or near the midregion of your body.
4. Lie flat on your back. Place your right hand on your abdomen and your left hand on the upper part of your chest. Breathe as naturally as possible. You'll notice a slow and regular expansion and contraction of the area under your right hand and very little movement of the area under your left hand.
5. (Not for the faint of heart). From a standing position, bend over and touch the floor—if you can! All the air should be out of your lungs. Concentrate on a column of breath as if it were a light entering your body. Slowly, slowly straighten up, inhaling, the light flooding your chest. As you're doing this, spread your arms up and out. Your lungs are full of air. Now begin to exhale. Move your arms back in, slowly bend your body forward until your fingertips touch the floor again. Your lungs are empty. Repeat several times.

The following exercises are for general practice:

6. Stand comfortably erect and as you breathe, try to keep most of the movement in the center of your body. Place your hands on your waistline, the fingers extended to the front and the thumbs to the rear. Notice the general expansion in this area.
7. Press a book against your abdominal area below the ribs. Inhale. The expansion in this area should force the book out from ¾ to 1¼ inches. Exhale. The contraction permits the book to go back in. Get the feel of the action.
8. Inhale deeply, and keeping the ribs raised, count to fifteen, gradually letting the ribs descend between fifteen and twenty.

CONTROLLING EXHALATION

You make sounds, of course, as you exhale. It's especially important that you control your outgoing breath. Exhale frugally. Be a miser. You must ration, or dole out, your breath. Don't allow air to escape before you start to make a sound or word, between words or phrases, or within a word itself.

9. You should be able to read this on one breath. Try it.
    A dog is smarter than some people. It wags its tail and not its tongue. No matter which screw in the head is loose, it's the tongue that rattles. Everybody agrees that a loose tongue can lead to a few loose teeth. A bit of advice:
    Say nothing often. There's much to be said for not saying much. It's better to remain silent and be thought a fool than to open your mouth and remove all doubt. If you don't say it, you won't have to unsay it. You never have to take a dose of your own medicine if you know when to keep your mouth shut.

If you didn't succeed, the following exercises will help you gain control over your flow of breath:

10. Take a deep breath and release it slowly, making the sound *s*. Keep it even and regular, free of jerkiness and bumpiness. Try it with the sound *f*.
11. An interesting experiment: Hold a small, lighted candle about six to eight inches in front of your mouth. Sustain *s* and then try *f*. Keep your exhalation regular and constant. The flame shouldn't flicker and certainly shouldn't go out.
12. With the second hand of a watch to guide you, allow yourself about thirty-five seconds to count aloud to fifty. Now try the count on one breath. (It *can* be done, but don't asphyxiate yourself!) Be sure that you don't allow breath to escape between numbers.
13. You'll notice that some words are relatively hissy, noisy, and wasteful of breath. The *s* in *six*, the *th* in *thirteen*, the *f* in *forty-four*, for example, are the culprits, especially if you allow too much breath to escape on these sounds. Now repeat Exercise 9. If you avoid producing any "hissers," you'll probably be able to read it in one breath. Repeat Exercise 12. You'll increase your count.
14. Be ultraconservative with your breath control, and read each of the following on a single breath. They'll be simple to do—at first!

    a. If you're going to do something tonight that you'll be sorry for tomorrow morning, sleep late.
    b. It pays not to leave a live dragon out of your plans, especially if you happen to live near one.
    c. As the poet said, "Only God can make a tree"—probably because it's so hard to figure out how to get the bark on.
    d. A college is truly a fountain of knowledge, and a great many of us go there to drink. Some students drink at the fountain of knowledge. Others just gargle.
    e. Americans have two chickens in every pot, two cars in every garage, and two headaches for every aspirin. The average American would drive his car to the bathroom if the door was wide enough.
    f. Little boys and girls who don't always tell the truth will probably grow up and become weather forecasters. Our tastes change as we mature. Little girls like dolls. Little boys like soldiers. When they grow up, the girls like the soldiers and the boys like the dolls.

g. The best rule in driving through five o'clock traffic is to try and avoid being a part of the six o'clock news. Statistics show that an average of thirty-nine thousand people are killed by gas annually. Sixty inhale it, forty light matches in it, and 38,900 step on it. A light foot on the gas beats two under the grass.

h. It seems that camels were once imported into the United States in the hope that they would be useful in desert fighting. On hearing the news, an Indian chief persuaded the army to give him one of the sturdy animals as a present for his wife. She was so fat that she had already ruined three horses. Alas, when she was hoisted aboard the new beast she achieved fame as the squaw that broke the camel's back.

i. There isn't much point in bothering with politics. It's much simpler to go directly into crime. A politician is a person who's got what it takes to take what you've got. Politics is like milking a cow. You can accomplish a lot if you have a little pull. Some Americans refer to Washington as the city of protocol, alcohol, and Geritol. We ought to be thankful that we're living in a country where folks can say what they think without thinking.

In speaking aloud you break sentences into phrases. What is a phrase? A phrase is a group of words expressing a thought unit, an idea, and occasionally several ideas. You generally inhale during the pauses between phrases.

One of the things that determines how often you must pause is your need for breath. Chapter 7 has exercises dealing with pauses and breathing.

HOW YOU PRODUCE SOUND

A typical day: you have been up and around, presumably awake, for sixteen hours. If you talk for fifteen minutes of each hour, saying 150 words per minute, and if each word has four sounds, you will be producing about 144,000 sounds per day!

Where do these sounds come from?

You've been grunting and gurgling meaningfully since you were a few weeks old. But how often do you consider the fascinating organ in your throat that makes the grunts and gurgles, as well as the more cultivated sounds? When you do, you may refer to it as the voice box. It's more correctly known as the *larynx,* and it's about the size of a large walnut.

THE LARYNX

The larynx, about two inches high and one inch in diameter, is the principal organ of sound. It functions as a kind of air valve by regulating the flow of air from your lungs as a faucet or a nozzle controls the flow of water from a pipe or hose. In addition, your larynx serves in three other capacities.

- The larynx is generally closed when you swallow, which prevents liquids, food, or foreign matter—fishbones, for example—from entering your windpipe and then your lungs, perhaps choking you to death.

- If you swallow a fishbone anyway, or if too large a chunk of sirloin steak gets stuck in your "wrong" or "Sunday" throat, your larynx and lungs set up a coughing reflex, producing a blast of compressed air to help expel the foreign object.

- When your larynx is closed, air is trapped or impounded in your chest cavity. You must be able to hold your breath for any kind of strenuous work such as lifting bricks, swimming underwater, and for such biological necessities as bearing down (in excretion or childbirth).

If you know how a car or a computer works, you can operate and control them more effectively. For that reason you should know at least a few basic things about the structures you use to produce sound.

Note the phrase "a few basic things." Not many of you reading this page right now are planning careers as laryngologists, tracheotomists, or otorhinolaryngologists. (Don't faint. Each of these jawbreakers describes a medical doctor who is primarily interested in the throat or larynx.) Therefore, the theory will be kept brief and simple.

I don't want to frighten you, but misuse or abuse of the voice-producing mechanisms can result in more than just poor vocal performance. Actual and serious damage can be done to the organs of the voice. If that happens to you, you *will* be visiting your local laryngologist, tracheotomist, or otorhinolaryngologist.

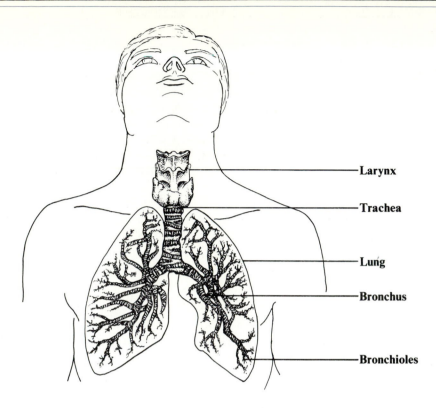

Figure 2.3 Frontal view of larynx, trachea, and lungs.

Back to the voice box, which is nothing more than the front and slightly bulging part of the larynx (it is more prominent in men than in women). Hum *m* or say *ah*. Place your thumb and forefinger on each side of your voice box. You'll feel a slight vibration. What is vibrating and what causes the vibration?

All sounds must have a motivating force. Breath, of course, is the sum and substance of sounds you make in your throat. After the breath is expelled from your lungs via the bronchial tubes, it passes through the trachea (windpipe)—a flexible tube. At the top of the windpipe, which is about four inches long and one inch in diameter, rests the larynx (figure 2.3).

The lowest of the laryngeal cartilages (a cartilage is something like gristle) is called the cricoid (figure 2.4). The cricoid is situated on top of the first ring of the trachea and is shaped like a signet ring, only the wide side is to the back and the narrow side is to the front. The cricoid is the base or foundation for the rest of the larynx. The bottom of the larynx is anchored to the cricoid and the top of the larynx is attached by muscles to the hyoid, which is a free-floating, horseshoe-shaped bone.

Ancient Greek physicians decided that each of the two connected sides of the larynx resembled a shield. The word *thyroid* comes from the Greek word for "large shield," *thyreos*. The shield, or butterfly-shaped, thyroid cartilage that forms the outside wall of the larynx is the largest cartilage of the larynx. It rests upon the cricoid. With your thumb and forefinger you can partially trace the outline of the thyroid cartilage.

At the top and front of the thyroid, your finger will hit a small notch or depression. The vocal folds, which are also known as vocal bands, lips, or cords (but never chords!) are attached within the larynx just behind and below this tiny V-shaped notch. From there, extending shelf-like back along each side wall of the thyroid, they slope slightly downward. At the rear they are attached to two small, triangular-shaped, movable cartilages known as arytenoid cartilages, which have to do with the opening and the closing of the vocal folds.

When you swallow, your larynx bobs up and down. This action is controlled by the *extrinsic* (outside) muscles. One of these, for example, attaches the larynx above to the hyoid bone. Thus, food or liquids pass over, rather than into, the larynx. The leaf-shaped epiglottis, which is at the base of and just behind your tongue, has little or no

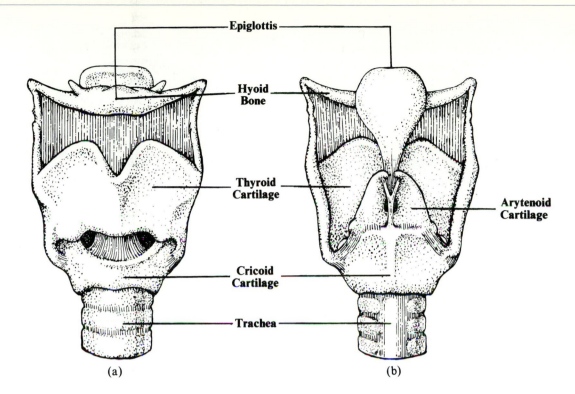

Figure 2.4   (a) Front view of the laryngeal cartilages; (b) back view of the laryngeal cartilages.

important function in speech. When you swallow, the larynx rises and the epiglottis moves backward, acting as a protective flap, or covering, over the larynx, preventing foreign substances (those fishbones again) from entering your lungs.

Place your finger on your larynx and swallow two or three times. Then try humming a high note. Jump quickly to a low note. You will notice that your larynx jumps or shifts position. What controls the movements of the larynx? The extrinsic muscles do, and they are able to raise or to lower as well as support the larynx. Extrinsic muscles have attachments outside the larynx, many of them to the hyoid bone.

The *intrinsic* (inside) muscles are attached to various points entirely within the structure of the larynx. These muscles are more directly concerned with the process of making sounds, and they are therefore of more interest to us.

THE VOCAL FOLDS

A student once defined opera this way: "In an opera when a guy gets stabbed in the back, instead of bleeding, he sings for half an hour." That comment doesn't do justice to the strength and stamina stage performances require. Consider Luciano Pavarotti, one of the finest tenors in the world today. "Super Throat" not only projects his voice over a seventy-five-piece orchestra, but also makes gorgeous sounds.

If you see a professional actor like Meryl Streep or Christopher Plummer on stage, you'll be deeply impressed with the powerful, full, rich sounds rolling out so effortlessly and through performances that last hours. One would almost be inclined to think that any of the owners of these golden voices have, by some miracle, giant pipe organs instead of small voice boxes hidden in their throats. It is incredible that voices such as these, as well as yours and mine, originate within the larynx and, more specifically, from a series of amazingly complicated movements by the two tiny intrinsic muscles commonly referred to as the vocal folds. Consider these facts:

- The average length of the folds in males is about nine-tenths of an inch (although they can vary from seven-eighths of an inch to one and one-fourth inch).
- The average length of the folds in females is about seven-tenths of an inch.

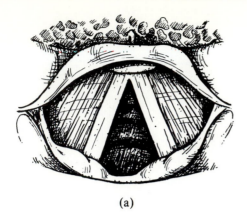
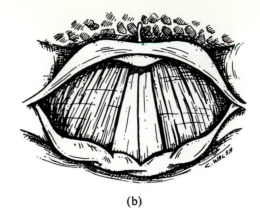

(a)   (b)

Figure 2.5   The vocal folds in position for (a) quiet breathing
(glottis opened), and (b) phonation or vocalization (glottis
closed).

The vocal folds, or cords, are long, narrow, smoothly rounded flaps of muscle tissue. They've also been described as "blobs" of muscle, because they're difficult to depict. They're not sharp and taut, and they don't resemble
rubber bands. The folds may be lengthened or shortened, tensed or relaxed. They may be drawn apart; they may
be drawn together. The inner edges are composed of a glossy, pinkish, fibrous material, and they're covered with
mucous membrane. If you're a heavy smoker, your vocal folds may appear to be pale red; if you have a sore throat
or laryngitis, a flaming red.

During quiet breathing, the vocal folds are drawn apart leaving an opening, the glottis, between them. In this
relaxed position, the folds form a V-shape with the point of the V at the front.

How the Vocal Folds Produce Sound

Relaxed, the vocal folds are relatively quiet and immobile, but when you're speaking, these intrinsic muscles vibrate
or flutter with incredible speed. If you hum middle C, the frequency of the vibration is approximately 256 cycles
per second! What is the nature of this vibration?

When you were a kid, did you ever place two blades of grass between your fingers and blow on them and
make them whistle? Or did you ever just blow out air between slightly tense lips to imitate the sound of a motorboat
or a diesel truck? If you ever studied a brass instrument such as a trombone or a trumpet, you may recall that your
initial efforts were largely confined to vibrating or fluttering your lips rapidly (as you might have in producing the
unpleasantly expressive Bronx cheer, except that while you were blowing into your mouthpiece, your tongue was
entirely inside your mouth). In any case, these examples may give you a rough idea of how the vocal folds vibrate
or flutter to produce sound.

This is how the vocal folds work:

- The vocal folds are apart during quiet breathing. Before sounds can be produced, the folds come together,
  somewhat like swinging-sliding doors, and completely close off the larynx (figure 2.5).
- When the vocal folds are tightly closed, air pressure builds up beneath them.
- When this pressure rises to a peak, it blows the vocal folds open, and a puff of air escapes into the vocal tract.
- The vocal folds are elastic, and as the air pressure beneath them decreases, they spring back together.
- As soon as the vocal folds are closed, the pressure beneath them builds up once more, and again the vocal
  folds are forced apart.

This cycle occurs again and again. The successive escaping puffs of air set the vocal folds into vibration, and they, in turn, cause the column of air in the voice tract to vibrate. It is this vibration which, when heard by listeners, is recognized as sound.

In general, the faster the folds vibrate or flutter, the higher the pitch. If you hum or sing middle C, your vocal folds vibrate 256 complete cycles per second. When a professional tenor hits high C, his folds vibrate at 512 times per second. Some sopranos can reach a high G above high C, which means a frequency of 1,568 vibrations per second. Some basses can drop to a low, low B, which means 60 cycles per second.

Your range of hearing extends, roughly speaking, from about 20 to 20,000 cycles per second. Dogs apparently can hear notes as high as 25,000 cycles per second. By using a special dog whistle, some hunters and trainers of dogs such as Lassie and Benji can give signals or commands to their dogs that human beings cannot hear. (Bats respond to tones as high as 100,000 cycles!)

RESONANCE AND RESONATORS

A popular, daytime TV program once presented a fascinating experiment in sound. Three musical instruments were displayed: a bassoon, a cello, and a trombone. Then "Twinkle, Twinkle, Little Star" was played on each instrument. Great dissimilarities of sound quality were noticeable among the three instruments. The bassoon, often used by composers for comic effects, growled. The rather plaintive cello had a husky richness. The brassy trombone was alternately brilliant and mellow.

The television audience was then asked to listen to a series of four special recordings of each instrument playing the same tune. The audience was also told that the sound had been tampered with. While listening to the first of these recordings, it was easy to tell that the bassoon had lost some of its growl, but it still sounded like a bassoon. The cello and the trombone, respectively, had lost some of their huskiness and brilliance, but not their identities. But when the fourth recording was played, the three instruments not only had lost all traces of their identifying characteristics but they also sounded exactly alike! What had happened? In the first of the special recordings, a number of overtones had been eliminated. In the second and third recordings, more and more of the overtones had been erased until only the fundamental remained in the fourth recording. Overtones? Fundamental? Read on.

Resonance

As the cellist draws the bow over a string, the string is set into vibration. If the full length of the string is vibrating at a frequency of about 256 cycles per second, the ear interprets the resulting sound as the pitch of middle C. Tone that results from vibration over the full length of the string is known as the *fundamental*. It is the fundamental that tells us the pitch of the note. Not only does the cello string vibrate over its full length, however; it also vibrates simultaneously in halves, thirds, fourths, or fifths. Each of these vibrating segments produces a pitch that is higher and weaker than the fundamental. These tones are known as *overtones* or *partials*. Thus, the tone we actually hear isn't a pure, simple, or single tone, but it's a composite type of tone, a blending together of a fundamental and overtones.

The vocal folds, being far more complex than cello strings, produce a greater number of different, simultaneous vibrations. The number and the relative strength of the overtones, in combination with the fundamental, help identify voices as well as instruments. As a simple example, very few overtones are produced in the piccolo or flute. The tone quality of these instruments is relatively pure and simple. That sometime musical clown, the bassoon, produces a good many overtones, however, and its tone quality is much more complex and difficult to describe.

Resonators

If you remove a string from a guitar and stretch it tightly between two chairs, even John Williams could produce only limpid and chirpy musical scratchings and scrapings from the string. Strip the sounding board from your Steinway grand, and you can still sit down and play. But the lush, sumptuous tones would be missing, and your Chopin would sound as if it were being played on eighty-eight tiny, tuned tin cans.

Some kind of sounding board or vibrator is needed to reflect and renovate the original tone or sound. The guitar string needs the body of the instrument. The piano keyboard and strings need their sounding board.

Resonance, then, refers to a process that includes:

■ Reinforcement and enrichment of sound. (It's something like what happens when you add speakers in a stereo.)

■ Modification and blending (selection and emphasis) of particular groups of overtones. Different parts of the original tone are emphasized or built up, and other parts are damped or filtered out.

Reinforcement, enrichment, and *modification* are key words to our understanding of the resonating process. How are these brought about in the human voice?

THE HUMAN RESONATORS

If you could whisk yourself inside of your larynx and listen to yourself speak, you would hear something like a series of buzzing noises. It would certainly not sound like the voice that you recognize as your own. The vocal folds need their soundboards, too: the throat, mouth, nasal cavities, and perhaps the chest.

Sound begins with the vibration of the vocal folds in the larynx. The sound waves pass up through the cavities of the pharynx (throat), oral cavity (mouth), and the nasal cavities (nose). These three cavities are the human resonators (figure 2.6).

The sounds produced by the vocal folds are initially weak and thin. They are reinforced by being echoed, reflected, or bounced off the surface of the cavities approximately in the manner of sound magnified by a megaphone. Simultaneously, the sounds are enriched and modified by changes in the size, shape, and surface tensions of the throat and mouth. The nasal cavities may also be used or completely closed off. All of these changes and adjustments produce characteristics that identify an individual's voice quality.

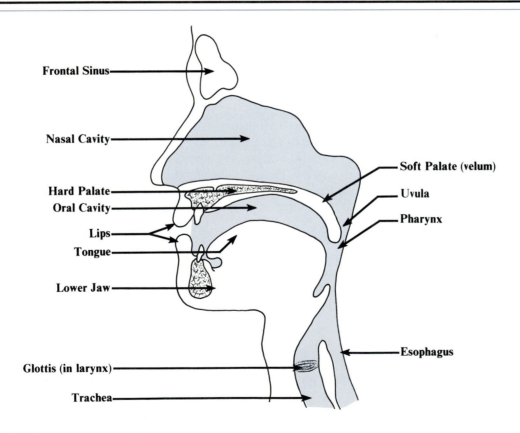

Figure 2.6   Section of head and neck showing resonance tract.

The Pharynx (Throat)

Description

The pharynx is a trumpet-shaped, tubelike, muscular passageway, about five inches long, with soft side and rear walls, which extends from the tops of the larynx and the esophagus to the cavity behind the nasal passage. The upper portion of the pharynx connects with the oral and nasal cavities. (The pharynx also forms the upper part of the digestive tract and has been described poetically as the "gateway to the gut.")

Function as a Resonator

An unnecessarily tight, constricted throat with tense, rigid walls will possibly emphasize and give prominence to the higher overtones and frequencies. The resulting vocal quality may be strident, harsh, or metallic.

Openness of throat, relative relaxation of the constrictor muscles, walls, and surfaces will emphasize and give prominence to the fundamental and lower overtones and damp out some of the higher overtones and frequencies. The resulting vocal quality may be relatively mellow, full, and rich.

The Oral Cavity (Mouth)

Description

The oral cavity is the most variable in size and shape of all the resonance chambers. It is bounded at the front by the lips and the jaws, below by the tongue, above by the hard and soft palates, and on the sides by the insides of the cheeks.

Function as a Resonator

As the most versatile and the largest cavity resonator, the mouth acts as a balancer or as a kind of coordinator for the other resonators. The hard palate (arched roof of the mouth) probably acts as an efficient reflector of sound. On the other hand, the tongue and the soft, inner surfaces of the cheeks and the lips may have an absorbing or damping effect on certain overtones. The possibilities and the combinations are as complex as they are infinite. The vowel sounds, of course, are produced by changing the size and shape of the oral cavity. If you will compare the vowel [i] in *eat* with the vowel [ɑ] in *calm,* you will feel the difference in the shape of your mouth. Most likely the vowel in *eat* makes greater use of certain overtones than the vowel in *calm.*

In a selective capacity, then, the oral cavity acts to reinforce particular overtones, which are primarily responsible for the distinguishing characteristics of the vowel sounds.

The Nasal Cavity (Nose)

Description

The nasal cavity actually consists of two cavities. The dividing wall of thin bone and cartilage between the nostrils extends back to where the velum is joined to the hard palate.

Function as a Resonator

The nasal cavity is the least versatile resonator and is primarily responsible for resonating [m], [n], and [ŋ]. Its total contribution to resonance is somewhat limited, although it can have a damping, or diminishing, effect on many sounds.

Other Resonators

When you speak or sing in a low tone, you can easily feel vibrations in your ribs and chest. Occasionally singers, teachers of voice, and actors like to talk about chest resonance. The cushioning effect, however, of flesh, tissue, and muscles, not to mention clothing, probably diminishes considerably the effectiveness of the chest as a resonator.

It's also possible that the facial bones are set into forced vibration by the action of the vocal folds. The terms *head resonance* or *sinus resonance* are not uncommon, but here again it's unlikely that the bones of the forehead or the sinuses themselves contribute significantly to the resonating process.

RESONANCE AND QUALITY

The voices of both Bugs Bunny and Dan Rather have resonance, but (and we may all be quite thankful) Dan Rather's voice quality is vastly different from that of the famous cartoon character. Bugs Bunny's voice, in reality, comes from the throat of a quite human and unrabbitlike gentleman, Mel Blanc, who provides the voice of many cartoon characters, human and animal. Blanc and Rather initiate fundamentals and overtones with their vocal folds, of course, and in both instances, the process of resonation selects, reinforces, and enriches the fundamentals and overtones. Therefore, we shouldn't say that Dan Rather's voice has more resonance than Bugs Bunny's voice. He probably has more of the right kind of resonance than Bugs. Or we might say that Bugs has too much of the wrong kind of resonance. Actually, Blanc creates the brassy voice of that pesky rabbit by deliberately interfering with and impeding resonance: he tightens the muscles of his mouth and throat. Similar techniques very likely produce the unforgettable voices of a couple of the gabbier and more outrageous Muppet characters, Gonzo and Miss Piggy.

The individual sounds that identify the voices of Dan Rather, Bugs Bunny, and the Muppet characters are characterized not by their resonance, but by their quality. In other words, then, *quality is the hearer's interpretation of resonance.* Thus, one voice does not have more quality than another, but a different type of quality.

How, then, do you develop the appropriate kind of sound quality? The next chapter answers that question.

WRAP-UP

1. The chest cavity, or thorax, has twelve pairs of ribs attached to the spinal column (backbone). The ten upper pairs are connected as well to the sternum, or breastbone. The two lowest pairs, which are not attached to the sternum, are called free, or floating, ribs.

2. The chest cavity is almost entirely filled by the two lungs, which are spongy and elastic air reservoirs. They are shaped something like cones that are narrow on top and wide at the bottom.

3. Lung tissues are passive. They neither suck in nor push out air.

4. The most important muscle of breathing is the diaphragm. It separates the chest cavity from the abdominal cavity. It is a thin but very tough muscle that resembles a dome or an upside-down bowl.

5. The primary reason we breathe is to stay alive. Secondarily, we breathe to speak.

6. In inhalation, you breathe in by increasing your chest capacity. Your diaphragm flattens, pulling down the floor of your chest cavity. The air pressure in your lungs is now lower than the pressure outside your body, and air rushes into your lungs.

7. In exhalation, you breathe out by decreasing your chest capacity. Your diaphragm is pushed back up. The air pressure in your lungs is now higher than the air pressure outside your body, and air rushes out of your lungs.

8. Life (nonspeech) breathing involves comparatively shallow breaths. You inhale about as fast as you exhale, approximately twelve times a minute.

9. Breathing to speak requires fuller and deeper breaths. Inhalation is quick. About one-sixth of your time is spent taking in air. Exhalation is slow. About five-sixths of your time is spent expelling breath as you speak.

10. Clavicular-shoulder breathing involves movements of the upper part of the chest. This method tends to provide shallow breathing, and it may lead to excessive tensions in the throat. The method is used infrequently by people with superior voices.

11. Central-deep breathing uses movements in the abdominal area. This method permits greater control, ease, and flexibility and is used frequently by people with superior voices.

12. The larynx, or voice box, is a structure of cartilages and muscles that sits on top of the windpipe. As the principal organ of sound, it houses the vocal folds, or bands.

13. The vocal folds, which average less than an inch in length, are made to vibrate by puffs of air coming up from the lungs and windpipe. The vibrating vocal folds act as a sound generator.

14. How slow or fast the vocal folds vibrate or flutter is determined by their length, their thickness or mass, and their tension when they start to vibrate. In general, the greater the number of vibrations of the folds, the higher the pitch. The fewer the number of vibrations of the folds, the lower the pitch.

15. The sounds produced by the vocal-fold vibrations are little more than weak buzzes or noises. These sounds have to be reinforced, amplified, modified, altered, and enriched by resonators before we recognize them as voice. The process is known as resonance.

16. Resonators are the soundboards that reinforce, modify, and enrich sounds. The three principal human resonators are the pharynx (throat), the oral cavity (mouth), and the nasal cavity (nose).

Assignment 1: Breathing

For home practice, select any of the exercises in this chapter that you believe will help you. Are you breathing efficiently?

Your final target is to achieve easy and natural control of breathing. This means that you shouldn't be consciously aware of how or when you breathe as you read, as you speak in class, or as you talk to people. Remember:

- Breath control must be coordinated with phonation (the making of speech sounds).
- It must never interfere with phonation. The outgoing breath must be used economically and not wasted.
- Breath control must be coordinated with phrasing. Inhalation must be accomplished quickly where a pause permits.

Prepare and practice material to be read in class. Two to three minutes of material, 300 to 450 words, is typical, but your instructor may modify the amount of material and the time limits.

Your instructor may also recommend specific material, but if you're on your own:

PLEASE SELECT INTERESTING MATERIAL (for future assignments as well). Informal prose is generally preferable to poetry. Choose something that is conversational and casual. Newspaper editorials or paragraphs from your microbiology and calculus textbooks are written in a more formal style for the eye rather than the ear. *Avoid these!*

You'll do a better job with an anecdote, a folk tale, the most unforgettable character you've ever met or a personal experience: an embarrassing or frightening moment, an amusing job experience.

You'll also get a far better response from your listeners, and this will encourage you and help you perform more effectively.

Suggested Checklist for Assignment 1

As you practice, you may want to work with this check list. Listen carefully to yourself, have a friend check you, and perhaps watch yourself in a mirror as you practice. Eventually, your goal will be to have a check mark in the **Yes** column for each category. (Optional: Perhaps your instructor will want to use the checklist to evaluate you during your classroom presentation.)

	Yes	No
Maintains alert, comfortably erect posture		
Upper chest and shoulders remain relatively motionless		
Most expansion-contraction activities occur in medial areas of the body		
Inhalation is silent, quick, unobtrusive		

AVOIDS—

	Yes	No
running out of breath in the middle of a word or phrase		
overbreathing: taking in too much breath, taking too much time to inhale		
breath leaks before or after sounds or during pauses		
breath leaks on such sounds as *s, sh, th, f*		
Coordinates phrasing and breathing so that the material is meaningful, natural, and interesting		

Additional comments or suggestions:

PUT YOUR BEST VOICE FORWARD!
Quality

WOULD YOU BELIEVE THAT

. . . Of the ten best speaking voices in the United States (chosen by five hundred speech communication experts), eight are the voices of actors? The complete list: actors Julie Andrews, Pernell Roberts, Sean Connery, James Earl Jones, Gregory Peck, Jane Fonda, John Forsythe, Burt Reynolds, and TV personalities John Chancellor and Connie Chung.

. . . There is only one voice in the world exactly like your voice—your own? Your voice is you. Courts of law now recognize a voice print as evidence that is as acceptable as a fingerprint for identifying an individual.

. . . If you breathe seventy-five percent helium, you'll quack like a duck, whether you want to or not?

. . . Those low-pitched, sexy and sultry female voices which galvanize the fellows often have pathological (medical) problems?

. . . Although most opera stars are absolute fanatics about the care of their voices, Enrico Caruso, the world's greatest tenor, was not? He smoked two packages of superstrong Egyptian cigarettes daily.

. . . Early in her acting career, the late Grace Kelly had a thin, bleaty, high-pitched voice? She studied voice and developed what came to be known as "that cream-of-tomato-soup voice"—smooth and rich.

IS YOUR VOICE PLEASANT TO LISTEN TO?

Your voice tells us a lot about you. It's a key to your identity. It's your calling card, your trademark, your personal logo. It's like a sandwich board—the kind you strut around with. It advertises something. In this case it proclaims to the world what kind of a person you are.

Quality is that certain something about voices that makes us rate a voice as first rate or second rate. People we respond to favorably often have agreeable voices. The people we avoid may possibly have voices that jar us or get on our nerves.

Thanks to movies and TV we associate a certain kind of voice with a specific character type. We see a timid, anemic-looking individual, and we expect a wishy-washy, mousy voice to come out of him. We watch Robert Duvall play an aggressive loudmouth, and we expect a harsh, raucous voice. Rhea Perlman of NBC's "Cheers" portrays a brassy character with a voice to match. Joan Collins is seductive; her voice is come-hither. George C. Scott and Charles Bronson use gruff voices to delineate grumpy, brusque individuals.

Quality is the texture of a sound or tone that distinguishes it from another tone having the same pitch, duration, and loudness.

Kathleen Battle, rising young star of the Metropolitan Opera, and Barbra Streisand and Linda Ronstadt, of less Olympian heights, have at least one thing in common: each of them is a soprano. Yet, if each of them made a recording of "America, the Beautiful" in the same key, few of us would mistake one of these singers for another.

Likewise, if a trumpet player, a violinist, and a saxophonist played middle C and sustained the tone for the same length of time and at the same level of loudness, you'd have no problem recognizing which was which. And if a close friend phones you, you can generally identify the person at once. Perhaps there is a warmth and richness about this particular voice. Another friend's voice, however, may have a rather hard and brassy quality. A third friend who calls may sound breathy and whispery. All of these characteristics help you identify the quality—tone, color, or timbre—of the voice.

We may sometimes overlook the unpleasant vocal quality of a speaker who is highly persuasive, funny, or fluent, or we may become engrossed with *what* is being said rather than *how* it's being said. Most of the time, however, an unpleasant voice is a liability.

Two things determine voice quality:

■ The production of the original tone by the vocal folds (*phonation*).
■ The process of selection, reinforcement, and enrichment of this tone by the resonators (throat, mouth, and nasal cavities).

Certain aspects of your vocal quality, which are determined by the structure of your body, cannot be changed, but some aspects can be substantially improved. Your vocal mechanism is an integrated, not an isolated, part of your body. In other words, things that affect you emotionally or physically may also affect, directly or indirectly, your speech processes. Simply stated, good emotional and physical health are generally necessary before you can produce effective voice. Rarely do you hear a great voice coming from a sickly, cadaverous body. The voice is an amazingly good index of the physical and mental health of a person.

NECESSARY AND UNNECESSARY TENSION

Are you worried or under pressure because of . . .

finances, friends, family problems, fitness, love life, looks, livelihood, teachers or *tests, bosses* or *bombs?*

I can't do anything about the lurking dangers of ICBM's, but I can help you learn how to relax and overcome some of the stress and strain.

Tension and stress are here to stay. They're the price you pay for being human. Dick Cavett clinches it: "Tension is the enemy. It's the most undesirable thing you can have. It contributes nothing."

Tension and stress are not only enemies of good health, they can also seriously interfere with your resonance and vocal quality. The Wrought-Up Robertas and the High-Strung Hirams of the world produce voices to match— undesirable and displeasing.

If you have a tight, constricted throat with rigid walls, for example, your voice may be strident, jarring and rasping.

Openness of throat and relaxation of the walls and surfaces will promote a mellow, velvety and molasses-rich quality.

RELAXATION

Relax—let go completely!

It can't be done!

If you didn't have some muscular tension, you couldn't walk, talk, or blow your nose. "If everything goes right there would be something wrong," as B. F. Skinner, Harvard psychologist, once said. "You must have tension to stay alive."

Let go completely really means: Try to get rid of *unessential* tension in those muscles not needed to perform your task.

Part of the difference between the professional and the amateur—be it an Olympic champion or a student of voice—is the ability to distinguish between what tension is necessary and what isn't. You're concerned with eliminating the undue tightness that hampers voice improvement. You're committed to finding the right kind of relaxation. But never confuse relaxation with inertia or laxness. Relaxation is *selective, conscious* and *controlled.*

The large muscles of the body are easier to get at and loosen, and you can't isolate and relax the relatively small muscles of your vocal equipment if the large ones are taut, so it's with these that we begin:

1. Stand. Deliberately tense the larger muscles of your body and then let go. Repeat several times.
2. While you're standing, have somebody raise one of your arms slowly and then release it. There should be no resistance, and your arm should fall limply to the side. Repeat, but this time offer some resistance, keeping the rest of your body relaxed. Gradually relax the resisting arm.
3. The YEC-C-C-CH! exercise: Pretend that you've accidentally plunged your arm into a barrel of gunk or slime. (It smells terrible and there are little green things wriggling around in it.) Shake your arm vigorously to get rid of the repulsive stuff. It helps to say "Yec-c-c-ch!" as you do this. Repeat, but this time the slime is on your legs, then your torso, and finally the neck and the head.
4. Sit. Tighten your body. Then relax, allowing your head to fall forward and your arms to dangle loosely at the sides.

Try Exercise 5 at home:

5. Select a quiet, comfortable room and lie down, face up on a sofa or bed. Loosen tight clothing. Unwind mentally. A background of soft, mood music helps. Or relive a previously serene and soothing experience.

   a. Stretch and yawn. The stretching should be intense, but the yawning gentle.
   b. Purposely stiffen the larger muscles of your body and then let go. Repeat this pattern several times.
   c. Lie on your left side and rotate your right shoulder slowly and tensely. After a few seconds, relax the shoulder and continue to rotate it. Try the left shoulder.
   d. Extend your right arm rigidly into the air. Relax it and then let it fall limply. Try the left arm.
   e. Assume a fetal or a near-fetal position. Bow your head forward, draw your arms and legs in toward your chin. Curl up. Tighten your entire body. Think of yourself as being absolutely compact and not much bigger than a basketball. Hold this tense position for six to eight seconds, then suddenly let your body go limp. Try to feel a wave of relaxation sweeping down from your forehead to your feet. Concentrate on removing any tensions around your forehead, eyes, mouth and jaw, neck, and back.

6. Now that you've removed the crinkles from the larger muscles, let's do the same for the smaller ones. These exercises will help you loosen the sound-producing mechanisms:

   a. Stretch your neck forward and downward, tensing your jaw and neck muscles. Let your head drop forward so that your chin touches your chest. Don't raise your shoulders as you move your head slowly to your right shoulder, to the rear, to the left shoulder, and forward to the chest again. Rotate your head in this manner several times, maintaining muscular rigidity and tightness. Now repeat these motions, but this time gradually relax the jaw and neck muscles.
   b. Say the following as though sighing. Stre-e-etch those vowel sounds:
      aw-haw-arm-cot-caw-maw-palm-tall-mush-mum-sup

7. This tranquil material will help you unwind. Read it quietly, calmly and slowly. Pro-o-o-long the vowels slightly. Concentrate on a general feeling of unbending and easing up.

   a. When it is dark enough, you can see the stars.
   b. What is life? It is the flash of a firefly in the night.
   c. Death tugs at my ear and says: "Live, I am coming."
   d. The Arctic expresses the sum of all wisdom: silence.
   e. Soft heads do more harm than soft muscles.
   f. Even if this is the dawn of a bright new world, most of us are still in the dark.
   g. People go to take sunbaths. Why have so few had the idea of taking baths of silence?
   h. One was asked, "What is hell?" The answer: "It is heaven that has come too late."
   i. Those who want the fewest things are nearest the gods.
   j. Let your speech be better than silence, or be silent.
   k. In real life it takes only one to make a quarrel.

l.   You have to adjust your running style when you're running on ice.

m.   Why is the place where I want to be so often so far from where I am?

n.   When you are deeply absorbed in what you are doing, time gives itself to you like a warm and willing lover.

Relaxing Throat and Mouth

As you've discovered in the last few pages, general, overall, bodily relaxation is the first step in developing a pleasing vocal quality. Now you can move to the next step:

Three conditions are necessary before you can build a satisfactory quality.

■ *Your throat and mouth passageways must be relatively open, selectively relaxed, and free of unnecessary tension.*

■ *Your lips and the jaw and, of course, your tongue must be agile and flexible.*

■ *Tone must be "projected" to the front of your mouth.*

8.   "Freeze" or tense your throat and jaw muscles and then swallow. Holding this extreme tension for a few seconds, say *ah*. What happens to your vocal quality?

9.   Now, for contrast, relax the jaw, and yawn gently as you inhale. With the same degree of ease, say *ah*. Notice the difference.

10. Keeping the feeling of ease and openness, say these words as though sighing:

who	now	odd	up	too
how	moo	oh	mush	oat
awl	rue	sue	call	loll
coo	saw	shawl	lass	sum

11. Let your jaw remain open and as motionless as possible, and keep the tip of your tongue behind your lower front teeth as you say:

a.   yah-yah-yah-yah-yah-yah-yah-yah

b.   you-you-you-you-you-you-you-you

c.   yoh-yoh-yoh-yoh-yoh-yoh-yoh-yoh

d.   hoo-hoo-hoo-hoo-hoo-hoo-hoo-hoo

e.   hoh-hoh-hoh-hoh-hoh-hoh-hoh-hoh

f.   hey-hey-hey-hey-hey-hey-hey-hey

12. Expa-a-a-nd your vowels and diphthongs slightly as you read these with an open and relaxed throat:

a.   Come up into the hills, O my young love.

b.   The river is a tide of moving waters.

c.   Come to us through the fields of night.

d.   The lights were sown like flung stars.

e.   The light was brown-gold like ground coffee.

f.   Darkness melted over the town like dew.

g.   The day was like gold and sapphires.

h.   The blue gulf of the sky was spread with light, massy clouds.

i.   The soft rays of the sun beat the gentle earth.

j.   The hush of dawn washed the murmuring brook in glowing pink.

k.   The quiet music of the stars nudged the heavy clouds of night.

l.   Froth and foam trickled through the thawing mash.

m.   The mountains were said to be in labor, and uttered the most dreadful groans. People came together far and near to see what birth would be produced; and, after they had waited a considerable time, in expectation, out crept a mouse. [Aesop]

The following exercises will help you develop agility and flexibility of your lips and jaw:

13. Open your mouth as widely as you can on the initial sound in each word.

opera	owl	always	hour	awl
awful	oddly	ouster	army	ought
almond	otter	office	ostrich	auk
auger	oxen	alder	object	ocelot

14. Give these a snappy reading, exaggerating your lip movements.

a. we-we-we-we-we-we-we-we

b. re-re-re-re-re-re-re-re

c. me-me-me-me-me-me-me-me

d. woo-woo-woo-woo-woo-woo-woo-woo

e. waw-waw-waw-waw-waw-waw-waw-waw

f. woo-waw-woo-waw-woo-waw-woo-waw

PROJECTING TONE

"Bounce your voice off the back wall of the room!"

IMPOSSIBLE!

You absolutely can't focus or bounce your voice—from a purely scientific point of view. For that matter, ventriloquists don't "throw" their voices either.

On the other hand, these words aren't just gimmicks. If you're told to focus, bounce, or project your voice, you'll respond by opening your mouth somewhat wider than you normally do. Your general articulation will also become more energetic and nimble. As you sharpen up with the material below, direct and aim your tones forward against the upper front teeth. This kind of practicing will give you greater clarity and brilliance of quality.

15. Chant these, but give the *oh* and *aw* sounds the same frontal placement and luster of *ee:*

a. ee-ee-ee-ee

b. oh-oh-oh-oh

c. aw-aw-aw-aw

d. lee-loh-law

e. bee-boh-baw

f. dee-doh-daw

g. wee-woh-waw

h. mee-moh-maw

i. tee-toh-taw

16. Can you carry over the forward placement and brightness of tone from the first sentence to the second and third sentence of each of these groups? Keep your throat relaxed. Build up the vowel tones, but avoid any hint of hardness or scratchiness.

a. What we really need in this country is a car that eats oats.
People who row the boat generally don't have time to rock it.
Once you get a reputation as an early riser, you can sleep till noon.

b. Please drive carefully—the IRS needs you.
If you want to forget all your other troubles, wear shoes that pinch.
A virgin forest is a forest in which the hand of man has never set foot.

c. When people agree with me, I always feel I must be wrong.
I'm not OK. You're not OK, and that's OK.
Sign on a church lawn: "Keep off the grass. This means thou."

d. If preachers preach and teachers teach, why don't we say that speakers speech?
The more I know the more I know I don't know.
Love conquers all things except poverty and toothache.

e. I would rather eat than fish, particularly eat fish.
What you don't see with your eyes, don't invent with your mouth.
There will be prayer in public schools, law or no law, as long as there are final exams.

f. We easily believe that which we wish.
Less is only more where more is no good.
It's better to be wanted for murder than not to be wanted at all.

g. The brain that doesn't feed itself, eats itself.
What happens to the hole when the cheese is gone?
I am going to speak my mind because I have nothing to lose.

h. The meek shall inherit the earth, but how long will they stay meek after they get it?
I shot an arrow into the air, and it stuck.
Whoever said money can't buy happiness didn't know where to shop.

THE SOUND OF YOUR VOICE

The human voice is the most beautiful instrument in the world.
Maybe you remember a poem by John Saxe. It begins:

It was six men of Indostan
To learning much inclined,
Who went to see the elephant
(Though all of them were blind),
That each by observation
Might satisfy his mind.

The side of the elephant felt like a wall to the first blind man. Number two grabbed a tusk and declared the elephant to be a spear. To the others, the trunk suggested a snake, the knee felt like a tree, the ear and the tail resembled a fan and a rope. And, as Saxe says later in his jingle, ". . . each was partly in the right, and all were in the wrong!"

Some fifteen hundred students in voice and diction classes were asked to be voice appraisers in the presidential campaigns as far back as 1972. They were told to jot down a few words describing their impressions of the candidates. The results were expectedly controversial.

On the donkey side of the ballot, the voices of candidates McGovern, Carter, Mondale and Ferraro were most often labelled: *warm, edgy, twangy, grating, silky, oily.*

On the elephant side, the voices of candidates Nixon, Ford, Reagan and Bush were most often labeled: *cellolike, slimy, metallic, whiny, syrupy, oily.*

One suspects that the political persuasion of the listeners might just possibly have something to do with their choice of adjectives. What is *growly* and *dead* to Patrick is *creamy* and *enticing* to Patricia. Yet, many of these terms do help us tag a certain kind of voice. But here are more specific terms widely used by voice experts (and you'll remember reading about them earlier in the book): BREATHY, GLOTTAL SHOCK (or ATTACK), STRIDENT, HARSH, VOCAL FRY, NASAL, DENASAL, THROATY, HOARSE.

Note: Assignments in this section should be selected according to individual needs. If you can, tape your voice. Your instructor will help you identify any specific problems, and will recommend exercises that will help you improve your voice quality. If you become aware of any vocal strain or discomfort, discontinue the exercises. Seek professional assistance. Your instructor will advise you how to contact a speech pathologist or a physician.

THE BREATHY VOICE

DO YOU SOUND FUZZY, WHISPERY, OR FEATHER-EDGED? YOU'RE BREATHY!

If you have this woolly quality, it's because when you're talking, you don't bring your vocal cords together firmly enough to form a tight seal, and unused air leaks between them.

A breathy voice isn't always unattractive. You've noticed how often TV and movie actresses cultivate this vocal cloudiness. Diane Keaton, Zsa Zsa Gabor and Goldie Hawn have this smoggy quality. It allegedly makes the voice sound sexy, and some members of the male sex claim to be stirred up by this type of downy charm.

Breathiness is less common among male voices, although many actors in soap operas, particularly in the steamier scenes, tend to produce voices that contain more soap suds than clear and solid tones.

ELIMINATING BREATHINESS

The answer is to get just the right amount of tension in your vocal cords. They should be neither too tight nor too relaxed. Don't try to be as limp and floppy as the Scarecrow of Oz. Inadequate tension may be responsible for the failure to bring the vocal cords together during tone production. Be aware of muscle adjustments in your throat. Exercises 17–20 will help you.

17. Sit like a robot in an armless chair. Grip the sides of the chair and tighten your body, especially your arms and shoulders. Say the pronoun *I* half a dozen times, using a strong voice. You'll feel some pressure in your throat and hear a firmer tone quality. Then substitute these sentences for *I:*

    a. Soup should be seen and not heard.
    b. Facts do not change; feelings do.
    c. If you can't stand the heat, get out of the oven.
    d. Behind every great man is a woman. Behind her is his wife.
    e. The family that stays together probably has only one car.

18. Stand erect. Extend your arms rigidly in front of you. Hold a fairly heavy book in your hands. Say *I* several times, and then repeat the short sentences in Exercise 17.

Try this exercise at home:

19. Remember Samson of Biblical fame? Stand in an open door with the palms of your hands placed flat against each side of the door. Push as firmly as you can. You'll feel the increased tension of muscles in the abdominal and chest areas. Hold the position for five to six seconds (your vocal folds should now be closed), then release the pressure. Relax. Repeat the Samson exercise half a dozen times.

20. Repeat, but as you let go, count from one to ten. Make the numbers hard and robust. Do this several times.

21. As soon as your voice sounds strong and sturdy with the numbers, try these:

    a. Do it now! Today will be yesterday tomorrow.
    b. Blind dates are better than no dates at all.
    c. Love teaches even asses to dance.
    d. One should eat to live, not live to eat.
    e. Never strike a child. You might miss and hurt yourself.

22. As you rehearse the first sentence in each trio, exaggerate and use a breathy, smoky, and sighing quality. Make the second sentence louder, and eliminate *some* of the featheriness. The third sentence should be spoken in a firm voice. Do away with all traces of fuzz and fluff.

    a. The more the change, the more it is the same thing.
       Beware the fury of a patient person.
       I'm an instant star. Just add water and stir. [Barbra Streisand]
    b. A nose that can see is worth two that sniff.
       Saint: A dead sinner revised and edited.
       If love makes the world go around, why are we going into outer space?
    c. Man will always delight in a woman whose voice is lined with velvet.
       A fox is a wolf who sends flowers.
       The world is getting better every day—and then worse again in the evening.
    d. You can never be too skinny or too rich.
       Quit worrying about your health. It'll go away.
       When the going gets tough, the smart get lost.
    e. Some people speak from experience. Others—from experience—don't speak.
       If you're there before it's over, you're on time.
       A good rooster crows in any hen house.

f. Energy is beauty. A Rolls Royce with an empty tank doesn't run.
Self-love is the greatest of all flatterers.
Fun is like life insurance: The older you get, the more it costs.

g. Money is always there, but the pockets change.
Marriage is two people agreeing to tell the same lie.
Start every day off with a smile and get it over with.

23. Certain consonants are breathier and hissier than others: *s, f, th, h, sh,* and *p.* They're simply molded puffs of air. The problem arises if an individual carries over the hissy sound to a next-door vowel or consonant. In the word *shall,* for example, the feathery quality of *sh* shouldn't color the rest of the word: *all.* Try doing it the wrong way. Expand the underlined sounds in these words:

a.	<u>s</u>ay	lat<u>ch</u>	wi<u>sh</u>	cal<u>f</u>	<u>s</u>ick
b.	<u>h</u>ill	<u>h</u>iss	<u>h</u>im	<u>k</u>id	<u>th</u>in
c.	<u>f</u>ad	<u>sh</u>ould	<u>f</u>ine	ro<u>p</u>e	<u>t</u>ale

24. This time cut short each sound with a diagonal line. Don't draw it out.

a.	ṣay	latℓh	wiṣh	calḟ	ṣick
b.	ḥill	ḥiss	ḥim	ḳid	ṭhin
c.	ḟad	ṣhould	ḟine	roṗe	ṭale

25. Read these word clusters at a moderately loud level. Keep each word entirely free of breathiness. The third and fourth words in each group need special attention.

a. I–die–sigh–high
b. am–dam–Pam–ham
c. ow–bow–sow–how
d. at–bat–fat–sat
e. ope–dope–soap–hope

f. ale–bale–pale–sail
g. air–bare–tear–hair
h. eyed–bide–side–hide
i. all–doll–Paul–hall
j. Ike–bike–tyke–hike

26. Sustain these sounds by beginning with a quiet, but nonbreathy, tone and by increasing the loudness of each:

ah   oh   ee   oo   uh

27. Use full volume as you start these selections, but after you've read a line or two, gradually reduce the loudness until you hit a moderate level of volume that is free of breathiness.

a. It's no secret that organized crime in this country takes in over one hundred million dollars a year. This is quite a nice profit, especially when you consider that the Mafia spends very little for office supplies.

b. How come it's always the loudest snorer who falls asleep first? Women can cure their husband's snoring by kindness, patience—or stuffing an old sock in his mouth.

c. It's said of Jane Austen that on her deathbed she made it plain that she wanted to say something, and what she wanted to say was that she had written that life was ninety-nine percent chance and wished to correct this figure to one hundred percent.

d. It's surprising how easy it is to tolerate people when you don't really have to. Always be tolerant with a person who disagrees with you. After all, he has his right to his ridiculous opinion.

e. The boy called out "Wolf, Wolf!" and the villagers came out to help him. A few days afterward he tried the same trick, and again they came to his help. Shortly after this a wolf actually came, but this time the villagers thought the boy was deceiving them again and nobody came to his aid. A liar will not be believed, even when he speaks the truth. [Aesop]

28. Read each of these in a clear, solid tone—one that is free of breathiness. Keep out the vocal vapors.

   a. If truth is beauty, how come people don't have their hair done in the library?
   b. I'm not very keen for doves or hawks. I think we need more owls.
   c. A person of sixty has spent twenty years in bed and over three years eating.
   d. Grow up as soon as you can. The only time you really live fully is from thirty to sixty.
   e. Americans are people with more timesaving devices and less time than any other people in the world.
   f. Running for office is like coaching a team. You have to be smart enough to know how to win and dumb enough to think it's important.
   g. Most people would rather defend to the death your right to say it than listen to it.
   h. After you hear two eyewitnesses to an automobile accident, you're not so sure about history.
   i. I expect to pass through this world but once. Any good therefore that I can do, or any kindness that I can show to any human being, let me do it now. Let me not defer or neglect it, for I shall not pass this way again.

Breathiness is often related to other voice problems. An inadequately loud voice, for example, is frequently breathy. If you have this type of voice, you should work on both problems simultaneously, and the exercises in Chapter 6 will be helpful. A voice that's improperly pitched, especially one that's excessively low, may occasionally be breathy. There's a serviceable and agreeable pitch level—the optimum level—for most of us, and if we use it, we'll generally not be breathy. See Chapter 7.

Assignment 2: Breathiness

Select interesting material, and as you practice it, use a relatively moderate level of loudness. Make your vowel sounds forceful and clear. Don't let breath escape between words or during pauses, and avoid blasting on voiceless sounds. When you perform before the class, do so in a voice that's free of breathiness and vocal fuzz.

The Suggested Checklist that includes Assignments 2–7 can be found at the end of the chapter. It may be useful to you as you practice.

GLOTTAL SHOCK

DO YOU MAKE EXPLOSIVE GRUNTS ON YOUR FRONTAL VOWELS? YOU HAVE *GLOTTAL SHOCK*.
   Read aloud the following sentences, inserting a slight pause between the words:
      Andy and Opal invited Eve to the eerie island in April.
      Ask Ann and Arthur to open the old apple with an axe.
      The owl eyed the eel and ate the olive in August.
If you notice a raspy little bark or a sharp, staccato click on the vowels at the beginning of each word, you may have glottal shock (also known as glottal attack, click, or stroke). In one sense, glottal shock is the opposite of breathiness, in which breath is allowed to escape before initial vowels are begun. In glottal shock, however, the glottis is closed firmly *before* the vowel is sounded. The subglottal breath pressure builds up, and the breath finally explodes its way through, blasting the vocal folds apart. Part of the problem in overcoming glottal shock, then, is a matter of timing and coordination. The air stream must begin to flow as the vocal folds are ready to receive it.

REDUCING TENSION

Frequently, a tense, strained throat and larynx are responsible for glottal shock. If the vocal folds are closed completely and too tensely as phonation (the production of vocal tones or sounds) begins, the blast will generally be pronounced. As an example, tense your throat muscles and repeat the same three sentences, deliberately attempting to start each word with a glottal shock. Repeat these until you are able to hear this attack.

   Now perform these exercises:

29. Start *aw* on a whisper, but gradually begin sound with the softest and gentlest tone you can make. Be especially careful that when your voice changes from a whisper to a vocal tone there's no clicking sound or rasp. Hold the nonwhispered sound for five or six seconds and then repeat. Try with *oo, ee, oh, a* (as in *ask*).

30. Try these, working for an easy, relaxed attack.

    a. ha–ha–ha–ha–ha–ha–ha–ha
    b. ho–ho–ho–ho–ho–ho–ho–ho
    c. he–he–he–he–he–he–he–he
    d. hi–hi–hi–hi–hi–hi–hi–hi
    e. hoo–hoo–hoo–hoo–hoo–hoo–hoo–hoo

    Repeat these syllables, dropping the *h*.

31. As you drill with these word pairs, you'll notice that it's easy to produce a clickless vowel if it follows *h*. Try to keep this easy, "doing-what-comes-naturally" approach as you say the second *h*-less word in the following pairs:

Hal–Al	holly–Ollie	ham–am	hoe–owe
hold–old	hide–ide	hunk–unk	hair–air
hide–I'd	honk–onk	hope–ope	hun–un
hat–at	heat–eat	handy–Andy	had–add

32. As you read aloud or speak conversationally, you tend to link or blend words together in phrases or clusters. Read the words in each of the columns. Don't permit a break between the phrases in the second and fourth columns. For example, *an* and *apple* in the second column should be blended together just as the syllables are in *Annapolis* in the first column. Avoid glottal shock.

Annapolis	an apple	tiara	tee are
thrash	three ashes	trio	tree oh
theater	the account	beautify	be at
Newark	new ark	Neanderthal	knee and
trapeze	trap easy	meander	me and

33. Read each of these phrases in one continuous and uninterrupted flow of breath. Be cautious with the attack on the initial vowel.

    a. in–an–open–alley
    b. evening–April–air–is–elegant
    c. add–an–owl–and–an–ogre
    d. Enid–eats–onions–and–omelettes
    e. oats–and–apples–are–extra
    f. I–am–in–agony
    g. ill–in–old–office
    h. odes–in–October–are–awesome

34. Pay close attention to the frontal sounds and work for an easy, shockless attack. Don't chop off the words, but blend or link them together without interruption.

    a. I owe, I owe, so it's off to work I go.
    b. Wherever I climb, I am followed by a dog called Ego.
    c. A word isn't a bird. If it flies out and escapes, you'll never catch it again.
    d. I often feel I'll just opt out of this rat race and buy another hunk of Utah. [Robert Redford]
    e. Professionals built the *Titanic*—amateurs the ark.
    f. There aren't any embarrassing questions—only embarrassing answers.
    g. It is only possible to live happily ever after on a day-to-day basis.

Assignment 3: Glottal Shock

Prepare material in which most of the words begin with vowels or diphthongs. You may use nonsense material. As you practice, link the words together, but be certain that the initial words are free of glottal shock. The Suggested Checklist for the assignment at the end of the chapter may be useful to you as you practice.

THE STRIDENT VOICE

DO YOU SOUND BRASSY, PIERCING OR STRAINED? YOU'RE *STRIDENT.*

A popular magazine polls its readers yearly. Who are the ten most admired living women? The results:

Queen Elizabeth	Elizabeth Dole
Nancy Reagan	Margaret Thatcher
Mother Theresa	Geraldine Ferraro
Katharine Hepburn	Sandra Day O'Connor
Jane Fonda	Ann Landers

The last name on the list, Ann Landers, is the widely read and popular columnist who dispenses common-sensical and often humorous advice on everything from heartbreak to herpes, paranoia to petting, and, occasionally, how to make meat loaf.

It comes as a bit of a shock to some of her fans to hear the lady in person. Here is an astringent and quite scratchy voice. (It comes as no shock to her. She's aware of it.)

Breathy voices don't always faze hearers, but listening to strident voices is something like having a root canal job without novocaine. It's earsplitting, steely, and forced.

Does your voice sound blaring and abrasive even when you're not waspish or uptight? You can often *see* stridency! Talk to your mirror. Do the veins and muscles in your neck seem to knot or bulge? If they do, your voice may have all the raucous charm of an outraged parrot.

This high-pitched harshness generally results from *excessive* muscular tension in the throat. It's far more characteristic of women's voices than men's, although there are males whose voices have a cawing crow quality.

We often associate this sharp and taut kind of voice with a high-strung, jittery and hypertense individual. (If you're persistently strident, you may have a psychological problem. In this case, professional counseling is recommended.)

REDUCING STRIDENCY

Stridency is often related to one or a combination of several factors:

- Using too much of the wrong kind of loudness. Squeezing and rasping the tone out of the throat with no feeling of bodily support. How do you get that body support? Chapter 6 will tell you.
- Speaking with a too-high pitch level. Chapter 7 will help you find a comfortable pitch level.
- Shallow breathing. Have you checked your breathing recently? Remember, clavicular breathing promotes throat tensions. Deep breathing doesn't. If you need to, check Exercises 1–8 in Chapter 2.
- Unnaturally tight throat. Review Exercises 6–12 in this chapter.

35. Locate the V-shaped notch at the top of your larynx. Say this sentence several times at a comfortably low pitch level: *She and he weeded the wiry seaweed.*

    If you can't find the notch, you may be raising your larynx too high in your throat. Again, too much tension is the villain. Practice until you're able to lower the larynx to its normal position.

36. With your tongue on the floor of your mouth, start an easy, gentle yawn. Your throat area is reasonably relaxed. Whisper *ah* and hold for about five seconds. Gradually add voice to the whisper, and build it up to a moderately loud level. But don't allow a feeling of tightness to creep into your throat. Repeat with these sounds:

    ee (meet) oh ah ow oo (moon) oi uh

37. As you do the first sentence in each group, *be a tad strident.* (DON'T OVERDO THE STRIDENCY! A little bit goes a long way. If you have a sore throat, don't do it at all.)

But read the second sentence with a breathy and hushed quality.

Now, for contrast, try the third sentence with a normal quality—no stridency, no breathiness.

a. **(strident)** "Be yourself!" is about the worst advice you can give some people.
   (breathy) People don't change. They just become more so.
   (normal) A hole is nothing at all, but you can break your neck in it.

b. **(strident)** Avenue: a street that formerly had trees on it.
   (breathy) Teeth placed before the tongue give good advice.
   (normal) The greatest of faults, I should say, is to be conscious of none.

c. **(strident)** It doesn't matter if you're rich or poor, as long as you've got money.
   (breathy) If your soul is in your belly, nobody can drive you out of your skull.
   (normal) Everything comes to one who waits—among other things, death.

d. **(strident)** A cynic: a person who knows the price of everything and the value of nothing.
   (breathy) The burnt child shuns the fire until the next day.
   (normal) Nets: holes surrounded by pieces of string.

e. **(strident)** If an atom bomb destroys the human race, will surviving turtles wear people-neck sweaters?
   (breathy) It is hard for an empty bag to stand upright.
   (normal) Don't borrow trouble. Borrow money, and trouble will come of its own accord.

f. **(strident)** The wheel that squeaks the loudest is the one that gets the grease.
   (breathy) Conscience is the inner voice that warns us that someone may be looking.
   (normal) Hit the ball over the fence, and you can take your time going around the bases.

g. **(strident)** A newscast always starts off with 'Good evening'—and then proceeds to tell you why it isn't.
   (breathy) Many motorists tend to drive much too close to the cars behind them.
   (normal) If we all obeyed the Ten Commandments, there'd be no ten o'clock news, would there?

h. **(strident)** A bee is never as busy as it seems; it's just that it can't buzz any slower.
   (breathy) Laugh and the world laughs with you. Snore and you sleep alone.
   (normal) A fox should not be on a jury at a goose's trial.

38. Inhale deeply and then sigh. After you've done this several times, vocalize the words below on the sigh. Start with a relatively high tone, and then glide downward to a low tone. Your vocal folds should become more relaxed as you lower the pitch.

well	law	full	show	shop
our	dart	fool	boy	prowl
who	boil	not	cart	doll
round	mellow	brawl	lodge	warm

39. Carefully avoid stridency as you read these sentences. Prolong the principal vowel sounds and give each one a downward inflection so that it sounds like a vocalized sigh, thus:

```
    \     \     \     \   \      \
The years flowed by like water.
```

   a. The empty vessel makes the greatest sound.
   b. People born to be hanged are safe in water.
   c. The trouble with being poor is that it takes up all of your time.
   d. "Let us cross the river," the general said, "and rest under the shade of the trees."
   e. Eat to please yourself, but dress to please others.
   f. I would rather sit on a pumpkin and have it all to myself than to be crowded on a velvet cushion.
   g. It takes twenty years to make an overnight success.

40. Deliver these in a leisurely manner and stre-e-e-tch your vowels and diphthongs slightly, but avoid extreme exaggeration. Pay careful attention to breathing and pitch level. Work for proper relaxation, an unconstricted throat, and, of course, a vocal quality that isn't caustic or strident.

   a. If you are afraid of being lonely, don't try to be right.
   b. All work and no play makes Jack a dull boy and Jill a wealthy widow.
   c. Night is the time of love, of strange thoughts, of dreams.
   d. Death comes like a thief in the night. Don't let yourself get mugged.
   e. Faith is the bird that feels the light when the dawn is still dark.
   f. In heaven they will bore you. In hell you will bore them.
   g. This thing called rain can make the days seem short and the nights seem long.
   h. Tell me what you think you are and I will tell you what you are not.
   i. Don't shout for help at night. You might wake your neighbors.
   j. If fortune turns against you, even jelly breaks your tooth.

THE HARSH VOICE

DO YOU SOUND ROUGH, RASPY, GRUNTY OR GROWLY? YOU'RE *HARSH*.

   Not to be outdone by the ladies, a popular man's magazine surveyed its subscribers. The ten most admired men are:

Ronald Reagan	Bob Hope
Pope John Paul II	Bill Cosby
Lee Iacocca	Jimmy Carter
Prince Charles	Senator Edward Kennedy
Billy Graham	John Wayne

   What accounts for the appeal of the only one in the list who's no longer living—John Wayne? It may be his true-blue, apple pie Americanism or his swivel-hipped walk. But his voice? HARSH!

   This type of voice is gruff, husky, and guttural. No pun is intended, but *guttural* is a fine choice of word, because a scraping voice seems to grind its way up from a vocal gutter.

   A harsh voice is invariably low-pitched. In a sense, then—
what strident is to the female voice, harsh is to the male voice.

   The owners of these corrosive voices sometimes create the impression that they're cold and unsympathetic individuals, if not downright "meanies." Movies and TV heavies like Charles Bronson, Robert Mitchum, Lee Marvin (and the miscellaneous pushers and pimps who appear in "Miami Vice") make use of a voice like a human hacksaw as one way to create their tough-guy characterizations.

   An interesting exception is Debra Winger who uses a harsh rather than a strident voice to create sympathetic roles.

   Oddly enough, a guttural voice occasionally identifies a lazy and careless individual, and now and then, an ill at ease person—one who seems to be afraid of the sound of his own voice.

REDUCING HARSHNESS

What causes harshness?

■ Not enough energy in your speech. Many people with harsh voices have improved substantially by speaking more energetically (and louder).

■ A too low pitch level. Sometimes it's necessary to raise the habitual pitch level (the pitch level most frequently used) two to four semitones. See Exercises 1–12 in Chapter 7.

■ Permitting your tongue to hump up in your throat. Pulling back the tongue muffles the sound and also contributes to mealymouthed articulation.

■ Burying your chin in your neck while speaking. If you do this (once again have a dialogue with a mirror and check that chin position), you're pulling the voice box down into an abnormally low position.

■ Too much relaxation of the throat.

■ Too much tension in the throat area. To assure openness of your throat and mouth passageways, flexibility of your jaw, and forward placement of tone, review Exercises 6–16 in this chapter.

If you're still harsh, Exercises 41–44 will set you on the right course.

41. RAGGEDY ANN—RAGGEDY ANDY: Be a rag doll and lower the upper part of your body so that your shoulders almost rest on your knees. Let your head flop around and your arms dangle loosely at the sides. Do you feel comfortably relaxed?
   Now sit up, but keep the same easy relaxed feeling that you had a second ago.

42. Do a rerun on Exercise 41, but this time while in the sitting up phase, hum *n* quietly. Hum on various pitches, taking a breath between each change of pitch, holding the hum for five to ten seconds.

43. Repeat the humming, but now do it louder and with more relish. Contrast and compare what you did in the previous exercise with what you're doing now. Can you *feel* a difference?

44. Lower your pitch a tone or two as you speak the first sentence in each group. Let the words fall back into your throat, and speak with as little gusto as possible. Sound exhausted! You'll find yourself simulating a grating, growly quality.
   The second sentence: Raise your pitch one or two tones and read in a *relatively* strong voice but don't overdo!
   The third sentence: Use a normal quality, with no trace of harshness. Concentrate on the second and third sentences in each group.

   a. If you don't feel pain, you don't feel anything, and that's not living.
      Etiquette: learning to yawn with your mouth closed.
      A critic is one who knows the way but can't drive the car.
   b. An alarm clock is a device that makes you rise and whine.
      Kissing a smoker is a little like making love to an ashtray.
      For Christmas, why not give the gift that keeps on giving? A female cat.
   c. You're never going to get anywhere if you think you're already there.
      Millions of Americans aren't working, but thank heavens they've got jobs.
      You're not drunk if you can lie on the floor without hanging on.
   d. If at first you don't succeed—push.
      Sign in a liquor store: "Preserve wildlife. Throw a party!"
      You're making progress if each mistake you make is a new one.
   e. A road sign in Texas: "Drive like hell, and you'll get there."
      Blessed are the teenagers, for they shall inherit the national debt.
      Carrots are good for the eyes. Have you ever seen a rabbit with glasses?
   f. The silent dog is the first to bite.
      Fate makes our relatives. Choice makes our friends.
      There is nobody who is not dangerous for someone.
   g. Silence gives consent, or a horrible feeling that nobody's listening.
      Living well is the best revenge.
      If a person thinks he can or can't, he's probably right.
   h. Age doesn't matter unless you're a cheese.
      Average: the poorest of the good and the best of the bad.
      Have you ever noticed that those who most fear the power of ideas never have any?

VOCAL FRY

DO YOU SOUND LIKE GREASE IN AN OVERHEATED FRYING PAN? YOU HAVE *VOCAL FRY*.

Here's an odd vocal foible—an offshoot of harshness—which one hears now and then. You don't have to be consistently harsh to be a victim of the "Irksome Quirk"—as it's so aptly nicknamed. At the end of a phrase or sentence, if you drop the pitch of your voice down into the cellar, the final sound is a gypsy croak—a noise from the back of the vacuum cleaner. It sounds something like bacon frying.

Sometimes the "fry" has to do with poor breath control. If your air supply is depleted, the last few words of a thought or phrase may be squeezed out of your throat with a popcorn-popping quality.

The drop in pitch that most of us use at the end of a sentence may be accompanied by this vocal fry quality. Its occasional appearance needn't alarm you, but a persistent basement buzzsaw rumble might indicate excessive tension of your vocal folds.

REDUCING VOCAL FRY

(Review Exercises 10–14, which deal with breath control, in Chapter 2 and Exercises 1–16, which deal with relaxation, in this chapter.)

45. Start each of these words on a fairly high pitch, and then slide your voice downward. When you've reached the lowest level you can—without the crackle—prolong the vowel or diphthong.

die	how	who	lie	do
roe	they	me	lay	doe
maw	why	sea	no	play
boy	new	low	buy	too

46. Now do the opposite of what you just did in Exercise 45. Slide your voice upward on each word. As you begin, let your voice fall back into your throat and rumble. Raise the pitch slowly, and as soon as you hear and feel the disappearance of the growling quality, hold the vowel or diphthong sound for a few seconds on that particular pitch level.

awe	sow	at	isle	keen
all	plow	add	ode	ire
caught	ow	ask	eel	mop
sought	now	aunt	ore	sop

47. Read these. The first sentence in each pair is loaded with front vowel sounds and the so-called tongue-tip consonants in which the front part of your tongue is most active. To say them clearly and sharply, you'll have to move your tongue quite far forward. Exaggerate this forward tongue movement, and aim for sturdy, untarnished sounds. Slightly more forceful projection will also help you eliminate vocal fry.

As you read the second sentence in each pair, concentrate on maintaining the same degree of brightness and vigor. Work also for crispness of articulation.

a. If I had my life to live over again, I would have eaten less cottage cheese.
   Soft soap is always a sign there's dirty water about.
b. We can't all be heroes because somebody has to sit on the curb and clap as they go by.
   People who know how much they're worth generally aren't worth very much.
c. Six feet of earth makes us all of one size.
   I wonder what language truck drivers use now that everybody's using theirs.
d. If George Washington were alive today, he'd turn over in his grave.
   Most people are too busy earning a living to make any money.
e. People who have little to do are great talkers. The less we think the more we talk.
   The finger that turns the dial rules the air.
f. Some people are so fond of ill-luck that they run halfway to meet it.
   Make the most of the best and the least of the worst.

g.   Fool me once, shame on you. Fool me twice, shame on me.
     There are more warmed-over ideas than hot ones.
h.   He who laughs has not yet heard the bad news.
     The trouble with country music is that it doesn't stay there.
i.   The fellow who brags about how smart he is wouldn't if he was.
     It's time to go on a diet when you start puffing going down stairs.
j.   Ideas are funny things. They don't work unless you do.
     Never get mad at anyone for knowing more than you do. It's not his fault.

Assignment 4: Stridency, Harshness, and Vocal Fry

If your voice is strident, prepare quiet and reflective material. Devote some of your practice period to the procedures suggested in Exercise 37: read a line or two (no more) in a relatively strident manner; read several lines in a breathy voice. Then reread the entire selection several times, using a quality that is free of stridency.

If your voice is harsh, or if you have vocal fry, prepare material that is lively and spirited. If you write your own material, be sure that you include many front-vowel words (*me, it, bed, take*) and tongue-tip consonant words (*tip, day, night*). In your classroom presentation, avoid exaggerating as you read, and avoid harshness or vocal fry.

The Suggested Checklist for this assignment is at the end of the chapter, and it may be useful to you as you practice.

THE NASAL VOICE

DO YOU SOUND LIKE A FOGHORN? DO YOU TWANG OR WHINE THROUGH YOUR NOSE? YOU'RE *NASAL.*

"A country singer," Dolly Parton says, "is a person who sings through his nose by ear."

Nasality is a loose word. The bottom line: there are two kinds—TOO MUCH and TOO LITTLE. First, I'll talk about the TOO MUCH kind.

48.   With your thumb and forefinger, pinch your nose, closing off your nostrils and say:
      Television is what gives you something to do when you aren't doing anything.
      Feel the vibrations in your nose—especially on *m, n,* and *ng?*
      Put a clean mirror in a freezer compartment for a few minutes. Then place it under your nostrils and read the test sentence again, not holding your nose. There should be small clouds on the mirror.
49.   Once again, pinch your nose and say:
      Hollywood's all right. It's the pictures that are bad.
      You should feel no vibrations. If you do, you're talking through your nose. You have *too much* nasality.
      With a cold, clean mirror reread the test sentence, not holding your nose. This time, there should be no cloudy spots on the mirror. If there are—you're nasal.

Three of our most pleasant and musical sounds are *m, n,* and *ng* (as in *sing*). They're also the only three legitimate nasal sounds in the English language.

Want proof? *m, n,* and *ng* must be directed through your nose. Hum *m* for a few seconds and then pinch your nostrils with thumb and forefinger. You'll cut off the sound.

Now sing *aw* for a few seconds and then pinch your nostrils. It makes no difference. *Aw* can be produced with the nasal passages closed off.

How do you produce a nasal consonant? The breath stream must be blocked at some point in your mouth, and your velum must be lowered and relaxed. If these conditions are present, tone will be directed through your nasal passages.

When you say *ah* and permit the velum to hang relaxed and slightly open, however, your nasal passages act as supplementary resonators, and in this capacity they may accentuate the overtones of other vowels, diphthongs, and consonants as well as *ah*. In recent research, high-speed motion picture X rays indicate that some speakers with normal voices leave the velum partially lowered during the production of vowel and dipthong sounds. The degree to which the velum is lowered or raised for the production of nonnasal sounds obviously varies from individual to individual.

What causes *excessive* nasality?

- Your tongue humps up in the rear of your mouth. Sound is blocked from coming out the mouth. It backfires and is directed through your nose.
- Your jaw is too rigid, and your teeth are clenched or nearly closed. The sound gets trapped in your throat.
- Dilapidated articulation and talking too softly *increase* nasality. A wider mouth opening, talking louder, and crisper articulation will help you *decrease* nasality.
- Excessive relaxation of the velum.

REDUCING NASALITY

If you're excessively nasal, listen to a recording of your voice and try to identify the vowels and diphthongs you speak with excessive nasality. You may even notice it on certain consonants other than *m, n,* and *ng.* Perhaps your instructor or a classmate can imitate your vocal quality. Listen carefully to the voices of various personalities in movies, radio, and TV, and pick out the voices with too much nasality. If your nasality is caused by a pulled-back tongue, a narrow mouth opening, or a rigid jaw, review Exercises 6–14 in this chapter.

50. Watching yourself in a mirror, open your mouth widely and say *aw–ng* (as in ring): *aw–ng, aw–ng.* What happens to the velum?
    To produce *aw,* you must raise the velum. To produce *ng,* you must lower the velum. (See figure 3.1.) Repeat the exercise until you get the feeling of this action.
51. Start to sound *b,* building up air pressure behind closed lips, but then let the air escape through your nose for *m.* Can you feel the action of the velum? Repeat this procedure, using *d* and *n* as a combination and then *g* and *ng.*
52. In this exercise nasal and nonnasal sounds are listed in alternate order. Practice saying them until you can differentiate clearly between them:
    m–aw–n–ee–ng–i–m–oh–n–eh–ng–oo–m–b–n–d–ng–g

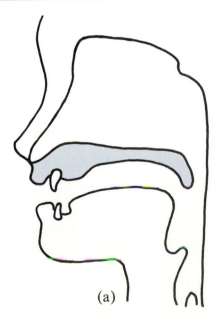
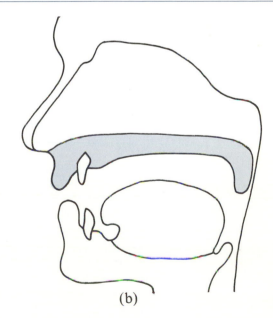

(a)   (b)

Figure 3.1   (a) Position of velum in production of the nasal consonants *m, n, ng;* (b) position of velum in production of oral sounds (for many individuals, the velum will be completely raised).

53. In these exercises, don't let your vowels become unduly nasal:

    a.   Hold *aw* briefly, pause, and then add the nasal sound. Repeat without the pause.

aw . . . m	aw . . . n	aw . . . ng
awm	awn	awng

    b.   Follow the pattern of Exercise (*a.*), but place the nasal at the beginning.

m . . . aw	n . . . aw	ng . . . aw
maw	naw	ngaw

    c.   Place the nasal sound between the vowels.

       aw . . . m . . . aw   aw . . . n . . . aw   aw . . . ng . . . aw

    d.   Place the vowel between the nasals.

       m . . . aw . . . m   n . . . aw . . . n   ng . . . aw . . . ng

54. The first sentence of each pair below is saturated with nasal sounds. As you read them, try to ricochet the tones through your nose. There are no nasal sounds in the second sentence of each pair; exaggerate the non-nasal quality as you read.
Repeat until you can *feel* and *hear* the difference.

    a.   A censor is a person who knows more than he thinks you ought to.
       If you drive a car, I'll tax the street. If you try to sit, I'll tax the seat.
    b.   One reason I don't drink is that I want to know when I'm having a good time. {Brooke Shields}
       Whoever gossips to you will gossip about you.
    c.   Don't be so humble. You're not that wonderful.
       I have a perfect cure for a sore throat. Cut it. {Alfred Hitchcock}
    d.   I base most of my fashion taste on what doesn't itch. {Phyllis Diller}
       He who laughs, lasts.
    e.   Other people's sins are before our eyes; our own are behind our back.
       Politics is like football. If you see daylight, go through the hole.
    f.   A rich person is nothing but a poor person with money.
       The best way to get praise is to die.
    g.   Here's a marvelous rule I recommend: never practice two vices at once. {Joan Collins}
       Bill Cosby to a heckler: "If your IQ rises to thirty, sell!"
    h.   The devil and me, we don't agree. I hate him and he hates me.
       Without red cells, blood would bleed to death.
    i.   Some people are like musical glasses: to produce their finest tones, you must keep them wet.
       If exercise is so good for us, why do star athletes retire at thirty-five?

55. These selections contain no nasal consonants. As you read them, have somebody listen to you. Practice until you're free of unpleasant nasality.

    a.   Several years ago I heard a preacher who was powerful good. I decided to give his church every dollar I had. But he refused to quit. A little bit later I decided to keep the bills but just give a few loose quarters. A quarter hour later I decided to keep the quarters too. A half hour later he stopped; the plate was passed. I was so exhausted that I took out five dollars out of sheer spite. {Mark Twain}
    b.   A Hare said to a Tortoise, "You are stupid because you are so slow." The Tortoise laughed. "We'll just see about that," he said. "Let's have a race."
       "Good!" said the Hare. "I'll show you what real speed is."
       They decided to race to the big forest which stood far away. The Tortoise started right away at his steady pace, but the Hare said boastfully, "I feel tired so I'll sleep for a little while. It'll still be easy to beat that stupid Tortoise."
       He stretched out, fell asleep, but woke up just as the daylight had started to fade. He raced to the edge of the forest as fast as he could go, but he was very surprised to discover that the Tortoise was already there. {Aesop}

c.   Friday was always a good luck day for Jack, a poor woodchopper. This particular Friday, he was over-joyed to discover a huge oak tree. "That tree is so large," he told his wife, "that we'd have wood to build a great house for a duke." "Why the delay?" she asked. "Cut it!"

He dashed back to the oak. He raised his axe. "Stop!" said a voice. A tree sprite appeared. "Please save the tree. It's where I live. If you do, I'll give you three wishes. Whatever you ask for is yours."

Jack spared the tree. His wife was furious. "Just for that, you idiot, you'll go without supper." "I wish I had a fat, juicy sausage," he said. A beautiful sausage appeared.

His wife was baffled, so he told her about the three wishes. Said she, "What a jackass you are to waste a wish. I wish that stupid sausage were stuck to your face."

It was, too.

He pulled as hard as he could, but the sausage stayed where it was. "I'll have to use the last wish. Let the sausage fall off."

It dropped off.

The couple, poor as ever, at least had a delicious sausage for their supper.

ASSIMILATION NASALITY

"Watch those nosy nasal neighbors," as one student put it.

Pronounce: *nan* and *lap*

You'll notice that the vowel *a* is more nasal in *nan* than it is in *lap*. The three nasals, *m, n,* and *ng* have a tendency to carry over and strongly affect neighboring vowels. Too much of this can give your voice a nasal aura.

Say *nan* again. Your velum must be lowered for *n*, raised for *a*, and lowered again for final *n*. Efficient, prompt control of the velum is essential.

56.   Read the following word pairs. Words to the left contain no nasals. Words to the right do. Stress or round out the vowels and hang onto the nasals briefly. But be careful not to jump the gun by allowing the words to become excessively nasal.

fat–fan	Ed–end	yet–yen
tip–tin	big–bin	code–cone
row–no	lake–lane	Vic–vim
dog–dawn	pod–pond	wade–wane

57.   As you read the first column of words, prolong the nasal consonants as indicated. Pause slightly and then say the vowel or diphthong.

As you read the second column, don't prolong the nasal sounds, but pause briefly before you say the final sound.

With the third column, eliminate the pause.

mmmmmmm / / y	m / / y	my
mmmmmmm / / e	m / / e	me
mmmmmmm / / oo	m / / oo	moo
nnnnnnn / / ight	n / / ight	night
nnnnnnn / / ail	n / / ail	nail
nnnnnnn / / o	n / / o	no

58.   The first time you say these words, overdo the nasal sounds. The second time, avoid overdoing. Be sure that there's no nasal spill.

am	ma'am	moat	next	mate
ran	mantle	nil	mouse	mask
Dan	nag	banned	mouth	mitt
pan	hang	ream	mound	met

59. Exaggerate the nasal quality the first time you read the following. Repeat, but avoid the nasality that lingers from a nearby *m, n,* or *ng.*

   a. I'd leave a man for a movie, but I'd never leave a movie for a man. {Elizabeth Taylor}
   b. There are moments when everything goes well. Don't be frightened. It won't last.
   c. Never eat anything at one sitting that you can't lift. {Miss Piggy}
   d. When angry, count to ten. When very angry, swear. {Mark Twain}
   e. We cannot unthink unless we are insane.
   f. When one burns one's bridges behind one, what a nice fire it makes!
   g. If you don't want to work, you have to earn enough money so that you won't have to work.
   h. A tax refund is the next best thing to being shot at and missed.
   i. If anything can go wrong, it will. In 1895, there were two automobiles in all of Michigan, and they collided.
   j. I think it can be stated without denial that no man ever saw a man he would be willing to marry if he were a woman.

THE DENASAL VOICE

DO YOU SOUND STUFFY, COLD-IN-THE-HEADISH, DEHYDRATED? YOU'RE *DENASAL.*

We've talked about the TOO MUCH kind—excessive nasality. Now let's talk about the TOO LITTLE kind—denasality.

"Good bawdig. Sprig has cub, ad I have a bad cold id by dose."

Ever sound like that? Your case of sniffles is temporary, of course, but once in awhile we hear a voice that always sounds blocked and congested.

Sylvester Stallone, in his *Rocky* movies, deliberately worked for the broken-nose, bottleneck effect. That's great for playing a punch-drunk boxer. Otherwise, denasality can seriously hamper understandability of speech.

Denasality happens if a small amount of air or no air at all enters the nasal passages as you talk. Sometimes a barrier is responsible: enlarged adenoids, swollen tonsils, hay fever, or a broken nose will give you this nasal roadblock.

Possibly surgical repair or medical treatment is needed. Unfortunately, even after such treatment, some individuals remain denasal. A little vocal retraining will generally solve the problem.

CORRECTING DENASALITY

60. Hum *m, n,* and *ng* (as in si*ng*) up and down the scale. You'll feel vibrations and tinglings on your lips and in your nasal passages.

61. You won't feel any ripples in your nose as you say the first word in each pair below. But as you say the second word, prolong *m, n,* and *ng,* and you'll feel prickling sensations there.

bay–May	dell–Nell	bag–bang
bad–mad	day–nay	rug–rung
bail–mail	dill–nil	big–bing
bake–make	door–nor	log–long
bike–Mike	dip–nip	gag–gang

62. Read these words twice, the first time slowly and the second time rapidly. In both readings make the nasal consonants as prominent as you can.

an	lime	noon	moll	length
sign	bone	mat	bend	strength
aunt	rhyme	moon	chin	finger
mom	plain	dawn	bring	ring

63. Speak each of these sentences twice. The first time stretch the nasal sounds so that you're definitely aware of nasal tremors.

Can you make the tone quality of the vowels and diphthongs as vibrant and ringing as it is on *m, n,* and *ng?* The second time: don't exaggerate, but be certain that *m, n,* and *ng* have normal nasality and that your vowels and diphthongs also have a bit of luster.

    a.   Today if you invent a better mousetrap, the government comes along with a better mouse.
    b.   May the fleas of a thousand camels infest your armpits. [Arab curse]
    c.   Some are bent with toil, and some get crooked trying to avoid it.
    d.   Classical music is the kind that we keep thinking will turn into a tune.
    e.   Today's trying times in about twenty years will have become the "good old days."
    f.   The best thing about movies: you're giving people little, tiny pieces of time that they'll never forget. [Paul Newman]
    g.   We didn't all come over on the same ship, but we're all in the same boat.
    h.   Many are saved from sin by being so inept at it.
    i.   Never take the advice of someone who has not had your kind of trouble.
    j.   Every man, woman, and child has at least one scheme that won't work.
    k.   Life is a meaningless comma in the sentence of time.
    l.   Do unto yourself as your neighbors do unto themselves and look pleasant.

Assignment 5: Nasality and Denasality

If you're excessively nasal, prepare two short selections. The first one should contain no nasal consonants (*m, n, ng*), but the second one should contain a moderate number of nasals. Listen to yourself carefully as you practice. If possible have someone else listen too.

If denasality has been one of your problems, select material that is loaded with nasals. Practice with this suggestion in mind: exaggerate the nasals somewhat, but try to make the vowels and diphthongs as bright and vibrant as the nasals.

When you do your assignment in class, concentrate on ease and naturalness.

The Suggested Checklist for this assignment is at the end of the chapter, and it may be useful to you as you practice.

THE THROATY VOICE

DO YOU SOUND MUFFLED, TRAPPED, ZOMBIELIKE? YOU'RE *THROATY*.

This is the voice-from-the-tomb quality—a heavy echo bouncing off the back wall of a cave. It almost sounds as if its owner has a physical obstacle in the mouth that prevents the voice from coming out.

Not surprisingly, when TV comedies want to portray a character as a dummy, a booby, or a nerd, the actors often use this sooty, throaty quality.

Outside the entertainment world, this dammed-up kind of voice can be objectionable to listeners because it generally lacks carrying power. It sounds swallowed and thick. The peculiar clogged quality attracts attention, if not necessarily approval. (Throatiness has been described as "vocal constipation.")

If you can "see" a strident voice, you can also "see" a throaty voice. The throaty person likes to bury the chin against the neck, and a hollow, voice-in-the-sewer-pipe sound emerges. "Keep your chin up," in other words, is fine advice in more ways than one. CHECK YOUR CHIN POSITION in a mirror.

REDUCING THROATINESS

64. Do the sentences below three times: the first time, pull your chin back against your neck.
The second time, go to the other extreme. Tilt your head back quite far, and raise your chin high.
The third time, strike a compromise posture. Your chin should be in a normal position. Your throatiness should disappear. If you're still having problems, repeat the techniques suggested for the second and third readings, but omit the first, chin-against-the-neck position.

   a. Easy doesn't do it.
   b. A penny saved is a penny taxed.
   c. By the time we've made it, we've had it.
   d. One thing this country needs is fewer needs.
   e. When you want salt, sugar won't do.
   f. You can't step twice into the same river.
   g. People who make no noise are dangerous.
   h. Oh, no! Not nuclear war! What about my career?

65. Is your tongue position correct?
If your tongue is consistently pulled too far back or humped up toward the rear of the mouth, certain of your important vowel sounds will be murky and inky. Try the sentences below three different ways:
First, retract the tongue. Pull it back as far as you can, and read the sentence. You'll notice that some of the sounds will be greatly distorted.
Second, move your tongue slightly forward as you read.
Finally, push your tongue far forward. Definitely get the feeling that most of the activity involves the front part of the tongue.

   a. Stand still and watch the world go by—and it will.
   b. Fame is all right if you don't inhale.
   c. We don't all think alike. In fact, we don't all think.
   d. Forgive your enemies, but never forget their names.
   e. What is a rebel? A man who says no.
   f. He who hesitates is not only lost, but miles from the next exit.

Throatiness sometimes occurs if a person speaks in an extremely low-pitch range. A person may be told by a well-meaning friend that his or her voice is too high. If the issue is pressed, the "guilty" party may react by forcing the voice into a bass or alto range. This is certainly not good practice. It can possibly damage the vocal machinery. If your particular problem of throatiness has to do with an improper pitch level, preview that section of Chapter 7 that deals with pitch range.

66. The first sentence in these pairs is chock-full of sounds that have warmth and sparkle—front vowels and tongue-tip consonants. You'll find it easy to avoid throatiness while reading this material.
The second sentence in each pair is studded with dark and dusty sounds—sounds that lack sheen.
Try to transfer at least some of the brightness and the feeling of the front-of-the-mouth production that you had with the first sentence. Repeat the exercises until you're able to read all of the material with a luminous quality.

   a. Deed: past tense of do. "Macbeth deed the bloody did."
      Never trouble trouble till trouble troubles you.
   b. The first and great commandment: don't let them scare you.
      A budget tells us what we can't afford, but it doesn't keep us from buying it.
   c. Rain is much nicer than snow because you don't have rain plows piling up rain in eight-foot piles.
      If God wanted us to be brave, why did he give us legs?
   d. Middle age is when you're sitting home on Saturday night and the telephone rings and you hope it isn't for you.
      I hate small towns because once you've seen the cannon in the park there's nothing else to do.

e. Tax reform: when you take the taxes off things that have been taxed in the past and put taxes on things that haven't been taxed before.
   Prayer of the modern American: "Dear God, I pray for patience, and I want it right now."

f. Washing your car and polishing it all up is a never failing sign of rain.
   Two can live as cheaply as one, but it costs twice as much.

g. Travel folder: a trip tease.
   If dogs could talk, perhaps we would find it as hard to get along with them as we do with people.

h. The tongue of man is a twisty thing.
   I must say that I hate money, but it's the lack of money I hate most.

i. Men who never get carried away should be.
   A true artist is one who will not prostitute his art except for money.

j. listen: there's a hell of a good universe next door. let's go {e. e. cummings}
   If you live to the age of a hundred you have it made because very few people die past the age of a hundred.

Assignment 6: Throatiness

If you're throaty, prepare material that contains many of the front vowels. (In the following words, front vowels are underlined: m__e__, __i__t, d__a__te, __e__gg, h__a__t.) Also include words that contain tongue-tip consonants: __t__in, __d__og, __l__ad, __n__ot. Run through your material a few times, using the procedures described in Exercise 64. Spend most of your time practicing the material as you plan to do it in class, *without* the two extremes of the chin-against-the-neck or the chin-raised-high.

The Suggested Checklist for this assignment is at the end of the chapter, and it may be useful to you as you practice.

THE HOARSE VOICE

DO YOU SOUND RUSTY AND RASPING? YOU'RE *HOARSE*.

This is the Gravel Gerty and Gravel Gordy voice. It's raw, husky, and gruff. Hoarse people don't talk—they croak! A hoarse voice has been described as a voice with acne, and it's often called a "smoker's voice," even if its owner is a nonsmoker.

Hoarseness due to a bad cold or sore throat will disappear. Chronic hoarseness, however, is dangerous. It's like committing vocal suicide.

> If your voice is affected by chronic hoarseness, see a physician.

Actor/rock star David Bowie played a 150-year-old man in a recent film. To suggest advanced age, Bowie came up with a bullfrog voice. How did he do it? By standing on the damp and chilly banks of the Thames River in London each night before filming and singing rock music as loudly as he could until his voice turned hoarse and raspy. Bowie's concern for realism is to be admired. His concern for his vocal health isn't. What will be the state of his voice in a year or two?

Persistent hoarseness may result from organic defects or structural abnormalities. Nodes, polyps, (benign, noncancerous growths—something like small knobs—on the vocal cords), or malignant tumors may be responsible for trouble. Surgical treatment is generally required for these more serious defects.

There is some controversy regarding the causes and the nature of certain of these growths, but there can be little question that vocal abuse has something to do with their presence. The kind of shouting and yelling that some of us indulge in at athletic events is one of the more obvious types of brutal vocal abuse. Screamer's nodes may result. Prolonged or excessive loud talking is another. Actors, both amateur and professional, occasionally lose their voices because of this. A pitch level that is unnecessarily high or low is still another example of vocal abuse.

REDUCING HOARSENESS

If your voice is affected by chronic hoarseness, let your instructor and your doctor help you. If some kind of vocal training is recommended, many of the discussions and exercises listed elsewhere in this book will be of value. The interested individual should review the following exercises:

- In this chapter: exercises for relaxation, 1–14
- In Chapter 6: exercises for loudness, 1–8
- In Chapter 7: exercises for pitch, 1–12

WRAP-UP

1. Quality of voice is the texture, tone color, or timbre that characterizes your voice and nobody else's. It's the distinctive sound of one voice that distinguishes it from all other voices.

2. Quality is determined by the production of the original tone by the vocal folds. As the tone passes through the throat, mouth, and nasal cavities, it's altered and modified, reinforced and enriched. The shape, size, and tension of these resonators determine the sound the listener hears.

3. It's human nature to judge others by how they sound. Right or wrong, we tend to associate a certain type of voice with a certain type of person.

4. Vocal quality is a surprisingly reliable indicator of the physical as well as the emotional health of a person.

5. Relaxation and good vocal habits usually go hand in hand, but only the right kind of selective relaxation. Such advice as "Let go. Relax completely!" really means "Relax those muscles not needed to perform your task," or "Try to get rid of unnecessary tension."

6. A breathy voice sounds whispery and fuzzy. If the vocal folds aren't sufficiently together during speech, unused air escapes. A breathy voice is inefficient and weak. It may tag its owner as lazy, extremely shy, or sickly.

7. Glottal shock, a raspy little click on vowels at the beginnings of words, is often caused by a tense, strained throat. If the vocal folds are closed too firmly or too tensely before the initial vowel is pronounced, the breath blasts the folds apart.

8. A strident voice is harsh, brassy, and high-pitched. It's more frequently associated with women's voices than men's. It generally results from excessive muscular tension in the throat.

9. A harsh voice is husky and guttural. It's often low-pitched and more often associated with men's than women's voices. Not speaking loudly enough, using too low a pitch level or excessive relaxation of the throat may produce harshness. With some people, however, too much tension of throat muscles, rather than laxness, causes this hacksaw quality.

10. Vocal fry is the voice quality that results if the pitch of the voice drops at the end of a phrase or sentence and the voice is allowed to weaken. The final sounds have a growly, bacon-frying, popping sound. Poor breath control and excessive tension of the vocal folds may be responsible.

11. The nasal voice is often described as talking through the nose. Excessive relaxation of the velum is a major cause of this bottled-up vocal quality of too much nasality.

12. In assimilation nasality, the nasal consonants *m, n,* and *ng* exert a strong influence on neighboring vowels. The velum must move rapidly in a word such as *man.* If it doesn't, the vowel sound will also be directed through the nose.

13. Denasality—too little nasality—produces a stuffed-up nose or muffled sound. A physical problem such as enlarged adenoids or a broken nose can promote denasality.

14. The throaty voice sounds swallowed, thick, and dull. It may also have a hollow, voice-from-the-tomb sound. Burying the chin in the neck while speaking, incorrect tongue position, and an excessively low pitch range all contribute to throatiness.

15. The hoarse voice is harsh, husky, and raspy. Acute hoarseness may be caused by a simple sore throat. Chronic (persistent) hoarseness may result from abnormal growths on the vocal folds.

Assignment 7: General Quality

This chapter has helped you answer the question: *Is my voice pleasant to listen to, or does it sound breathy, strident, harsh, excessively nasal, denasal, throaty,* or *hoarse?*

Now, as the final assignment for this specific unit, prepare material that you especially enjoy. As you rehearse, concentrate on the overall impression your voice is making on others, rather than on relaxation, resonance, or specific vocal faults. Your objectives shouldn't be the so-called pear-shaped tones, which are apt to be distortions, but ease and naturalness.

The Suggested Checklist for this assignment may be useful to you as you practice your material.

Suggested Checklist for Assignments 2, 3, 4, 5, 6, and 7

As you practice by yourself, you may want to work with this checklist. Listen carefully to yourself. If it is feasible, record the assignment, or get a classmate or friend to listen to you as you read the material. Eventually, your goal will be to have a check mark in the **Yes** column for each category that applies to you. (Optional: Perhaps your instructor will want to use the checklist to evaluate you during any classroom presentations.)

Breathiness

	Yes	No

Avoids—

inefficient breathing habits, such as shallow or clavicular breathing

rigid or sloppy posture that may interfere with inhalation

noisy inhalation

overbreathing: taking in too much breath

excessively low loudness level

excessively low pitch level

wasting breath on voiceless consonants such as [s f th-θ h sh-$\int$ k p t]

carrying over breathy quality from the voiceless consonants to adjacent vowels and consonants

Glottal Shock

Avoids—

excessive tension or strain in throat or larynx

too-high pitch level (which sometimes accompanies glottal shock)

Stridency

	Yes	No

Avoids—

excessive tensions and constrictions of pharynx and soft palate

shallow or clavicular breathing

excessive or improper loudness

too-high pitch level

Harshness and Vocal Fry

Avoids—

too-low loudness level

too-low pitch level

pulling chin back against neck

excessive relaxation (laxness) of throat

excessive tensions and constrictions of lower part of pharynx

shallow or clavicular breathing

Nasality (too much Nasality)

Avoids—

attitude of carelessness and general muscular sluggishness

permitting tongue to hump in rear of mouth

excessively rigid jaw and clenched teeth

nasalizing vowels before or after nasal consonants

too-high pitch level

too-low loudness level

	Yes	No

Denasality (too little Nasality)

Avoids—

    excessive tension in nasopharynx

Throatiness

Avoids—

    pulling chin back against neck

    excessive tongue humping toward back of mouth

    too-low pitch level

CONSERVE YOUR CONSONANTS
ARTICULATION

WOULD YOU BELIEVE THAT

. . . The trickiest tongue twister in the English language is not: *Peter Piper picked a peck of pickled peppers?* It's this one. Try it: *The sixth sick shiek's sixth sheep's sick.*

. . . Dogs don't bark "bow-wow" or "woof-woof" in foreign languages? In French, it's "oua-oua," in Russian—"gav-gav." Dutch canines say, "waf-waf"; in Japan—"wan-wan."

. . . The ugly Bronx cheer or raspberry has a highbrow name—*bilabial fricative?* To make it you compress your tongue between your lips and push out some air.

. . . The ten most beautiful words in the English language are: *chimes, dawn, hush, lullaby, luminous, melody, mist, murmuring, tranquil, golden?*

. . . The ten ugliest words in the English language are: *gripe, crunch, jazz, schizoid, mugged, plump, jerk, screech, cacophony, flatulent?*

ARTICULATION

WHAJASAY?

Joe and Ed in this scene are not rejects from *"Aliens, Part III."* They're from Zap, North Dakota, and one of them is a fisherman. Can you translate?

Joe: Hiyed.

Ed: Lojo. Whatimezit?

Joe: Boutaquar nine.

Ed: Whajasay?

Joe: Quarnine. Howzt gon?

Ed: Nasaha.

Joe: Whasamatta?

Ed: Jescopla bites.

Joe: Gonexra beer?

Ed: Godaball Beefearjin. Wanna snor?

Joe: Nah. Godago.

Ed: Wazzarush?

Joe: Gotpoinment adenis. See yamorrow.

Ed: Tekedezy.

Joe: Gluk!

Joe and Ed are afflicted with a tiresome and commonplace verbal disease: sloppy, indistinct, garbled, mushy speech. More formally, it is referred to as poor articulation.

Articulation is the process by which individual speech sounds are produced by the tongue, lips, teeth, and soft palate modifying the outgoing breath stream.

I use the term *articulation* in its broadest sense. It means the same thing as the terms *enunciation* and *diction*. All of these terms refer to clarity, intelligibility, and distinctness of speech.

Sharp, lucid speech is generally a reliable indication of the mental and physical alertness of the individual, so how did the gentlemen get this way? Laziness? Apathy?

Nervous tension and problems of health and hearing, of course, contribute to gummy, dilapidated speech. What about environment? If Joe and Ed's parents, their playmates and their teachers have contaminated speech, it tells us why Joe and Ed mutilate their speech.

About three people in one hundred have good or superior articulation. More than one-third speak so indistinctly that they are in need of some kind of special help.

Startling? Yes, indeed—in view of the fact that at least ninety percent of all the communicating we do is oral! And all listeners like to hear sharp and crisp sounds, because it obviously makes the job of listening easier.

Are You a Mumbler?

If your speech is mushy and slushy, it won't be easy to convince you that your articulation needs overhauling. People are rarely conscious of their speech habits and if their attention is called to them, they may shrug off the problems. After all, they're always intelligible to themselves. Even if they couldn't hear themselves, they'd still know what they were thinking. As one of these mushmouths once said to me: "Mebbe issa consadence, but se'ral m'bes frens are gittin deaf. They kin ne'er unerstan anathin I sayn keep askin me ta r'peat alla time."

He had never heard his recorded voice. I taped him. When we played it back, at first he was aghast, then furious. Mr. Mumbles accused me of either hexing his tape or sneaking in somebody else's voice!

I arranged for two of his friends to be present as witnesses and then taped him again. It took the three of us to persuade him that what he heard was truly himself. He enrolled in a voice and diction course, and in sixteen weeks tidied up his articulation.

If sluggish speech irritates more listeners than most other speech faults combined, only slightly less annoying is arty, elegant and mincing speech. It's much too precise and clipped. It suggests snobbishness and a superiority complex. This type of articulation, however, is seldom found among students.

William Buckley, the well-known TV commentator of "Firing Line," bothers many people with his highly polished and glossy diction. Each syllable shimmers like a sword blade. Articulation that calls attention to itself is generally undesirable.

Good articulation requires precision, but a precision that isn't excessive. Natural articulation avoids either of two extremes: sloppiness and artificiality. It's neither *undercooked* nor *overcooked*. It's simply speech that is as clear and sharp-edged as it's apparently easy and unforced. It doesn't distract the listener.

OVERLAPPING SPEECH (ASSIMILATION)

Always bear in mind that you speak most often in phrases and sentences and not in disconnected words. Your language tends to flow along smoothly. It's fluid and supple. Words seemingly melt or blend into one another.

Would you really say at lunch, for example: (Pause where you see the double vertical lines).

Please | | pass | | the | | salt | | and | | pepper.

Probably not. The chances are you'd say:

Pleasepassthesalt'n'pepper.

Overlapping, connected speech isn't a slow-moving, old-fashioned freight train—an open space between each boxcar. Instead, it's a slick Amtrak streamliner.

Speech sounds are rarely given their full value in overlapping or interconnected speech. One sound modifies and colors its neighboring sounds in a word. The process is also known as *assimilation,* or *coarticulation.* Assimilation helps to make sounds and sound combinations easier to pronounce because it facilitates the various movements of the articulators. Assimilation, because it telescopes sounds, reduces the travel time between sounds, increasing the speed and overall efficiency of articulation. It's easier to say

bustop	than bus⌐ ⌐stop
what'r'ya doing?	than what⌐ ⌐are⌐ ⌐you⌐ ⌐doing?
black 'n' blue	than black⌐ ⌐and⌐ ⌐blue

If overlapping is common and necessary in our speaking, what was wrong with the way Joe and Ed were talking? These two mumblemouths were overlapping to the *n*th degree.

If you say "jeat?" instead of "Did you eat?," "Fyull" for "if you'll," and "T'sup?" for "What's up?" your overlapping is extreme. If assimilation is practiced to such a degree that it interferes with intelligibility, it's wrong.

Everyday, conversational speaking permits more overlapping than formal situations. Don't forget, as you set to work with the material in this chapter—connected speech is natural and smooth-flowing. The word *articulation,* after all, also means *joined.*

THE ARTICULATORS

You form and sculpt speech sounds by the movements of your

. . . LIPS which pout and protrude, squeeze and stretch, relax and rebound. They pucker: *weep, wool, oats.* They touch: *pill, beet, man.* They spread: *cheese, he, eel.*

. . . FRONT TEETH which help out when your tongue or lower lip touch them. Say *Velma, cook the veal very thoroughly.* You'll feel your lower lip or your tongue tip contact your upper teeth.

. . . LOWER JAW which opens and closes in varying degrees. Drops on *awl* and *calm,* but is almost closed for *oven* and *few.*

. . . TONGUE which flattens, flits, narrows and furrows; stretches and spreads; pushes and pulls. Ever watch the darting tongue of a chameleon? Your tongue's movements, if not quite as visible, are almost as spectacular. If you say *da-da-da* as fast as you can, the way a baby might babble, the tip of your tongue is moving about eight times a second! Notice the variety of tongue positions as you say: *think, these, bust, buzz, fool, show, noon, suit.*

. . . VELUM. As you say the words *my, nine, ring,* the velum (soft palate) lowers like a curtain and diverts the breath stream into the nasal cavities. (All of the articulators are shown in figure 4.1).

Returning a moment to Joe and Ed, let's assume that their articulators are normal. What is it about their organs of articulation that makes their speech so slushy?

You've observed and heard the person who speaks with almost limp lips. Joe and Ed are excessively lax and loose-lipped.

Sports commentator O. J. Simpson, for all his charm and good looks, now and then is guilty of spongy enunciation.

Then you know the speaker who draws his lips into two narrow, iron bands. Invariably, the jaw is also rigid and unmoving. Barbara Walters, another prominent TV personality, has often been accused of speaking with tight lips and a frozen jaw.

Some people learn to speak quite nimbly with a pipe or cigar clenched between the teeth. Others don't even need a prop to do it. This kind of locked-jaw articulation worked well for the late Humphrey Bogart with his ice-cold voice, and it comes in handy for convicts engaged in prison yard talk. For the rest of us, a rusty jaw may strangle the sound. Open your mouth!

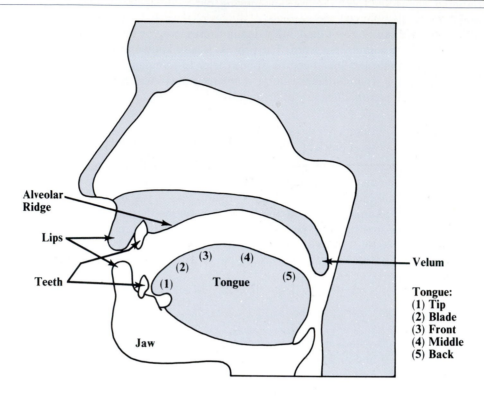

Figure 4.1   Organs of articulation.

EXERCISES FOR THE ARTICULATORS

Here are some setting-up exercises, or articulatory push-ups, that will help you limber up your articulators.

Exercises for the Lips

1. Push your lips out as far as you can, and then pull them back tightly into an extreme smiling position. Repeat.
2. Exaggerate lip movements as you say

   a.   too–tee–too–tee–too–tee–too–tee
   b.   bee–boo–tee–too–bee–boo–tee–too
   c.   too–boo–boo–too–too–boo–boo–too
   d.   wee–way–wee–way–wee–way–wee–way
   e.   The one who eats is the one who works.
   f.   A man without a wife is like a man in winter without a fur hat. (Russian proverb)
   g.   Television has proved that people will look at anything rather than each other.
   h.   At a dinner party one should eat wisely, but not too well, and talk well but not too wisely.
   i.   If this is coffee, please bring me some tea. If this is tea, please bring me some coffee. (Lincoln)
   j.   People who work sitting down get paid more than people who work standing up.

Exercises for the Jaw

3. Drop your jaw easily as if you were going to say *aw*. Move the relaxed jaw from left to right with your hand.
4. Exaggerate jaw movements as you say

   a.   taw–taw–taw–taw–taw–taw–taw–taw
   b.   goo–gaw–goo–gaw–goo–gaw–goo–gaw
   c.   gee–gaw–goo–gaw–gee–gaw–goo–gaw
   d.   Cars and bars mean stars and scars.

e.   It's awfully difficult for the tolerant to tolerate the intolerant.
f.   Sign in a car on an out-of-the-way parking lot: "Attention, car thieves—this car is already stolen."
g.   The wrong sort of people are always in power because they wouldn't be in power if they weren't the wrong sort of people.
h.   Do you solve problems or are you one of them?
i.   Automobiles continue to be driven at two speeds—lawful and awful.

Exercises for the Tongue

5.   Double your tongue back against your soft palate as far as you can. Then thrust your tongue firmly against the inside of your left cheek and then against the inside of your right cheek.
6.   Exaggerate tongue movements as you say

   a.   daw–daw–daw–daw–daw–daw–daw–daw
   b.   raw–raw–raw–raw–raw–raw–raw–raw
   c.   Behind the phony tinsel of Hollywood lies the real tinsel.
   d.   Saints are all right in heaven, but they're hell on earth.
   e.   The world is a funny paper read backwards—and that way it isn't so funny.
   f.   Once you're over the hill you pick up speed.
   g.   The only time a woman really succeeds in changing a man is when he's a baby.

Exercises for the Velum (Soft Palate)

7.   Watch yourself in a mirror as you yawn. Note that your velum rises. Repeat the yawn.
8.   Still observing yourself in the mirror, make the sound *aw*. Be sure that your soft palate is raised high. Repeat. Say *m*. Your soft palate is now lowered. Repeat.
9.   Try to feel the contrasting actions of the soft palate as you say

   a.   aw–m–aw–m–aw–m–aw–m
   b.   n–aw–n–aw–n–aw–n–aw
   c.   b–m–b–m–b–m–b–m
   d.   ee–m–ee–m–ee–m–ee–m

10. Be certain that your soft palate is lowered for *m, n,* and *ng,* but is in a relatively higher position for all other sounds as you read these sentences.

   a.   There is no glory in outstripping donkeys.
   b.   *Moll Flanders* is not a novel for small children.
   c.   To my friends, I say "thanks." To my enemies, I say "wait."
   d.   A Yankee is a Northerner who visits the South; a damn Yankee is one who stays.
   e.   Being unable to sleep at night is wonderful. It encourages thinking, including thinking about not thinking.

SOUNDS AND SYMBOLS

There are two major families of sounds: vowels and consonants. Almost fifty different sounds are found in the English language, but the English alphabet provides symbols for only twenty-six sounds—five vowels *(a, e, i, o,* and *u)* and twenty-one consonants.

How many different ways can you pronounce u in this nonsense sentence?

Surely, busy students bury thugs and then buy furs.

The sentence contains seven different u sounds!

A young German once wrote a jingle to help his German friends who also were struggling to learn English.

"Gear and tear, but wear and tear . . .
Meat and feat, but sweat and great.
(That last word rhymes with freight and weight.)
Quite different again is height
Which sounds like bite, indict, and light . . .
Crew and blew and few, but sew,
Cow and row, but sow and row. . . . "

It's no wonder that English spelling is a highly unreliable guide to pronunciation and that English spelling is the world's most awesome mess, as a Columbia University professor declared.

English. It's a glorious language—the language of Shakespeare, Lincoln, and Churchill—but it *is* loaded with eccentric spellings.

The Italian language has twenty-seven sounds and fortunately has an alphabet of twenty-seven letters. German has thirty-six sounds represented by an alphabet of thirty-eight letters.

At this point, the only logical way to represent the almost fifty sounds of American English is to use an alphabet of symbols in which each symbol represents one, distinct sound and one sound only.

THE INTERNATIONAL PHONETIC ALPHABET (IPA)

In *My Fair Lady,* Professor Higgins gets the plot rolling when he attempts to copy down and then mimic the cockney dialect of Eliza Doolittle, the flower girl.

Ow, eez ye-ooa san, is e? Wal, fewd dan y' de-ooty bawmz a mather should, eed now bettern to spawl a pore gel's flahrzn than ran awy athaht pyin. Will ye-oo py me f'them?

(Oh, he's your son, is he? Well, if you'd done your duty by him as a mother should, he'd know better than to spoil a poor girl's flowers and then run away without paying. Will you pay me for them?)

Professor Higgins is a phonetics expert, and he remarks that phonetics is the science of speech. More accurately, ***phonetics*** *is the study of the sounds of spoken language.*

The most widely used phonetic alphabet, the International Phonetic Alphabet (IPA), contains hundreds of symbols. If you learn the entire alphabet, you can write out phonetically any language on earth, from Afghanistan to Zulu. For this course, however, you can get by with learning fewer than fifty symbols. A reasonable degree of familiarity with these symbols will aid you in identifying precisely the sounds you hear and make.

Each symbol represents a *phoneme*—a basic unit or sound family. As an example, the *d* sound in *dog* and in *bad* is a phoneme. Actually you can't produce the same *d* in both words any more than nature produces two identical snowflakes, but you can recognize and understand both sounds as *d.*

You'll need to recognize forty-three phonemes. Twenty-five are consonants and eighteen are vowels and diphthongs. Learning the IPA symbols isn't difficult. *You're already familiar with sixteen of the IPA symbols for consonants,* since they're the same as the diacritical markings, or symbols, used to indicate pronunciation in dictionaries. These sixteen IPA symbols and their dictionary equivalents are shown in table 4.1. (A more detailed presentation of dictionary symbols can be found in Appendix A.)

The IPA symbols for the remaining nine consonants may not be so familiar to you. Some of the symbols are modifications of familiar letters, and two symbols are borrowed from the Greek alphabet and the Old English alphabet. These symbols, along with their corresponding symbols, are shown in table 4.2.

The vowel symbols represent fifteen vowels (see table 4.3) and three diphthongs (see table 4.4). (Diphthongs are vowels which change their sound during production, beginning with one sound and shifting to another.)

When placed above and to the left of a syllable, this mark (ˋ) indicates that this syllable is to receive the principal or primary emphasis, or accent.

ˋdʌblɪn (Dublin)

dɪ ˋtrɔɪt (Detroit)

Table 4.1   Consonants: Identical Phonetic and Dictionary Symbols

Phonetic Symbols	Dictionary Symbols	Key Word	Examples
{p}	p	p̲ig	p̲en, p̲a̲p̲er, sli̲p̲
{b}	b	b̲et	b̲ag, ro̲b̲b̲er, la̲b̲
{t}	t	t̲ip	t̲ow, pre̲t̲t̲y, a̲t̲
{d}	d	d̲in	d̲ay, me̲d̲d̲le, li̲d̲
{k}	k	k̲in	c̲hoir, li̲q̲uor, pic̲k̲
{g}	g	g̲one	g̲host, da̲g̲g̲er, plag̲ue
{f}	f	f̲ell	p̲h̲ony, di̲f̲f̲er, toug̲h̲
{v}	v	v̲ain	v̲at, dri̲v̲er, li̲v̲e
{s}	s	s̲in	s̲cene, mi̲s̲ter, ni̲c̲e
{z}	z	z̲one	z̲any, si̲z̲z̲le, ha̲s̲
{h}	h	h̲im	h̲all, w̲h̲o, a̲h̲ead
{l}	l	l̲ate	l̲ook, ho̲l̲l̲y, sou̲l̲
{r}	r	r̲an	w̲r̲eck, glo̲r̲y, nea̲r̲
{w}	w	w̲in	w̲ant, a̲w̲ay, q̲uiet
{m}	m	m̲ad	m̲y, hu̲m̲m̲er, hy̲m̲n̲
{n}	n	n̲od	n̲ail, ma̲n̲n̲er, sig̲n̲

Table 4.2   Consonants: Different Phonetic and Dictionary Symbols

Phonetic Symbols	Dictionary Symbols	Key Word	Examples
{θ}	th	th̲rill	th̲ink, e̲th̲er, ba̲th̲
{ð}	~~th~~	th̲em	th̲ey, fa̲th̲er, ba̲th̲e
{ʃ}	sh	sh̲ell	sh̲ed, ma̲ch̲ine, mu̲sh̲
{ʒ}	zh	beig̲e	ca̲s̲ual, vi̲s̲ion, roug̲e
{tʃ}	ch	ch̲ain	ch̲um, righ̲t̲eous, cat̲ch̲
{dʒ}	j	g̲em	j̲ilt, sol̲d̲ier, ed̲g̲e
{ʍ}	hw	wh̲ile	wh̲ere, somew̲h̲at, wh̲ich̲
{j}	y	y̲es	y̲et, u̲n̲ion, be̲y̲ond
{ŋ}	ŋ or ng	rin̲g̲	kin̲g̲, ba̲n̲k̲er, sin̲g̲er

Table 4.3   Vowels: Phonetic and Dictionary Symbols

Phonetic Symbols	Dictionary Symbols	Key Word	Examples
{i}	ē	tee	eat, meet, be
{ɪ}	i or ĭ	it	if, sieve, pity
{e}	ā	fate	ape, gauge, weigh
{ɛ}	e or ĕ	bet	ebb, many, steady
{æ}	a or ă	sad	at, plaid, rang
{ɑ}	ä	ah	alms, far, sergeant
{ɔ}	ô	jaw	all, brought, saw
{o}	ō	obey	oasis, vocation, show
{ʊ}	oo	put	look, would, wolf
{u}	o͞o	tool	ooze, fruit, who
{ɝ—ɜ}	ûr	murder	ermine, herd, deter
{ɚ}	ər	ever	perform, singer, error
{ə}	ə	ahead	among, carnival, banana
{ʌ}	u or ŭ	cut	under, sum, flood

Table 4.4   Diphthongs: Phonetic and Dictionary Symbols

Phonetic Symbols	Dictionary Symbols	Key Word	Examples
{ɑɪ}	ī	ride	isle, while, die
{ɑʊ}	ou	now	out, house, sow
{ɔɪ}	oi	boy	oyster, noise, joy

When placed below and to the left of a syllable, this mark (ˌ) indicates that this syllable is to receive a secondary accent, that is, one that is weaker than the primary accent.

     mɪsəˈsɪpɪ (Mississippi)

     ˈækrəˌbæt (acrobat)

> Practice material for transcribing with phonetic or dictionary symbols is located in Appendix A.

CONSONANTS

"Consonants can be made either by stopping the breath or by disturbing it, making it explode, or making it buzz or hum," Charlton Laird writes in his delightful *The Miracle of Language.*

> *In making* **consonants,** *the lips, front teeth, lower jaw, tongue, or the velum must interfere with, obstruct, or modify the outgoing breath stream to produce a sound or noise.*

Or as one student wrote, "Consonants are the clinks and clangs, huffs and puffs, plinks and plunks of our language."

Table 4.5   Classification of Consonants by Place and Manner of Articulation
(Dictionary symbols are listed to the right of phonetic symbols only if they differ from the IPA symbols.)

Place of Articulation	Plosives		Glides		Nasals		Fricatives		Affricates	
	Voiceless	*Voiced*	*Voiceless*	*Voiced*	*Voiceless*	*Voiced*	*Voiceless*	*Voiced*	*Voiceless*	*Voiced*
Lips (Bilabial)	p	b	ʍ hw	w		m				
Lower Lips and Upper Teeth (Labiodental)							f	v		
Tongue and Teeth (Linguadental)							θ th	ð ͭ͟ʜ		
Tongue Tip and Upper or Lower Gum Ridge (Lingua-alveolar)	t	d		l		n	s	z	tʃ ch	dʒ j
Tongue Blade and Hard Palate (Linguapalatal)				r j y			ʃ sh	ʒ zh		
Back of Tongue and Soft Palate (Linguavelar)	k	g				ŋ				
Space Between Vocal Folds (Glottal)							h			

Consonants make for clearness and intelligibility in our speech. They act as dividing units and frequently separate vowel sounds. Consonants are the skeleton, and vowels the flesh of our speech. Almost 65 percent of all English sounds are consonants, and about 35 percent are vowels.

Problems and defects of articulation involve consonants far more often than vowels.

Oddly enough, your vocal cords aren't involved for ten of the consonants, the *voiceless* sounds. But fifteen consonants are *voiced* sounds, where the cords are actively involved.

How can you tell the difference? Try this:

Place your fingertips lightly against your Adam's apple. Pronounce the sounds in Column 1. (Say the sound, not the name of the letter.) You'll feel no movement or vibration because your vocal cords aren't working. They're resting. The result is that *t, p, k, s, f* are only little molded puffs of air, *voiceless* consonants.

But as you run through the *voiced* consonants in Column 2, you'll feel some movement and vibration. For *d, b, g, z, v* your vocal cords are working and producing extra sound to accompany the puffs of air. They're *voiced* consonants.

Column 1	Column 2
t	d
p	b
k	g
s	z
f	v

It's also convenient to classify consonants according to their physical characteristics and the manner in which they're produced (table 4.5).

PLOSIVES

The **plosives** (also known as *stops* or *stop-plosives*) are made by briefly blocking the outgoing air stream and thus building up air pressure. The velum is raised, preventing the escape of air through the nose. Then the tongue is dropped or the lips opened suddenly, and the built-up air is released with a little explosion.

There are six plosives in English,

Voiceless	*Voiced*
{p}	{b}
{t}	{d}
{k}	{g}

and in the following sections they will be considered in pairs, according to their places of articulation.

Place of Articulation   lips (bilabial)

Classification   {p} voiceless
    {b} voiced

Examples   {p} Pam happened to slip when Pete put pepper on the apple.
    {b} Buddy booed before Abe bounced the ball off the cupboard.

How to . . .

Press your lower and upper lips firmly together. As a rule, your teeth are slightly parted. The breath is compressed within your mouth. Part your lips suddenly, and the air bursts out with a light pop.

Faults and Foibles

1. "Clean up with a *damn* sponge" is the wind-up of a popular TV commercial in which an attractive lady is demonstrating a carpet cleaner. She obviously means *damp,* but that's not what we hear.
    Don't be a sound snipper! It's only too easy to chop off the final {p} and {b}: sleep, crab, pipe, tube.
    They're even more apt to be obliterated if they follow another consonant: chirp, bulb, trump, verb.
    If you want clean and neat {p} and {b} sounds, be sure that your lips make solid contact with each other as you shape the plosives.

    a. When a friend makes a mistake, don't rub it in, rub it out.
    b. Sound sleep is the sleep you're in when it's time to get up.
    c. You can't clean up this old world with soft soap. It takes grit.
    d. If you count sheep two at a time, you'll fall asleep twice as fast.
    e. "It'll soon be too hot to do the job it was too cold to do last winter," said Barb to Rip.
    f. A compliment is the soft soap that will wipe out the dirty look.
    g. Give a quack enough rope and he'll hang up a shingle.
    h. A bachelor is a man who can take a nap on top of a bedspread.
    i. Rub-a-dub-dub. Three men in a tub. How kinky.
    j. Your ship won't come in if you don't send a ship out.
    k. Problems would lessen if people would listen.
    l. Too many people attempt to fight the battle of life with a bottle.
    m. The proprietor of a flower shop was terrified after being held up by an armed robber. You might describe the person as a petrified florist.
    n. Beverly Hills is the only place in the world where the police have an unlisted phone number.
    o. A scandal is a breeze whipped up by two or more windbags.

[p] and [b] substitutions

If your first language is German, you may confuse [p] and [b]. If the first or initial sound of the word is [p], a [b] may be substituted. An initial [b] may be replaced with [p].

Result: *pay* [pe] and *bike* [baɪk] become *bay* [b] and *pike* [paɪk]

Remember that the initial [p] is voiceless, but the initial [b] is voiced. There will, of course, be a greater emission of breath with the voiceless [p].

2. For contrast, practice these, differentiating clearly between the initial voiceless [p] and the initial voiced [b].

pun	pail	pig–big	pore–bore
but	bill	pin–bin	pet–bet
pill	pine	pot–bought	pad–bad
bop	bit	pack–back	pull–bull

[b] and [v] substitutions

If you have a Spanish language background, you may possibly replace a middle [b] with [v], an error that results if the lips are not completely closed for [b].

Result: *rubbing* [rʌbɪŋ] becomes *ruving* [rʌvɪŋ]

fibbing [fɪbɪŋ] becomes *fiving* [fɪvɪŋ]

The voiceless [p] is commonly substituted for the voiced [b] in the final position too.

Result: *cab* [kæb] becomes *cap* [kæp]

knob [nɔb] becomes *knop* [nɔp]

3. As you practice these words and sentences, be certain that the lips are firmly closed for middle [b]. Don't confuse the *voiceless* final [p] with the *voiced* final [b].

   a.

sober	nap–nab	lop–lob	sip–sib
habit	bop–Bob	dip–dib	rip–rib
ribbon	cap–cab	pup–pub	nip–nib
table	rope–robe	gap–gab	rep–reb

   b. Mab, help Abe grab the rope crib.
   c. Herb, tape the tub before you tab the map.
   d. Bob the cop could not grab the sub from the ship.
   e. Did the Arab nap near the pub or the cab?
   f. In April she will stoop in the steep sloop and sip from the supper table.
   g. The robe fits Pope Peter Paul better than the tailor expected.
   h. The happy rabbit popped the slipper into the paper shop.
   i. The roped robber in the abyss sipped a drop from the dribbling sap.
   j. Habit: At first it's a cobweb, then it's a cable.

Omitted [b]

4. One of the most abused words in our language? *Probably*. Most people say *probly* or, worse, *proly*. Running a close second is *numer* for *number*.

   Although we can understand these warped versions, they imply sloppiness. What is responsible for most demolished [p] and [b] sounds? Comatose lips and general lukewarm activity, and both result from carelessness and indifference.

   Snappy, vigorous articulation is needed for the sentences below. Your lips must be locked together for [p] and [b] and then opened quickly.

   a. Be a pianist, not a piano.
   b. Beethoven's Fifth is not a bottle of Jim Beam.
   c. The person with push will pass the person with pull.
   d. To whip people with iron ribs use whips of steel.
   e. Never work before breakfast. If you have to work before breakfast, get your breakfast first.
   f. It wasn't the apple on the tree, but the pair on the ground, I believe, that caused all the trouble.

g. No human being believes that any other human being has a right to be in bed when he himself is up.
h. Babe Ruth was born for baseball, just as Bach was born for music.
i. Last night I dreamed I ate a ten pound marshmallow, and when I woke up, the pillow was gone.
j. Betty Botter bought a pound of butter. "But," she said, "this butter's bitter. If I put it in my batter, it will make my batter bitter. But a pound of better butter will make my batter better." So Betty Botter bought a pound of better butter, and it made her batter better.
k. Good manners is being able to put up with bad ones.
l. It's unlucky to postpone a wedding, but not if you keep on doing it.
m. It's sad when a person has a head like a doorknob. Anybody can turn it.
n. Some battle their way to the top. Others bottle their way to the bottom.
o. Reputation is a large bubble which bursts when you try to blow it up yourself.

Place of Articulation   tongue tip and upper gum ridge (lingua-alveolar)

Classification   [t] voiceless
[d] voiced

Examples   [t] They tell you that drugs turn you on. They don't tell you that later they turn on you.

[d] Judging by the divorce rate, a lot of people who said, "I do"—didn't.

How to . . .

Press the tip of your tongue against your upper gum ridge. The sides of your tongue should touch the upper molars. The air stream is now momentarily dammed up. Drop the tongue tip and your lower front jaw. The breath will be released in a small burst.

Faults and Foibles

Dentalization

As you already know, pressing the tip of the tongue against the upper gum ridge will produce a good, clear [t] or [d] sound. A few people, however, place the tongue tip on the back of the upper front teeth. A slushy sound results, and [t] and [d] may resemble [ts] and [dz]. This is known as *dentalization*. Dentalization is fine for the [θ] in thin, but not for the [t] in tin.

5. Do you make slushy, wet [t] and [d] sounds? This will happen if you place your tongue tip on the back of your upper teeth.
    tin and *did* sound more like *tsin* and *dzid*.
       Press the tip of your tongue against your upper gum ridge, about a third of an inch behind your teeth. You'll produce a tidy and dry [t] or [d] sound. Work for a brisk upward movement of your tongue as you read these. "Trippingly on the tongue"—advice from Shakespeare is still appropriate.

a.	teal–deal	tan–Dan	teen–dean
	ten–den	Tim–dim	toll–dole
	toe–doe	talk–dock	till–dill
	tuck–duck	tie–die	ton–done
	tore–door	tog–dog	tub–dub

b. Heaven defend me from a busy doctor.
c. Don't slam the door. You might want to go back.
d. What can be done at any time is never done at all.
e. The sins you do two by two you must pay for one by one.
f. If you drink, don't drive. Don't even putt.
g. Lead us not into temptation. Just tell us where it is; we'll find it.
h. I'm a champion. I play in the low 80s. If it's any hotter than that, I won't play.
i. If you don't get everything you want, think of all the things you get that you don't want.
j. I had only one friend, my dog. My wife, Dottie, was mad at me, and I told her a man ought to have at least two friends. Dottie agreed and bought me another dog.

Middle {t} and {d} Omitted

6. Read this: *Teddy noticed Betty standing near the bottled water.*
    If you swallowed or omitted those middle plosives, you may have sounded something like this:
    Te'y no'iced Be'y stan'ing near the bo'led wa'er.
    Many of the good citizens of *Baltimore, Seattle* and *Houston,* for example, mispronounce the names of their cities as *Bal'more, Se'al* and *Hous'n.*
    Now let's restore these sounds. Give each middle {t} and {d} a brief but solid tap as you read:

    a.
matter	after	wider	body
winter	history	couldn't	hadn't
wouldn't	biting	Teddy	pardon
potato	shouldn't	whittle	candy
Betty	data	certain	Arctic

    b. The atomic age is here to stay—but are we? The way to win an atomic war is to make certain that it never starts.
    c. Politics is an uncertain game. One day you're a rooster, the next you're a feather duster.
    d. "Don't worry" is a better motto if you add the word "others."
    e. History is the short trudge from Adam to the atom.
    f. One of the better things about getting older is that you find you're more interesting than most of the people you meet.
    g. The cemeteries are full of people who thought the world couldn't get along without them.
    h. Veterinarians now prescribe birth control pills for dogs. It's part of an anti-litter campaign.
    i. There ought to be a better way of starting the day than having to get up.
    j. Life started from a cell, and if justice is done, a lot of it is going to end there.
    k. Some Americans refer to Washington as the city of protocol, alcohol and Geritol.
    l. Russian girls are more interested in boys than in politics. It's better to be wed than red.
    m. We shudder to think what would happen if the Soviets broke our ZIP code.

{d} for {t} substitution

7. Did you know that a Corot landscape is PRIDDY? A twenty-five cent piece is also called a QUARDER? If {t} occurs in the medial position and especially if it's preceded and followed by voiced sounds, there's a common tendency to substitute {d}.

    a. For contrast, do these word pairs. The words on the left need an energetic {t} in the middle. Be sure it's there, and be sure it's the *voiceless* {t} and not the *voiced* {d}. And don't make it too prominent.

matter–madder	bitter–bidder	seating–seeding
latter–ladder	debtor–deader	wetting–wedding
batter–badder	rater–raider	writer–rider
daughter–dodder	rutty–ruddy	mutter–mudder

There are no medial {d} sounds in the following material, but it's saturated with middle {t} sounds. Bounce them off your gum ridge. Don't substitute {d}.

b. You're well adjusted if you can make the same mistake twice without getting nervous.
c. North Dakota's a nice place to be in winter time, especially if you're a shovel.
d. It's better to be beautiful than good, but it's better to be good than ugly.
e. History repeats itself. That's one of the things that's wrong with history.
f. Did chatter among the twenty bitter citizens betray Walter Sutton?
g. If George Washington never told a lie, what's his picture doing on a dollar bill that's worth only forty-three cents?
h. Statistics are like witnesses. They'll testify for either side.
i. Gangster "Pretty Boy" Floyd insisted that he had started out in life as an unwanted child, but by the time he was twenty-four, he was wanted in eighteen states.
j. Morton and Horton had a pretty boat with a little bottom.

Omitted {t} Followed by {s}

If {t} is preceded or followed by {s}, it is commonly omitted. In general {s-t-s} combinations are tricky.

Result: *fists* {fɪsts} may sound something like *fiss* {fɪs}

vests {vɛsts} may sound something like *vess* {vɛs}

8. To correct this fault, pronounce {s-t-s} slowly and carefully as separate sound units. When you're certain that you're forming a sharp, clear {t}, pronounce the sounds in a connected manner. As you practice the following, be sure that the {t} is not omitted when it occurs in difficult sound combinations:

a.
waists	masts	rusts	pastes
gifts	acts	busts	erupts
posts	lists	dusts	tastes
crusts	wrists	rejects	anesthetics
chests	trusts	boosts	asterisk

b. Janet insists that the lists of tests were placed in the chests.
c. Dot boasts that she fasts on crusts at feasts.
d. The crests, the masts, and the beasts could not be seen in the mists.
e. Kristi rests while Betsy sews vests in the forests.
f. Do pets hate posts, pests, and gates?
g. Misty Reston paints masts with pots of paints.
h. It is easy to stand a pain, but difficult to stand an itch; it is easy to bear the bitter taste, but difficult to bear the sour taste.

Omission and Mispronunciation of {əd}

If *-ed* {əd} is used to form the past tense of a verb, it's sometimes omitted or mispronounced.

If the *-ed* is preceded by

. . . {t} or {d}, it's generally pronounced as a separate syllable:

hunted is pronounced *huntud* {ˈhʌntəd}

skidded is pronounced *skiddud* {ˈskɪdəd}

. . . a voiceless sound, it's pronounced as {t}:

whipped is pronounced *whipt* {hwɪpt}

asked is pronounced *askt* {æskt}

. . . a voiced sound, it's pronounced as {d}:

nagged is pronounced *nagd* {nægd}

filled is pronounced *fild* {fɪld}

9. Pronounce the -ed endings correctly in the following words and sentences:

   a.
lurched	matted	hoed	iced
edged	razzed	trapped	drowned
shaded	loved	rammed	ranted
crashed	attacked	fitted	debauched

   b. One who is born to be hanged will never be drowned.
   c. A good deed never goes unpunished.
   d. Success has killed more people than bullets.
   e. The image of woman as we know it is an image created by men and designed to suit their needs.
   f. A man in love is incomplete until he is married. Then he is finished. [Zsa Zsa Gabor]
   g. The person who is all wrapped up in himself is overdressed.
   h. A jury recently reported back to the judge. "We just don't want to get involved."
   i. A watched pot often causes one to join Weight Watchers.
   j. A pessimist carried a card in his wallet that said, "In case of accident, I'm not surprised."

[t] and [d] omitted at end of a word

10. If [t] and [d] occur at the end of a word, they're often omitted, especially if they're preceded by other consonants. You'll say *jus, fac,* and *frien* instead of *just, fact,* and *friend.*
    Make your final plosives crystal clear and audible in these:

    a.
crept	just	world	ground
moist	crossed	sold	fad
pelt	quart	heard	crazed
raft	fact	hand	athlete

    b. Don't go to bed mad. Stay up and fight.
    c. Crime wouldn't pay if we let the government run it.
    d. Don't bite the hand that has your allowance in it.
    e. The only way to get rid of a temptation is to yield to it.
    f. If you don't say anything, you won't be called on to repeat it.
    g. Don't lead me; I may not follow. Don't walk behind me; I may not lead. Walk beside me and be my friend.
    h. I used to be Snow White, but I drifted. [Mae West]
    i. Backward, turn backward, O Time, in your flight, and tell me just one thing I studied last night.

[t] and [d] in various positions and sound combinations

11. You'll find it helpful to exaggerate somewhat as you read aloud this drill material. Eventually, however, you'll want to strive for ease and naturalness and articulate [t] and [d] sounds that don't call attention to themselves.

    a. If the world seems cold to you, kindle fires to warm it.
    b. It is not the bad that is bad, for the bad rarely deceives us. The mediocre is bad, because it can seem to be good.
    c. The husband who boasts that he never made a mistake has a wife who did.
    d. The past is never dead; it's not even past.
    e. I'm not afraid to die; I just don't want to be there when it happens.
    f. It is all right to hold a conversation, but you should let go of it now and then.
    g. The law can make you quit drinking, but it can't make you quit being the kind that needs a law to make you quit drinking.
    h. Rembrandt painted three hundred pictures and Americans have all seven hundred of them.
    i. The auto industry accounts for one out of every twenty jobs in the United States, and this does not include morticians.

j. Stradivarius could have turned out a lot more violins if he had quit fiddling around.

k. A guy asked the meat cutter at the supermarket if he had any veal. A lady standing nearby turned to him and said sharply: "Has it ever occurred to you where that veal comes from when you're eating it?" The man pointed to a carton of eggs in the woman's cart and replied. "Has it ever occurred to you where those come from when you're eating them?"

Place of Articulation   back of tongue and soft palate (linguavelar)

Classification   {k} voiceless
{g} voiced

Examples   {k} Kate walked back into the cave after six members of the chorus ate the biscuits.
{g} Golden eagles eat bugs and exist in ghettos during big plagues.

How to . . .

Press the back of your tongue against your soft palate (toward the rear of your mouth). Build up air pressure behind the tongue, and lower it abruptly, releasing the breath with a small blast.

Faults and Foibles

{g} and {k} substitution

12. Have a foreign language background? You may be switching {g} with {k}. You'll pronounce *local* {ˈlokl} as *logal* {ˈlogl}. Or you may be switching {k} with {g}. *Pig* {pɪg} becomes *pick* {pɪk}.

It isn't difficult to straighten them out. Don't forget that {k} is *voiceless*—a bantam breeze. There is no sound in your throat as you produce it. {g} is *voiced*. You make a mini-grunt.

As you practice these words and sentences, make sure that the back portion of your tongue presses firmly against the velum on the {k} and {g} sounds. Try to keep the {k} or {g} relatively light and clean-cut, and avoid producing a muddy, heavy sound.

a.

game–came	snigger–snicker	bag–back
God–cod	stagger–stacker	nag–knack
gate–Kate	lagging–lacking	sag–sack
goat–coat	logging–locking	brig–brick
gill–kill	haggle–hackle	hog–hock
gall–call	trigger–tricker	lug–luck

b. Hard work never killed anybody, but why take a chance?

c. A person takes a drink, the drink takes a drink, and the drink takes the person.

d. A vacation is what you take when you can no longer take what you've been taking.

e. Doing a movie is a gamble. It's exactly like being pregnant. You're all agog, but you've got that long wait to see if it's ugly. {Carol Burnett}

f. A college boy in Kentucky called his folks. He was flunking out, because it was discovered he had a clinker in his thinker.

Spelling and Faulty Pronunciation of {k} and x

The strange spelling given to a sound that is actually a {k} or a {g} may sometimes confuse us and may account for faulty pronunciation of words containing these sounds.

The principal troublemakers are words such as *accept* that contain the *cc* spelling. A common fault is to omit the {k} sound in these words.

Result: *accelerate* is incorrectly pronounced as {æ`sɛlǝret} instead of correctly as {æk`sɛlǝret}

accessory is incorrectly pronounced as {æ`sɛsǝrɪ} instead of correctly as {æk`sɛsǝrɪ}

Other problem words are ones such as *exert* and *extra*. In *exert,* the correct sound for *x* is {gz}: {ɪg`zɝt}. In *extra,* the correct sound for *x* is {ks}: {`ɛkstrǝ}.

There are two simple rules that will help you distinguish *x* words that require the {gz} pronunciation and *x* words that take the {ks} pronunciation.

If the vowel sound following the *x* is stressed, the *x* will be pronounced {gz}.

    exactly {ɪg`zæktlɪ}        *exempt* {ɪg`zɛmpt}

If *x* is followed by a pronounced consonant or if it is found in the final position, it will be pronounced {ks}.

    excite {ɪk`saɪt}   *box* {bɑks}
    expect {ɪk`spɛkt}   *fix* {fɪks}

13.   The sentences below are crammed with {k} and {g} sounds, but the kaleidoscopic spellings don't always warn you that {k} or {g} are lurking in the background. Be sure that you form these two plosives properly. The back of your tongue must touch your soft palate. You'll be able to feel this happen. Hear them correctly, too!

    a.   The best substitute for experience is being sixteen.
    b.   Most people have great respect for old age—particularly if it's bottled.
    c.   There are two good finishes for automobiles: lacquer and liquor.
    d.   Puberty: the time when kids stop asking questions and begin to question answers.
    e.   People who squawk about their income tax can be divided into two classes: men and women.
    f.   Experience is what enables you to recognize a mistake when you make it again.
    g.   A Cadillac is what a doctor buys not to make house calls in.
    h.   You can say "quick as a wink" two-fifths of a second faster than you can say "Jack Robinson."
    i.   Here Skugg lies as snug as a bug in a rug.
    j.   Fanatic: one with a kink, a quirk, and a crack in the cranium.

GRAB BAG: PRACTICE MATERIAL FOR THE PLOSIVES

The plosives are the forgotten underdogs of all the sound families. Too often these useful sounds are aborted or annihilated. They shouldn't be. The plosives are the "drum beats" of our language.

14.   The material coming up contains all six plosives—{t}, {d}, {p}, {b}, {k}, {g}—in a variety of positions and sound combinations.

THE TRIPLE PLAY:
Do each sentence three times.
first time: Exaggerate your medial and final plosives considerably. Make them pop like a balloon. *Remember, this is for practice purposes only.*
second time: Use moderate exaggeration. Your medial and final plosives should be medium loud pops.
third time: No exaggeration. *Be natural.* Tap your plosives with a feather, but tap them!

---

    a.   If it looks like a duck, walks like a duck and quacks like a duck—it is a duck.
    b.   If you hit two keys with the typewriter, the one you don't want hits the paper.
    c.   Dog catcher: a person with a seeing-dog eye.
    d.   Getting an award from TV is like being kissed by somebody with bad breath.
    e.   Fewer marriages would skid if more who said "I do" did.
    f.   A cocktail party is an excuse to drink for a lot of people who don't need an excuse.
    g.   I have always thought of a dog lover as a dog that was in love with another dog.
    h.   Television isn't so bad if you don't turn it on.
    i.   If you worry about missing the boat, remember the Titanic.
    j.   The skunk sat on a stump. The skunk thunk the stump stunk, but the stump thunk the skunk stunk.

k. Diamonds are chunks of coal that stuck to their job.
l. If a cat spoke, it would say things like, "Hey, I don't see the problem here."
m. The only reason I would take up jogging is so that I could hear heavy breathing again. (Erma Bombeck)
n. Most kids can't understand why a country that makes atomic bombs would ban firecrackers.
o. Public opinion is what folks think folks think.
p. When you stop to think, don't forget to start again.
q. Big toe: a device for finding furniture in the dark.
r. They say that women talk too much. If you worked in Congress, you know that the filibuster was invented by men.
s. The company that prints those wallet cards that read: I AM A DEVOUT CATHOLIC. IN CASE OF ACCIDENT, CALL A PRIEST has expanded its line to include a card which reads: I AM A DEVOUT ATHEIST. IN CASE OF ACCIDENT, GOODBYE.
t. That old bromide about truck drivers leading you to the good eats was cooked up in the same kettle as the wild tales about toads causing warts and goats eating tin cans. Don't believe it. Follow the truckers and you'll wind up at truck stops.

Assignment 8: Plosives

Prepare material that contains many examples of the six plosives (p b t d k g) in various positions and sound combinations. If you've found one or two of them to be unusually troublesome, be certain that your material is loaded with them. You may find it easier to write your own material. Nonsense material is generally acceptable, but emphasize simplicity. As you practice, try the Triple Play. At first make firm, crisp and relatively hard sounds. As you continue practicing, gradually decrease the exaggeration. Plosives are the *snap, crackle,* and *pop* sounds of the consonant families, but remember that normal, connected speech is natural speech.

Suggested Checklist for Assignment 8

As you practice by yourself, you may want to work with this checklist. Listen carefully to yourself. If it is feasible, record the assignment or get a classmate or friend to listen to you as you read the material. Eventually, your goal will be to have a check mark in the **Yes** column for each category. (Optional: Perhaps your instructor will want to use the checklist to evaluate you during your classroom presentation.)

	Yes	No
Initial plosives firmly articulated		
Medial plosives firmly articulated		
Final plosives firmly articulated		
Differentiates between—		
voiceless (p) and voiced (b)		
voiceless (t) and voiced (d)		
voiceless (k) and voiced (g)		

__Avoids—__

overemphasis resulting from excessive pressure

substituting {θ} for {t}

substituting {f} or {v} for {p} or {b}

Pronounces _ed_ endings correctly

Additional comments or suggestions:

GLIDES (SEMIVOWELS)

A __glide__ is a sound produced by a continuous gliding movement of the articulators from the position of one sound to that of another. The glides have been described as vowels in motion.

There are four glides in English:

{l}	{w}
{r}	{j} y

When you say {r}, {w}, or {j}, for example, your tongue is in motion as these sounds are being formed.

Make the {w} sound in _well_. Hold it for a few seconds, as if you were going to say the whole word in slow motion. You'll discover that {w} really sounds like the _oo_ {u} in _moon_ {mun}. Now move into the _ell_. What's your tongue doing? Moving or gliding, as it were. Even your lips and jaw are in motion—a smooth, continuous gliding motion.

__Place of Articulation__	lips (bilabial)
__Classification__	voiced
__Example__	<u>W</u>ilma <u>w</u>ailed q<u>u</u>ietly as <u>o</u>ne tear <u>w</u>obbled down her q<u>u</u>ivering cheek.

__How to . . .__

Round and protrude your lips. The back of your tongue should be arched toward the soft palate. It's the rapid widening of your lips that gives {w} its character. An excellent {w} can be produced with little or no movement of your tongue.

__Faults and Foibles__

__{w} _confused with_ {v} _or_ {f}__

Individuals with a Germanic language background (and occasionally other foreign languages) often confuse {w} with {v} or {f}. Note and compare the rounded lip position used for the English {w} with the position for {v} or {f}.

For {v} or {f}, the lower lip is held lightly against the edges of the upper front teeth. For {w}, the lips mustn't touch the teeth.

Another little tip: As you do the words beginning with {w} in the material below, first say the *oo* of *moon*, hold for two seconds and then glide into the next sound. For example: *oo-ail (wail), oo-ell* (well).

15. Watch yourself in a mirror as you say

    a. | vail–wail | vary–wary | vest–west | fade–wade |
        |-----------|-----------|-----------|-----------|
        | veal–weal | vault–Walt | vine–wine | fin–win |
        | vane–wane | veld–weld | vaunt–want | food–wooed |
        | vet–wet | vent–went | vee–we | fell–well |

    b. Will Velma Weems give Wilbur West's vest to the vet?
    c. Why did Violet weigh Warren Vernon and Vesta Watson?
    d. Van weeps when vines and weeds are watered in winter.
    e. Verna Winston whispered, "We must wander with Wendy toward Venice."
    f. Everybody wants to live a long time but nobody wants to get old.

16. The *qu* spelling in such words as *quit, Quaker,* and *queen* doesn't indicate the presence of {w}, but the sound is present in every English word that begins with *qu.* Notice the phonetic spelling of these words.

    {kwɪt   `kwekɚ   kwin}

    There's a tendency in careless speech to weaken the {w} sound in {kw} clusters. Be sure that the sound is firm as you practice this material. Don't forget to push out and round the lips for {w}.

    a. | quad | quilt | quick |
        |------|-------|-------|
        | quaint | quart | quantity |
        | quality | quite | quell |
        | quarter | quest | quill |

    b. She quivered as she quietly paid a quarter for the quilt.
    c. Quickly got—quickly lost: Quite quoteworthy.
    d. The duck quaked and quacked as it fell into the quicksand.
    e. Quakers will not quarrel and quibble while quizzed.
    f. There are two kinds of marriages—where the husband quotes the wife, or where the wife quotes the husband.

Flabby {w}

Chronic mumblers will generally produce weak and flabby {w} sounds. If the lips are allowed to hang like two pieces of inanimate liver, a clear {w} cannot be produced. Lip movement must be vigorous, rapid, and forceful. Amateur ventriloquists generally try to avoid material loaded with {w} at the beginnings of words.

17. Read the material in this exercise twice. The first time, exaggerate lip rounding and protruding, and prolong {w} sounds slightly. The second time, avoid exaggeration, but work for sharpness of articulation. Watch out for medial {w}, as in for*w*ard and house*w*ife.

    a. He preaches well who lives well.
    b. Always give the public what they want, even if they don't want it.
    c. Winning isn't everything but wanting to win is.
    d. Laugh and the whole world laughs with you. Cry and your mascara runs.
    e. The choir was persuaded to switch plans quickly.
    f. Whatever is worth doing at all, is worth doing well.
    g. If your head is wax, don't walk in the sun.
    h. The time you enjoyed wasting wasn't wasted.
    i. The longest word in the world is "a word from our sponsor."
    j. We don't know who it was who discovered water, but we're pretty sure it wasn't fish.
    k. A person with one watch knows what time it is. A person with two watches is never sure.

l.   A few weeks ago we went to a well-known German restaurant. The appetizer made us queasy, and the wurst was yet to come.

m.   People become well-to-do by doing what they do well.

n.   Even the woodpecker has discovered that the only way to succeed is to use one's head.

o.   They now have a lie detector without wires. It's called a wife.

p.   There is no need to worry, because the only thing to worry about is whether you are rich or poor. If you are rich, there is nothing to worry about. If you are poor, all there is to worry about is whether you are sick or well. If you are well, there is nothing to worry about. If you are sick, all you have to worry about is if you are going to get well or die. If you get well, there is no need to worry. If you die, all you have to worry about is if you go to heaven or hell. If you go to heaven, there is nothing to worry about. If you go to hell, you will be so busy shaking hands with your friends that you won't have time to worry.

hw

Place of Articulation   lips (bilabial)

Classification   an {h} approach to {w}; a fricative glide

Example   <u>Wh</u>y did the <u>wh</u>ite <u>wh</u>ale <u>wh</u>irl around <u>wh</u>en fed <u>wh</u>itefish?

How to . . .
Your lips assume the rounded position for {w}, but the initial part of the following gliding movement is accompanied by the voiceless {h}.

Faults and Foibles
How do you handle these word pairs?

where–wear
whet–wet
whacks–wax

A vast majority of us pronounce *where/wear* the same way: {wɛr}

If you're a stickler for precision, you may want to pronounce that {h} in *wh* words. If so, you'll have to sound the {h} before, not after, the {w}. A thousand years ago in Old English, most of the present-day words beginning with *wh* were spelled with the two letters reversed and pronounced that way: *hwaer* (where).

Many speakers, readers and actors concerned with finesse do pronounce *wh* words with the {h} sounded first (as if the everyday English spelling were *hwere, hwet, hwacks*).

But if you listen carefully to good speakers and well-trained voices, you'll discover that the {h} in *wh* combinations is disappearing from pronunciation rather rapidly.

However, let's be reasonable. *It's neither incorrect to use it nor is it incorrect to drop it*. Use it if you will.

18.   For those who will: Make a distinction between the *wh* combinations and the single *w* in the following.

a.
whether–weather	where–wear	whet–wet
wheel–weal	whale–wail	whir–were
when–wen	what–watt	whey–way
whine–wine	whish–wish	why–y
whit–wit	whin–win	whig–wig
whirled–world	whoa–woe	while–wile

b.   Where did the white wight wear the wispy whiskers?

c.   Which witch whined when the wine was spilled on the wheel?

d. "I don't care a whit for your wit or whims," said Will White.

e. I wish I were what I was when I wanted to be what I am now.

f. I keep six honest servants: They taught me all I know. Their names are What, Why, When, How, Where, and Who.

g. In the United States there is more space where nobody is than where anybody is. That is what makes America what it is. [Gertrude Stein]

Place of Articulation tongue and upper gum ridge (lingua-alveolar)

Classification voiced

Example Lena filled the pickle barrel with plump apples.

How to . . .

Place the tip of your tongue tip lightly against your upper gum ridge. Keep the sides of your tongue down to allow the breath stream to flow freely over the sides.

Faults and Foibles

Clearness and Darkness

If [1] is found at or near the end of a word as in *ball, tale,* and *cold,* it's a dark [1]. A dark [1] in itself certainly isn't incorrect, but if it's so dark that it's muffled and gluey, it'll probably hinder intelligibility. You'll make a too dusky [1] if your tongue tip doesn't contact the gum ridge.

19. To help you hear as well as feel the difference between a clear [1] and a dark [1], read the following. The first word of each pair begins with a clear [1]. Be sure that the back of your tongue is held relatively low. The second word ends with a dark [1]. Your entire tongue should be pulled farther back in your mouth than it is for a clear [1]. The back portion of your tongue is also higher for the dark sound than for the clear one.

lean–seal	lag–gal	lock–call
let–fell	lot–tall	lime–mile
lid–dill	lip–pill	lead–deal
late–tale	loot–tool	lost–stall

Swallowed [1]

Don't slight [1] if it's followed by another consonant: *help, silk, wolf, film.*

Do you say *bid, code, jade* and *wed* for *build, cold, jailed* and *weld?* If you do, you're blotching or bleaching that important [1] sound.

20. Caution: Your tongue tip MUST make proper contact with the gum ridge as you form [1] in the following:

a.				
wealth	twelve	jailed	revolve	dolphin
self	helm	shelve	malt	alb
Ralph	scald	alm	pelvis	pelf
gulp	milk	film	gold	belt

b. We are told that history always repeats itself. But, then, so does television.

c. A hothead seldom sets the world on fire.

d. There are three things most men love but never understand: females, girls, and women.

e. Always use first names: Remember, if God had meant us to use last names, He would have used one Himself.
f. A telephone pole never hits an automobile except in self-defense.
g. Driving your car can help you see the world, but how you drive will determine which world.

21. Do you say *aw* right for *all* right, baseb*a* for baseba*ll?* Then you're diluting or eliminating that final {l}. DON'T!
As you read these, don't let those tail end {l} sounds droop or lurk in the back of your throat. PUSH them forward! Give them a bit of glitter.

a. Since it's better to speak well of the dead, let's knock them while they're still alive.
b. Hot tempers will mean cool friends.
c. Any fool can make a rule.
d. Surely it's better to tell the truth behind peoples' backs than never tell it at all.
e. Why is it that a scandal runs, while truth must crawl?
f. Every child has a right to be both well-fed and well-led.
g. There is no fool like an old fool. Ask any young fool.
h. A rascal I know says he's too old for castor oil and too young for Geritol.
i. Tip to young male drivers: forget the girl and hug the road.
j. In college football the real triple threat is one who can run, kick and pass all his exams.
k. Tell me what you eat, and I will tell you what you are.
l. Conscience is the still, small voice that makes us feel still smaller.
m. Joan Rivers says that a yo-yo is one who's not playing with a full deck . . . a few pickles short of a barrel . . . got one wheel in the sand . . . a little loose in the loafers.

Substitutions for {l}

Individuals whose first language is Oriental rather than English may confuse {l} and {r}. The Oriental allegedly says *velly good laundly* for *very good laundry* or *flied lice* for *fried rice.* Most Oriental languages don't contain sounds that are exactly like the English {l} and {r}. They do, however, contain a consonant that resembles and has some characteristics of both—hence the confusion.

22. For anybody who needs to work on this aspect of English pronunciation: Remember that for {l} the tip of your tongue must touch the upper gum ridge. For {r}, the central portion of your tongue is raised, and the tip is pointed upward but should not contact either the gum ridge or the hard palate immediately above the gum ridge. With these differences in mind, practice this material.

a.

lamb–ram	line–Rhine	lewd–rude	glimmer–grimmer
lope–rope	lack–wrack	Lyle–rile	plank–prank
lip–rip	loan–roan	leap–reap	fly–fry
lag–rag	limb–rim	blink–brink	climb–crime

b. Do not cram the clams into the crock near the clock.
c. Cleo hauled the long load of blue brew down the wrong road.
d. Telling your troubles is swelling your troubles.
e. Lily Ringling arrived alive even though she had ripped the lid.
f. The heated lead turned red as the glow began to grow.
g. Life can only be understood backwards, but it must be lived forwards.

23. *Pwease, yet's go for a riddow wide.*
If a four-year-old says this, it's cute. If a forty-year-old says it, it isn't.
{l} is a troublesome sound. It's also one of the last sounds children learn to make. A tot will often substitute {w} and {j} and, less frequently, {r} for the {l} sound.
Result: *lad* {læd} becomes *yad* {yæd}, *wad* {wæd} or *rad* {ræd}
Well-meaning parents sometimes encourage this kind of baby talk, and the defective {l} may carry over into adulthood. Newscaster Tom Brokaw articulates {l} sounds which lean unmistakably in the direction of {w}. *Billion* turns into *biwyun.*

Read the material below. Do NOT substitute lip movement for tongue movement on your {l} sounds. Keep lip activity to an absolute minimum. And remember, the tip of your tongue must touch your upper gum ridge for each and every {l}.

a.

way–lay	yank–lank	rot–lot	wink–link
wake–lake	yet–let	rung–lung	yeast–least
wick–lick	year–leer	rip–lip	rain–lain
wore–lore	yard–lard	rap–lap	yawn–lawn

b. A marriage may be a holy wedlock or an unholy deadlock.
c. Golf is a sport in which a small white ball is chased by men who are too old to chase anything else.
d. If money is all you want, money is all you'll get.
e. Cleopatra loved to sing duets all by herself.
f. It has been said that there is no fool like an old fool, except a young fool. But the young fool has first to grow up to be an old fool to realize what a damn fool he was when he was a young fool. {Dwight Eisenhower}

Other Faults

■ In careless speech, the schwa {ə} is occasionally inserted between {l} and a preceding initial consonant. Thus, *clean* {klin} becomes *cuh-lean* {kə'lin} and *plenty* {'plɛnti} becomes *puh-lenty* {pə'lɛnti}.

■ If {l} is the final sound in a word, and if it's preceded by {t} or {d}, some speakers will omit the plosives.
Result: *little* {'lɪtl} sounds like *li-ul* {'lɪəl} or *li'l* {lɪl}
   saddle {'sædl} sounds like *sa-ul* {'sæəl} or *sa'l* {sæl}

24. Careful listening is necessary to correct these faults. Again, check the position of your tongue, especially the tip. Try for accurate and acceptable {l} sounds as you say these sentences:

a. I never give them hell. I just tell the truth, and they think it's hell. {Harry S Truman}
b. All the things I really like to do are immoral, illegal or fattening.
c. An alcoholic is like a whiskey bottle: all neck and belly and no head.
d. Sports do not build character. They reveal it. If Howard Cosell was a sport, it would be roller derby.
e. Until you walk a mile in another man's moccasins you can't imagine the smell.
f. In a shop on Lexington Avenue in New York is this sign: We undersell the store that undersells the store that will not be undersold.
g. All the world may not love a lover, but all the world loves to watch a lover.
h. We should all just smell well and enjoy ourselves a lot more.
i. The lion and the calf shall lie down together, but the calf won't get much sleep.
j. Is Melville's *Moby Dick* a tale about a real whale or a whale of a tale about a whale's tail?
k. There never was a devil who didn't advise people to keep out of hell.
l. The world is as good as you are. You've got to learn to like yourself. I'm a little bit screwed up, but I'm beautiful. {Tom Cruise}
m. Love is like the measles: all the worse when it comes late in life.
n. He who has a thing to sell and whispers it in a well is not so apt to get dollars as he who climbs a tree and hollers.
o. What is moral is what you feel good after, and what is immoral is what you feel bad after.

Place of Articulation   tip or blade of tongue behind upper gum ridge (linguapalatal)

Classification   voiced

Example   Raymond could not bear rock and roll music so Gertrude wrote an opera for him.

How to . . .

One Manner of Production

The central portion of your tongue is tensed slightly and raised toward the hard palate (the roof of the mouth). The tip of your tongue may be lowered and drawn back somewhat from the lower teeth.

Another Manner of Production

The tip of your tongue may be brought close to the gum ridge and turned back slightly toward the middle of the hard palate.

Both of these are starting positions. As soon as the sound is begun, your tongue glides or moves to the position necessary to make the following sound. The exact position of your lips and jaw also depends largely upon the sound that follows.

A *gremlin* in our language?

The |r| sound is a genuine mischief-maker. It's also controversial.

Run through these five words, and you'll come up with five entirely different |r| sounds: *rim, turn, matter, four* (some Easterners pronounce it as *fo-wa*), *fire* (in some Southern speech, the |r| disappears completely at the ends of words—it floats off to the nearest magnolia tree—as in *fah-yuh*).

The section of the country in which you live may strongly influence your |r| sounds.

Faults and Foibles

A lazy, lifeless tongue will do much to destroy a clear and identifiable |r|. Let your lips be lazy, but your tongue needs to toil.

25. A little extravagance is called for here.

Before you sound the initial |r| in such words as *red* and *right,* make the sound of *er* |ɝ| as in *ermine* and *fern.*

To make *er:* Raise the middle portion of your tongue toward the roof of your mouth. If this seems unnatural to you, simply make sure that the front of your tongue is higher than the back. Some individuals point the tip of the tongue upwards; others curl it slightly backwards.

Do each of the words and sentences in this exercise twice. In the first reading, make an exaggerated *er* |ɝ| sound before the initial |r|:

Er–round the er–rough and er–rugged er–rock the er–ragged er–rascal er–ran.

The second time, keep the same tongue position on the initial |r| which you used on the *er* |ɝ| sounds, but cut the preliminary *er* quite short.

a.	rent	rim	rail	ripe
	rift	wren	rant	rock
	raw	wrack	run	rink
	rabbit	road	ride	wrought

b. A rose is a rose is a rose is a rose. |Gertrude Stein|
c. Weathermen are never wrong. It's the weather that's wrong!
d. Running for money doesn't make you run fast. It makes you run first.
e. Real embarrassment is when you tell a girl her stockings are wrinkled and she's not wearing any.
f. A problem teenager is one who refuses to let his parents use the car.
g. The rich in our society are really different. Among the Republicans in Beverly Hills, the Internal Revenue Service is known as a terrorist organization.
h. Freedom is the right to be wrong, not the right to do wrong.
i. A reckless driver is seldom reckless for very long.
j. If the left side of the brain controls the right side of the body, then only left-handed people are in their right mind.

{pr, br, fr} clusters

As you've noticed, {p} and {b} require rather strong lip activity. As the articulators adjust from the initial consonant to the {r}, a sound much like {w} may be heard. *Pride, brim* and *fry* become *pwide, bwim* and *fwy*.

The {w} substitution is to be avoided, of course. Remember—and this is not as tricky as it may seem—the tongue articulates {r} in these clusters at the same time that the lips articulate {p}, {b}, and {f}. In other words, before you have finished making {p}, {b}, and {f}, the {r} sound has already begun.

26.   Try these words and sentences.

a.	pride	brought	freak
	prank	brick	frill
	prod	brunt	fright
	prattle	broom	from

b.   The brown bricks pressed against the pretty grass frame.
c.   "Are you proud of the prank?" asked the bragging friar.
d.   Is it progress or improvement if a cannibal uses a knife and fork?
e.   Thieves respect property. They merely wish the property to become their property that they may more perfectly respect it.

{kr, gr} clusters

Again, the initial consonant must virtually overlap with the {r}. This very close blend isn't difficult to form if the {r} is articulated with your tongue pulled back as it would be if {k} and {g} were being sounded.

27.   Don't hold the initial sounds too long as you practice the following:

a.	cross	crate	grill	grace
	crust	crack	grim	groom
	crude	creek	grade	gripe
	croak	cry	grant	congratulate

b.   When you're green, you're growing. When you're ripe, you rot.
c.   Greta Gray crams for her courses but Craig Crockett is a grind.
d.   When angry, count ten before you speak. If very angry, count one hundred.
e.   Perhaps the world's second worst crime is boredom. The worst crime is being a bore.

{tr, dr} clusters

The {r} that most of us produce in words such as *try* and *drip* is still another kind of {r} and with a personality of its own. Friction noises can sometimes be heard with this sound, and in its manner of production it's similar to the fricative family.

Lower the tip of your tongue just enough to produce the {t} or {d}. Then retract it quickly with the tip of your tongue near but not in actual contact with the gum ridge. Incidentally, many individuals find it easy to produce a successful {r} if the tongue touches the gum ridge lightly.

28.   As you drill with this material, avoid two fairly common faults:
       Don't make the {r} clusters conspicuous—too noisy or sustained.
       Don't insert a sound resembling *uh*—the schwa {ə}—between an initial consonant and the {r}.
       When this is done, such words as *try* and *dream* become *tuh-ry* and *duh-ream*.

a.	trim	dram	treat
	trod	dreary	droop
	trout	draft	tray
	trek	drink	drawl

b.   A trout is a fish known mainly by hearsay; a trout must be caught by tickling.

c. Never have children, only grandchildren.

d. When choosing between two evils, I always try to choose the one I've never tried before. [Mae West]

e. The trouble with treating people as equals is that the first thing you know they may be doing the same thing to you.

[w] substitutions

Bugs Bunny has respectable (New Yorkish) *r* sounds. His nemesis, the muddled Elmer Fudd, doesn't. Elmer substitutes *w:* "I won't west until I get wid of that wascally wabbit."

In more elevated circles, TV newscaster Barbara Walters begets *r* sounds that tilt decidedly toward *w*. This may explain why the "Saturday Night Live" comics, some years back, always referred to her as "Ba-Ba Wa-Wa."

29. If you find that you're substituting *w* for *r*, here's how to convert to *r:* Keep your lips immobile, don't raise the back of your tongue, and emphasize movements of the *front* of your tongue as you make *r*.

a.

wad–rod	way–ray	wide–ride
wade–raid	wane–rain	woo–rue
wine–Rhine	week–reek	will–rill
won–run	woe–row	wing–ring

b. Rita wailed after the wild ride through the waning rain.

c. Are there reeds or weeds near the willows on the rill?

d. While waiting for the whales, Rhonda and Wanda rode the rails.

e. Randy Ware wooed Rhea Wheeler during the ride on the wide wagon.

Trilled [r]

30. If you have a foreign language background and trill the sound—and trilling seems to be a cross between fluttering and gargling—modify your way of making *r*. Say *uh*, prolong it, and try to curl back the tip of your tongue.

a.

rot	trap	forest
ran	drop	foundry
rail	crop	Lorna
rue	grade	wearing

b. It's a rare person who hears what he doesn't want to hear.

c. Never lend your car to anyone to whom you have given birth.

d. To err is human, but to really foul things up requires a computer.

e. Rock journalism is people who can't write interviewing people who can't talk for people who can't read.

f. The really wretched thing about being rich is that you have to live with rich people.

Regional [r]

"You can't fool all the people all the time. Once every four years is enough."

How true! Every four years we watch and hear the two major political parties nominate candidates. There is enough hell-bubbling pageantry and speech-making for everybody. Most interesting to some of us, however, is the wonderful conglomeration of dialects or "accents."

The delegate from Boston who talks about problems that *Americer* has with *Cuber* and *Libyer* is just as colorful as the senator from South Carolina who tells the convention about his great *feah of nucleah wah*. The chairperson identifies herself as a native *Noo Yawkuh*, with an absence of recognizable [r] sounds, but the visiting governor of Iowa hangs on to the [r] in *R-R-R-Republican* as though his life depends on it. (That hard, midwestern [r] has been nicknamed the "snarling [r].")

Who has the correct [r] sound? All of them, as long as they're intelligible.

If [r] follows a vowel and occurs in or near the final position of a word, such as in *fair* and *cart,* and if you use General American dialect, you'll probably articulate the [r] with definite [r] coloring. If you use Eastern or Southern dialects, you may possibly articulate an [r] in *fair* and *cart* that resembles *uh.*

General American		Eastern and Southern	
far	= [fɑr]	far	= [fɑə]
park	= [pɑrk]	park	= [pɑək]
beard	= [bird]	beard	= [biəd]

Maybe you have no problem with this variation of the [r] family. Let your instructor advise you. If you're told that your [r] sound is too hard and prominent or is accompanied by unpleasant friction noises, you may be curling the tongue tip back excessively as well as prolonging the sound. As you read the drill material, try to get the feel of your tongue activity and position. The tongue tip should not curl back on itself.

31. If your [r] sound is weak and pallid, is too close to *uh,* or is otherwise conspicuous for the area in which you live, raise the central portion of your tongue, and point the tip of your tongue in the direction of the gum ridge. It may help you to prolong the [r] sound briefly as you read aloud the following:

   a.   fear   queer   leer   bare
        rare   mar   poor   floor
        liar   start   port   mire
        air   bored   barn   sire

   b.   Too many people pick a quarrel before it's ripe.
   c.   Popular song title before World War I: "Take Back Your Heart. I Ordered Liver."
   d.   There's no harm in talking to yourself, but try to avoid telling yourself jokes that you've heard before.
   e.   A good question to ask ourselves: What kind of a world would this be if everybody was just like me?
   f.   The friendly cow all red and white
        I love with all my heart.
        She gives me cream with all her might
        To eat with apple tart.

Intrusive {r}

Back to Boston: Cub*er* and Liby*er.*

This is the *intrusive r*—an *r* sound where it doesn't belong. It's common in parts of New England and in the New York City area.

Hardly a criminal offense, it often provides amusement for outsiders. The [r] is inserted between two words if the first one ends with a vowel and the second one begins with a vowel. This seems to ease the transition between consecutive vowels. Thus, we hear *sofa-r in the living room, idea-r of his, law-r of the state.* Speakers who use the intrusive [r] may also hook it on the end of a single word: *potater* [pə ˋtet ɚ] for *potato* and *arear* [ˋɛri ɚ] for *area.*

Those who use General American or Southern dialect will rarely use the intrusive [r].

32. If you use Eastern dialect, you may be inserting this extra [r] sound. If you want to eliminate it, practice these sentences. Let somebody listen to you. Work until the tacked-on sound disappears.

   a.   Hannah Adams and Papa ought to dance the polka all day.
   b.   The gorilla understood how to eat a banana in the arena.
   c.   "The idea of doing a drama in an Alabama open-air theater is great," Anna answered.
   d.   Ole ate raw oysters in Alaska and Canada.
   e.   Georgia Upton wore the toga in the plaza in Cuba.
   f.   Eva bought the china in Vienna after the tourists went to Russia.

Acceptable {r} *Sounds*

Whatever the nature of your [r] sounds, be certain they're not so quirky and nonconformist that you're hard to understand. The sound should never be lengthened or deafening. Most importantly, if your [r] stands out like a beacon light, practice until you can produce a suitable [r] sound.

33. This material contains [r] in many combinations and positions.

   a.
   shop–sharp   code–cord   load–lord
   Don–darn   pock–park   ought–art
   hod–hard   toe–tore   mock–mark
   saw–a–car   foe–fore   tomato–and–corn
   era–of–war   Moe–more   radio–in–there

   b. The lion shall lie down to rest with the lamb, but every morning they'll have to provide a fresh lamb.
   c. Sign outside a Hollywood church: "Last chance to pray before entering the freeway."
   d. Depend on the rabbit's foot if you will, but remember it didn't work for the rabbit.
   e. The trouble with alarm clocks is that they always go off when you're asleep.
   f. George Washington never told a lie, but then he never had to file a Form 1040.
   g. A church bulletin: "The Lord loveth a cheerful giver. He also accepteth from a grouch."
   h. Never put off till tomorrow what you can do the day after tomorrow.
   i. You can get away with murder in Detroit, unless you're parked next to a fire hydrant at the time.
   j. Don't believe the world owes you a living; the world owes you nothing—it was here first.
   k. Men are like wine. Some turn to vinegar, but the best improve with age.
   l. It's real nice for children to have pets until the pets start having children.
   m. I strongly support air bags in all new cars. I really ought to know. I married one. [Elizabeth Dole]
   n. You can get a lot more done with a kind word and a gun than with a kind word alone. [Al Capone]
   o. Remember—don't call a restless man nervous; he may be wearing scratchy underwear.
   p. A restaurant on Delaware Bay promoting oysters the year around with this poster: "Oysters available in Mayr, Jurne, Jury and Augurst."

Y

Place of Articulation	front of tongue and hard palate (linguapalatal)
Classification	voiced
Example	Yank York, the valiant young champion, sailed the yellow yacht that was loaded with bullion.

How to . . .

Raise the front of your tongue toward the front of your hard palate. The position is similar to the one used for the vowel sound in *fee* [fi]. Your tongue shifts rapidly into the position for whatever vowel follows.

Faults and Foibles

By itself, [j] presents no special difficulties. Some persons with Scandinavian backgrounds may confuse [j] with [dʒ]. In all four Scandinavian languages, the *j* spelling is used to represent the sound [j]. Thus, a Norwegian may say *yoke* [jok] for *joke* [dʒok]; *Yune* [jun] for *June* [dʒun].

(The Scandinavian influence shows up at a North Dakota zoo that has a pair of yaks. He's called Yak and she's called Yill.)

34. It'll help to remember that for [j] the front part of your tongue is raised high toward, but not in actual contact with, the hard palate. For [dʒ], the tip of your tongue is pressed rather firmly against the gum ridge and then moves downward rapidly.

   a.
   yak–Jack   year–jeer   yo–Joe   yet–jet
   yoke–joke   yaws–jaws   yip–gyp   yard–jarred
   yam–jam   yell–jell   yowl–jowl   yea–jay

   b. Joe dropped the yo-yo into the yam-flavored jam.

c. June will yell if the youth drops the yolk on the jacket.
d. Jill yawns whenever Jane yearns for Jerry.
e. Yesterday, Yorick the Jester said that the jet from Yale had not yet arrived.
f. He did not care a jot if the yellow jewels fall off Jenny's yacht.

[ju] combination

What differences in pronunciation do you note between the vowel sounds in each of these pairs of words?

food–feud
boot–butte
who–hue

You can hear *oo* [u] in all of the words, but in the words to the right you hear an extra sound inserted just before the [u]. This sound, of course, is [j] or a sound closely resembling it. Together, [j] and [u] form a combination sound that is pronounced exactly like the common pronoun *you.*

When do you use [u], and when do you use [ju]? As a rule, when the spelling of a word uses *oo,* such as in *boot, loot, food,* and *mood,* do not use [ju]. The simple vowel [u] is also generally used when preceded by [s], [z], [l], or [θ].

When [u] follows other consonants, however, there is almost as much inconsistency as there is controversy about preference. The person who declares that "It is the *duty* [d-you-ty] of each *student* [st-you-dent] to read the *newspaper* [n-youz-paper] on *Tuesday* (t-youz-day]" is, it seems to me, working rather hard to achieve precision and finesse. Of course, if your education or environment dictates the use of [ju] in such words, there is probably nothing wrong with your doing so. The conclusion that can be made about [ju], when its use is optional, is probably the same as about the *h* in certain *wh* combinations. Its use seems to be fading.

35. In these sentences when [ju] is required, pronounce it accordingly. When it's not required, let your own personal sincerity be your guide.

a. The puny student was aroused to fury when the ice cube was dropped on the new uniform.
b. She knew that it was her duty to cut coupons out of the duke's newspaper.
c. Is it stupid to muse and view the future of curfews with amusement?
d. The union said that the barbecue was useless and confusing.
e. The pure air in the large fuel tube was humid.
f. You are unique. You are the first you that ever was.
g. When stupid people do something they are ashamed of, they always argue that it is their duty.
h. A university is not engaged in making ideas safe for students. A university is engaged in making students safe for ideas.

GRAB BAG: PRACTICE MATERIAL FOR THE GLIDES

This material contains all of the glides in a variety of positions and sound combinations.

36. Practice for clear and accurate articulation of sounds, but avoid exaggeration.

a. When one will not, two cannot quarrel.
b. If you want to live wisely, ignore sayings—including this one.
c. A quorum means enough people are there to start a quarrel.
d. A fairy tale is a horror story to prepare children for the newspapers.
e. Results! Why, I have gotten lots of results. I know several thousand things that won't work. [Thomas Alva Edison]
f. There is no such thing as a moral or an immoral book. Books are well-written or badly written. That is all.
g. Marriage is a friendship recognized by the police.
h. Hollywood's a place where they'll pay you a thousand dollars for a kiss, and one dollar for your soul.
i. Acting is hell. You spend all your time trying to do what they put people in asylums for.
j. When playing in a high-stakes poker game, remember that a Smith and Wesson beats four aces.
k. If Robin Hood were alive today, he'd steal from the poor because the rich carry only credit cards.

l. As the hen said when she stopped in the middle of the highway, "Let me lay it on the line."

m. You don't fall trees. You fell them. However, if you fell them, you're not a feller, but a faller.

n. From *Weekly Farm News:* Nebraska bachelor wants wife. Must be interested in farming and own tractor. Please enclose picture of tractor.

o. When Lincoln said you can't fool all the people all of the time, the cloverleaf highway hadn't been invented yet.

p. The honeymoon is definitely over when she lets you lick the beaters on the electric mixer without turning off the switch.

q. Highway sign near Walla Walla, Washington: "Thirty days hath September, June, and November— and anyone exceeding the speed limit."

r. Save a little money each month and at the end of the year you'll be surprised at how little you have.

s. Love is the feeling that you feel when you feel that you are going to feel a feeling that you never felt before.

t. Don't be fooled into believing alcohol is an effective aphrodisiac. A moderate amount reduces the inhibitions—but as Shakespeare said, it increases the desire, but damages the performance.

Assignment 9: Glides

Prepare material that contains all of the glides in various positions. (Remember that [w] and [j] do not occur as glides in final positions.) Be sure that there's an abundance of those glides that you've found troublesome. You'll recall that [l] and [r] are two of the trickiest sounds in our language. The glide [w] is relatively easy for most people, but if you've been criticized for having flabby articulation, it would be a particularly good sound for you to emphasize in this assignment. When you practice by yourself, the Triple Play is fun, but when you do your assignment in class, be sure that your glides are accurate, natural and not unnecessarily noticeable.

Suggested Checklist for Assignment 9

As you practice by yourself, you may want to work with this checklist. Listen carefully to yourself. If it is feasible, record the assignment or get a classmate or friend to listen to you as you read the material. Eventually, your goal will be to have a check mark in the **Yes** column for each category. (Optional: Perhaps your instructor will want to use the checklist to evaluate you during your classroom presentation.)

	Yes	No
Articulates glides which are accurate, natural, and not unduly conspicuous.		
Avoids substituting—		
[l] for [r] or [w]		
[w] or [j] for [l]		
[w] for [r]		
[v] or [f] for [w]		
[u] for [ju]		

<u>Avoids</u>—

inserting the schwa [ə] before [l] or [r]

confusing [j] with [dʒ]

intrusive [r]

trilled production of [r]

Additional comments or suggestions:

NASALS

Hold [ɑ] as in *calm* for a few seconds, and then pinch your nostrils quite firmly. What happens? Nothing.

Now hang onto [m] as in *hum* for a few seconds, and pinch your nostrils. What happens? Everything. You can't make [m] if your nasal passages are stopped.

[m], [n], and [ŋ] are known as nasal consonants because they are directed mostly through the nose rather than the mouth. The soft palate (velum) lowers, hanging something like a curtain, and diverts the breath stream through the nasal cavities as you say the nasals in *my, nine, ring.*

Want to see your soft palate in action? Watch yourself in a mirror and say [ɑ]—*aw.* Your soft palate will rise. Say [m], and even though you can't see your soft palate perform with this sound, you'll sense that it's lowered. Saw *aw-m-aw-m-aw-m* and you'll be able to feel the contrasting actions of the velum.

The nasals not only have superb carrying power, they're not difficult to make. This explains why they're so often taken for granted.

Place of Articulation	lips (bilabial)
Classification	voiced
Example	<u>M</u>any ta<u>m</u>e la<u>m</u>bs ca<u>m</u>e ho<u>m</u>e when <u>Em</u>ma s<u>m</u>iled at the<u>m</u>.

How to . . .

Close your lips as if you were going to make a [b] sound. Your teeth should be slightly apart. Your tongue is generally relaxed on the floor of the mouth. The vocal tone comes out through your nasal passages.

Faults and Foibles

Disappearing [m]

The sound [m] is by no means as troublesome as [r], the most fickle sound in the language. Now and then, however, and especially in careless and hurried speech, the [m] may lose its identity or disappear. This happens most commonly when [m] is followed by another consonant.

Result: *lamp* [læmp] may sound something like *lap* [læp]

humble [ˈhʌmbl] may sound something like *hu'bl* [ˈhʌbl]

37. Your missing [m] can be restored if you're careful to make a firm and complete closure of your lips as you articulate [m] in this material:

a.	seemly	doomlike	hymnal
	sometime	gemlike	ramp
	I'm trying	lumber	climbed
	whimper	company	employ

b. They seemed to have aimed the empty pumpkin at the blimp.
c. Some think that I'm taking some things for granted.
d. Romney grumbled about the rumlike drink and clam dip.
e. When in doubt, mumble.
f. They call me a prima donna? Look at my face. Not a mark on it. No other champ ever looked this way. I am the champ. [Muhammad Ali]
g. A lamp doesn't complain because it must shine at night.
h. Computers are useless. They can only give you answers. [Picasso]
i. The breakfast of champions is not cereal. It's the opposition.
j. I prefer the word *homemaker,* because *housewife* always implies that there may be a wife someplace else. [Bella Abzug]

Full-value [m]

38. Singers in pop groups and other vocal ensembles are often partial to [m], as well as to the other nasals. If [m] occurs at the end of a word, phrase or line, it can be stretched out into infinity. And, of course, this nasal is the sound most frequently used in humming.

Obviously in everyday talking prolonged [m] sounds would be ridiculously hammy. On the other hand, don't prune them. Basically a pleasant and mellifluous sound, give this nasal its full value and you'll enrich the sound of your speech.

The Triple Play works nicely here. Read the sentences below three times. The first time draw out the [m] for three or four seconds. On the second reading, hold it for about two seconds. The third time: No exaggeration, but don't lop it off.

Remember—your lips must be tightly closed as you make [m].

a. Counting time is not so important as making time count.
b. Spank: to impress upon the mind from the bottom up.
c. If there is no hell, many ministers are obtaining money under false pretenses.
d. As the cow said to the Maine farmer, "Thank you for a warm hand on a cold morning."
e. Heroism: Not giving a damn before witnesses. Heroism consists in hanging on one minute longer.
f. I have made mistakes, but I have never made the mistake of claiming that I never made one.
g. What is mind? Doesn't matter. What is matter? Never mind. [Bertrand Russell]
h. A camel looks like a horse that was planned by a committee.
i. Every person is a fool for at least five minutes every day. Wisdom consists in not exceeding the limit.
j. The best way to keep children home is to make the home atmosphere pleasant—and let the air out of the tires.
k. The chief problem about death is the fear there may be no afterlife. Maybe I don't believe in an afterlife, but I am bringing a change of underwear.
l. The main thing wrong with most monthly budgets is that there's always too much month left at the end of your money.

Place of Articulation tongue tip and upper gum ridge (lingua-alveolar)

Classification voiced

Example   Newton was knighted by Queen Anne and presented with a golden uniform.

How to . . .

Press the tip of your tongue against your gum ridge as you would for [d] or [t]. The sides of your tongue may touch the inner edges of your teeth. Your soft palate is lowered so that the air can exit through your nasal passages.

Faults and Foibles

Disappearing |n|

39. Like its cousin [m], [n] is repeatedly bruised and battered. When [n] precedes another consonant, it may be dropped altogether or transformed to an [m].

Government, infantry, can meet
                    become
goverment, imfantry, cameet
Remind yourself that [n] is a tongue tip-upper gum ridge sound.

   a.   stand   tenth   unpin   lunch
        Sunday   ninety   consider   happened
        tension   infer   gigantic   unbound
        concoct   ungainly   monstrous   environment
   b.   Never cry over anything that can't cry over you.
   c.   Nonsense is good only because common sense is almost unheard of.
   d.   The first ninety percent of the task takes ninety percent of the time, and the last ten percent takes the other ninety percent.
   e.   The most important part of being a salesman is confidence. Confidence is going after Moby Dick with a rowboat, a harpoon, and a jar of tartar sauce.
   f.   Finance is the art of passing money from one hand to another until it finally disappears.
   g.   I always keep a supply of gin handy in case I see a snake—which I also keep handy. [W. C. Fields]
   h.   Homicide is always a mistake. One should never do anything that one can't talk about after dinner.
   i.   One reason the Ten Commandments are so short and clear is that Moses didn't have to send them through the United Nations.

40. In final and medial positions, [n] is often too thin and slim. Like [m], it's a gratifying sound, and it adds a bit of color to your speech.
      Do the Triple Play again, and when you get to the third step, give [n] its maximum rather than its minimum value.

   a.   The saints are the sinners who keep on going.
   b.   Two pieces of coin in a bag make more noise than a hundred.
   c.   Never return a kindness; pass it on.
   d.   Nothing matters to a person who says nothing matters.
   e.   If your parents didn't have any children, there's a good chance you won't have any.
   f.   The newspapers are full of what we would like to happen to us and what we hope will never happen to us.
   g.   Have as many enemies in front of you as you can tackle, but never leave one behind you if you can help it.
   h.   It is futile to build a fence around a cemetery, for those inside can't come out and those outside don't want to get in.
   i.   The dangerous age is any time between one and ninety-nine.
   j.   Accidents happen every hunting season because both hunter and gun are loaded.
   k.   The dentist's favorite marching song is "The Yanks are Coming."
   l.   When everyone is in the wrong, everyone is in the right.

[ŋ]

ŋ – ng

Place of Articulation	back of the tongue and soft palate (linguavelar)
Classification	voiced
Example	U<u>n</u>cle Bi<u>ng</u> sa<u>ng</u> the dri<u>nk</u>ing so<u>ng</u> on the ba<u>n</u>k of the Li<u>n</u>coln River.

How to . . .

Raise the back of your tongue so that it touches the lowered soft palate. The breath stream is directed through your nose. The position of your tongue for [ŋ] is very much like that used for [k] and [g].

Faults and Foibles

[n] for final [ŋ] substitution

He: You dancin'?
She: You askin'?
He: I'm askin'.
She: I'm dancin'.

The misguided souls who talk this way are victims of articulatory herpes. Substituting [n], as in *sin,* for final [ŋ], as in *sing,* won't necessarily make your speech incomprehensible, but it will label your way of talking as flawed and careless.

Educated and cultured people may pronounce *Tuesday* as *tooz-day* [ˈtuzdɪ] instead of *t-youz-day* [tjuzdɪ], and they may pronounce *when* as *wen* [wɛn] instead of *hwen* [hwɛn]. Very few intelligent listeners will criticize. But those who persist in saying *comin', goin', thinkin', sleepin'* may be ASKIN' for trouble. They'll generally attract the wrong kind of attention to their speech not to mention unfavorable criticism.

College graduate job-seekers, otherwise well qualified, have been rejected at interviews because their speech was marred by this particular mannerism.

This fault is known as "dropping the g"—a totally inaccurate description, by the way, because there is rarely a [g] plosive in most [ŋ] sounds.

It has been hinted that the so-called "dropping the g" is typical of all Southern speech. 'Tain't necessarily so. It is just as common in Midwestern and Eastern speech—not to mention West coast speech.

Probably many people who cheat on the final "ng" know better, too. So why do they say "I'll be seein' you"? It may have a lot to do with the "Let's-be-one-of-the-crowd" or the "I-don't-want-to-be-different-from-the-others" syndrome.

Even professional actors and actresses in soaps cheat. There are some highly talented performers among them, and *they,* of all people, really ought to know better!

41. Say slowly [n-ŋ-n-ŋ-n-ŋ-n-ŋ].
    Notice the basic difference in tongue position between the two sounds?
    [n] is formed with the front part, the tip, or the point of your tongue.
    [ŋ] is shaped with the back of your tongue.
    Remember this distinction as you practice these:

    a.
sin–sing	lawn–long	gun–gung	tan–tang
run–rung	hun–hung	gone–gong	ton–tongue
sun–sung	thin–thing	pin–ping	win–wing
ban–bang	bin–bing	pan–pang	ran–rang

b. Read this nonsense material slowly. (Note: Read *across* the columns, from left to right.) Concentrate on the difference between the articulation of [n] and [ŋ].

Get the feel of [n] as a *tip-of-the-tongue* sound and of [ŋ] as a *back-of-the-tongue* sound.

fan	fang	fan–in	fang–in	fang–ing
sin	sing	sin–in	sing–in	sing–ing
ban	bang	ban–in	bang–in	bang–ing
gon	gong	gon–in	gong–in	gong–ing
lin	ling	lin–in	ling–in	ling–ing

The person who insists on saying *wearin'* for *wearing* would have no problem at all if asked to pronounce only the last four letters of the word. He or she would certainly say *ring* rather than *rin*.

Exaggerate as you practice this material. The words are divided in a purely mechanical fashion. Wherever you see two diagonal lines, pause for a second or two, eliminating any kind of vocal sound.

c. ring/ /ring/ /ring/ /ring:fear/ /ring   soar/ /ring   hear/ /ring
                          bar/ /ring   sour/ /ring   pour/ /ring
                          mar/ /ring   stir/ /ring   star/ /ring

d. Now, eliminating the pause that divides the word, connect the two syllables and say them rather rapidly. Are you able to make a firm [ŋ] at the end of each word?

fearing	soaring	hearing
barring	souring	pouring
marring	stirring	starring

42. The nasal [ŋ] is found only in central or final positions. As you work with this material, be supercautious. Don't let [n] weasel its way in and take over for [ŋ].

a. In teaching, the greatest sin is to be boring.

b. When children are doing nothing, they are doing mischief.

c. It was as helpful as throwing both ends of a rope to a drowning person.

d. Caring is everything; nothing matters but caring.

e. Idleness is not doing nothing. Idleness is being free to do anything.

f. Having read so much about the bad effects of smoking, they decided to give up reading.

g. Gambling: the sure way of getting nothing for something.

h. The cost of living is going up, and the chance of living is going down.

i. There is no fun in having nothing to do; the fun is having lots to do and not doing it.

j. I'm living so far beyond my income that we may almost be said to be living apart.

k. Some people spend the day in complaining of a headache, and the night in drinking the wine that gives it.

l. Some folks get what's coming to them by waiting; others, while crossing the street.

m. Shunning women, liquor, gambling, smoking and eating will not make one live longer. It will only seem like it.

n. Unhappiness is being trapped on a rainy highway with a slow-moving truck in front of you and a fast-moving truck coming up behind you.

o. A digital clock is something they have in an office so you can tell how long you must wait before you can start stopping work by stalling until.

p. Retreating and beating and meeting and sheeting,
Delaying and straying and playing and spraying,
Advancing and prancing and glancing and dancing,
Recoiling, turmoiling, toiling, and boiling,
And gleaming and steaming and streaming and beaming,
And rushing and flushing and brushing and gushing,
And flapping and rapping and clapping and slapping,
And curling and whirling and purling and twirling,

And thumping and plumping and bumping and jumping;
And dashing and flashing and splashing and clashing;
And is never ending, but always descending,
All at once and all o'er, with a mighty uproar,
And this way the water comes down at Lodore. [Southey]

The ng-click

Say: *singer, linger*

Both words have [ŋ]. Did you notice, however, that [ŋ] is not pronounced the same way?

In *singer,* the [ŋ] is simply the nasal sound we've been working on. There is no plosive [g] in the word. You say SING er. [ˈsɪŋɚ].

In *linger,* the [ŋ] is a combination of the nasal [ŋ] PLUS the plosive [g]. You say LING ger. [ˈlɪŋgɚ]

No wonder, then, that we sporadically have trouble with [ŋ]. Fiendish English spelling doesn't help either. To add to the turmoil, in certain foreign languages and dialects, [ŋ] is almost invariably followed by a [g] or a [k]. Individuals whose language backgrounds include Yiddish, Slavic, Spanish, Hungarian, or Italian—even though they may be native born—often add the villainous "Long GUY-land click." *Gong* becomes *gong-G* or *gong-K, ring* becomes *ring-G* or *ring-K.*

How can the hard [g] be purged?

Your sense of hearing and feeling will help. You'll remember that the back of your tongue is raised against the velum or soft palate to make [ŋ]. Say *sing* and you'll feel the contact.

Say *sing* again, but this time listen quite conscientiously to the nasal sound, extend it a few seconds, and as you're holding [ŋ], pull your tongue away from the velum. If this is done, you won't add the hard [g].

43. Read this material slowly, always drawing out the [ŋ]. Don't forget to pull your tongue away from the velum <u>during</u> the production of the sound rather than <u>after</u>. You'll eliminate the click.

thing	sing	ring
bang	long	bong
wrong	rang	clang
lung	wing	young

44. Now that you've been told how to remove the after-click, let's put it back in! You do NOT use it with such words as *long, young* and *strong.* But you DO use it with the comparative and superlative forms:

longer [ˈlɔŋgɚ]   *longest* [ˈlɔŋgəst]

stronger [ˈstrɔŋgɚ]   *strongest* [ˈstrɔŋgəst]

If you find [ŋ] within the root or the middle of a word, it's generally pronounced with the click: [ŋ-g].

finger	monger	kangaroo	English
fungus	anger	mingle	tingle
hunger	single	angry	bungle
jingle	jungle	angle	extinguish

And to spoil the fun—the exceptions:
gingham, Washington, hangar, strength, length
Even outstanding speakers slip on these pesky and temperamental sounds. When in doubt, consult your dictionary.

GRAB BAG: PRACTICE MATERIAL FOR THE NASALS

Don't neglect your nasals! Nourish them!

As a reminder—

[m]: your lips must be firmly closed.

[n]: the tip of your tongue must be placed against your upper gum ridge.

[ŋ]: the rear of your tongue must make contact with your velum.

45. The Triple Play works beautifully with these sounds. And at the third level—even without the overplaying—make [m], [n], and [ŋ] glisten. Above all, be accurate.

   a. What this country needs is a good five-second television commercial.
   b. Never murder a man who is committing suicide.
   c. We all learn by experience, but some of us have to go to summer school.
   d. If you drive with one arm, you end up either walking up a church aisle or being carried up it.
   e. My mother loved children—she would have given anything if I had been one. [Phyllis Diller]
   f. It's not true that life is one damn thing after another—it's one damn thing over and over.
   g. Forgive me my nonsense as I also forgive the nonsense of those who think they talk sense.
   h. Basically my wife is immature. I'd be home in the bath and she'd come in and sink my boats. [Woody Allen]
   i. Women generally manage to love the guys they marry. They manage to love the guy they marry more than they manage to marry the guy they love. [Clare Booth Luce]
   j. My advice to you: Don't ask "Who am I, What am I doing here, Where am I going?" Just enjoy your ice cream while it's on your plate—that's my philosophy. [Thornton Wilder]
   k. Nobody will ever win the Battle of the Sexes. There's just too much fraternizing with the enemy. [Shirley MacLaine]
   l. Dentistry means drilling, filling, and billing.
   m. If you know beans about chili, you know that chili has no beans.
   n. There are still a few people who believe in getting up and getting, while a great many people prefer sitting down and sitting.
   o. An alcoholic is not one who drinks too much, but one who can't drink enough.
   p. Never buy anything with a handle on it. It might mean work.
   q. The four most important words in the English language seem to be: I, me, mine, and money.
   r. Commencement speaker in Michigan: "My advice to young people going out into the world today—don't go!"
   s. Tact is something that if it's there, nobody notices it. But if it isn't there, everybody notices it.
   t. If I've learned one thing, it's always be nice to snipers.

Assignment 10: Nasals

Prepare material containing numerous nasal consonants: [m n ŋ]. If you've had no special difficulty with these sounds, stress them slightly as you practice to bring out their pleasant quality, but avoid gross exaggeration. If you've found any of them troublesome—and [n] and [ŋ] in certain words, especially the latter as a final sound, are often faulty—work for sounds that are accurate and correct.

Suggested Checklist for Assignment 10

As you practice by yourself, you may want to work with this checklist. Listen carefully to yourself. If it's feasible, record the assignment, or get somebody to listen to you as you read the material. Eventually, your goal will be to have a check mark in the **Yes** column for each category. (Optional: Perhaps your instructor will want to use this checklist to evaluate you during your classroom presentation.)

	Yes	No
Avoids substituting—		
[m] for [n]		
[n] for [ŋ]		
Avoids—		
omitting [m] and [n]		
"Long GUY-land click"		
Avoids weak production of—		
[m] in medial or final position		
[n] in medial or final position		
[ŋ] in medial or final position		

Additional comments or suggestions:

FRICATIVES

Say *sizzle*. You'll notice that you're putting obstructions in your mouth that interrupt the outgoing breath stream. The air is forced through a small, narrow opening or slit. A friction noise is produced.

The fricatives have been described as the buzzers and blasters of the consonant tribes. If improperly produced, they <u>can</u> be noisy and offensive.

There are nine members of the fricative family. Here, the dictionary symbol is shown next to the bracketed phonetic symbol for a fricative when the two differ:

Voiceless	*Voiced*
[f]	[v]
[θ] th	[ð] ~~th~~
[s]	[z]
[ʃ] sh	[ʒ] zh
[h]	

In the sections that follow, the dictionary symbols for the fricatives will be shown on the right-hand side of the page when they differ from the phonetic symbols.

Place of Articulation	lower lip and upper teeth (labiodental)

Classification	[f] voiceless
	[v] voiced

Examples	[f] Frank coughed and offered Flora enough fudge to comfort her.
	[v] Velda shoved Stephen into the vat with more vigor than love.

How to . . .

Raise your lower lip, drawing it inward, and place it lightly against the edges of your upper front teeth. Then force the breath stream between the lip and teeth.

Faults and Foibles

Substitutions

Anyone who learns English as a second language (especially if the first is German or Spanish) tends to pronounce [v] as [f] or [b].

Fince can proof that foodoo is a file fice. (Some German speakers)

or

Bince can prob that boodoo is a bile bice. (Some Spanish speakers)

For [b–v] confusion: [b] is a plosive, of course, and to make it you must press your lips closely together. To sound [v], you should feel your lower lip touching your upper teeth.

For [f–v] confusion: You'll be able to feel as well as hear the difference. [f] is a voiceless air puff—no vibration in your throat as you make the sound. [v] is voiced—there'll be a mini-commotion in your Adam's apple.

46. Distinguish carefully between the voiceless [f] and the voiced [v] in this material. Don't confuse the two sounds, and don't substitute [b] for [f] or [v]. And remind yourself that [b] is a lips-firmly-together sound, but [f] and [v] are lower-lip-against-upper-teeth sounds.

   a. ban–van   lubber–lover   define–divine   rifle–rival
       dub–dove   best–vest   feel–veal   strife–strive
       base–vase   saber–saver   fan–van   half–have
       beer–veer   berry–very   folly–volley   fife–five
   b. Is life worth living? That depends on the liver.
   c. You haven't lived until you've died in California.
   d. Reckless drivers drive like living is going out of style.
   e. Shakespeare said that the evil men do lives after them. On TV this is called a rerun.
   f. Have you noticed that people who have stopped smoking haven't stopped talking about it?
   g. The male lovebug on the average devotes fifty-six hours of its life to making love. The lifespan of the lovebug is fifty-seven hours.
   h. Never exaggerate your faults. Leave that for your friends.

|v| omission

   A lotta people have a lotta free time.

   A lot of people also love to carve up that poor, impotent little word *of.* True, it's runty and inconspicuous, but that doesn't justify squashing it. *Of,* although spelled with an *f,* is pronounced with a *v.*

47. Go over this material slowly a few times, and then gradually increase your speed to a normal rate. Be conscious of the lip-to-teeth articulation as you make a *v* at the end of each *of*.

a. full of people	bunch of girls	full of smoke
bag of peanuts	tired of him	one of those
lots of money	rows of seats	box of candy
half of those	can of soup	pat of butter

b. For the sort of people who like this sort of thing, this is the sort of thing that sort of people will like. [Lincoln]

c. Beware of the high cost of low living.

d. Lots of us think that our national anthem should be "Deep in the Heart of Taxes."

e. I am a member of the human race. That means a little of the angel and a little of the devil.

f. There are Ten Commandments, right? Well, it's sort of like an exam. You get eight out of ten right, you're just about top of the class.

g. Good breeding consists of concealing how much we think of ourselves and how little we think of the other person. [Mark Twain]

Blurred [f] or [v]

48. Bear in mind that a clean-cut [f] or [v] depend mostly on the activity of the lower lip. If your lip is protruded or drawn back too far, you'll be producing fuzzy fricatives. That lower lip <u>must</u> make an easy contact with your upper lip as you come out with the sounds.

a. fact	valve	fluff	above
fair	very	avoid	dove
fin	suffer	cover	behave
four	before	saving	defense

b. Even the lion has to defend itself against flies.

c. Figures won't lie, but liars will figure.

d. Do not take life too seriously. You will never get out of it alive.

e. When our vices have left us, we flatter ourselves that we have left them.

f. You might as well fall flat on your face as lean too far backwards.

g. Wagner's music has some wonderful moments but awful hours.

h. It is better to deserve honors and not have them than to have them and not deserve them.

i. Drive toward others as you would have others drive toward you.

j. It isn't the cough that carries you off; it's the coffin they carry you off in.

th – th

Place of Articulation	tongue tip between teeth (linguadental)
Classification	[θ] voiceless [ð] voiced
Examples	[θ] <u>Th</u>elma <u>th</u>ought Mar<u>th</u>a <u>th</u>rew a boo<u>th</u> into Lake A<u>th</u>ens. [ð] <u>Th</u>ey saw Fa<u>th</u>er put <u>th</u>e la<u>th</u>er on <u>th</u>e smoo<u>th</u> lea<u>th</u>er.

How to . . .

Place the tip of your tongue lightly against the back or edges of your upper front teeth, or thrust the flattened tongue tip slightly between your teeth so that the upper side makes a soft contact with the lower edges of your upper teeth. Drive the breath between the tongue tip and your teeth.

Faults and Foibles

What's the hardest-to-pronounce short word in the English language? *Sixths.*

It's a fine example of a one-word tongue twister. The chances are that you don't pronounce it correctly. If you say it this way: S-I-K-S

you're wrong.

Now say it in slow motion: S-I-K-S-TH-S

and you're right.

(But try it rapidly and see what happens!)

A tough sound to pronounce in *sixths* [sıksθs] is [θ]. The fricative [θ] and its voiced counterpart [ð] can be almost as formidable in simple words.

If you've ever seen old-time gangster movies from the thirties—James Cagney and Edward G. Robinson starred in a few dozen—you'll recall that many of the characters couldn't say *these, them,* or *mother.* They used a Brooklyn Mafia-Chicago mobster dialect that turned [θ] and [ð] into [d]: *dese, dem, mudder.*

One doesn't have to be a thug to mess up [θ] and [ð] sounds. The [d] substitution is heard not infrequently among those who use Eastern dialect. (Remember a Bronx-born, Hollywood star who achieved immortality for his delivery of this line: "Yonduh lies duh castle of muh fadduh."?)

[t] or [d] for [θ] or [ð] substitution

Some Easterners permit the tongue to make too firm a contact against the edges of the teeth. A sound something like [t] or [d] will result. Remind yourself that [t] and [d] require a close tongue tip contact, but that the contact for [θ] or [ð] must be light as fluff.

49. If you're substituting [t] or [d] for [θ] or [ð], try this:

    Extend your tongue so that the broad part of it touches your upper front teeth. Force out air as you gradually retract your tongue until the tip reaches the upper teeth. When you can make a healthy sound, try the material in this exercise. Be certain that the contact is gentle for good [θ] and [ð] sounds, but solid for [t] and [d].

    a.
thin–tin	oath–oat	death–debt	mother–mudder
thought–taught	thank–tank	three–tree	their–dare
thigh–tie	theme–team	author–otter	breathe–breed
through–true	worthy–wordy	lather–latter	those–doze

    b. Miss Diss said this: "Thanks for putting the tanks near the three trees."
    c. The truth hurts—especially on the bathroom scales.
    d. The thicker one gets with some people, the thinner they become.
    e. The Lord giveth and the IRS taketh away.
    f. The trouble with facts is that there are so many of them.
    g. She sifted seven thick-stalked thistles through a strong, thick sieve.

[s] or [z] substitution

50. "Zee trouble wis zee French is zat zay seem wiser zan zay are," the late Charles DeGaulle once said.

    Very few foreign languages have our [θ] or [ð] sounds. If your first language is French or German, for example, you may be saying *zeez* and *sink* for *these* and *think.*

    If you're substituting [s] or [z] for [θ] or [ð], you're doing something wrong with the tip of your tongue.

    For [s] or [z]: *Raise your tongue toward, but not in actual contact with, the upper gum ridge.*

    For [θ] or [ð]: *Place your tongue tip lightly against the back or the edges of your upper front teeth.*

    Remember, [θ] is voiceless; [ð] is voiced.

Check your tongue position carefully as you read this material:

a.
thigh–sigh	think–sink	teethe–tease
myth–miss	thumb–sum	rather–razzer
thought–sought	breathe–breeze	bathe–baize
lathe–lays	seethe–seize	south–souse

b. Truth crushed to earth will rise again—but so will a lie.

c. If health is wealth, how come it's tax-free?

d. The race may not be to the swift nor the victory to the strong but that's how you bet.

e. The young never understand youth in others; that is their tragedy. The old always do; that is theirs.

f. Few people think more than three times a year. I have made a great reputation for myself by thinking three times a week. [Gloria Steinem]

[f] for [θ] and [ð] substitution

A three-year-old child who says "I fro the ball," meaning "I throw the ball," is merely cute, but an adult who says it will be labeled as infantile. It's true that baby talk among adults isn't often encountered, but the substitution of [f] for [θ] happens now and then in sloppy speech.

Compare the manner in which [f] and [θ] are produced:

To produce [f]: Raise the lower lip, drawing it inward, and place it lightly against the edges of the upper front teeth.

To produce [θ]: Review the description of this sound, and remember that the tongue tip but not the lower lip contacts the upper teeth.

51. As you read this material, contrast carefully between [f] and [θ]. Use this simple formula to help you:
[f]—Lower lip against front teeth
[θ]—Tongue tip against front teeth

a.
thin–fin	wrath–raff	think–fink
three–free	wreath–reef	death–deaf
thaw–faugh	myth–miff	thrum–from

b. Fran fought for the right to throw the thread to and fro.

c. Faults are thick where love is thin.

d. Did the fancy frills on the wreath thrill Phyllis as she sat near the reef?

e. The thin fin on the three fenders caused the death of the deaf oaf.

f. Thinking is the hardest work there is, which is the reason why so few do it.

Confusion of [θ] and [ð]

52. Spelling never tells you which is which. Your ear does, however. It's no problem hearing the difference between the two sounds.

There seems to be a trend toward using the voiceless [θ] at the expense of the voiced [ð]. Avoid mistaking one for the other as you do these:

a. Things are not as bad as they seem. They are worse.

b. When you get there—North Dakota—there isn't any there there.

c. What, oh what, is thought? It is the only thing—and yet nothing.

d. The person who thinketh by the inch and speaketh by the yard should be kicketh by the foot.

e. Writers seldom write the things they think. They simply write the things they think other people think they think.

f. There's no such thing as a tough child. If you parboil them first for three or four hours, they always come out tender. [W. C. Fields]

g. Tragedy is comedy turned upside down. If you see a great performance of Macbeth, for example, you should experience catharsis—an emotional Ex-Lax.

h. If you burn the candle at both ends you are not as bright as you think.

i. The trouble with some people is they don't think until they hear what they've had to say.

[S — Z]

Place of Articulation	tip or blade of tongue, gum ridge (lingua-alveolar)
Classificaton	[s] voiceless [z] voiced
Examples	[s] Sarah asked the cigar-smoking singer for the next dance. [z] Zelda was busy raising daisies in the zoo near Zion.

How to . . .

Raise the sides of your tongue so that they touch the middle and back upper teeth. A thin stream of air is forced through the V-shaped groove along the midline of the tongue. Your tongue tip is in a similar position for [t].

The most troublesome and the most frequently defective sound in our language is probably [s]. (Whatever is said here about the articulation of [s] generally applies also to [z].) Producing an acceptable [s] sound requires not only a keen sense of hearing, but also rather precise adjustments of the articulators.

Faults and Foibles

Breath Guzzlers? The fricatives [s] and [z] are one-sound cyclones.

Listen to a group of people recite material in unison—responsive readings by a congregation are a fine example—and you'll hear waves of hisses that belong in a snake pit.

A majority of the hissers are probably articulating the sound correctly. What they're doing incorrectly is simply producing too much of it. Even a respectable, normal [s] is rackety and turbulent. If you're making an [s] that sounds like a tornado, reduce your breath pressure. Don't emphasize the sound. Don't hang onto it! Usually, [s] should be cut short, touched lightly and briefly, but not allowed to vanish entirely.

53.   For contrast and to help you hear the difference between a good, skimpy [s] and a long, fat [s], read these word pairs aloud. Build up the [s] in the first word of each pair as the spelling indicates. Make it sound like a minor monsoon.

In the second word of the pair, tap the sound as if touching a hot stove, and hurry on to the following vowel sounds. Stress the vowels instead.

a.   s-s-s-s-see—see   s-s-s-s-sad—sad
      s-s-s-s-so—so   s-s-s-s-saw—saw
      s-s-s-s-say—say   S-S-S-S-Sue—Sue
      s-s-s-s-sot—sot   s-s-s-s-sin—sin

Work for an unobtrusive [s] and [z]. Don't blow them to smithereens. Condense and compress. Make them quiet.

b.

Sam	zone	zigzag	hiss	fizz
sort	Zulu	using	face	has
sod	zany	music	lass	craze
sill	zest	lazy	dross	maze

   c.   There's an old Southern saying: If it isn't busted, why fix it?
   d.   You can't steal second base if you keep one foot on first.
   e.   The past is the only dead thing that smells sweet.
   f.   The noblest of all dogs is the hot dog. It feeds the hand that bites it.
   g.   Cats are smarter than dogs. You can't get eight cats to pull a sled through snow.
   h.   It is dangerous to be sincere unless you are also stupid. [G. B. Shaw]
   i.   It's what the guests say as they swing out of the driveway that counts.

j. Scratch the surface, and if you're lucky, you'll find more surface.
k. Please be careful about calling yourself an expert. An ex is a has-been, and a spurt is a drip under pressure.
l. She's somewhere between the age of consent and collapse.
m. Kings live in palaces, and pigs in sties. And youth in expectation. Youth is wise.

The whistling [s]

Whistler's [s] is even more galling than the overdone, gusty [s] described in the previous exercise. The speech of individuals with gaps between their front teeth or people with poorly fitting dentures often is afflicted with whistler's [s].

It's an irksome and high-pitched sound. To anyone who works with a microphone, it's a serious handicap. Electronic amplification can turn a minor whistle into a howling wind.

Is your tongue too tense? Or are you pressing the tip of your tongue tightly against your upper teeth? You'll produce a thin or sharp squeak. Relaxing your tongue a bit may get rid of it. Whistler's [s] also occurs if you let your lower lip touch your upper front teeth while making the sound. Bear in mind that clean [s] sounds require that the lips be curled away from the teeth sufficiently to keep the edges of the teeth free.

54. Before you read the material in this exercise, hiss [s], holding your tongue in slightly different positions. Then draw the tip back. Listen carefully as you experiment until you can find a satisfactory position.

a.
moss	hits	loose	fuss
sass	mats	mace	waltz
loss	ropes	deuce	vase
less	roots	boss	advice

b. The devil does a nice business, considering he has such a lousy location.
c. I see nothing in space as promising as the view from a Ferris wheel.
d. About peace, when all is said and done, more is said than done.
e. The very moment everything looks serene, all hell breaks loose.
f. In politics, if you want anything said, ask a man; if you want anything done, ask a woman. [Margaret Thatcher]
g. A university is a college with a stadium seating more than sixty thousand.
h. The difference between a horse race and a political race: in a horse race the entire horse runs.
i. The best of married life is the fights. The rest is merely so-so.

[s] clusters

Asks is a surprisingly tricky little word. No wonder you occasionally hear: "The teacher *axe* questions." By itself [s] is a pesky sound, but hook [tr], [kr], [ks] or [ts] onto it, and your tongue has to perform double somersaults to get the sound out of the mouth.

Try these examples:

strip	*screech*	*tasks*	*destroy*
streak	*skates*	*rusts*	*describe*

The [s] in such awkward combinations is often distorted or dropped completely.

55. [str]: If you're in a rush to get to the [t], you'll flatten your tongue too soon. *Street* [strit] may sound like *shtreet* [ʃtrit].

Reading across the line, say the first word with a complete pause, as indicated. Say the second with no pause. In each one make the [s] sharp and short, and make a brisk [t] and a clear [r].

s| |trike–strike	s| |traw–straw	s| |tring–string
s| |trut–strut	s| |trip–strip	s| |trive–strive
s| |troll–stroll	s| |tray–stray	s| |trength–strength

56. [skr]: If you target the [k] too quickly you'll inadvertently raise the back of the tongue. *Scrap* [skræp] becomes *shkrap* [ʃkræp].

Using the procedure suggested in Exercise 55, try these. The [k] needs to be brittle.

s| |cratch–scratch	s| |cruple–scruple	s| |cript–script
s| |cram–scram	s| |crimp–scrimp	s| |crub–scrub
s| |crod–scrod	s| |crag–scrag	s| |creech–screech

57. [sts]: If you drop the [t] altogether you'll say *fiss* [fɪs] instead of *fist* [fɪst]. By now you know all about plosive [t]. Try the double pauses below and restore it.

ghos||t||s–ghosts	bus||t||s–busts
hos||t||s–hosts	mis||t||s–mists
cas||t||s–casts	lus||t||s–lusts
lis||t||s–lists	mas||t||s–masts

58. [sks]: If you omit the first [s]; you'll say *flaks* [flæks] in place of *flasks* [flæsks]. Don't overlook the first [s] in each cluster.

mas||k||s–masks	dis||k||s–disks
bus||k||s–busks	ris||k||s–risks
bas||k||s–basks	mus||k||s–musks
tas||k||s–tasks	hus||k||s–husks

59. Read carefully, avoiding omissions and distortions.

    a. Striking while the iron is hot may be all right, but don't strike while the head is hot.
    b. If he scraps while playing Scrabble, he scrawls afterwards.
    c. At hunters' feasts, there are many boasts and toasts by the guests.
    d. The host frisks everybody before he empties the casks to fill the flasks.
    e. Screeching beasts struggle with strong tusks.
    f. To show strength, scrawny knights wore masks in their jousts.

The final letter {s}

How is the final *s* pronounced when it is added to a noun or a verb?

In such words as *buys, boys, loves, dolls, runs, pencils, hides,* the final sound is pronounced as [z] because the sound immediately preceding it is <u>voiced</u>. It is easier for the vocal folds to continue vibrating the final sound. When you sound each of these words, articulate a [z] sound rather than [s] because a voiced sound precedes the final [s].

    lids   robs   fills   bathes   loves   shows

In such words as *hits, spoofs, pipes, decks, sifts,* the final sound is pronounced as [s] because the sound immediately preceding it is <u>voiceless</u>. It is easier for the vocal folds to remain at rest for the final sound. When you sound each of these words, articulate [s] because it is preceded by a voiceless sound.

    bats   laps   kicks   baths   huffs   escapes

In such words as *bosses, fizzes, churches, edges,* the final sound, if preceded by most fricatives, is pronounced as [ɪz] or [əz], and the ending actually becomes an extra syllable.

    wishes   passes   judges   smashes   scratches

60. This material contains [s] and [z] in a variety of positions and combinations. As you practice the material, don't forget—they're NOT plosives. Don't let them sound like nuclear blasts. Fricatives should be pint-sized and knife-edged. But don't disregard them.

And finally, is your tongue position correct? That [t] position will help you with most [s] and [z] sounds.

a. Ask me no question and I'll tell you no fibs.
b. The secret of success is to start from scratch and keep on scratching.
c. More homes are destroyed by fusses than by funerals or fires.
d. He is such a decent, honest guy that he'd steal a car and keep up the payments.
e. Two things indicate weakness: to be silent when it's time to speak and to speak when it's time to be silent.
f. God may forgive you your sins, but your nervous system won't.
g. The first sign of maturity is the discovery that the volume knob also turns to the left.
h. The first screw to get loose in your head is the one that holds your tongue in place.
i. Gossip is when you hear something you like about someone you don't.
j. The longer one lives the more one is inclined to think that this sphere is used by other planets as an insane asylum.
k. The fool says: "Don't put all of your eggs in one basket." But the wise person says, "Put all your eggs in one basket and—*watch that basket!*"
l. Assassination is the extreme form of censorship.
m. In times like these, it always helps to recall that there have always been times like these.
n. It is with narrow-souled people as with narrow-necked bottles; the less they have in them the more noise they make in pouring out.
o. Sign in a bakery window in San Francisco: "Cakes—sixty-six cents. Upside Down Cakes—ninety-nine cents."
p. Rock music is amazing. It includes a zestful vocalist who sings off key and a noisy drummer who hates music.
q. Swan swim over the sea;
Swim, swan, swim.
Swan swim back again;
Well swam, swan.

 # Sh – Zh

Place of Articulation   tip or blade of tongue behind gum ridge (linguapalatal)

Classification   [ʃ] voiceless
[ʒ] voiced

Examples   [ʃ] "Sure," said Sherry, "Let's rush the machines across the ocean."
[ʒ] The Persian lady pinned the corsage onto the beige dress.

Once again, spelling doesn't help you. In the following twelve words, the underlined sound is always pronounced "sh" [ʃ]:

chaperone	conscious	issue	mansion	mustache	nation
nauseous	ocean	pshaw	schist	shoe	sure

How to . . .

For an interesting approach to [ʃ], compare it with [s], as in *she* and *sea, shy* and *sigh.* You'll notice that your whole tongue is drawn back slightly farther for [ʃ] than for [s]. Your tongue surface is flattened somewhat, and the sides of the tongue should touch the inner borders of the upper back teeth. The air stream passes over a relatively wide but shallow central passage rather than through the narrow fissure that characterizes [s]. Your lips are slightly rounded and protruded.

Faults and Foibles

{s} for {ʃ} substitution

A fairly common fault is the substitution of [s], or a sound close to it, for [ʃ]. Non-English-speaking students may also substitute [z] for [ʒ]. To overcome these faults, contrast again the manner in which each of the two sounds is produced.

61. Watch yourself in a mirror as you articulate [s] and [ʃ] again and again. Note the obvious differences in the positions of the articulators. It's especially important that you feel the difference of greater tongue retraction and lip rounding for [ʃ] than for [s].

a.			
sack–shack	crass–crash	rues–rouge	puss–push
suit–shoot	lass–lash	bays–beige	muss–mush
sin–shin	lease–leash	lows–loge	seer–sheer
sore–shore	mess–mesh	lasses–lashes	say–shay

    b. Caution: don't forget that [ʒ] must be voiced.

leisure	explosion	prestige	version
camouflage	Asia	occasion	casual
collision	entourage	confusion	decision

    c. If fifty million people say a foolish thing, it's still a foolish thing.
    d. What we need today is a transmission that will automatically shift the blame.
    e. The vanishing American is one who pays cash for everything he buys.
    f. Confessions may be good for the soul, but they are bad for the reputation.
    g. Discretion: Putting two and two together and keeping your mouth shut.
    h. Did Shane hide the negligee in the garage when the invasion began?

High-pitched {ʃ}

Sometimes the tongue is permitted to rise too high toward the hard palate. This also may be accompanied by excessive tension of the tongue. The resulting sound is higher than an acceptable [ʃ], and it is frequently characterized by too much friction.

62. Listen to yourself as you sound [ʃ], and experiment by lowering your tongue from a position relatively high in your mouth to one that is somewhat lower.
    a. To make pleasures pleasant, shorten them.
    b. Your vision of treasure on the azure shore is only a mirage.
    c. A sharp tongue and a dull mind are usually found in the same head.
    d. You're very foolish if you try to beat around the bush. You just meet yourself coming around the bush the other way. [Betty Ford]
    e. Nice guys don't always finish last. Sometimes they don't finish. Sometimes they don't get a chance to start.
    f. We cannot reform the world. Uncle Sugar is as dangerous a role for us to play as Uncle Shylock. [John F. Kennedy]

[h]

Place of   glottis (glottal)
Articulation

Classification   voiceless

Example   Harry hated to see Hedda hop along in a humble manner.

How to . . .

No movement of the lips, jaws, or tongue is required to produce this sound. The vocal folds are brought closely enough together to restrict the outgoing breath. This makes an audible friction noise. The articulators are more or less preset in position for the vowel sound that follows the [h], and the outgoing breath stream produces a slight, whispery noise before the succeeding sound is vocalized.

Faults and Foibles

Omitted [h]

Individuals with a non-English or a Cockney English background may omit [h], a fault that's more likely to call attention to itself if the sound occurs in a prominent, stressed word.

If *Harry is happy because Helen came home* sounds like *'Arry is 'appy because 'elen came 'ome,* the absence of [h] is conspicuous.

63.   Initial and medial [h] should be sounded but not emphasized in this material.

    a.

old–hold	odd–hod	it–hit	ahead
at–hat	is–his	ope–hope	behave
ill–hill	am–ham	as–has	anyhow
id–hid	ode–hoed	arm–harm	inhale

    b.   Unhappy Horace inhabited the unheated lighthouse.
    c.   In Hollywood, if you don't have happiness, you send out for it.
    d.   Hope is the feeling you have that the feeling you have isn't permanent.
    e.   Home is the place where, when you have to go there, they have to take you in.
    f.   The hand will not reach for what the heart doesn't long for.
    g.   It's not how old you are, it's how hard you work at it.
    h.   To err is human. To blame it on somebody else is even more human.
    i.   When you honestly think about it, Adolf Hitler was the first pop star. Heaven knows, it certainly wasn't his politics. He was a media pop star. [David Bowie]

64.   Now and then [h] becomes defective for one of the same reasons [s] does: there is too much of it. Like [s], touch it lightly and briefly. A little bit of [h] goes a long way.

    a.   Humor is laughing at what you haven't got when you ought to have it.
    b.   Home is where the college student home for the holidays isn't.
    c.   What I have been taught, I have forgotten; what I know, I have guessed.
    d.   The secret source of humor is not joy but sorrow; there is no humor in heaven.
    e.   The mind is its own place, and in itself can make a heaven of hell, a hell of heaven.
    f.   The game of life is not so much in holding a good hand as in playing a poor hand well.
    g.   What you say here, what you do here, what you hear here, let it stay here when you leave here.
    h.   Katharine Hepburn once asked Lillian Hellman if she did not think her sense of humor had lengthened her life. "Heavens, no," Hellman replied, "my life has lengthened my sense of humor."

AFFRICATES

An affricate is a closely and rapidly blended combination of a plosive and a fricative. The two sounds merge; you don't completely finish the plosive and then begin the fricative.

The tongue momentarily blocks the breath as it does for the plosives, but then the tongue quickly assumes the fricative position and the impounded air is released somewhat explosively.

Place of Articulation	tongue tip and upper gum ridge plosives combined with tongue blade and front part of palate fricatives (lingua-alveolar)
Classification	[tʃ] voiceless [dʒ] voiced
Examples	[tʃ] Charles, feeling righteous, hid the hatchet under the batch of peaches in the kitchen. [dʒ] Joyce fed ginger and jelly to George as he planted cabbage at the edge of the lodge.

How to . . .

The tip and the blade of your tongue must be pressed quite firmly against the gum ridge. The body of your tongue assumes a position similar to that for [ʃ]. As the tip is lowered, a modified explosion, less sharp than that for [t] or [d], is heard.

Faults and Foibles

Defective fricative portions

If [tʃ] or [dʒ] are defective, generally only the fricative portions of those sounds are at fault. If necessary, review Exercises 60 and 61 in this chapter.

Coarse or prolonged affricates

Some individuals have a tendency to exaggerate the plosive qualities of [t] and [d] and to make [ʃ] and [ʒ] too conspicuous. By the time they get to the fricative part of the affricate, they produce minor vocal hurricanes.

65. Be sure that your affricates are sharp and relatively delicate rather than heavy and stressed as you read this material:

    a.
chill	birches	hitch	gist
choke	nature	lunch	giblet
cheap	richer	adjust	gigantic
chant	urchin	joke	gesture

    b. Generally speaking, it is dangerous to generalize.
    c. Do not ask if a person has been through college; ask if a college has been through a person.
    d. The key to everything is patience. You get the chicken by hatching the egg—not by smashing it.
    e. Charles, an agile merchant, jumped into the jeep.
    f. Mushrooms are spongy fungi.
    g. Longevity: an achievement to which there is no shortcut.
    h. They say judgment comes from experience, but experience comes from poor judgment.
    i. Diet tip: to indulge is to bulge.
    j. An engagement is an urge on the verge of a merge.

Distortions and substitutions

The Scandinavian stereotype who says *Yack Yones* for *Jack Jones* and the German stock character who says *larch* for *large* may reflect more fact than fiction. Many languages, including French, lack the [tʃ] or [dʒ] or both. The weirdly inconsistent English spelling of these sounds only compounds the confusion. Note, for example, the [dʒ] in these words: *jest, gesture, soldier, adjoin, grandeur.*

66. If English is your second language, study the following lists. Be sure that somebody with a reasonably good ear listens critically to you as you practice.
Differentiate carefully between these sounds as they occur in the word pairs or sentences.

   a. [ʃ] is often substituted for [tʃ].

share–chair	mush–much	mash–match
Shaw–chaw	wash–watch	shop–chop
Schick–chick	bash–batch	dish–ditch
shirk–chirk	cash–catch	hash–hatch

   b. [j], the initial sound in *yes,* is often substituted for [dʒ].

you–Jew	yip–gyp	Yale–jail
yell–jell	yoke–joke	yellow–Jello
yo–Joe	yam–jam	yawn–John
yaw–jaw	Ute–jute	yowl–jowl

   c. [ts] and [dz] are sometimes substituted for [tʃ] and [dʒ].

mats–match	wades–wage
wits–witch	raids–rage
hits–hitch	cads–cadge
mitts–Mitch	seeds–siege

   d. [ʒ] is sometimes substituted for [dʒ].
   (1) The Persian jigged and jested when he saw the magic vision.
   (2) Jealousy is the injured lover's hell.
   (3) Judge a jest after you have finished laughing.
   (4) If I am right, the Germans will say I was a German, and the French will say I was a Jew. If I am wrong, the Germans will say I was a Jew, and the French will say I was a German. [Albert Einstein]

   e. [ʃ] is often substituted for [ʒ] in the final position.
   [tʃ] is often substituted for [dʒ] in the final position.
   (1) To reach the edge before lunch, the huge bunch must charge the bridge.
   (2) I shall dash into the garage and fish the corsage out of the beige-colored trash can.
   (3) A batch of cabbage is no match for fresh oranges and fudge.
   (4) If you have a stiff neck, it will be my pleasure to give you a casual massage.

GRAB BAG: PRACTICE MATERIAL FOR THE FRICATIVES AND AFFRICATES

Fricatives and affricates are important to your speech, and when they are handled with precision, exactness, and sensitivity, they needn't sound like vocalized belching, exaggerated hissing or buzzing.

67. The drill material contains all of the fricatives and affricates in a variety of positions and sound combinations. Remember that these consonants have often been described as the ugliest sounds in the English language. None of them has to be offensively noisy or unpleasant. Nip and snip these windy sounds. Be stingy!

   a. A bee is a buzzy busybody.
   b. Macho does not prove mucho. [Debra Winger]
   c. We are all geniuses up to the age of ten.
   d. Happiness is having a scratch for every itch.
   e. A brain is that with which we think we think.

f. If you aren't fired with enthusiasm, you will be fired with enthusiasm.
g. Alarm clock: a device for awakening childless households.
h. An exaggeration is a truth that has lost its temper.
i. Remember this—if you shut your mouth, you have your choice.
j. College: a washing machine—you get out of it just what you put in, but you'd never recognize it.
k. California smog: it's as if God had squeezed a big onion over Los Angeles.
l. A cabbage is a familiar kitchen-garden vegetable about as large and wise as a person's head.
m. It is better to speak wisdom foolishly like the saints than to speak folly wisely like the deans.
n. Credit buying is much like being drunk. The buzz happens immediately, and it gives you a lift. The hangover comes the day after. [Dr. Joyce Brothers]
o. Grant me the strength to change what can be changed. Give me the strength to bear what can't be changed. And grant me the wisdom to know the difference.
p. If only God would give me a clear sign. Like making a large deposit in my name in a Swiss bank. [Woody Allen]
q. Roses are red, violets are blue. I'm a schizophrenic, and so am I.
r. My dog thinks I'm his best friend. Which is pretty amazing, considering I'm the one who had him fixed.
s. The closest to perfection a person ever comes is when he's filling out a job application form.
t. It doesn't take brains to criticize; any old vulture can find a carcass.
u. Bachelors should be heavily taxed. It's not fair that some men should be happier than others.
v. Girls tend to marry men like their fathers. That's why mothers cry at weddings.
w. I wasn't on the chess team in college. The coach told me I was too short. [Woody Allen]
x. How a child handles hate may determine if he'll go to Harvard or San Quentin.
y. Arthritis is nothing more than twinges in the hinges.
z. There's music all around you if you just listen. There's as much music in belching as in Beethoven, munching meatballs as in Mozart, in the sound of a toilet flushing as in Tchaikovsky. All noise is music if you know how to listen to it. [John Cage]

Assignment 11: Fricatives and Affricates

Select material that contains many examples of the nine fricatives [f v θ ð s z ʃ ʒ h] and the two affricates [tʃ dʒ] in a variety of positions. If you have been experiencing difficulty with one or more of these sounds, be sure that your material is loaded with them. Articulate them with as much care and finesse as you can, but avoid excessive noisiness.

Suggested Checklist for Assignment 11

As you practice by yourself, you may want to work with this checklist. Listen carefully to yourself. If it is feasible, record the assignment, or get a classmate or friend to listen to you as you read the material. Eventually, your goal will be to have a check mark in the **Yes** column for each category. (Optional: Perhaps your instructor will want to use the checklist to evaluate you during your classroom presentation.)

	Yes	No

Initial, medial and final fricatives are short, sharp, and clear in articulation.

Pronounces correctly final *s* or *es* as added to verbs and nouns.

Differentiates between—

voiceless [f] and voiced [v]

voiceless [θ] and voiced [ð]

voiceless [s] and voiced [z]

voiceless [ʃ] and voiced [ʒ]

Avoids—

excessive pressure in production of fricatives

omitting initial, medial and final fricatives

Avoids substituting—

fricatives for nonfricatives*

nonfricatives for fricatives*

*If there are substitutions, a few of the more common ones are listed here. Check or indicate those which occur:

[b] for [f] or [v] ____	[t] for [θ] or [ð] ____	[s] for [θ] ____	[w] for [v] ____
[d] for [θ] or [ð] ____	[v] for [f] ____	[s] for [ð] ____	[z] for [s] ____
[f] for [θ] or [ð] ____	[v] for [w] ____	[s] for [z] ____	[z] for [ð] ____

Other substitutions:

Additional comments or suggestions:

Smorgasbord: Review Material for all the Consonants

Bilabial Sounds

68. This material highlights sounds that are produced by the action of your lips. The lips are more than just two fleshy flaps forming the margin of your mouth. For adept, precise articulation, make their movements spry and perky.

[p]   [b]   [m]   [w]   [ʍ]

   a. Be brief when you cannot be good.
   b. Heartbreak: the end of happiness and the beginning of peace.
   c. If you will please people, you must please them in their own way.
   d. When you're about to meet your maker it makes you meeker.
   e. One of the quickest ways to learn how to think on your feet is to become a pedestrian.
   f. The people who think they can wind up ahead of the race include everybody who has ever won a bet.
   g. Born poor, but of honored and humble people, I am particularly proud to die poor. [Pope John XXIII]
   h. The world is full of willing people—some willing to work, the rest willing to let them.
   i. Politics has become so expensive that it takes a lot of money even to get beaten.
   j. Politician's prayer: yea, even though I graze in pastures with jackasses, I pray that I will not bray like one.
   k. A bank is a place where they lend you an umbrella in fair weather and ask for it back again when it begins to rain.
   l. There was a pious man who went to bed thinking that he had God Almighty by the little finger, but woke up to find that he had the devil by the big toe.

Labiodental Sounds

69. This material features sounds made by placing the lower lip against the upper teeth. These two sounds have a tendency to become buzzy. Don't inflate them.

[f]   [v]

   a. I never vote for anyone. I always vote against. [Bill Cosby]
   b. Fog: stuff that is dangerous to drive in—especially if it's mental.
   c. It costs more to satisfy a vice than to feed a family.
   d. Furthermore is much farther than further.
   e. Fancy free: a fancy way to say "playing the field."
   f. Who is more foolish, the child afraid of the dark or the adult afraid of the light?
   g. Don't tell your friends their social faults; they will cure the fault and never forgive you.
   h. Football: a game where the spectators have four quarters in which to kill a fifth.
   i. One of the strangest things about life is that the poor who need money the most are the very ones that never have it.
   j. TV: where you can see the movies you've been avoiding for years.
   k. Have you fifty friends? It is not enough. Have you one enemy? It is too much.
   l. Love does not begin and end the way we seem to think it does. Love is a battle, love is a war; love is a growing up.

Linguadental Sounds

70. This material underscores sounds that are formed by placing the tip of the tongue between or against the front teeth. Be meticulous about tongue placement. Don't overpower these sounds.

[θ]   th   [ð]   th̸

   a. A closed mouth gathers no feet.
   b. One good thing about being a man is that men don't have to talk to each other.
   c. Everything is miraculous. It is miraculous that one does not melt in one's bath. [Picasso]
   d. There are mighty few people who think what they think they think.

e. Take care of the sense, and the sounds will take care of themselves.

f. Thief: one who has the habit of finding things just before people miss them.

g. The afternoon: that part of the day we spend thinking about how we wasted the morning.

h. Some people study all their life, and at their death they have learned everything except to think.

i. I can give you a six-word formula for success: "Think things through—then follow through."

j. The marvelous thing about a joke with a double meaning is that it can mean only one thing.

k. Sending an offspring through college is very educational. It teaches both the mother and the father how to do without a lot of things.

l. There are two kinds of directors in the theater: those who think they are God and those who are sure of it.

Lingua-Alveolar Sounds

71. This material accentuates sounds that are shaped by placing the tip or blade of the tongue on or near the upper gum ridge. A deft and dexterous tongue will help. (And don't turn [s] into a hurricane, please!)

[t] [d] [l] [s] [z] [n]

a. The city is not a concrete jungle; it is a human zoo.

b. One who cannot cut the bread evenly cannot get along well with people.

c. There are three kinds of lies: lies, damned lies, and statistics.

d. The length of a minute depends on which side of the bathroom door you're on.

e. Footprints in the sands of time are never made by sitting down.

f. Since God made Adam out of dust He had to make Eve to settle him.

g. I get my exercise acting as pallbearer to my friends who exercise.

h. I'm so used to being tense that when I'm calm I get nervous.

i. Always keep your head up, but be careful to keep your nose on a friendly level.

j. Fools write nonsense in better language than the unlearned, but it is still nonsense.

k. Try as much as possible to be wholly alive with all your might, and when you laugh, laugh like hell and when you get angry, get good and angry. Try to be alive. You will be dead soon enough. [Joan Rivers]

l. California is the only state in the union where you can fall asleep under a rose bush in full bloom and freeze to death.

Linguapalatal Sounds

72. This material emphasizes sounds that are produced by placing the tip or blade of the tongue on or near the hard palate. Check tongue placement carefully.

[ʃ] sh [ʒ] zh [j] y [r]

a. Pleasure is more trouble than trouble.

b. A wrong reason is worse than no reason at all.

c. It's not the size of the ocean; it's the motion of the ocean.

d. No wise person ever wished to be younger.

e. One of the finest accomplishments is making a long story short.

f. Shouting: raising the level of the voice instead of the intelligence.

g. There is only one religion, though there are a hundred versions of it.

h. To establish oneself in the world, one does all one can to seem established there.

i. Nothing beats a cold shower before breakfast except no cold shower before breakfast.

j. Being powerful is like being a lady. If you have to tell people you are, you ain't. [Douglas Fraser]

k. Drive carefully! Remember: it's not only a car that can be recalled by its maker.

l. You have a gambling problem if you buy a paper and learn that your horse lost, and instead of believing it, buy another paper.

Linguavelar Sounds

73. This material dwells on sounds that are molded by pressing the back of the tongue against the soft palate or velum. Make muscular sounds of [k] and [g], and don't let [ŋ] do a disappearing act. Remember, [ŋ] is NOT [n]!

    [k] [g] [ŋ] ng

    a. The saying that beauty is but skin deep is but a skin-deep saying.
    b. In the kingdom of the deaf, the person with one ear is king.
    c. Almost everything comes from almost nothing.
    d. The proof of the pudding is in the eating.
    e. Escapist: a person who looks the facts of life in the back of the neck.
    f. If I cannot brag of knowing something, then I brag of not knowing it. At any rate—brag!
    g. A secret may be sometimes best kept by keeping the secret of its being a secret.
    h. One way to prevent conversation from being boring is to say the wrong thing.
    i. If love means never having to say you're sorry, then saying you're sorry means never having to do anything to change what you are sorry about.
    j. Colleges teach the dead languages as if they were buried and the living ones as if they were dead.
    k. The brain is a wonderful organ; it starts working the moment you get up in the morning, and doesn't quit until you get to the office.
    l. The Lord gave us two ends—one for sitting and the other for thinking.

Glottal Sound

74. The folds are open just enough so that the air in passing through the glottis produces a frictionlike sound. Don't ignore this sound; don't explode it.

    [h]

    a. Heaven's help is better than early rising.
    b. Hand: a grappling hook attached to the human arm.
    c. A sight of happiness is happiness.
    d. It has been my experience that folks who have no vices have very few virtues.
    e. The ass went seeking for horns and lost his ears.
    f. Heaven has no rage like love turned to hatred.
    g. Human nature: what we have; other people have faults.
    h. It takes a wise person to handle a lie; a fool had better remain honest.
    i. Horse Sense: that rare intelligence which keeps horses from betting on human beings.
    j. The wicked often work harder to go to hell than the holy do to go to heaven.
    k. There is only one quality worse than hardness of heart and that is softness of head.
    l. Nothing happens to you that hasn't happened to someone else.

WRAP-UP

1. Articulation means clarity, intelligibility, and distinctness of speech. In a general sense, it's the same thing as *enunciation* and *diction*.

2. Overlapping speech (also known as assimilation or coarticulation) is fluid, connected speech. It telescopes sounds, increasing the smoothness and overall efficiency of articulation. It's easier to say
   I'll beat'ya ina game of dungeons 'n' dragons
   than
   I will beat you in a game of Dungeons and Dragons.

3. Speech sounds are formed, molded, separated, and joined by the movements and contacts of the most important articulators: the lips, the front teeth, the lower jaw, the tongue, and the velum.

4. The lips pucker as in the first sound in *will,* touch together as in *pipe,* and spread as in *pizza.* The lower lip contacts the upper teeth as in *vim.*

5. The front teeth assist enunciation as the tip of the tongue touches them as in *thanks, Thelma,* or the air stream hits them as in *save Sally.*

6. The lower jaw drops as in *awe* and *palm,* but is almost closed for *dew.*

7. The tongue is the most active, versatile, and important of the articulators. Run through these words and note the variety of tongue positions:

   then, fuzz, feet, should, soon, tuck.

8. The velum (soft palate) lowers and blocks the oral cavity, forcing the breath stream through the nasal cavities as in *may, night, sing.*

9. The English alphabet has twenty-six letters, but there are almost fifty different sounds in our language. Forty-three of these sounds and sound combinations can be represented by the symbols of the International Phonetic Alphabet (IPA). Twenty-five are consonants. Eighteen are vowels and diphthongs.

10. The articulators interfere with or disturb the outgoing breath stream to produce consonants.

11. Consonants are voiceless or voiced. For voiceless sounds such as

[p]	[θ]	th
[f]	[ʃ]	sh
[s]		

    the vocal folds are at rest and do not vibrate. For voiced sounds such as

[b]	[ð]	th
[v]	[ʒ]	zh
[z]		

    the vocal folds are moving and vibrating.

12. To produce plosives the outgoing air column is blocked in the mouth briefly. Then the pressure of the lips and tongue is relaxed suddenly, and the compressed air is released with an explosive noise.

[p]	[b]
[t]	[d]
[k]	[g]

13. Sounds produced by rapid movements of the articulators are glides. They are brief transitions from one vowel to another.

[l]	[w]	
[r]	[j]	y

14. For the nasals the velum is lowered and the oral cavity is blocked by the lips or the front or back of the tongue. The breath stream exits via the nasal cavity.

[m]	[ŋ]	ng
[n]		

15. For fricatives the oral cavity is not blocked completely, and these sounds are produced when the air is forced through a small opening or slit under pressure.

[f]		[h]	
[θ]	th	[ð]	th
[s]		[z]	zh
[ʃ]	sh	[ʒ]	

16. For affricates—(combinations of a plosive and a fricative) the tongue blocks the breath briefly, and then the impounded air is released rather slowly.

[tʃ]	ch
[dʒ]	j

VARNISH YOUR VOWELS
DISCIPLINE YOUR DIPHTHONGS

WOULD YOU BELIEVE THAT

. . . Only a few words in our language contain all five vowel letters in alphabetical order? One of them is *facetious*.

. . . One vowel sound is common to almost every language in the world? It's the *a* in c*a*lm.

. . . The letters *ough* represent seven different pronunciations?: *although, enough, through, cough, thought, hiccough, bough.*

VOWELS

Say <u>ah-h</u> as you do when the doctor checks your throat. You've made a vowel sound, and you noticed that there was virtually no obstruction of the breath stream as you formed the *ah.*

Now make these sounds: [p] and [z]. You have to set up an obstacle course inside your mouth to block the airstream in order to produce consonants. *Vowels are made with more or less open mouth and without blocking the airstream. Vowels are free from friction noises.*

Vowels can be sung. (You can't sing the plosives, for example.) The consonants may provide beginnings, middles, and endings of words. They're often the boundary markers of speech. When we talk about intelligibility, crispness and distinctness of speech, we're primarily concerned with consonants.

"Consonants," said Alexander Graham Bell, "constitute the backbone of the spoken language—vowels, the flesh and blood."

POSITIONS FOR ARTICULATION

We may classify vowels on the following bases:

■ *Place of Articulation.* There are front, middle or central, and back vowels, depending on which part of the tongue is most actively involved in producing the particular vowel.

■ *Height of Tongue.* If you say *meet,* you will be aware that the front of your tongue is high in your mouth as you produce the vowel sound. If you say *mate,* the front of your tongue is in a mid-high position on the vowel sound. If you say *mat,* the front of your tongue is almost flat on the floor of your mouth on the vowel sound. Contrast also *feet* with *fate, way* with *woe.*

■ *Tension of Tongue Muscles.* The tongue muscles are more tense for the vowel in *meet* than in *met.* More tension is present for the vowel in *moon* than in *moan.*

If you'll remember that a vowel diagram suggests typical, but not exact, positions and that the differences in tongue positions from one vowel to another are comparatively slight, examine figure 5.1.

The top of the diagram suggests the roof of the mouth. The bottom suggests the floor of the mouth.

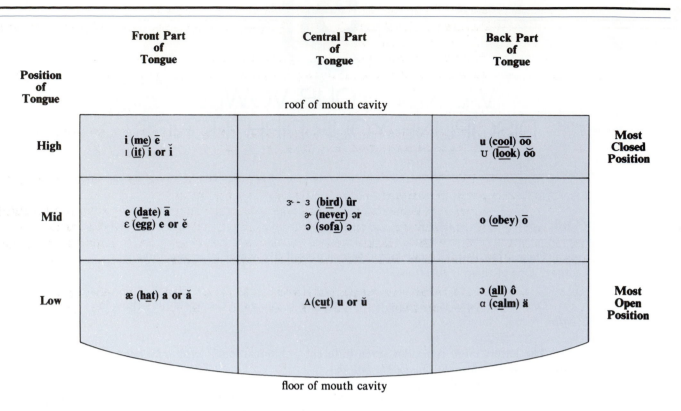

	Front Part of Tongue	Central Part of Tongue	Back Part of Tongue	
Position of Tongue		roof of mouth cavity		
High	i (**me**) ē ɪ (**it**) i or ĭ		u (**cool**) ōo ʊ (**look**) ŏo	**Most Closed Position**
Mid	e (**date**) ā ɛ (**egg**) e or ĕ	ɝ - ɜ (**bird**) ûr ɚ (**never**) ər ə (**sofa**) ə	o (**obey**) ō	
Low	æ (**hat**) a or ă	ʌ (**cut**) u or ŭ	ɔ (**all**) ô ɑ (**calm**) ä	**Most Open Position**
		floor of mouth cavity		

Figure 5.1   Various positions of tongue and mouth for vowel sounds. (Phonetic symbols are placed to the left of the key word. Dictionary symbols are placed to the right.)

The Front Vowels

The left side of the diagram represents the front part of the mouth. The sounds are front vowels. To produce these sounds, the tongue is somewhat forward in the mouth, and the front portion of the tongue is most active.

Beginning with [i], say the front vowels shown in the diagram and note what takes place. Your tongue arches high and far forward, but as you say the others down the list you'll feel the front of your tongue lower, your jaw drop, and your mouth gradually open. Your lips for [i] suggest a narrow rectangle. As you say the other vowels, your lips change from a narrow slit to more relaxed and open positions.

The Back Vowels

The right side of the diagram represents the back part of the mouth. The sounds are back vowels. To produce these sounds, the back portion of the tongue is most active.

Say the back vowels shown in the diagram, beginning with [ɑ] and ending with [u]. As you proceed from [ɑ] through [u], note how the back of your tongue and your jaw gradually rise. Your lips are relatively open and relaxed for [ɑ], but by the time you reach [u], they're protruded and rounded.

The Central Vowels

The center of the diagram represents the middle of the mouth. The sounds are central vowels. To produce these sounds, the middle portion of the tongue is most active.

As you begin with [ɝ], you'll note that your tongue may be arched relatively high in the middle of the oral cavity. With the other sounds your tongue drops slightly. When you reach [ə] and [ʌ], you'll be aware that your tongue, lips, and jaw are in quite relaxed positions.

Figure 5.2 will show you approximate tongue positions for the vowels.

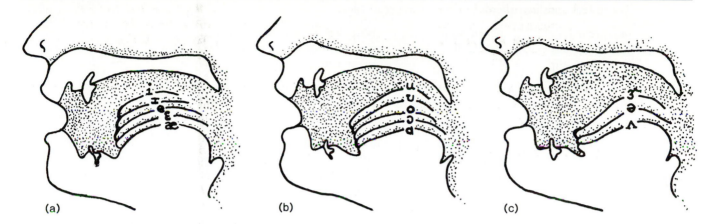

Figure 5.2 Approximate tongue positions for the vowels:
(a) front vowels; (b) back vowels; (c) middle or central vowels.

FRONT VOWELS

$$\left[\,\mathrm{i}\,\right]$$

ē

Example   Steve and Keith believe that Caesar feasted in the deep ravine near Phoenix.

How to . . .

Arch the front of your tongue high and far forward so that it almost touches the hard palate. Your tongue should be tensed. Your lips are spread slightly, and your upper and lower teeth are quite close together.

Faults and Foibles

Added Sound

"Did Mr. Kee-*uhl* stee-*uhl* your whee-*uhls*?"

Some Southerners and quite a few users of General American dialect—particularly those in midwestern regions—occasionally insert an extra little sound—the schwa [ə]—after the [i], especially if it's followed by [l].

The [ə] is legitimate in words such as *about* [əˈbaut], *lion* [ˈlaɪən], *sofa* [ˈsofə]. But if you stick it in where it doesn't belong, it isn't. Incidentally, many educated people add the [ə] in certain words: *we'll kneel* becomes *we-uhl knee-uhl*. This generally doesn't interfere with understanding. So—to *uh* or not to *uh*? It's up to you.

1. Read the word pairs below. You'll have no difficulty pronouncing the [i] in the first word of each pair. Then transfer the same [i] to the second word without inserting [ə]. *Hold your jaw steady on each second word.* If your jaw drops, this means you're stuffing in a [ə] where it shouldn't be.

keen–keel	read–real	eke–eel
peek–peel	seen–seal	teak–teal
feed–feel	dean–deal	heat–heel
mean–meal	wheat–wheel	Zeke–zeal

[ɪ] for [i] substitution

People with certain non-English language backgrounds may confuse [i] as in b**ee**t with [ɪ] as in b**i**t.

    Result: *feet* [fit] may sound more like *fit* [fɪt]

           meat [mit] may sound more like *mit* [mɪt]

2. For [i], your tongue is high and far forward, but for [ɪ], it's slightly lower and further back in your mouth. Try to feel and hear the difference as you read these:

    a. | | | | |
        |---|---|---|---|
        | reap–rip | sheen–shin | heap–hip | leap–lip |
        | seep–sip | deal–dill | seat–sit | beet–bit |
        | deep–dip | feel–fill | ream–rim | leak–lick |
        | bean–bin | seek–sick | seen–sin | wheat–wit |

    Practice these sentences. Distinguish carefully between [i] and [ɪ].

    b. Zest: the peel of an orange squeezed into wine.
    c. Why do we kill people who kill people to show that killing people is wrong?
    d. Few really believe. The most only believe that they believe or even make believe.
    e. Sleep faster. We need the pillow. [Yiddish proverb]
    f. If you're angry—speak. You will make the best speech you will ever regret.
    g. A person always has two reasons for doing anything—a good reason and the real reason.
    h. We are both great people, but I have succeeded better in keeping it a profound secret than you.
    i. An appeaser is one who feeds a crocodile, hoping it will eat him or her last.
    j. Whenever I get eager and feel like exercise, I lie down until the feeling passes.
    k. Please, Lord, teach me so that my words will be easy, tender, and sweet, for tomorrow I may have to eat them.
    l. Some preachers and teachers don't talk in their sleep; they talk in other people's sleep.
    m. It's easy to save face. Just keep the lower half of it closed.
    n. There is a demon who puts wings on certain stories and who launches them like eagles in the air.
    o. One thing that is hard to keep under your hat is a big head.

Example   Is Bill's pretty singer guilty of singing English hymns in business buildings?

How to . . .

Say the [i] of *meet* [mit]. Now, lower your tongue slightly and pull it back a bit as you sound the [ɪ] in *it* [ɪt]. Your lips and tongue should also be more relaxed for this sound than for [i].

Faults and Foibles

3. Non-native speakers may confuse [I] of *bit* with [i] of *beet*.
    Result: *feel* becomes *fill; seat* becomes *sit.*
    As you now know, for [i] the tongue is high and far forward, but for [I] it is lower and farther back in the mouth. Feel and hear the difference as you read these:

    a. | | | | |
        |---|---|---|---|
        | reap–rip | keen–kin | bean–bin | seen–sin |
        | seek–sick | deal–dill | heat–hit | teal–till |

    The Spanish language doesn't contain a vowel sound exactly like the English [I]. Hispanics sometimes have trouble with [ɪ] and substitute [i]. *Gyp* sounds more like *jeep; itch* sounds more like *each.*

    b. As you make the underlined sound in the word column below—

[i]	[I]
Spread your lips a bit—almost smiling.	Spread your lips slightly, but less than for [i].
Arch the blade of your tongue high in the front of your mouth. The tongue is tense.	Your tongue is lower and more relaxed than it is for [i].

(First read down each column—then across the page.)

gr<u>ee</u>t	gr<u>i</u>t
J<u>ea</u>n	g<u>i</u>n
wh<u>ee</u>l	w<u>i</u>ll
b<u>ea</u>d	b<u>i</u>d
d<u>ea</u>n	d<u>i</u>n
ch<u>ea</u>p	ch<u>i</u>p
l<u>ea</u>n	Lynn
st<u>ea</u>l	st<u>i</u>ll
P<u>e</u>te	p<u>i</u>t
s<u>ee</u>n	s<u>i</u>n

[ε] *for* [I] *substitution*

Careless individuals often substitute the [ε] of *egg* for [I]. The tongue positions for the two sounds are somewhat alike, but if you say *s<u>i</u>t-s<u>e</u>t, b<u>i</u>t-b<u>e</u>t, m<u>i</u>tt-m<u>e</u>t,* you will discover that the tongue is higher and farther forward for [ı] than for [ε].

4. Don't confuse the two sounds as you read.

    a.

did–dead	rid–read	kin–Ken
itch–etch	lid–led	pit–pet
bit–bet	sill–sell	hid–head
gym–gem	limb–Lem	pick–peck

    b. A bit better bittersweet will make your bitter sweetie better.
    c. It is easier to stay out than get out.
    d. A true friend will not laugh at your joke until he or she retells it.
    e. Television: A medium, so called because it is neither rare nor well done.
    f. What a pity the only way to get to heaven is in a hearse.
    g. Even though a number of people have tried, no one has yet found a way to drink for a living.
    h. If people are unwilling to hear you, better it is to hold your tongue than them.
    i. Kissing a girl is like opening a jar of olives—hard to get the first one, but the rest come easy.
    j. Never chase a lie. Let it alone and it will run itself to death.

Muffled [I]

At times [I] is permitted to sound muffled or swallowed. This may happen if you pull your tongue too far back toward a central position and round your lips on the vowel. This is most apt to occur if [I] is preceded or followed by [r] or [l] or by the lip and lip-teeth consonants [m, w, f, v, p, b].

5. As you read this drill material, work for an [I] sound that retains the [I] quality and avoid muffled or swallowed distortions.

    a.

pill	bitter	risk	milk
hip	fib	lip	whip
fifty	vim	gist	video
live	sniff	sieve	pin

    b. Income: something that you can't live without or within.
    c. If you're not big enough to lose, you're not big enough to win.
    d. The only ism in which Hollywood believes is plagiarism.
    e. Schizophrenia: a condition in which two can live as cheaply as one.
    f. Graffiti on wall of an abandoned church: We didn't invent sin. We're just trying to perfect it.
    g. Advice to a soldier: If it moves, salute it. If it doesn't move, pick it up. If you can't pick it up, paint it.
    h. A baby sitter is not experienced until she knows which kid to sit with and which kid to sit on.
    i. A cocktail lounge is a half-lit room full of half-lit people. The main trouble with liquor is that it makes you see double and feel single. Liquor will kill germs, but you can't get them to drink it.

$$\overline{a}$$

Example   K<u>a</u>te and the <u>ei</u>ght <u>a</u>pes from <u>A</u>sia <u>a</u>te the st<u>ea</u>k in <u>A</u>pril.

How to . . .

Lower your tongue slightly from the [ɪ] position to a midhigh position, and pull it farther back as you sound [e]. The muscles of your tongue are tense. Your jaw is open, and your lips are more relaxed than when sounding [I]. In unstressed positions, [e] is often a relatively pure vowel. In certain stressed positions, however, it becomes a diphthong [eI]—a rapid blending of two vowels in the same syllable.

Faults and Foibles

Nasalized ⎮e⎮

A common fault is the tendency to nasalize it in words in which it's preceded or followed by [m], [n], or [ŋ]. The velum must be raised for correct production of [e], and excessive tension in your throat and tongue is to be avoided.

6.   The [e] in the second word of each of these pairs should be as free of undesirable nasality as the [e] in the first word of each pair.

   a.   day–dame   fray–frame   gay–game   day–Dane
        ade–made   Kay–came   pay–pain   ail–nail
        ape–nape   ray–rain   shay–shame   say–same
        ate–mate   air–mare   ale–male   ache–make

Guard against excessively nasalized and strident [e] sounds as you practice this material.

   b.   *Two Danes and a Dame* is a maimed version of Shakespeare's famous *Hamlet*.
   c.   An expert is a man who has made all the mistakes which can be made in a very narrow field.
   d.   Do not forget to entertain strangers. Without knowing it, you may be entertaining angels or saints.
   e.   To say "Keep changing" is not a cliché. When you're through changing, you're through.
   f.   Filet mignon: an opera by Beethoven.
   g.   Will Rogers used to say: "Maybe *ain't* ain't so correct, but I notice that lots of folks who ain't using *ain't* ain't eating."
   h.   When the gardeners are praying for rain, the picnickers are praying for sunshine, so what is the poor Lord to do?

Variations

Vowel or Diphthong?

   They mailed the plate on May Day is entirely acceptable if the so-called *a* sounds are not diphthongized. There is no block to understanding if one says,

   [ðe meld ðə plet ɔn me de] instead of [ðeɪ meɪld ðə pleɪt ɔn meɪ deɪ]

   If excessively prolonged, [eɪ] also may become a triphthong.

   Result: *fate* becomes *fa-i-uht* [feɪət]

   This isn't uncommon in some Southern speech, and is used quite often by educated people in the South. If your speech is non-Southern, you're probably producing a relatively pure vowel sound.

   Some speakers let [e] drop and shorten to [ɛ] if it comes before [l].

   You'll go to jail, Dale, if you fail turns into *You'll go to jell, Dell, if you fell.*

7. Find out if you're making [e] a vowel, a diphthong, or a triphthong or shortening it to [ɛ]. Then correct as necessary.

   a.
fate	dale	ray	pail
Hades	April	slay	mate
mail	bathe	crayon	they
came	bane	same	rein

   b. About encores: "It's better that they should want and we don't play than we should play and they don't want." [Isaac Stern]
   c. The most heinous liar in the world is They Say.
   d. When angels play for themselves, they play Bach; when they play for God, they play Mozart.
   e. The ideal neighbor is the one who makes noise at the same time you do.
   f. A person should work eight hours and sleep eight hours, but not the same eight hours.
   g. If I had to live my life over again, I'd make the same mistakes, only sooner.
   h. The most important thing is honesty. If you can fake that, you've got it made. [Walter Cronkite]

Example   Bess and her friend found an empty treasure chest buried next to the chemistry lab.

How to . . .
Let the back of your tongue touch your upper molars. The tongue tip should be behind the lower front teeth. Your jaw drops slightly.

Faults and Foibles
Ayd, don't forgit to git some brayd and aygs. Translation: *Ed, don't forget to get some bread and eggs.*

This is the kind of talk you'll hear now and then in Appalachia—a region in the Eastern United States which extends roughly from Southern Pennsylvania to Northeastern Alabama.

If [e] is substituted for [ɛ]: *leg* and *dead* become *layg* and *dayd.*

In the Midwest, South, and Southwest many speakers also tend to switch [ɪ] for [ɛ]. Result: *ten* and *red* become *tin* and *rid.*

8. Contrast [ɛ] with [e] and [ɪ] in the following. Don't shuffle the sounds around.

   a.
[ɛ] words	[e] words	[ɪ] words
Rear of tongue touches upper molars.	Tongue midhigh. Tongue muscles tense.	Front of tongue high but relaxed.
Ben	bane	bin
den	Dane	din
bet	bait	bit
sell	sale	sill
net	Nate	nit
fen	fain	fin

   b. Never face facts; if you do you'll never get up in the morning.
   c. There are only two kinds of men—the dead and the deadly.
   d. Hell: they should have an express line for people with six sins or less.
   e. When you have only two pennies left in the world, buy bread with one and a lily with the other. [Chinese proverb]

f. Sex appeal is fifty percent of what you've got and fifty percent of what people think you've got.

g. Many of us are at the metallic age—gold in our teeth, silver in our hair, and lead in our pants.

h. It's sobering to remember that when Mendelssohn was my age, he had already been dead for ten years. [Victor Borge]

i. Does beer make you strong? Yes. Try this experiment. Order a keg of your favorite brew. You'll observe that it's very heavy. Tap it and start drinking. Before too long, you'll be able to roll the keg around the room with ease.

Nasalized |ɛ|

9. The nasals are pleasant, congenial sounds, but they do tend to spill over into nearby vowels. [ɛ] is one of the most frequently assaulted. Run through these, each of which contains an [ɛ], and pause where you see / /.

```
e/  /t           e/  /t           e/  /n
n/  /e/  /t       m/  /e/  /t      m/  /e/  /n
```

Say them again, omitting the pauses: *net, met, men.*
Is your [ɛ] clear and cloudless—absolutely free of nasality?
As you practice this material, be sure that the sound isn't nasalized excessively.

a. Egg: a day's adventure for a hen.

b. If you think education is expensive—try ignorance.

c. Headlines are frequently twice the size of events.

d. Obscenity can be found in every book except the telephone directory.

e. Early to bed, early to rise, makes one healthy, wealthy, and dead.

f. May you get to heaven a half hour before the devil knows you're dead.

g. God may help those who help themselves, but the courts are rough on shoplifters.

h. Memento: the keepsake of an event, such as a hotel room Bible.

i. A gentleman from Memphis said about his last Vegas vacation, "Out by jet, back in debt."

j. I have seventy days for this tour, and I have visited ten countries. That makes seven days in each country, and when you start blocking traffic—well, the first day people enjoy it, but by the third day they get bloody tired of it. The art of being a good guest is to know when to leave. [Prince Philip]

 a – ă

Example   The <u>a</u>ngry m<u>a</u>n sl<u>a</u>mmed the pl<u>ai</u>d b<u>a</u>sket of tr<u>a</u>sh into the c<u>a</u>n.

How to . . .

Let your tongue lie almost flat on the floor of your mouth, but keep it well forward. Your tongue muscles should be quite lax.

Faults and Foibles

Nasal and Tense |æ|

The most common problem with [æ] is making it with a nervous, nasal and meow-like quality. This is particularly noticeable in eastern speech. Not a few citizens of the New York, Philadelphia and Middle Atlantic regions (and it's spread into the Southwest) are apt to fashion a very taut and unattractive sound.

They distort such a simple sentence as *Ask the man about the tan cat* [æsk ðə mæn ə`bɑut ðə tæn kæt] into Eh-usk the meh-un about the teh-un ceh-ut. [ɛ-əsk ðə mɛ-ən ə`bɑut ðə tɛ-ən kɛ-ət]

This type of bleak, dry and disagreeable distortion often results from an overtense tongue that is raised too high. A closed and locked jaw also adds to the screechy-scratchy, cat-on-a-hot-tin-roof quality.

Speakers in all sections of the country must be careful with this sound. If [æ] is near a nasal consonant or a plosive, it can easily slip into a tinny, jangling mutilation.

10. Try this experiment with the word pairs below.
The negative: On the first word of each pair, deliberately tense your tongue, tighten and close your jaw somewhat, and be as nasal as you can. As you pounce on each of the [ɛ] sounds, think of saying the word *egg* [ɛg] between clenched teeth.

The positive: On the second member of each pair, work for a tranquil, almost-lazy tongue. Open your jaw, and be on guard against nasality.

a.

[bɛən–bæn]	[dɛən–dæn]	[mɛəd–mæd]
[fɛən–fæn]	[rɛən–ræn]	[rɛəm–ræm]
[tɛən–tæn]	[hɛəd–hæd]	[tɛəŋ–tæŋ]
[mɛən–mæn]	[fɛəd–fæd]	[grɛənd–grænd]
[klɛəm–klæm]	[sɛət–sæt]	[slɛəŋ–slæŋ]

b. Using the more agreeable, relaxed, and pleasant [æ] of the second word in each pair in section *a,* say these rapidly.
ban-shan-han-van-can-lamb-tram
jam-jab-sap-tab-Ann-sack-hack
add-mad-scram-bat-map-lass-lab
lag-dad-crab-Nan-and-prance-an
lack-sack-back-wrack-crack-tack-jack
ma'm-map-mack-mass-mab-man-mat

c. Happiness is no laughing matter.
d. Mack thought that thin was in, but Nat said that fat is where it's at.
e. There are those who make things happen. There are those who watch things happen, and there are those who wonder what happened.
f. It isn't the lack of love, but the lack of friendship that makes unhappy marriages.
g. Anger makes your mouth work faster than your mind.
h. Before you kiss the handsome prince, you have to kiss a lot of toads.
i. Man is like a tack. He can only go as far as his head will let him.
j. A bachelor is a rolling stone that gathers no boss.
k. Advertising is what turns a yawn into a yearn.
l. Give a quack enough rope and he'll hang up a shingle.

[ʌ], [ɛ], *or* [ɪ] *substitutions*

11. "If I Had My Druthers," a popular tune of the 1950s, suggested that Appalachian mountain folk pronounce *rather* as *ruther.* This is possibly true, but folksy mispronunciation is also encountered in other sections of the country.

The paired words below do *not* rhyme.
Reminder: For [æ]—your tongue is almost flat on the floor of your mouth.
For [ʌ]—raise the center of your tongue slightly.

a.

Sam–some	rag–rug
dam–dumb	clack–cluck
fan–fun	ram–rum
bad–bud	cram–crumb

Some people turn *had* into *head* and *can* into *kin.*
For [ɛ]—the back of your tongue touches your upper molars.

b.

bat–bet	sand–send
dack–deck	fan–fen
chat–chet	ham–hem
sat–set	lamb–Lem

For [ɪ]—the front of your tongue is relatively high.

  c.   sack–sick   salve–sieve
        mat–mit   flam–flim
        had–hid   dad–did
        dapper–dipper   fan–fit

12.   Monitor yourself diligently as you read these sentences. Don't let [ʌ], [ɛ], or [ɪ] sneak in and replace [æ].

     a.   Tex Thaxter, the actor, pays taxes on taxis in Texas.
     b.   Sam Goldwyn once said: "This makes me so mad that it gets my dandruff up."
     c.   People with tact have less to retract.
     d.   Mick Jagger had a bad accident recently. One of his pals slammed the car door on his hair.
     e.   Never gamble in heavy traffic. The cars may be stacked against you.
     f.   In acting Lady Macbeth, Gilda Radner ran through the gamut of emotions from a to b.

[ɑ] *for* [æ] *substitution*

13.   [æ] doesn't occur in some foreign languages, so if English is your second language, you may possibly be substituting [ɑ] for [æ]. In this case you would say *shock, cot* [ʃɑk, kɑt] for *shack, cat* [ʃæk, kæt]. For [ɑ] your tongue should be low, flat, and relaxed on the floor of your mouth. For [æ] your tongue is low, but there may be a slight elevation of the front part.
     Contrast the sounds in these word pairs.

mop–map	ox–ax	flog–flag
sock–sack	rock–rack	not–gnat
clod–clad	rot–rat	cop–cap
pod–pad	mod–mad	bottle–battle

14.   Don't wring [æ] out of shape. Avoid undue tongue and jaw tensions or nasality as you read these sentences. Stay with them until you can make a pleasant, untarnished [æ].

     a.   One can't go halfway around the world to count the cats in Zanzibar.
     b.   Every man has it in his power to make one woman happy by remaining a bachelor.
     c.   Talent is like money; you don't have to have any to talk about it.
     d.   The family you come from isn't half as important as the family you're going to have.
     e.   *Tax reform* means: Don't tax you, don't tax me, tax that man behind the tree.
     f.   The first half of our lives is ruined by our parents and the second half by our children.
     g.   Half of the world is composed of people who have something to say and can't, and the other half who have nothing to say and keep on saying it.
     h.   He who laughs last didn't get the joke.
     i.   Marriage is like canned hash. You've got to take a chance.
     j.   As for bad taste, it is, in fact, like bad breath—better than no breath at all.

BACK VOWELS

ä

Example   F<u>a</u>ther c<u>a</u>lmly c<u>a</u>rted T<u>o</u>m's <u>o</u>minous looking b<u>o</u>mb into the b<u>a</u>rn.

How to . . .
Your tongue should be low, relatively flat, and relaxed on the floor of your mouth. The back of the tongue is slightly raised. Your lips are rather far apart and unrounded. Your jaw is dropped to its most relaxed position.

Faults and Foibles

The [ɑ] sound is widely used and pleasant. American English has many so-called "short o" words such as c*ot*, n*ot*, d*ot*, h*ot*, and a majority of us pronounce these words with [ɑ].

Similarly, we have an abundance of common words in which the letter *a* is followed by *r: warm, car, part, large,* and with many of these, too, the [ɑ] is generally used.

Easterners, especially New Englanders, may use [ɔ] and [ʌ] in "short o" words.

Nasalized [ɑ]

If [ɑ] is near [m], [n], or [ŋ], there's a tendency to push the vowel through the nose. If you'll remember that the velum must be lowered for the production of the nasal consonants, but not for other sounds, you should be able to avoid an unpleasant quality with this vowel.

15. Check for nasalization as you read these:
   a. When you knock, ask to see God—not one of the servants.
   b. A deluxe model car costs no more than the standard model—you just pay a little longer.
   c. If it's art it's not for all, and if it's for all, it's not art.
   d. A burglar's business is to earn a living doing unwanted work.
   e. When a small boy doesn't object to soap, he's probably blowing bubbles.
   f. Progress might have been all right once, but it's gone on too long.
   g. Moll put the mop and the bond in the parched marsh.
   h. It is extremely difficult for the tolerant to tolerate the intolerant.
   i. An honest prayer: "Stop my neighbor, O Lord, from buying things I can't afford."
   j. A politician is a person who's got what it takes to take what you've got.
   k. A juvenile delinquent is a teenager who wants what he wants when he wants it and won't wait to get it.
   l. Politics is like milking a cow. You can accomplish a lot if you have a little pull.

Example   The outl*aw*'s sc*a*lded j*aw* looked rather r*aw* to P*au*l in the m*o*rning.

How to . . .

Raise the back of your tongue a bit. Your lips should be slightly rounded.

Faults and Foibles

The [ɔ] sound is notoriously fickle. The area of the country in which you live will have some influence on your pronunciation of this unstable vowel. To add a little more confusion: If you were to ask each member of your class to say *Paul,* you'd hear at least three different vowel sounds. Even within geographical areas, there are differences.

Many individuals use [ɑ] in place of [ɔ]. A few persons don't seem to use [ɔ] at all. Fortunately, [ɔ] causes few problems.

In certain sections of the East, it is not uncommon to hear [ɚ] added to [ɔ]. (This problem is discussed in greater detail in Exercise 31, Chapter 4.)

   Result: *law* [lɔ] may become *law-r* [lɔɚ]
          jaw [dʒɔ] may become *jaw-r* [dʒɔɚ]
   Occasionally [ə] or [ʊ] may be added to [ɔ].
   Result: *ball* [bɔl] may become *ba-uhl* [bɔəl]
          daughter [ˈdɔtɚ] may become *da-ooter* [ˈdɔʊtɚ]
   Those whose speech is Southern may wish to avoid inserting [w] as well as the schwa [ə].
   Result: *tall* [tɔl] becomes *ta-wuhl* [tɔwəl]
          taught [tɔt] becomes *ta-wuht* [tɔwət]

16. If you use any of these additions and would like to eliminate them, practice the drill material. Have somebody listen to you carefully and tell you if you're deleting unwanted sounds.

a.
draw	shawl	thought	moth
gone	caught	broad	cough
maw	Saul	falcon	morgue
awl	yawn	loss	wrong

b. The thoughtful outlaw ate the morsel of warm sauce.
c. The author saw the flaw in Shaw's play about the Indian squaw.
d. The hawk often gnawed the awning on the auburn halter.
e. Dawn does not come twice to awaken a person.
f. In the spring a young man's fancy turns to thoughts of love while the middle-ager wonders if the lawn-mower will start.
g. The late Orson Welles said: "If it hadn't been for women, we'd still be squatting in caves, eating raw dog meat. We made civilization to impress our girl friends."
h. A good lawyer knows the law; a clever one takes the judge to lunch.
i. A dog is a dog except when he's facing you. Then he's Mr. Dog. [Jamaican proverb]
j. The only walk more expensive than a walk down a church aisle is a walk down a supermarket aisle.
k. Epitaph on G. B. Shaw's tombstone: This is all over my head. I knew if I stayed around long enough, something like this would happen.

 $\overline{O}$

Example   Most of the boats floated in the ocean near the hotel.

How to . . .

Round and protrude your lips. Raise your jaw to a slightly higher position than it was for [ɔ]. The back of your tongue should be raised mid-high toward the palate.

Generally speaking, this sound is most likely to be found in unaccented or lightly stressed positions: *opinion*, *obey*, *omit*. Occasionally, it's heard as a simple vowel when followed by a voiceless consonant as in *lotion*, *bloated*, *coach*, or when followed by [r] as in *door*, *core*.

Faults and Foibles

Diphthong [ou] *or triphthong* [εou]

In stressed syllables, the diphthong [ou] is heard more often than the vowel [o]. However, *Go row the old boat* is certainly acceptable even if the so-called *o* sounds aren't diphthongized. There's no block to understanding if one says:

[go ro ðə old bot] instead of [gou rou ðə ould bout]

Very commonly in the East and in the Middle Atlantic section of the United States, this diphthong becomes a triphthong. A sound something like [ε] is inserted before the [o], and the resulting distortion is [gεou rεou ðə εould bεout]

If it's accompanied by too much nasality and tension—and it generally is—it becomes an extremely jarring sound.

17. Work for simple, uncluttered [o] or [ou] sounds as you read this material. Round your lips. Use a <u>relaxed</u> approach, and don't let that undesirable [ɛ] sneak in before an [o]. Don't let the sound go through your nose.

a.
snow	oath	over	ogle	beau
soul	bowl	goal	host	Joe
foe	row	woke	owe	ego
coat	oak	toe	no	sew

b. Polo: Ping-Pong with ponies.
c. Oboe: an ill woodwind that nobody blows well.
d. Whatever poet or orator may say of it, old age is still old age.
e. If you don't go to other people's funerals, they won't go to yours.
f. From hero to zero is about the average hero's fate.
g. The golden rule is that there are no golden rules.
h. What I know about work: Live by this code. You can't have bread—and loaf.
i. One who knows only one's own side of the case knows little of that.
j. Ghosts were created when the first person woke at night.
k. In Wyoming rodeos they say there's never been a horse that can't be rode, and never been a rider that can't be throwed.
l. The more you know, the more you ought to know.
m. If you don't know, simply say so.
n. A folk singer is a guy who sings through his nose by ear.
o. Most men are either old and bent, or young and broke.
p. The problem with not knowing where you're going is that you're never going to know when you get there.

Example Couldn't she put the cookies and the pudding on the sooty cushion?

How to . . .

Your tongue is lax, and the back portion of the tongue is lifted high toward the palate—higher than for the vowel [o]. Your lips are slightly protruded.

Faults and Foibles

The [ʊ] of book is often substituted for the [u] of moon. The exercise material will help make the differences clear. Another fault is that of weakening [ʊ] to [ʌ] or [ə]. If this occurs—
    would may sound something like wuhd [wʌd]

18. Don't substitute [u] or [ʌ] for [ʊ] as you read this material. You'll be able to avoid such substitutions if you keep your lips rounded for [ʊ].

a. It's not the time you put in, but what you put in the time.
b. Instead of putting others in their place, put yourself in their place.
c. The roof fell on the poor wolf in Little Red Riding Hood.
d. It is only the people with push who have pull.
e. Good art is not what it looks like, but what it does to you.
f. One who is good at making excuses is seldom good for anything else.

g. Ginger ale: a good, sugary drink that tastes like your foot feels when it's asleep.
h. It surely would be a good world if everybody was as pleasant as the person who's trying to rook you.
i. The only way to avoid Hollywood—you should live there.
j. The cook was a good cook, as cooks go; and as cooks go, she went.
k. Bad books sell more copies than good books for the simple reason that bad books tells us what we like to hear, while good books tell us what we ought to hear.
l. When I get a little money, I buy books. If any is left, I buy food. A house without books is like a room without windows.
m. Lou, the crook, would have wooed Sue, but she pushed him into a brook.
n. If a woodchuck could chuck wood, how much wood would a woodchuck chuck if a woodchuck could and would? But if a woodchuck could and would chuck wood, no reason why he should. How much wood could a woodchuck chuck if a woodchuck could and would chuck wood?

Example   Ruth saw the gloomy crew loot the suits from the blue room.

How to . . .

Raise the back of your tongue high toward the palate. The front of your tongue should be depressed and retracted. Your lips are more protruded and rounded for this sound than any other vowel.

Faults and Foibles

[uə] and [uwə] for [u]

Some speakers not only diphthongize [u] if it's followed by [l] or [n], but insert a [w] sound. *Tool* and *moon* become *too-wuhl* [tuwəl] and *moo-wuhn* [muwən]. If you're guilty, you'll want to work for a shorter vowel sound.

19. Try these:

a. cool	rude	pool	spoon
boot	coo	grew	spool
bloom	June	noon	fool
whose	woo	boost	tune

b. Bite off more than you can chew, then chew it.
c. Plan more than you can do, then do it.
d. So you think money is the root of all evil? Have you ever asked what is the root of money?
e. Once the toothpaste is out of the tube, it's much too hard to get it back in.
f. Dr. Dooley, my dentist, said, "It's a matter of the tooth, the whole tooth, and nothing but the tooth."
g. We get too soon old and too late smart.
h. You can eat as much as you want to as long as you don't swallow it.
i. Ninety-five percent of the movies produced in Hollywood are so foolish that it's stupid to review them in any publication not intended to be read while chewing bubble gum.
j. Most of today's news is too true to be good.
k. Love: a word made up of two vowels, two consonants and two fools.
l. The city of Washington is divided into two parts: "Who's who" and "Who's through."
m. The reason some people drink booze is that they don't know what else to do with it. Boozers are losers.

[u] or [ʊ]?

There is some controversy over a handful of *oo* words. How should we pronounce *roof, room,* and *root,* for example?

roof [ruf] or [rʊf]   *room* [rum] or [rʊm]   *root* [rut] or [rʊt]

The Random House Dictionary and *Webster's Third New International Dictionary* list [ruf], [rum], and [rut] as first choices, and [rʊf], [rʊm], and [rʊt] as second choices. This simply means that both choices are standard.

You'll have to let your own ears serve as your guide. With the following words, try both sounds, but if one of them sounds strange to you, try the other one.

room	roof	root	broom
groom	hoof	coop	hoop
soot	rooster	soon	hooves

20. If you have a non-English language background, however, you may confuse [u] and [ʊ]. Remember that if your lips are insufficiently rounded or if your tongue is allowed to become too lax, [u] will sound more like [ʊ], the vowel sound in *took.* Your tongue and lips should be relatively tense for [u], but more relaxed for [ʊ].

   a.

[u]	[ʊ]	[u]	[ʊ]
fool	full	Luke	look
wooed	wood	pool	pull
stewed	stood	cooed	could
shooed	should	who'd	hood

   b. If it looks too good to be true, it is too good to be true.
   c. Luke looked at the hood who'd wooed Lucy Cook.
   d. The troop of Sioux threw two bouquets and plumes to Ruth.
   e. Never let a fool kiss you or a kiss fool you.
   f. I know only two tunes. One of them is "Yankee Doodle," and the other isn't. [Ulysses S. Grant]
   g. How old would you be if you didn't know how old you were?
   h. Fools look to tomorrow. Wise men use tonight.
   i. The trouble with being a good sport is that you have to lose to prove it.

MIDDLE (CENTRAL) VOWELS

Example   [ɝ]: <u>Ea</u>rly b<u>ir</u>ds who ch<u>ir</u>p in f<u>ir</u> trees do not catch eme<u>rg</u>ing w<u>or</u>ms.

How to . . .

Your tongue should be slightly retracted, and the central portion should be raised mid-high toward the palate. Curl the tongue tip back slightly toward the hard palate. Your lips should be unrounded and open. The vowel [ɝ] occurs only in stressed syllables.

Regional Differences

If you use General American dialect, the [r] element of your [ɝ] is apt to be prominent. If you're from New England, New York or some southern states, you'll use less [r].

Faults and Foibles

Prolonged [ɝ]

Some speakers produce a satisfactory [ɝ] by curling the front of the tongue backward toward the hard palate. If the degree of tongue-curling is excessive, a hard and unpleasant sound may result. The sound shouldn't be prolonged, the tongue held too tensely or retracted too far.

21. Avoid a hard or stretched-out [ɝ] as you read these.

   a. If you learn from hard knocks, you can also learn from soft touches.
   b. A happy life is one spent in learning, earning, and yearning. [Lillian Gish]
   c. Burping in church during the sermon is a faux pas.
   d. One must try to worry about things that aren't important so one won't worry too much about things that are.
   e. I don't deserve this award, but I have arthritis and I don't deserve that either. [Bob Hope]
   f. He referred to the murder that occurred in Jersey.
   g. Colonel Merle Virgil purchased the ermine furs for Myrtle and Irma.
   h. Hollywood is where a boy grows up and marries the girl next door and the girl next door to her.

Inversions and Insertions

The salesperson who says

> A hund**er**d p**re**cent p**er**fer our product.

instead of

> A hund**re**d p**er**cent p**re**fer our product.

is inverting *re* or *er*—in other words, saying them backward. English spelling isn't always helpful as far as pronunciation is concerned. Now and then, however, it's a reliable guide. With that in mind, read the following. Which pronunciation (and don't say *pernunciation*) is standard?

child**er**n–child**re**n	p**re**fect–p**er**fect
p**er**tend–p**re**tend	p**er**scription–p**re**scription
p**re**form–p**er**form	p**er**vail–p**re**vail
mod**re**n–mod**er**n	t**er**mendous–t**re**mendous

Insertions: Don't insert an extra and unwanted sound before or after the vowel in question. Easterners, and especially those in the New York City-New Jersey area, should avoid saying *bird* [bɝd] so that it sounds something like *be-id* [bɝɪd], *be-uhd* [bɝəd], *buh-id* [bʌɪd] or worse, *boid* [bɔɪd]

   (It's only fair to say that, except for *oi*, these insertions seem to be acceptable in some Southern speech.)

22. Don't reverse *er* and *re* sounds as you read this material. Avoid adding an extra sound before or after [ɝ], unless educated people in your area do so.

   a.
heard	gird	Bert	lurk
whirl	jerk	earth	verse
dirt	curl	fur	pearl
third	burn	curse	girl

   b. To earn while you learn is worthy; to learn while you earn is perfect.
   c. A bird in the hand is worth what it will bring.
   d. The service we render to others is really the rent we pay for our room on this earth.
   e. Perfume: any smell that is used to drown a worse one.
   f. If a little bird whispers some gossip in your ear, be sure it isn't a cuckoo bird.
   g. Her capacity for affection is superb. When her third husband died, her hair turned quite gold from grief.
   h. A good nurse does more than take your temperature. A good nurse can make sickness a pleasure.
   i. She tried to preserve the perfume that spoiled the pattern on the apron.
   j. "Perhaps this prescription will prevent you from dying," said the Presbyterian.
   k. The weather expert, who is one hundred percent right, says to prepare for precipitation.

$\ni r$

Example   Robert Baker, the other actor, played the killer better in *Murder in Amsterdam*.

How to . . .

Almost the same as for [ɜ], but it's more relaxed, and your tongue position may be lower. The vowel sound [ɚ] occurs only in unstressed syllables and is shorter in duration and not as loud as [ɜ]

Say *murder* [ˈmɜdɚ] and you'll hear the difference.

The vowel [ɚ] occurs mostly in General American speech. Speakers from eastern New England, large areas of the South, and sections of New York City tend to use [ə] without "r coloring." Words such as *rather* and *other* sound like *rathuh* [ˈræðə] and *othuh* [ˈʌðə].

Faults and Foibles

Don't make a big production of [ɚ]. Don't emphasize it; don't prolong it.

23.   As you practice this material, don't neglect [ɚ], but don't draw it out.

    a.   The worst-tempered people I've ever met were people who knew they were wrong.
    b.   Who never makes an error never plays ball.
    c.   For a dancer, but not a scholar, a good calf is better than a good head.
    d.   An elephant never forgets—but after all, what has it got to remember?
    e.   A nightingale dies for shame if another bird sings better.
    f.   Go to your business, pleasure, while I go to my pleasure, business.
    g.   Don't go berserk. Don't force it. Get a larger hammer.
    h.   Erlene murmured that Herbert had tossed the dollar mirror into the harbor.

$u - \breve{u}$

Example   Uncle Chuck discovered the lucky buck buried under a ton of mud.

How to . . .

Open your mouth, and relax your jaw and tongue. Raise the central part of your tongue slightly. The lips are unrounded.

Faults and Foibles

Substitutions

[ɪ] or [ɛ] is sometimes substituted for [ʌ].

    Result: *just* [dʒʌst] will be mispronounced as *jist* [dʒɪst] or *jest* [dʒɛst].

24.   There are many [ʌ] sounds in this material. Be careful to articulate [ʌ] rather than [ɪ] or [ɛ].

    a.   Never miss a good chance to shut up.
    b.   You don't judge a book by its cover, so why pay for the cover?
    c.   Suburbs are things to come to the city from.
    d.   More muggings are taking place in broad daylight. Muggers are afraid to be out at night with all that money on them.

e. Let us so live that when we come to die even the undertaker will be sorry.
f. You're never too old to become younger. [Gloria Steinem]
g. If fortune smiles, who doesn't? If fortune doesn't, who does?
h. The old-time mother, who used to wonder where her boy was, now has a grandson who wonders where his mother is.

Many other languages don't have [ʌ], and students with non-English language backgrounds may substitute [ɑ] for [ʌ]. Remember, [ʌ] is a relaxed central vowel that may need a slight raising of the central portion of your tongue. Also, raise the tongue higher for [ʌ] than for [ɑ].

25. Don't confuse [ɑ] with [ʌ] as you read:

a.
calm–come	dock–duck	shot–shut
knot–nut	mock–muck	log–lug
sop–sup	got–gut	rock–ruck
cob–cub	hot–hut	cop–cup

b. Middle age occurs when you are too young to take up golf and too old to rush up to the net.
c. The dog dug in the sod and gnawed under the tree before Don was done.
d. The perils of duck hunting are great, especially for the duck.
e. One does not get a headache from what other people have drunk.
f. The Great Author of all made everything out of nothing, but many a human author makes nothing out of everything.
g. One who drinks a little too much drinks much too much.
h. So many people are taking drugs, it's no wonder they believe the Martians are coming.
i. The chances of getting eaten up by a lion on Main Street aren't one in a million, but once would be enough.

 ə

Example   Anita was amazed to find Eva, the adult baboon, eating bananas in the arena.

How to . . .
[ə] is formed the same way as [ʌ], but it's shorter and weaker.

The sound is known as a *schwa.* This odd little word comes from a German word *schwach,* which means weak. Compare the schwa of *ago* [əˈgo] with the [ʌ] of *up* [ʌp] and you'll notice that it's weaker, shorter in duration and receives less stress.

The schwa is the most commonly used vowel in our language. English spelling doesn't indicate how often we use it. Take the word *about.* Even if you say it slowly, you won't pronounce the initial *a* with the same sound you use in *ask* [æsk]:[æˈbaʊt]. So we say [əˈbaʊt].

How do we pronounce the underlined *o* in *welcome?* To use the *o* that we use in *go* or *not* would make your pronunciation stilted. Again, the unstressed vowel becomes [ə]: [ˈwɛlkəm].

There's a definite tendency for vowel sounds in unstressed positions to lose their individual coloring and identities and become [ə].

Faults and Foibles
There are two problems involving [ə].

Speakers with slovenly diction often omit or swallow the sound. It's a helpful little sound, and there's no reason for eliminating it.

The schwa may be unnecessarily tacked on to the beginnings of many verbs. One of the speech mannerisms of those who try to create an impression of being "folksy" or quaint is the insertion of [ə]. In certain "folksy" speech we hear:

I'm *a*-comin' and then we're *a*-goin' *a*-fishin'.

If there is such a thing as small-town General American dialect, this is certainly one of its characteristics. The intruded [ə] is heard frequently not only in the Midwest, but it is also widely heard in certain areas of the South and Southwest. This mannerism should be eliminated.

26. Watch for unstressed vowels as you read the exercise material. If the schwa substitution is acceptable, use it, but don't emphasize it. A "tap," a short vocal grunt, will do. Don't hang [ə] onto certain verbs.

   a.

again	about	cruel	data
lion	omen	terrible	Idaho
camera	sofa	Carolina	parade
symbol	riot	annoy	poem

   b. Nora admitted that the breakfast chocolate was appalling.
   c. We are all terrified by the idea of being terrified.
   d. It is now possible for a flight attendant to get a pilot pregnant. [Richard Ferris, President, United Air Lines]
   e. There is nothing more cranky than a constipated gorilla.
   f. Texas: Second-largest state in the Union—where Alaskans should spend the winter.
   g. The cobra will bite you whether you call it cobra or Mr. Cobra. [Indian proverb]
   h. The adults were in a coma as they sat under the umbrellas washing potatoes.
   i. Rita adores dancing and singing when the orchestra is playing.

27. The most common word in the English language? *I*. The second most common? *The*.
   Few of us have trouble with the pronoun. Quite a few of us get addled with the article.
   If you say "THEE higher you get in THUH evening, THEE lower your feel in THEE morning"—your THEE and THUH are reversed.
   The rules are simple.
   The is pronounced THUH [ðə] if it's followed by a consonant: THUH girl, THUH book, THUH zebra.
   The is pronounced THEE [ði] if it's followed by a vowel: THEE apple, THEE Indian, THEE onion.
   Read these:

   a. The emptier the pot, the quicker the boil—watch your temper.
   b. It's not the ups and downs of life that bother the average man. It's the jerks.
   c. The expressway is a highway with three lanes—the right lane, the left lane and the one you're in when you see the exit.
   d. It's often the last key on the ring that opens the door.
   e. You can't deal with the serious things in the world unless you understand the amusing things first.
   f. Juvenile delinquency starts in the high chair and could end in the electric chair.

Smorgasbord: Review Material for All the Vowels

28. **Front Vowels**
   The material in this section emphasizes vowels in which the front part of your tongue is most active.

[i]	ē	[ɛ]	e or ĕ
[ɪ]	i or ĭ	[æ]	a or ă
[e]	ā		

   a. Fill what's empty. Empty what's full. And scratch where it itches.
   b. Any man who pits his intelligence against a fish and loses has it coming.
   c. A baby sitter feeds the baby at ten, twelve, and two—and herself at nine, eleven and one.
   d. Some people say that the squeaky wheel gets the grease, but others point out that it's the first one to be replaced.

e. Sleeping at the wheel is a good way to keep from growing old.
f. If the world laughs at you, laugh right back—it's as funny as you are.
g. A real friend will tell you when you have spinach stuck in your teeth.
h. If you think a seat belt is uncomfortable, you've never tried a stretcher.
i. Germs attack the weakest part of the body—which is the reason for head colds.
j. The difference between a king and a president is this: a king is the son of his father—a president isn't.
k. Bette Midler's ten favorite dinner guests from all history: "I realize that I might have a seating problem with this creep heap, but on the other hand, the table chitchat would be a blast." Ivan the Terrible, Jack the Ripper, John Wilkes Booth, Adolf Hitler, Lizzie Borden, Nero, Joe Stalin, Dracula, Lady Macbeth, Charles Manson.

29. **Back Vowels**
The material in this section emphasizes vowels in which the back part of your tongue is most active.

[u] o͞o   [ɔ] ô
[ʊ] o͝o   [ɑ] ä
[o] ō

a. Moonshine is all moonshine to me.
b. Modern art: oodles of doodles.
c. Let us be thankful for fools; but for them, the rest of us could not succeed.
d. Tact consists in knowing how far to go too far.
e. Never go to a doctor whose office plants have died.
f. Some are born good, some make good, and some are caught with the goods.
g. Even those who prefer smooth peanut butter are now faced with a crunch.
h. Some people are so dry that you might soak them in a joke for a month and it would not get through their skins.
i. People are called fools in one age for not knowing what they were called fools for in the age before.
j. Yesterday I was a dog. Today I'm a dog. Tomorrow I'll probably still be a dog. There's so little hope for advancement. [Snoopy]
k. Kissing is where two people get so close together that they can't see anything wrong with each other.
l. It takes more hot water to make cold water hot than it takes cold water to make hot water cold.

30. **Middle (Central) Vowels**
The material in this section emphasizes vowels in which the central part of your tongue is most active.

[ɝ-ɜ] ûr   [ɚ] ər
[ʌ]   u or ŭ   [ə] ə

a. Birds of a feather will gather together.
b. To the bachelor, horror films are pictures of a wedding.
c. Good luck is a lazy person's estimate of a worker's success.
d. People murder a child when they tell it to keep out of the dirt. In dirt is life.
e. Love your enemy—it will drive the person nuts.
f. A dog is the only thing on earth that loves you more than it loves itself.
g. California is a fine place to live in—if you happen to be an orange.
h. Everyone is crazy but me and thee, and sometimes I suspect thee a little.
i. If you're a surgeon, never say "oops!" in the operating room.
j. For three days after death, hair and fingernails continue to grow, but phone calls taper off.
k. We must have respect for both our plumbers and our philosophers or neither our pipes nor our theories will hold water.
l. We are hurried and worried until we're buried, and then there's no curtain call.

Assignment 12: Vowels

Prepare material containing many examples of the vowels that you have found troublesome. As a reminder, here is a key:

Front Vowels	**Back Vowels**	**Middle (Central) Vowels**
[i] ē as in *be*	[u] ōō as in m<u>oo</u>n	[ɝ-ɜ] ûr as in f<u>ir</u>
[ɪ] i or ĭ as in *hit*	[ʊ] oo as in l<u>oo</u>k	[ʌ] u or ŭ as in <u>up</u>
[e] ā as in c<u>a</u>ke	[o] ō as in c<u>o</u>ld	[ɚ] ər as in ev<u>er</u>
[ɛ] e or ĕ as in l<u>e</u>d	[ɔ] ô as in <u>a</u>ll	[ə] ə as in ide<u>a</u>
[æ] a or ă as in <u>a</u>sk	[ɑ] ä as in <u>a</u>lms	

Suggested Checklist for Assignment 12

As you practice by yourself, you may want to work with this checklist. Listen carefully to yourself. If it is feasible, record the assignment, or get a classmate or friend to listen to you as you read the material. Eventually, your goal will be to have a check mark in the **Yes** column for each category. (Optional: Perhaps your instructor will want to use the checklist to evaluate you during your classroom presentation.)

	Yes	No
Front Vowels		
Avoids—		
nasalizing [e], [ɛ], or [æ]		
adding schwa [ə] to [i] or [ɪ]		
distorting [æ]		
muffled [ɪ]		
Avoids Substituting—		
[ɪ] for [i], [i] for [ɪ], or [ɛ] for [ɪ]		
[e] for [ɛ] or [ɛ] for [e]		
[æ] or [ɪ] for [ɛ]		
[ʌ], [ɛ], [ɪ], or [ɑ] for [æ]		

	Yes	No

Back Vowels

<u>Avoids</u>—

    nasalizing [ɑ], [ɔ], [o], [ʊ] or [u]

    adding [ɚ] to [ɔ] or [ɑ]

    inserting [ə] and [wə] after [u]

    inserting [ɛ] before [o]

Avoids Substituting—

    [ʊ] for [u], [u] for [ʊ]

    [ʌ] for [ʊ] or [u]

    [ɪ] and [ɛ] for [ʌ]

Middle (Central) Vowels

<u>Avoids</u>—

    prolonging [ɝ] or [ɚ]

    inserting [ə] where it doesn't belong

    omitting the schwa [ə]

    confusing [i] and [ə] in "the" words

    confusing [ɝ] and [ɜ]

    inverting <u>re</u> and <u>er</u> sounds

Avoids Substituting—

    [ɔI] for [ɝ] or [ɜ]

    [ɪ], [ɛ], [ɔ], or [ɑ] for [ʌ]

Additional comments or suggestions:

DIPHTHONGS

HOW NOW, BROWN COW? Check your *ow* sound!

Say the words slowly, and you'll discover that the two vowels you're merging in each word are [ɑ] as in *ah* + [ʊ] as in *book*. Now meld [ɑ] quickly with [ʊ], and you'll make the diphthong [ɑʊ].

A diphthong is a rapid blending together of two separate vowel sounds within the same syllable.

However, a diphthong isn't always represented by two letters in everyday spelling. The *i* in *night* is also a diphthong. Say the sound in slow motion, and you'll hear both vowels: [ɑ] as in *ah* + [ɪ] as in *it*.

Blend the two rapidly and you'll produce [ɑɪ].

 or  $\bar{\imath}$

Example   Lila guided the five skydivers down the aisle to the high wire.

(NOTE: [ɑɪ] is most commonly heard in New England. Both [ɑɪ] and [ɑɪ] are used by educated speakers in all parts of the country.)

How to . . .

Start out with [ɑ]. Lower your tongue to a flat position and drop your jaw quite far. Now move to the [ɪ] position and lift your tongue relatively high.

Faults and Foibles

You don't have to be a UN interpreter to translate the following sentences, but it would help.

Ah fahnally opened mah ahs.
He fahred his rahfle at the lah-uhn.
The qwahr sang qwah-uhtly Frahday nah-ut.

Puzzled?
Try them again. Wherever you see *ah* or *ah-uh,* substitute [ɑɪ].
Southern? Southeastern? Southwestern?
Many speakers in these areas linger so long on the first vowel component—the [ɑ]—that they cheat on the second one, turning it into *uh* [ə].

like becomes *lah-uhk* [lɑək]
dine becomes *dah-uhn* [dɑən]

In more extreme cases, the second vowel component—the [ɪ]—is allowed to evaporate completely. We hear *lahk, dahn* [lɑk, dɑn].

31. Depending on your geographical locale, you may or may not wish to modify your [ɑɪ] diphthong. If you do, avoid overstressing or dropping either element of [ɑɪ] as you practice this material.

    a.
sign	admire	buy	china	geyser
height	biceps	lie	style	rhyme
kite	fly	isle	eye	pie
try	quite	icicle	choir	miser

    b.   A lie in time saves nine.
    c.   Trying to define yourself is like trying to bite your own teeth.
    d.   Don't wait for pie in the sky when you die! Get yours now, with ice cream on top.
    e.   The fly that doesn't want to be swatted is most secure when it lights on the fly swatter.
    f.   I not only try to use all the brains I have, but all I can borrow.

g. My interest is in the future because I am going to spend the rest of my life there.
h. No matter which side of an argument you're on, you always find quite a few people on your side that you wish were on the other side.
i. One who says "What's mine is yours and what's yours is yours" is a saint. The one who says "What's yours is mine and what's mine is mine" is a vile person.
j. Try to be kind to everybody. You never know who might show up on the jury at your trial.
k. "I mourn death, I disperse the lightning, I announce the Sabbath, I rouse the lazy, I scatter the winds, I appease the bloodthirsty." [Inscription on old bell]
l. Fame is chiefly a matter of dying at the right time.
m. Have you ever noticed that a fire department never fights fire with fire?
n. Times are especially trying for those who aren't trying.
o. I've tried relaxing, but—I don't know—I feel more comfortable tense. [Michael Jackson]
p. Some folks commit a crime and go to jail; others commit a crime, write a book and get rich.

 or $[\mathrm{a\upsilon}]$ ou

Example Howard Gow, the outlaw, hid our brown sow south of the mound of flowers.
(NOTE: Both [ɑʊ] and [aʊ] are used by educated speakers in all parts of the country.)

How to . . .
Start with the [ɑ] position. Your tongue should be fairly low and your lips unrounded. Then as you move toward the position for [ʊ], elevate your tongue and round your lips.

Faults and Foibles

[æ + ʊ] *or* [ɛ + ʊ] *substitutions*
In certain sections of the East, notably in the New York City, Philadelphia, and Baltimore areas, as well as in a few scattered regions of the South, [ɑʊ] is often made as an extremely piercing, hooty sound. Instead of using [ɑ] as the first vowel element, some speakers from these areas use the [æ] of *as* or the [ɛ] of *egg*.

A combination of [æ + ʊ] or of [ɛ + ʊ] in place of [ɑ + ʊ] generally results in a sound that is exceedingly disagreeable. It often happens if your tongue is raised too high or held too tensely. A tight, taut jaw will also give this diphthong a vinegary edginess. The sound has been likened to the "meow" of an irritable cat.

32. In the following, pronounce:
ah as [ɑ]
oo as [ʊ]
ow or *ou* as [ɑʊ]
    Read across the page. Don't forget: Your jaw *must* drop on [ɑ].

(Stretch the *ah* sounds)	(Say slowly)	(Say rapidly)
dah	dah–oo	down
clah	clah–oo	clown
mah	mah–oo	mound
sah	sah–oo	sound
hah	hah–oo	hound
nah	nah–oo	noun
pah	pah–oo	pound
rah	rah–oo	round
crah	crah–oo	crowd
jah	jah–oo	joust

33. As you read the material below, painstakingly avoid [æ] or [ɛ] as the first vowel element of the *ou* or *ow* blends. Always start with that relaxed and open-jawed [ɑ].

a.

scout	tower	outrage	plow	bough
owl	louse	scowl	ouch	bower
devout	county	foul	wow	tout
dowel	gout	cowl	glower	fountain

b. Outer space: our largest suburb.

c. Cowards do not count in battle; they are there but not in it.

d. Live around wolves and you'll soon learn how to howl.

e. Some men have a den in their house, while others just growl all over the house.

f. A mousetrap; easy to enter but not easy to get out of.

g. Better to be a devout coward than a corpse.

h. By the time you know what it's all about, it's about all over.

i. Holding down public office is like dancing on a crowded dance floor. No matter how you move around, you're bound to rub someone the wrong way.

j. Seven out of ten people in our country can't remember life without television.

k. We lie loudest when we lie to ourselves.

l. Hours and flowers soon fade away.

m. Politician: one who tells it like it is after he found out what it was.

n. The darkest hour in the life of a youth is when that person sits down to study how to get money without honestly earning it.

o. One of the major problems we face each summer is how to get the watermelon into the refrigerator without taking the beer cans out.

p. Tax the farmer; tax his fowl;
Tax his dog; tax his howl.
Tax the coffins; tax the shrouds.
Tax the souls beyond the clouds.
Tax them all and tax them well,
And do your best to make life hell.

q. Everything great that we know has come to us from neurotics. They alone have founded our religions and created our masterpieces. Never will the world be aware of how much it owes to them, nor above all, how much they suffered in order to bestow their gifts on it. [Marcel Proust]

Exaggerated Nasality

Substituting the brittle [æ] or [ɛ] for the [ɑ] portion of [ɑʊ] produces an ugly, fingernails-on-the-chalkboard sound, but there's another complication. The vowels [æ] and [ɛ] are often nasalized, especially if a nasal sound [m], [n], or [ŋ] precedes or follows them. Add excessive nasality to [æʊ] or [ɛʊ], and a metallic and tense diphthong results.

34. Practice this material, avoiding [æ-ɛ] variations or exaggerated nasality in *ou* and *ow* words.

a. The brown mouse ran around the mountain town.

b. When you're down and out, lift up your head and shout, "I'm down and out!"

c. I swapped my cat and got me a mouse. Its tail caught fire and burned down the house.

d. There's a big difference between good, sound reasons and reasons that sound good.

e. We join the noisy crowd to drown out the loudness of our own silence.

f. Liz Downes announced that she would count the crowns in the lounge.

g. It sounded as if Joan Mount wanted to impound a large amount of beef.

h. Each of us should have personal sounds to listen for. The wind outside is one of my sounds—a lonely sound, perhaps, but soothing. One of the greatest sounds of all—and to me it is a sound—is utter silence. [Emily Dickinson]

[ɔɪ]

oi

Example   The n<u>oi</u>sy b<u>oy</u>s br<u>oi</u>led R<u>oy</u>'s sirl<u>oi</u>n in the s<u>oy</u> sauce.

How to . . .

Start the sound from the position for [ɔ] as in *awe*. The back of your tongue is generally elevated, and your lips are slightly rounded. Then let your tongue glide effortlessly to the position for [ɪ] as in *it*.

Faults and Foibles

Annoys is defined by some New Yorkers as the lady who checks your pulse in the hospital.

The "beautiful goil with the poils on toity-toid street" type of speech in the New York City area isn't quite as common as non-New Yorkers like to think. But it does show up. And some citizens of the Big Apple pronounce *girl* without an [r]: *ge-il* [gɛɪl].

And the same beautiful goil—with or without the poils—may drive her car into a *soivice* station to have her *erl* [ɝl] checked. Her cousin, a Dallas debutante, may ask the attendant to check the *all* [ɔl] in her Ferrari.

In some provincial or countrified speech, [ɑɪ] replaces [ɔɪ]. The friendly mountain folk of West Virginia, for example, may readily ask you to *jine* [dʒɑɪn] instead of *join* [dʒɔɪn] them.

35. If you've been told that your [ɔɪ] is quaint, rustic or otherwise attention-getting, rehearse the drill material below.

For comparison and contrast, read the following words across the page. Most problems with [ɔɪ] result from too much lip rounding. Remember that as you say [ɔɪ], your lips should move from a slightly rounded to a relaxed and unrounded position.

boil	Burl	bile	ball	boil
foil	furl	file	fall	foil
loin	learn	line	lawn	loin
poise	purrs	pies	paws	poise

36. As soon as you feel that you have a stable and unblemished [ɔɪ], read these:

    a.

loiter	point	destroy	gargoyle
toyed	soy	foist	Roy
doily	void	choice	loin
voice	envoy	toil	poignant

    b. What kind of a noise annoys a foiled oyster?
    c. The biggest difference between men and boys is the cost of their toys.
    d. If oil spoils water, perhaps the answer to oil spills is to paper train the oil tankers.
    e. Airfares have increased considerably. Even the cost of going up is going up.
    f. Many have pointed out that boys will be boys, but they don't have to be the James boys.
    g. There's many a boy here today who looks on war with great joy, but, boys, it is all hell.
    h. Your greatest desire is your path to joy, but don't let it destroy you.
    i. Detroit is Cleveland without the glitter.
    j. Satan has no unemployment problem.
    k. Gamblers are like toilets—broke one day and flush the next.

Smorgasbord: Review Material for All the Diphthongs

37. Read this material:

   a. In baiting a mousetrap with cheese, always leave room for the mouse.
   b. Playboy: a plowboy with a Rolls Royce.
   c. I'm trying to arrange my life so that I don't even have to be present.
   d. Most of the time I don't have much fun. The rest of the time I don't have any fun at all. [Woody Allen]
   e. I hate television. I hate it as much as I hate peanuts. But I can't stop eating peanuts. [Jackie Gleason]
   f. Small children, small annoys; big children, big annoys.
   g. The important thing is not to let oneself be poisoned. Hatred poisons.
   h. The devil doesn't know how to sing, only how to howl.
   i. When a person is down in the world, an ounce of help is better than a pound of preaching.
   j. I went to a fight the other night and a hockey game broke out.
   k. An orator tries to see how long he can talk without saying anything.
   l. Thanks to the moisturizing creams my wife buys, she's oily to bed and oily to rise. [Rodney Dangerfield]
   m. It's much wiser to love thy neighbor than his wife.
   n. It's funny how a bottle of brew can lead to bubble, bubble, toil and trouble.
   o. How can you rejoice, if you've never joiced? How can your reconnoiter, if you've never connoitered?
   p. I haven't been wrong since 1979 when I thought I made a mistake.
   q. Life's what's important. Walking, houses, family. Birth and pain and joy—and then dying. Acting is just standing around waiting for custard pie. That's what it's all about. [Katharine Hepburn]
   r. If you like it, they don't have it in your size. If you like it and it's in your size, it doesn't quite fit. If you like it and it fits, you can't afford to buy it. If you like it, it fits, and you can afford to buy it, it falls apart the first time you try to wear it.
   s. Let's have a merry journey, and shout about how light is good and dark is not. What we should do is not future ourselves so much. We should now ourselves more. "Now thyself" is more important than "Know thyself." Get high on now. Reason is what tells us to ignore the present and live in the future. So all we do is make plans. We think that somewhere there are going to be green pastures. Why? It's crazy. Heaven is nothing but a grand instance of the future. Listen, now is good. Now is wonderful. Enjoy now. [Mel Brooks]
   t. The tourist stopped his car on a road and asked a boy how far it was to Mountainville. With a twinkle in his eye, the little boy smiled and said, "It's about twenty-five thousand miles the way you're going, but if you turn around, it's about four."
   u. Prayer of high school senior: Please lead me out of this constant coma, And give me a chance at my diploma. Let others fight about church and state. I pray only to graduate.

Assignment 13: Diphthongs

Prepare material containing many examples of those diphthongs with which you particularly need work. As a reminder, here is a key.

[ɑɪ]	ī as in my	[ɑʊ]	ou as in cow
[ɔɪ]	oi as in oil		

Suggested Checklist for Assignment 13

As you practice by yourself, you may want to work with this checklist. Listen carefully to yourself. If it is feasible, record the assignment, or get a classmate or friend to listen to you as you read the material. Eventually, your goal will be to have a check mark in the **Yes** column for each category. (Optional: Perhaps your instructor will want to use the checklist to evaluate you during your classroom presentation.)

Avoids—

nasalizing diphthongs

Avoids Substituting—

[ɝ], [ɛɪ], or [ɑɪ] for [ɔɪ]

[æʊ] or [ɛʊ] for [ɑʊ]

Avoids Overstressing, Weakening, or Dropping—

either vowel element of [ɑɪ]

either vowel element of [ɑʊ]

either vowel element of [ɔɪ]

Additional comments or suggestions:

WRAP-UP

1. A vowel is a vocal sound produced by relatively free passage of the breath stream through the vocal tract. Changes in the size and shape of the oral cavity help to make one vowel different from another.

2. To produce these front vowels, the front portion of the tongue is most active.

[i]	ē
[ɪ]	i or ĭ
[e]	ā
[ɛ]	e or ĕ
[æ]	a or ă

    To produce these back vowels, the back portion of the tongue is most active.

[u]	o͞o
[ʊ]	oo
[o]	ō
[ɔ]	ô
[ɑ]	ä

    To produce these middle or central vowels, the middle portion of the tongue is most active.

[ɝ-ɜ]	ûr
[ɚ]	ər
[ʌ]	u or ŭ
[ə]	ə

3. Diphthongs are smooth blends of two different vowel sounds within the same syllable. A diphthong changes quality during production. The first vowel receives greater stress than the second.

[ɑɪ]	ī
[ɑʊ]	ou
[ɔɪ]	oi

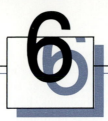

SPEAK UP! LOUDNESS

WOULD YOU BELIEVE THAT

. . . There is documented evidence of permanent deafness striking rock musicians who perform on an average of about twelve hours a week for one year?

. . . The barrel-chested tenor, Enrico Caruso, never at any time in his career shattered a wine glass or a mirror by singing high C at full volume? Nor is there any evidence that any other singer has ever accomplished this feat.

. . . The most powerful orator of all times, Demosthenes, was a weak, awkward, and skinny youth? He not only stuffed pebbles in his mouth to slow himself down, but also to increase his vocal strength and volume. He enjoyed giving speeches above the roar of the sea, and he ran up and down hills, declaiming at the top of his voice.

. . . Astronauts, when in outer space, don't snore? Weightlessness lets the uvula float.

. . . The word *decibel* is derived from the inventor of the telephone—Alexander Graham Bell? Volume or loudness is measured in units known as decibels.
> A whisper measures about 20 decibels
> Ordinary conversation—60 decibels
> Lawnmowers—90 decibels
> Symphony orchestra (playing Wagner full blast)—100 decibels
> Sting (playing Sting full blast)—120 decibels
> Pain level—140 decibels ("The Who" rock group has been clocked at 141 decibels!)

APPROPRIATE LOUDNESS

"Sorry, can't hear you!"
"What did you say?"
"Would you speak a little louder, please?"

How often do people say these to you?

So you turn up your volume. Or maybe you just think you do. How well DOES your voice carry?

For many students, urban living has meant growing up in an environment of apartments, condominiums and nearby neighbors. Youngsters who from ages two to twenty are constantly being shushed by parents become, in time, intimidated enough to reduce their loudness levels and speak in vocalized whispers. Another bad habit launched.

Let's consider Lisa in the back row of the classroom. As far as she's concerned, she's physically unable to talk any louder. Possibly she has a mental block. *She doesn't want to hear herself any louder.* Her own value system and her own personal code of behavior dictate that a quiet, soft speaking level is ideal and that loudness has something to do with aggressive, sometimes even obnoxious, behavior. Lisa simply doesn't feel comfortable speaking loudly to a group of people. Extraverts are always loudmouths, thinks Lisa. Sometimes they are.

And two hundred-pound Mike, seated front-and-center, may have the same block. He doesn't want to speak in a way that conflicts with his own self-image. He's a gentleman, and gentlemen don't raise their voices. In both cases, shyness or reserve may have a lot to do with inadequate loudness.

Something else bugs the Lisas and the Mikes (and they may react by turning down their own volume): the noisy, blaring, raucous world around them of radios and record players, Rock and Rachmaninoff being played simultaneously (full blast), TV sets, low-flying 747's, Yamaha bikes, souped-up cars with exploding mufflers, sirens, bells, and whistles. Added to these are the yells, grunts, squeaks, and squawks of the human sonic boom: those bratty neighborhood kids, the mob at the shopping mall or at the park on Sundays, and the crazy parties next door.

(Overheard in Classroom)

Lori: Who's partying this weekend?

Dan: Who isn't?

Help! "He that hath ears to hear, let him stuff them with cotton," indeed! Lisa and Mike gave up a long time ago. Can you blame them? Undoubtedly under some circumstances silence *is* the best solution.

It's an eye-opening—or maybe I should say an "ear-opening"—experience to attend some public meetings. Listen to Joan and John Hancock try to get in their "two-bits worth" from the floor. In many cases, you may listen, but you won't necessarily hear. A startling number of these well-intentioned speakers can't be heard throughout the room. Their voices simply don't carry. Microphones aren't always available. And have you noticed? They don't always work when they're supposed to.

A person who can't be heard is wasting the listener's time. Communication is a two-way street. If A can't hear what B is saying, there is no communication!

It's impossible for you to judge your own levels of loudness. Your voice is amplified by the bones in your skull, and it always seems as loud as World War II to your own ears. Anyway, you know what you're thinking, so why shouldn't you know what you're saying?

Talking too softly suggests that you're an insecure person, unsure of yourself. And what's worse—it signals your listeners that you don't genuinely believe in what you're saying.

On the other hand, the person who is constantly bellowing and roaring is, literally, a pain in the ear. Have you ever been stuck with a telephone "blaster"? He hears himself so loudly that he can't hear anyone else. To preserve your eardrums, not to mention your sanity, you have to hold the telephone at arm's length.

You're not being asked to develop loudness merely for the sake of loudness. Your voice, however, mustn't be so weak that it can't be heard under ordinary speaking circumstances, nor should it be so loud that it calls undesirable attention to itself.

Loudness must be adequate for the situation, but it must also be tempered and varied.

VOCAL ABUSE

Whatever time of the year it is when you read this page, the chances are that you are in the football, basketball, hockey, or baseball seasons.

Maybe you're going to a game this weekend. Plan to do some yelling? Lots of luck! What you'll probably find yourself doing is going from loud to louder to loudest! Swept along by the enthusiasm of the crowd, we find ourselves shouting at the top of our lungs. A prominent vocal therapist has a few words of warning.

> Cheerleaders stand to lose more than their voices. Most of them damage their vocal cords, and this can lead to a host of professional or personal problems. Nobody can scream for two or three hours without doing a lot of damage.

In more than one sense, the noisemaking is half the fun of attending a sports event. Now and then, however, some of us report to classes or work the following Monday morning with a vocal "hangover." The throat is raw and inflamed, and the voice—what is left of it—is unpleasantly hoarse. It hurts to talk. When this happens, we generally attribute our sore throats to excessive yelling, shrug it off, and assume that in a day or two most of the hoarseness and rawness will disappear. Vocal hangovers are by no means confined to sports enthusiasts. Lawyers, teachers, actors, and speakers—more often the green, inexperienced novice than the seasoned professional—become victims of acute hoarseness. If this happens often enough, the novice may also be committing vocal suicide.

Yet, there are thousands of individuals who don't develop hoarseness, even though their occupations tax the larynx. How about Broadway stars who must get their voices across to a theater audience as often as eight times a week? How about election-year politicians and their door-to-door, stump-to-stump campaigning? How about teachers who must often lecture several hours daily in good-sized classrooms? Athletic coaches? Announcers? Ministers? Salespeople? Telephone operators?

Seldom do these individuals come down with vocal hangovers. The logical conclusion, then, is that it's quality rather than the quantity of loudness that leads to hoarseness.

STRENGTHENING THE VOICE
What factors are involved in developing an adequately loud voice?

Articulation
A person with a weak voice often doesn't open the mouth widely enough in speaking. The voice doesn't carry because, in a sense, it doesn't have much chance to get out of the mouth in the first place. Maybe it's true that convicts are sometimes forced to communicate with each other in this ventriloquist, not-moving-the-lips fashion, but it's poor practice for anyone else (unless you're planning a career of crime).

As an experiment, try the old tongue twister *Peter Piper picked a peck of pickled peppers* in three different ways.

- Say it as if your lips are glued together and your jaw wired shut.
- Say it with normal lip and jaw activity.
- Exaggerate lip and jaw activity. Open your mouth as widely as you can.

Can you feel and hear the difference?

If your class has already gone through the chapter on articulation, then you should know all about how to open your mouth and let the sounds come out. You should be an expert by now. But in case you haven't done Chapter 4, or if you feel in need of a little brushup, review Exercises 1–6 at the beginning of Chapter 4.

Proper Pitch Level
"Speak Low" is a smart song title, and it's good advice if you're lucky enough to own a naturally deep voice.

But it's not so good if you're trying to produce the voice-from-the-mummy's-tomb and speaking at a level that's too low for you. Or if you're a soprano who lets your voice soar into outer space—you may be speaking (or squeaking?) at a pitch level that's too high for you. If you have a loudness problem and believe that it has to do with your pitch level, investigate Chapter 7, Exercises 1–12.

Even if you're using your best pitch level, do you still permit your pitch to jump upward five or six tones when you read or speak with considerable loudness? The resulting sound is generally terrible. And talking this way can also be dangerous to the speaker. Remember the comment about vocal suicide?

Maximum Use of Resonance
Loudness, in part, results from the reinforcement of the original tone by the resonators. Openness of throat and freedom from undue muscular constrictions are important in developing loudness. If you need to, review Exercises 8–14 in Chapter 3.

Increase in Breath Pressure Below the Vocal Folds

A burly and seasoned drill sergeant whose job was teaching potential drill instructors once told me: "I don't tell 'em anything scientific about shoutin' commands. I just tell 'em to pack the tone from the guts. And it works!"

It probably does, too.

To put it more delicately, however, the sergeant was advising his students to get their propulsive power from their midregions. The strength and vitality that produce loud, firm tones *come from the muscles of breathing, mostly in the middle areas of your body,* and not from the muscles of your throat.

Clear Tone Quality

The individual whose voice is breathy, harsh, or hoarse may also have a problem getting the voice across. In particular, a breathy voice is generally a weak voice; a weak voice is generally a breathy voice. Which came first—the chicken or the egg? Of one thing you can be certain: if you're deliberately trying to be soft-voiced, wasted breath will help you reach your goal.

Conscious Control of Rate and Articulation

"Speak slower!"

Marvelous advice, and most of us pay as much attention to it as we do to "Drive carefully!" If you're told to slow down while talking, what you probably do is put longer pauses *between* words and phrases. (Try producing a loud pause and see what comes out.)

As far as loudness is concerned, what "Speak slower!" really means is slowing down *on* the words. Point up your vowels and diphthongs by hanging onto them and stre-e-e-etching them. They are the sounds that cut through.

Say *Stop.* You can make a lot more of the right kind of noise on the *o* than you can on the *st-p.* Try it.

Sufficient Energy and Animation

The tricky problems of personality and life-style enter the scene once more. You met Lisa and Mike a couple of pages ago. Shy, bashful individuals, however, aren't always the only ones unable to make themselves heard. Vocal laziness, not to mention indifference, hinders good projection. Another complication. The minute vocally lazy persons are urged to speak loudly enough, they protest: "But I'm screaming!" But *to their hearers,* they're not screaming.

If your emotional and physical health is good, you'll have excellent projection if you speak with more force and energy. Your entire body must respond! A well-projected voice doesn't merely reach its hearers, it penetrates them. Animation and power are there for the asking if you have something to say, a purpose in saying it and, above all, a strong desire to say it.

Billy Graham was asked how he attracted such mammoth audiences and held them spellbound. "I set myself on fire," he replied, "and they come to watch me burn!"

WHAT YOU'RE SAYING, WHERE YOU'RE SAYING IT, AND THE SIZE OF YOUR AUDIENCE

Nature of Material Being Presented

Material that expresses relatively strong and forceful emotions or ideas (happiness, elation, rage, anger, conviction) is often more effective if relatively loud levels are used. Material that expresses sadness, despair, profundity, moodiness, or sincerity is frequently more effective if relatively quiet levels are used.

Room or Area: Size and Acoustics

Speaking to an audience in an auditorium that seats two thousand or to a few friends in a small living room are two entirely different situations. Everybody knows that, and yet some speakers who find themselves in an unfamiliar room or area, make no effort to adjust their volume and who, without the aid of a mike, can't be heard. Rather than laziness, their problem is a lack of experience or an inability to adapt to circumstances.

Audience Size and Proximity (Nearness)

You shouldn't have to turn up your volume in a Coke, coffee, or Coors conversation with three friends in a booth to the same extent that you do if you're talking to thirty or three hundred people in a large hall. The nearness of the audience is also important. To a partner five feet away, you can pitch a baseball with a mere flick of the wrist. If the partner is standing fifty feet away, more energy and strength are required.

Competing Noises

Did you know that the general noise level in cities is rising at the rate of one decibel a year? This noise level includes banging air conditioners inside your classroom and gabby students in the hallway outside of your classroom. In the face of this, you must try to be heard without screaming or straining your voice.

LEVELS OF LOUDNESS

In some of these exercises, we'll experiment with three levels of loudness:

- Soft (avoid whispering)
- Medium loud
- Loud

1. As a sergeant in charge of a firing squad, you're about to give the commands *Ready! Aim! Fire!* three times. The first time, you're standing next to your squad. The first level of loudness will work. The second time, you're standing about ten yards from your squad. Second level of loudness. The third time, you're standing about twenty yards away. Third level. As you give the commands three times, don't try to control the pitch levels, and on the third one, let the sound "blast."

   As a result of this negative practice (*and don't try it more than once!*), you'll certainly feel or hear several things: an excessive upward swoop in pitch, a strangled and strident vocal quality on level three and a possible slight irritation in your throat. All of these are highly undesirable elements in achieving loudness.

2. Begin *ah* softly, and then increase it to your loudest tone of good quality. Hold the tone for a few seconds, and then decrease it to your softest tone of good quality. Repeat several times, keeping the pitch constant. Try it with *ee, oh, uh.*

3. Sustain *ah, ee, oh,* and *uh* at a comfortable pitch level for about five seconds. Keep the throat open, keep the pitch steady, and avoid strain.

   Try it at the three levels of loudness.

4. Musicians are concerned with signs and symbols as well as notes. The sign < indicates a gradual increase in loudness or intensity (a crescendo). The sign > indicates a gradual decrease in loudness or intensity (a decrescendo). As you practice:

- Keep your pitch level constant
- Avoid tightening your throat
- Think of the support coming from the muscles of breathing

Read the material as indicated.

a.

a b C D E F   G H I J k ı

b.

M N O P q r   S T U V w x

c.

a a B B C C   d d E E F F

d.

G G H H i i   j j K K L L

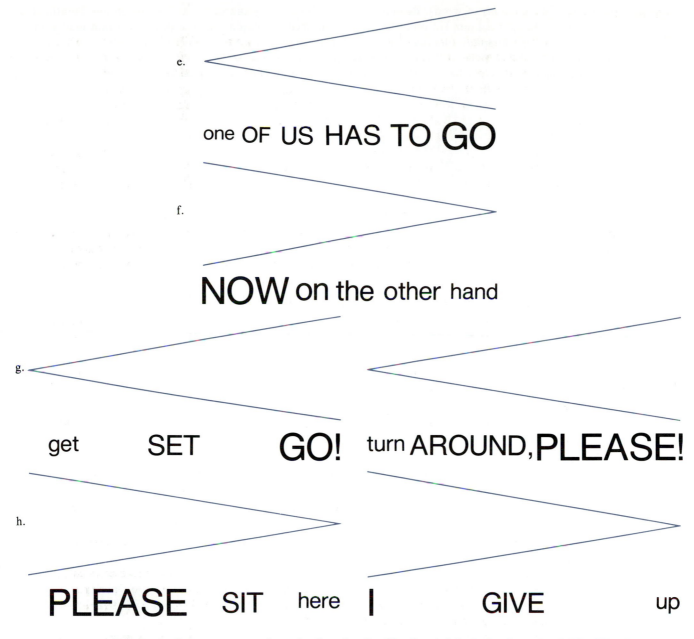

e.

one OF US HAS TO GO

f.

NOW on the other hand

g.

get   SET   GO!   turn AROUND, PLEASE!

h.

PLEASE   SIT   here   I   GIVE   up

5. In reading each of these commands at the three levels of loudness, inhale deeply and quickly. Give them some clout. Say them briskly but keep the throat as relaxed as possible. Notice the sudden contraction of your abdominal muscles as you project the phrases.

a. Bug off!	d. Eyes right!	g. Order arms!
b. Hands up!	e. All aboard!	h. Get lost!
c. Company, halt!	f. On the double!	i. Left face!

Exercises 6 through 8 coming up.

Staying in? If you've been reasonably comfortable with Exercises 1–5, you might be ready for a little change. Keep this uppermost in mind: Loudness is a *relative* term.

As a little switch, let's go for four levels of loudness.

■ *soft*

■ medium loud

■ LOUD

■ VERY LOUD

6. Below are four columns of words. Read across the columns. Say the same four words on one breath. Read the words in the first column (in italics) softly, in the second column (regular print) medium loudly, in the third column (small capitals) loudly, and in the fourth column (capitals) very loudly.

A little bodily activity will help you. Make fists, and as you say the word, punch out straight ahead of you. The louder the word, the bigger your punch. Sound silly? Of course it does. But it works. Try it.

hey	hey	HEY	HEY
no	no	NO	NO
sit	sit	SIT	SIT
leave	leave	LEAVE	LEAVE
out	out	OUT	OUT
die	die	DIE	DIE
ho	ho	HO	HO
now	now	NOW	NOW
arm	arm	ARM	ARM
play	play	PLAY	PLAY
push	push	PUSH	PUSH
deal	deal	DEAL	DEAL
roll	roll	ROLL	ROLL
hi	hi	HI	HI
row	row	ROW	ROW
nay	nay	NAY	NAY

7. Drill with these short sentences. The instructions in parentheses preceding each sentence in section *a* suggest a loudness level.

   a. **(Telephone conversation: quiet)** I'll see you in five minutes.
   (Casual, face-to-face) That prof's a rough grader.
   (Vigorous) You know better than that!
   (Strong determination) I refuse to listen to you!

As you read these sentences, repeat the pattern suggested in *a:*

   b. I have no idea where she is.
   Let's go on a picnic tonight.
   He always cheats in tests.
   I've never been so mad.
   c. Sorry, but I'm busy tonight.
   Sorry, but I'm busy tonight.
   Sorry, but I'm busy tonight.
   Sorry, but I'm busy tonight.
   d. I was just taking a nap.
   Where did you get that good-looking tie?
   Gosh, I can't wait for vacation.
   I want my money, and I want it now.
   e. I haven't seen you in months.
   Why is that card up your sleeve?
   I don't care what you think.
   I don't care what anyone thinks.
   f. Do you know what I saw today?
   They used to go together.
   UFO'S? I don't believe in them!
   Don't bother me. Let me alone!

g.   I don't watch TV any more.
       I heard that she was seriously ill.
       UFO'S? I believe in them!
       I'll never wait for you again.

h.   I'm getting a new roommate.
       Isn't the food around here terrible?
       You've said that a hundred times.
       Listen to me: we're all through!

i.   I'm going to level with you.
       What can I do about it?
       Go away!
       He's got a gun!

j.   Why are you staring at me like that?
       Why are you staring at me like that?
       Why are you staring at me like that?
       Why are you staring at me like that?

k.   Honey, wake up, there's a burglar in the basement.
       I don't want to tell you again.
       It's all over. You're under arrest!
       I smell smoke. Let's get out of here!

l.   Do you hear something ticking in that case?
       Come along. The boys downtown want to talk to you.
       What do you mean—you lost it?
       If it's the last thing I ever do, I'll get you for this!

m.   There's something you ought to know.
       Don't move until I tell you to.
       You're the last person in the world I'd suspect.
       Don't touch! It's a live wire!

n.   What's that scratching at the door?
       Whatever it is—don't open that door!
       I'm not afraid of anything. I'm opening the door!
       He-e-elp!

8.   If possible, go to a large room or auditorium to practice this exercise. The members of the class should be scattered around the room. Stand at one end, and read each of the lines at the four levels of loudness. The first level should easily reach those seated nearest to you. The second level should easily reach those who are seated somewhat farther away, and so on for each of the subsequent levels. As you continue practicing, you'll learn how to project material read at the first level to those seated the greatest distance from you. They may not hear your first and second levels as comfortably as your last two levels, but if you're doing a good job, you'll find that even a whisper can be made to carry over a considerable area.

DON'Ts and DOs

- DON'T let your voice take off like a skyrocket.
- DO speak at a suitable general pitch level and stay there.
- DON'T get your support from your throat.
- DO get your pushing power from your midregion.
- DON'T tighten up.
- DO loosen up.
- DON'T compress the stressed vowels and diphthongs.
- DO expand them.

a. Arm! Arm! It is the cannon's opening roar!
b. Cry "God for Harry, England, and Saint George!"
c. Roll on, thou deep and dark blue ocean, roll!
d. Life is real! Life is earnest! And the grave is not its goal.
e. Alas! Alas! With me the light of day is o'er.
f. Ring, happy bells, across the snow; the year is going, let him go.
g. Break, break, break, on thy cold, gray stones, O sea!
h. Lord God of Hosts, be with us yet, lest we forget!
i. I must go down to the seas again, to the lonely sea and the sky!
j. Flame out, you glorious skies; welcome our brave!
k. A horse! a horse! my kingdom for a horse!
l. March we along, fifty score strong; great-hearted gentlemen, singing this song!
m. Heave at the windlass! Heave all at once, with a will!
n. A Yankee ship and a Yankee crew! Ye ho, ye hoo! Ye ho, ye hoo!
o. Ye crags and peaks, I'm with you once again.
p. The anchor heaves! The ship swings free! To sea, to sea!
q. Come live, be merry and join with me to swing the sweet chorus of "Ha, ha, ha!"
r. Forward, the light brigade! Charge for the guns!
s. Who cares for nothing alone is free—sit down, good friends and drink with me!
t. Fifteen men on the dead man's chest—Yo-ho-ho, and a bottle of rum!

PROJECTION

The term *projection* has already been used. Obviously, it has something to do with loudness, but because it also has a rather special meaning, it is given some extra consideration.

A bride tosses her bouquet. Customarily, she throws it in the general direction of the bridesmaids, not necessarily at a specific woman. A baseball pitcher throws a ball, but aims it in the direction of a specific individual—the catcher.

If you speak loudly, you are, in a sense, "tossing" your voice in a general direction and over a general area with sufficient strength and power so that most of those present can hear and understand what you're saying. If you're projecting your voice, you're beaming it to a particular individual or group or to a rather specific area.

Projection is controlled energy that gives impact and intelligibility to sound. It involves a deliberate concentration and a strong desire to communicate with your listeners.

Athletic, crisp articulation is also essential for effective projection.

Directors and actors use the word *project* constantly. We've all attended amateur and professional plays and complained that we couldn't hear some of the actors. Their loudness may have been adequate—maybe they were even shouting—but their voices only reached, rather than penetrated us. Yet the actor who knows how to project rather than merely speak loudly can be understood easily even when speaking *sotto voce*—in a low, soft voice.

A former student is now a district attorney in a large city. He's required to speak in a courtroom almost every day—without a mike. Says he, "I refuse to scream, but I do use my voice as a weapon. I've found that the more aggressively I project and beam my voice at the judge and jury, the more convictions I get."

Vitalize Your Vowels, Dust Off Your Diphthongs

Earlier in the chapter you were told to point up your vowels and diphthongs by stretching them. They are the sounds that carry and project.

9. Say the following as vigorously as possible. This is an artificial device, but the dashes will remind you to le-e-engthen and pro-olo-ong your vowels and diphthongs. Exaggerate.

   a. Ou–out, da–amned spot, ou–out, I say!
   b. Loo–ook too–oo this–is day–ay! Fo–or i–it i–is the ve–ery wa–ay o–of li–ife!
   c. Go–old! Go–old! Go–old! Bri–ight a–and ye–ellow–ow, ha–ard a–and co–old!

    d.   Whe–en i–in dou–oubt, do–on't.

    e.   Whe–en I–Irish e–eyes a–are smi–iling, wa–atch yo–our ste–ep.

    f.   May-ay the de–evil cha–ase you–ou e–every day–ay o–of yo–our li–ife a–and ne–ever ca–atch you–ou.

    g.   Show–owing u–up i–is ni–inety per ce–ent o–of li–ife.

    h.   E–even the–e be–est fa–amily tree–ee ha–as i–its sa–ap.

    i.   I–if you–ou ca–an la–augh a–at i–it, you–ou ca–an li–ive wi–ith i–it.

Repeat *without exaggerating,* but make your vowels and diphthongs spirited and springy. Be sure that they carry.

10.   *The blond fox of Oz said, "Gosh!" as he squashed the kumquat.*

        Nonsense? of course! But you can have some fun with it. What's the point? After all, we don't communicate with each other using gobbledegook.

        The point: Practicing nonsense material, you'll quickly discover that loudness alone won't put it over. Once again you'll be compelled to fatten your vowels and diphthongs and, above all, to tackle your consonants with force and energy.

        Your primary target with the jabberwocky below is the gusty and robust projection of speech sounds. Forget about meanings!

        Read these as dynamically as you can:

    a.   Olive, the odd otter, sat on the oblong palm at the opera.

    b.   Ong gnawed the eggnog in Sergeant Saul's ominous vault.

    c.   A hundred muggers threw marshmallows at Bonnie, the fluttering usher.

    d.   Cobblers often knock Tom the Jock on Wanda's yacht.

    e.   Audrey and Austin waltzed in grandpa's long johns in Austria.

    f.   Don Juan coughed as he drank the awful coffee in Boston.

    g.   The limp forest reeked of hooting owls and warped whistles.

    h.   Wells of soda gurgled toward doghats and green oxen.

    i.   The lead feather washed a fish snorkel on no sneezy axe.

    j.   Did Kay rake wires and tar toes with omens?

Obviously we don't spend our lives communicating with people through the use of nonsense sentences. But maybe this exercise has made you more sensitive to the need for sprightly and bouncy articulation in order to project intelligibly. Can you carry over this awareness into non-nonsense material, some of which is conversational? It's not always the public speaker who fails to project; it's often the person in private or everyday conversation.

Assignment 14: Projection

If possible, your performance should be given in a large room or auditorium.

1.   Prepare vigorous and energetic material that lends itself to forceful projection. Divide your material into four sections, and present it using the four levels of loudness (soft, medium loud, loud, very loud).
    or

2.   Prepare nonsense material (you may wish to write your own) or select appropriate material that is suitable for lively projection. Beam it at individual members or sections of your group, but before you've finished, you should make sure that each listener feels that you have spoken to him or her personally at least once during your presentation.

        The Suggested Checklist for this assignment, which is at the end of the chapter, may be useful to you as you practice your material.

PSYCHOLOGICAL CONTRAST

Composer Franz Joseph Haydn worked a charming stunt in his "Surprise" symphony. Fearing that the audience might snooze during the quiet section of the work, he inserted several extremely loud, crashing chords where they would be least expected. "That's sure to make them jump," he said.

And jump they did!

Your vocal thunder has to be sufficiently high-powered so that your listeners can hear you, but it also has to be varied and tempered. You have to learn when to purr and when to roar and what to do in between. An orchestra never plays so loudly that it blasts the audience out of the concert hall; it never plays so quietly that the audience can't hear it, but its 110 instrumentalists do vary their volume.

Obviously, you'll need to use something close to the fourth level of loudness if you call out to a friend a block away. In a telephone booth, however, the first level will do. But what of the speaker in a large room? Must he use the fourth level exclusively? By no means. It would be unnecessary and extremely monotonous.

In reality, dealing with loudness in terms of four levels is an artificial device. There are probably forty or perhaps four hundred levels. In other words, the nuances and shadings are endless.

Here are some suggestions that will help you vary your loudness:

11. Talk at a relatively low level of loudness for a minute or two. Then, at a key word or punch line, raise your volume to a near-shout. This will jolt your listeners.

   For example, as you read the material below, start close to Level 1, and pause when you get to the pause marks: / /
   Read the final phrases, after the pause, in the vicinity of Levels 3 or 4.

   a. I was—I am Mary of Scotland—and I came to you for mercy. This you have denied me. You tore me from my people. You cast me into a prison. However, let us forget all the cruelties I have suffered. You will never use the power you have to kill me. I give up all claims to your throne. You've done your worst. You have destroyed me. My sins were human. Can as much be said of yours? You did not inherit virtue from your mother. We know only too well what brought the head of Anne Boleyn to the block! If there were justice, you would be kneeling here before me because I am your lawful queen./   / The English have been cheated by a juggler! A bastard—yes, a bastard, soils the British throne. [Schiller, *Mary Stuart*]

   b. I can see him there . . . he grins . . . he is looking at my nose . . . that skeleton. What's that you say? Hopeless? Why, very well! But a man does not fight merely to win! No no . . . better to know one fights in vain! You there! Who are you? A hundred against one! I know them now, my ancient enemies! Falsehood! Prejudice! Cowardice! What's that? Surrender? No! Never, never!/   / Yet in spite of you, there is one crown I bear away with me, and tonight when I enter before God, my salute shall sweep all the stars away from the blue threshold! One thing without stain, unblemished, unspotted . . . and that is . . . my white plume! [Rostand, *Cyrano de Bergerac*]

12. Read the selections in Exercise 11 again, but this time read the material before the pause at relatively loud levels. The final phrases should be read at a soft level.

13. Use Level 3 or 4 briefly and just before getting to a major point (after the pause) drop your volume to a near-whisper, a subdued Level 1. Your hearers will lean forward, feeling that they're being taken into your private confidence.

   a. Oh, Rip tells a good story and sings a lusty song. He's a glorious fellow! Did you ever see the wife or children of a glorious fellow? Their home is the gutter. I've tried everything to save him, but he's as stubborn as a Dutch pig. What's even worse is his good nature. It drives me frantic when night after night he comes home drunk and hopelessly good-natured. I can't stand that/   /. I drove Rip from his own house. If he would only mend his ways, he would see how much I love him and how much I forgive him. [Irving, "Rip van Winkle"]

   b. The manuscript? Well . . . I have torn your precious manuscript into a thousand pieces. I have torn my own life to pieces. So why shouldn't I tear my lifework too? Yes, I tell you! A thousand pieces— and scattered them on the fjord. There is cool seawater at any rate—let the pieces drift on it, drift with the current and the wind./   / And then presently they will sink—deeper and deeper—as I will, Hedda. [Ibsen, *Hedda Gabler*]

14. Read the selections in Exercise 13 again, but this time read the material before the pause at a near-whisper. After the pause, raise your volume to Levels 3 or 4.

15. Start near Level 1 and *gradually* increase your volume to Level 3 or 4. Here, too, your listeners will enjoy the suspense, waiting for the climactic moment.

    a.   A great ox, grazing in a swamp, put down his foot on a family of young frogs, and crushed most of them to death. One escaped and ran off to his mother with the terrible news. "Mother," he said, "you never saw such a big beast as the beast that did it."

           "Big?" said the foolish old mother frog. She puffed herself to twice her size and said, "Was it as big as this?"

           "Oh, much bigger," said the little frog.

           She puffed herself some more, and said, "As big as this?"

           "Oh no, Mother, much, much bigger."

           So she puffed again, and puffed so hard that suddenly with a great POP! she burst into little pieces.

    b.   Well, I'll be darned! What's on the schedule now? Why are all these men trying to surround me? What do you men want? What's all the commotion about? Why are you closing in on me all of a sudden? What's the rush? Where are we going? Some rumble! Hell's bells! They've grabbed me. Damn it all! Citizens, friends, to the rescue! Save me, fellow citizens! Help! Let me go, you donkeys, you asses! [Plautus, *The Menaechmi*]

16. Begin close to Level 3 or 4 and *gradually* decrease the volume. Your followers may tilt toward you—not just in anticipation—but because they're concerned that they might not hear your last sentence or two.

    (The following story was told in a student speech about child abuse.)

    a.   Neighbors had reported Jonah's mother several times for beating him unmercifully. One evening she beat him with a broomstick for failing to clean up his room, the living room and the kitchen. After knocking him unconscious, she put him on the back porch and left to go partying at 9:00 P.M. At midnight, hearing moans, the neighbors investigated and found Jonah on the back porch, alone and uncovered in thirty degree weather. He was rushed to the hospital but died two hours later. Apparently he had regained consciousness at one point and reentered the house, for police found a note on the kitchen table. It read:

           Mom,

           I'm sorry for not cleaning up. I love you.

                        Jonah

    b.   The world's richest man, King Midas, was also the greediest. He prayed to Bacchus, "I'm poor. Give me gold!"

           The god replied, "Your wish is granted."

           A delighted Midas sat down to dine. The food and wine he put to his lips turned into gold. His little daughter climbed up onto his lap and turned into a gold statue.

           "Bacchus!" cried the king. "You are a monster!"

           The angry god changed Midas' ears into those of an ass. The king was so humiliated that he hid his hairy ears under a cap. Only the royal barber knew Midas' secret. And he was sworn to silence. But one day he could stand it no more and he dug a hole in the field and spoke his secret into it. He filled up the hole, but in the spring reeds grew there, and every time they were stirred by a breeze, they whispered to the whole world, "King Midas has asses' ears! King Midas has asses' ears!"

17. Tricks have a somewhat mechanical basis. A good conversationalist or speaker doesn't concentrate on four levels of loudness. These techniques, when used judiciously, will help.

    The selections below are not marked in any way. No guidelines are given. As you read, forget about gimmicks. Can you achieve loudness that is ample? Diverse and different?

    a.   My young friend, about seventy-five years ago I learned I was not God. And so, when the people of the various states want to do something and I can't find anything in the Constitution forbidding them to do it, I say, whether I like it or not: "Damn it, let 'em do it!" [Oliver Wendell Holmes, Jr.]

    b.   Virginia Moss was hotly attacking the reputation of a rival writer, Gertrude Kennedy, when her friend, surprised at this sharp outburst, interrupted to say that she had no idea that Moss even knew Kennedy. "Know her!" Moss exclaimed, "Of course I don't know her. I never could hate anyone I knew."

c. Somebody once asked Beethoven, "Master, how, when, where did you think of the beautiful theme in your third symphony?"
"Well, it was like this. I walked out to the woods, and when it got hot and I got hungry, I sat down by a little brook and unpacked my cheese and sausage. And just as I opened the greasy paper, that darn tune pops into my head!"

d. Really, I'm a square. I'm a yo-yo! But it's the squares and the yo-yos who carry the burden of the world, and the bores who become the heroes. If the Creator had a purpose in equipping us with a neck, He surely meant us to stick it out. [Katharine Hepburn]

e. When you command a dog to "sit up," the poor idiot thinks he has to do it. The average cat ignores you, pretends to be stupid and not to understand what you want. He really understands you only too well, but he sees nothing in it for him. So why sit up?

f. An old woman was accused by her nieces of not being logical. For some time she couldn't quite understand what they meant. Suddenly, it came to her, and she exclaimed: "Logic! Good gracious! What rubbish! How can I tell what I think until I see what I say?"

g. My dear husband, how can you say a thing like that about me? How could I have done anything wrong when I was with you—the man I married? I would never stoop to the behavior you're accusing me of. Is it your idea to catch me in adultery? You never will! What's more, you're probably thinking I'll shrug this off just like so much water under the bridge. I will not! And keep your hands off me! I'm saying good-bye now. Keep your part of the property, and please return mine at once! [Plautus, *Amphitryon*]

h. I don't deny the charges. I admit them. I buried my brother's body. If it's a crime, then it's a crime that God commands! What I can't stand is meekly submitting to my brother's body being unburied. You smile at me. If you think I am a fool, maybe it is because a fool condemns me! You find me guilty of treason? I have defied you. And for this I am being dragged off by force. I shall never marry. I shall never bear children. I'm to be buried alive! I just want to ask what moral law I have broken? I have done no wrong. I have not sinned before God. But if I have, I will know the truth in death. [Sophocles, *Antigone*]

i. My Lords, you cannot, I venture to say, you cannot conquer America. What is your present situation there? We do not know the worst, but we know that in three campaigns we have done nothing and suffered much. You may swell every expense and strain every effort; you may traffic and barter with every pitiful German Prince who sells and sends his subjects to the shambles of a foreign country. Your efforts are forever vain! For it irritates the minds of your enemies to overrun them with the sordid sons of plunder! If I were an American as I am an Englishman, while a foreign troop was landed in my country, I never would lay down my arms!—never! never! never! [William Pitt (1777)]

j. Ye Gods! That's it! Now nobody, but nobody, is going to stop me from going straight to your wife and telling her the truth . . . the whole story about you and your little schemes. You just wait, you parasite, until this stuff starts coming back at you. That banquet you enjoyed and I never got to is going to give you bad dreams. Wait and see! [Plautus, *The Menaechmi*]

k. I'm shuddering all over, but I just can't go away. I'm afraid to be quiet and alone. I was born here. My grandparents lived here. I love this old house. My husband . . . died in this room. My boy . . . my only son . . . was drowned here. Oh, don't be so rough on me, Peter. I love you as though you were one of us. I'd gladly let you marry Anna—only, you do nothing. You're simply tossed from place to place. Strange, isn't it? And you must do something with your beard to make it grow longer. You look so funny. [Chekhov, *The Cherry Orchard*]

l. The knife, where's the knife? I left it here. It'll give me away! What is this place? I hear something . . . something that's moving! But now it's quiet . . . so very quiet! Marie, Marie . . . why are you so pale? Where did you get those red beads that you are wearing around your neck, Marie? Did you earn them with your sins? Your sins made you black, Marie, and I made you pale. But the knife, the knife! There! I've got it. Now, into the water with it! Ha, it'll get rusty! Nobody will ever find it! But why didn't I break it first? And am I still bloody? I've got to wash myself. There's a spot, there, and there's another. [Buechner, *Woyzeck*]

m. I had one attack while I was away. It didn't last long, but it filled me with . . . terror. If it had only been an ordinary illness—even a fatal one—I wouldn't have minded so much. I'm not afraid of death. But to become a child again—a helpless child—to have to be fed! I can't stand the thought of lingering on like that! And if you die, Mother, I would be left alone. The doctor said I might live for years. He called it softening of the brain. What a way to put it! It makes me think of cherry-colored velvet curtains—soft and delicate to the stroke! [Ibsen, *Ghosts*]

n. Do you think it was done coldly, cunningly? I was not the same person then that I am now, standing right here and telling you this. Do you know something? I think there are two sorts of will, of desire, in everyone. I wanted that woman out of the way, but I never really thought it would happen. With every step I took, I felt as if something seemed to shriek inside me. No further! Not a step further! But I could not stop. I had to go just a little further. Just one step, and then another, always one more. And so it happened. That's the way things like that do happen. [Ibsen, *Rosmersholm*]

o. Do you want me to prove that none of you is completely sane? If you are sane and rational, you would have control over your own mind, right? Yes. Now I want all of you to concentrate real hard and think of an elephant. O.K. Start visualizing. Think about the elephant's size, color, that long trunk, those big floppy ears. Do you have a picture of an elephant in your mind? And now: Do NOT think of an elephant for the next five seconds as I count to five. Can you do it? Here goes. One . . . two . . . three . . . four . . . five. Did anyone succeed in NOT thinking of an elephant? Just as I thought: everyone of you has a crinkle in the cranium, a pimple in your personality. Remember: one out of every four people in this country is mentally unbalanced. Think of your three closest friends. If they seem O.K., then . . . you're the one!

p. Why are we so violent? Why do most of us enjoy violence so much? Everybody in his life, everybody here has at least once kicked, slapped or scratched another human being. And don't deny it. (And did you notice how much better you felt after you did it?) A Chicago paper recently took a survey. They interviewed college couples—those going steady or sharing an apartment. More than fifty percent admitted that they had used violence on each other, and not just those big, hairy guys on the poor, helpless girls. There were a surprising number of cases in which those poor, helpless girls beat up on those big, hairy guys. Maybe it all goes back to what we watch on TV. One week of evening TV alone will bring you an average of eighty-four killings and 372 other acts of violence. Have you hugged someone today? Don't. Beat 'em up instead!

WRAP-UP

1. Loudness is also referred to as intensity, volume, force, strength, and projection.
2. Some individuals are too soft-spoken, under-projected and, at times, impossible to hear. The reasons:
   a. Concerned parents may continually have hushed their normally noisy children.
   b. Personal value systems that identify a loud voice as a sign of an extravert or an aggressive person.
   c. Excessive competition from the noisy environment frustrates many people. They compensate by speaking quietly.
   d. Shyness or insecurity may encourage a speaker to adopt a hushed and whispery manner of talking.
3. Loudness is measured in decibels—a decibel being a unit to express the intensity of a sound wave.
4. Excessive yelling or shouting is vocal abuse. It can damage the vocal cords.
5. Adequate loudness can be achieved if you observe the following conditions:
   a. Openness of mouth: tight lips and a frozen jaw block the sound. Sharp and crisp articulation is a forerunner of satisfactory loudness.
   b. Speaking slower. Don't squeeze your vowel sounds. They have greater carrying power than most of the consonants.
   c. Don't let the pitch of your voice zoom skyward like a rocket. Keep a comfortable pitch level.
   d. Support the tone. Think of the energy and power being concentrated in the midregion of your body, not your throat.
   e. Be alert! Be animated!

6. The amount of loudness you need also depends on:
   a. Size of the room or area in which you are talking.
   b. Your audience. How many? How near?
   c. What you're talking about. If you need to be persuasive or forceful, turn up the volume. If you want to meditate or be romantic, turn down the volume.
   d. How much competition do you have from sources over which you have no control—the noisy world around you?
7. Projection gives thrust, precision, and intelligibility to sound. The speaker has a strong desire to communicate. A projected voice is beamed to listeners. It does more than reach them; it penetrates them.
8. Loudness is relative, and it must always be varied and subtle. Contrast is important. The range of loudness extends from very soft soft to very loud loud.

Assignment 15: Loudness

Prepare material that lends itself to energetic projection. Avoid purely descriptive or expository material. A narrative, especially one containing dialogue, is often effective for this type of assignment. Read it with enough overall loudness to be heard in a reasonably large room, but work for as much contrast and variety in loudness as you can.

The Suggested Checklist for this assignment may be helpful to you as you practice your material.

Suggested Checklist for Assignments 14 and 15

As you practice by yourself, you may want to work with this checklist. Listen carefully to yourself. If it is feasible, record this assignment or get a classmate or friend to listen to you as you read the material. Eventually your goal will be to have a check mark in the **Yes** column for each category. (Optional: Perhaps your instructor will want to use the checklist to evaluate you during your classroom presentation.)

	Yes	No
Adjusts To—		
size and proximity of audience		
size and acoustical qualities of room		
nature of material being presented		
Varies loudness		
Propulsive force comes from muscles near midregions of body		

	Yes	No
Avoids—		
undue muscular constriction and tension of throat		
rigid jaw, clenched teeth, immobile lips		
too-low pitch level		
too-high pitch level		
excessive upward jumps in pitch		

Additional comments or suggestions:

BE VARIED AND VIVID   EXPRESSIVENESS

WOULD YOU BELIEVE THAT

. . . You can get an excellent response from an audience even if you're talking to them in a language they don't understand? Helena Modjeska, a great Polish actress, was once asked quite unexpectedly at a dinner party to do one of her favorite scenes from Shakespeare. She performed in Polish for about ten minutes before an English-speaking audience. Her performance was so emotional that she had her listeners in tears. Later she confessed that she had merely recited the Polish alphabet over and over again!

. . . You can also get a strong audience response by simply reading the telephone directory aloud? The late Richard Burton did it and charged his words with gun powder. Charlton Heston also accomplished the feat—except that he read from a Montgomery Ward catalogue.

. . . Mozart, the greatest child prodigy of all time (he composed an opera when he was twelve), had perfect pitch? His ear was so fine that he could distinguish a difference in pitch of one-eighth of a tone. One could whistle, hum, or play a note on any musical instrument, and Mozart could tell exactly what note it was.

. . . Great careers have been demolished because of voices? In silent films, John Gilbert was one of the most passionate screen lovers of all times. Shortly before talking pictures came along, Gilbert signed a five-year contract with MGM for a million dollars a year (megabucks in those days). Then he made his first sound film. His scrawny, high-pitched voice cracked up audiences, and Gilbert's career soon ground to a halt.

. . . *Castrati* (emasculated male singers) were the rock stars of the seventeenth and eighteenth centuries? The cruel operation was done when a boy was between seven and twelve to prevent his soprano or alto voice from changing. As an adult, however, he had all the physical power and strength of a grown man. When *castrati* sang particularly well in an opera, Italian audiences liked to shout, *"Viva il coltello!"* ("Long live the knife!")

. . . If you tell a lie the pitch of your voice tends to rise? This, according to voice print experts who work with courts of law.

. . . "The Star Spangled Banner" is the world's most unsingable national athem? The range—an octave and a half—is beyond the capabilities of nine out of ten Americans. The melody, an old English drinking song, had been "borrowed" for twenty-six other songs before F. Scott Key borrowed it for "The Star Spangled Banner."

VOCAL MONOTONY

Now I lay me down to sleep,
The lecture dull, the subject deep;
If he should quit before I wake,
Give me a poke, for heaven's sake!

That three word phrase at the beginning of the second line: THE LECTURE DULL . . . is a key to what this chapter is about.

Recent surveys at fifty colleges and universities gave 2,500 students the opportunity to rate their instructors on "teaching personality" and to explain or comment briefly upon their ratings. Table 7.1 is a simple breakdown of the responses.

Table 7.1   Criteria for Rating Instructors

General Ratings of Instructors	*Reasons or Comments*
Superior, Excellent, Good	Enthusiastic delivery, alive, brisk, peppy, alert, vocally animated, dynamic way of talking, has warmth and rapport, vivid, energetic.
Fair, Inferior	A monotone, drones and chants, indifferent, lacks animation, singsong, bored, sounds the same in everything, no enthusiasm, dead, wooden, bland.

Vocal monotony is a plague that strikes clergy, lawyers, nurses, legislators, astronauts, housepersons, butchers, bakers and candlestick makers, and—you knew this was coming—*students!*

Actually the identities of these vocal bores—let's call them *drones*—are less important than why they are the way they are. Everytime they say something, they pound coffin nails into their remarks. Vocal monotony has its roots in:

- personality characteristics
- the purpose of the speaker, including the subject matter and the general nature of the material
- the attitudes, moods, and emotions of the speaker
- faulty habits
- health and hearing

Each factor has its own drones' gallery.

PERSONALITY CHARACTERISTICS

Are you bashful?

Do you tend to think, move and talk slowly?

Have you ever been told that you have a "cold" personality?

An important word from your sponsor. There are surely hundreds of Bashful Beths around us, but it would be wrong to think that all shy, modest, or reserved people are drones. Beth may be excessively bashful in her everyday relationships with friends and classmates, but she may suddenly become supercharged and emit sparks on a speaker's platform or on a stage. Likewise, not all slow-paced people—the slow movers and speakers—are bores in front of audiences. Frigid Freddy, too, and his "cold" colleagues are sometimes able to catch fire in performance situations.

PURPOSE OF THE SPEAKER

Some individuals don't try very hard to communicate with their listeners. They're unimaginative. As Lee Iacocca has said, "If you have no fire in yourself, you certainly can't warm others."

A colleague—the students have nicknamed her Repetitious Rita—teaches Economics 101 and has been teaching it for almost as many years. As the students put it, "She makes us feel numb on one end and dumb on the other." She's slowly slid into the wrong kind of groove without being aware of it. Her argument is that it's impossible to sound lively in something you've been saying over and over again, year in and year out. In reality, she's no longer interested in what she has to say. She's stagnant. She needs her batteries recharged!

ATTITUDES AND EMOTIONS

Do you know the type who's a fireball in conversation but suddenly freezes and becomes highly inexpressive in front of a speech class? Or the "I'm-so-bored" type? Audiences bore him to death and he approaches them condescendingly. Or the *bewildered* type? His principal crime is mental flabbiness and a general inadequacy of intellectual response.

FAULTY HABITS

Some students are indifferent and careless listeners. Their argument—and it isn't a bad one—may be that their ears are bombarded hour after hour, day after day, with voices and the blare of their roommate's radio or stereo. Thus, when they want to study or concentrate, they can't always be put down for trying to shut out unwanted sounds or noises. Unfortunately, however, there may be an undesirable carryover into other more general situations.

HEALTH AND HEARING

- Individuals suffering from general ill health
- Individuals suffering from partial hearing loss

People with problems of health and hearing generally need medical aid or the assistance of specially trained speech therapists who can set up a program of hearing rehabilitation.

FACING THE PROBLEM

Do *you,* by any remote chance, belong to the Drones' Gallery? Maybe you're just a part-time monopitch. Be honest. No one likes to be tagged as drab, colorless or cadaverous. The world's second worst crime is boredom. The first is being a bore.

Make a realistic attempt to face the problem head-on. The old saw, "A leopard can't change its spots," is quite true—for leopards. If you're receptive as you work on the material in this chapter, you'll remove yourself from the Drones' Gallery (and enjoy yourself in the process!)

FACTORS OF EXPRESSIVENESS

Typically, many drones use a range of only two, three, or four tones as they speak. The singsong drone may use many more, but his or her up-down-up-down vocal pattern is just as monotonous as the voice of the three-note drone. The trained voice is capable of using tones within a range of an octave and one-half or more. Almost everyone should be able to develop and use effectively a range of at least one octave. Before you can work on specific techniques that will help you achieve greater vocal flexibility, you should consider, however, the interesting subject of pitch.

PITCH

The legendary tenor Enrico Caruso was singing an opera in Philadelphia. Before the performance started, the bass complained of laryngitis. There was no understudy. The show had to go on. The bass was particularly worried about his big aria in act 4. Caruso told him to do the best he could, but if he felt his voice giving out, to alert him with a stage whisper. The bass struggled through the opera and finally got to the big solo. His voice disappeared, and he frantically signaled Caruso. The performance wasn't stopped. Caruso sang the bass aria in a deep voice, while the stricken singer simply mouthed the words. Not a soul in the audience knew the difference, and the aria was greeted with tremendous applause.

Caruso, with that 24-karat voice, had built a reputation as a tenor and not as a bass. He looked like a tenor, acted like a tenor, sang like a tenor, and had the vocal equipment of a tenor. We all understand that a tenor voice is higher in pitch than a baritone and that an alto is lower in pitch than a soprano. But what, specifically, does *pitch* refer to?

Pitch *refers to the highness or lowness of tone or sound.* The slower the vibration cycles of the vocal folds, the lower the pitch; the faster the vibration cycles, the higher the pitch. Find middle C on the piano and hum a corresponding pitch. Your vocal folds are meeting and separating in vibratory cycles of approximately 256 times per second. If you hum the C above middle C, they are vibrating about 512 times per second.

What Determines Pitch?

As a youngster, did you ever indulge in a little hero or heroine worship? You may have modeled your speech after a teacher, a TV, movie or sports celebrity or a parent. If your model had a well-pitched voice—fine and dandy! If the model didn't, you may have copied his problems.

Age, sex, and general emotional states are the more obvious factors that determine pitch, but you must also reckon with three other relatively subtle factors: the length, thickness and mass, and degree of tension of your vocal folds.

- *Length.* Pitch is lowered if length is increased. A man's larger vocal folds produce lower tones than a woman's smaller vocal folds. (The longest piano strings produce the lowest bass tones; the shorter strings produce the highest treble tones.)

- *Thickness and Mass.* Pitch is generally lowered by greater weight, that is, greater thickness and mass of the vocal folds. (The strings on a bass viol are thicker and heavier than the strings on a violin.)

- *Tension.* Pitch is raised as tension of the vocal folds is increased. (As a guitar string is tightened, the pitch is raised.)

In general, pitch is largely the result of variations in tensions and of changes in pressure beneath the vocal folds.

The most important thing for you is to use a pitch level that is suitable for *your* voice. Voices, like musical instruments, have a range or span of tones in which they sound their best. For example, strike three or four keys at the top and bottom of a piano keyboard, and you'll immediately realize why composers rarely write compositions calling for the use of those particular keys.

You've heard individuals who speak in a harsh growl—a sort of glottal gargle. They're probably using the lower extremes of their vocal ranges. More irritating are the persons who habitually use the upper extremes, producing shrill, squeaky voices.

The Optimum Pitch Level

The optimum pitch level (it's also known as the natural pitch level) is simply the most desirable and serviceable level of pitch for the individual voice.

Your voice functions most dynamically and efficiently at this level.

Young people are often interested in cultivating relatively deep-pitched voices. Many radio announcers, disc jockeys, TV, movie, and stage personalities massage our ears with sultry bass rumbles. Favorite female performers have voices reminding us of Lauren Bacall or Joan Collins. Their male counterparts bring to mind the younger Lee Marvin or Michael J. Fox with a bad cold. All of these voices seem to emerge from cavernous depths. These are voices in which deep bells ring.

The late Tallulah Bankhead, a flamboyant stage and movie actress with a *basso profundo* voice, once received a telephone call from Earl Wilson. Wilson, a well-known New York gossip columnist, had a shrill, high-pitched voice.

Wilson: "Tallulah, have you ever been mistaken for a man?"
Tallulah: "No, Earl. Have you?"

There is surely nothing wrong with a mighty Wurlitzer bass or a smoky contralto voice. At the same time, there's nothing wrong either with a well-used tenor or soprano voice. A large number of successful speakers or entertainers—Tom Selleck has already been mentioned—have voices that are relatively high pitched. Being tall and macho doesn't guarantee you a deep, plummy voice. One of the most satiny, lush bass voices I've ever heard came from a young man who stood 5'4" and weighed 135 pounds!

Your business with this section of the chapter is not how to develop an enticing or commercial voice. Your business is *how to make the best of what you already have.*

The Habitual Pitch Level

You'll notice that as you speak or read a few lines of material the pitch of the voice varies in highness and lowness. The upward and downward inflections, however, seem to cluster about one average or central pitch level. It's the pitch level you most frequently use. You move up and down from it, but you most often return to it. This is your *habitual pitch level.*

Finding Your Habitual Pitch Level

1. Sit comfortably erect in a chair. Inhale deeply two or three times and then sigh. (Vocalize! Don't whisper.) Listen carefully to the pitch level of the sigh. Repeat the process and sigh several times. You'll discover that the sighs are being vocalized at approximately the same pitch level. This level is *close* to your habitual level.

2. Read sentences *a–e* in a normal and relaxed manner. Emphasize the italicized words, but try to concentrate on the nonitalicized words. You'll be quite close to your habitual level on the unemphasized words. (The final syllable or word in a sentence, however, is often pitched lower than the habitual level.)

    a.   Life is like a camel. It *won't* back up.
    b.   Bees can't make honey and *sting* at the same time.
    c.   Old jokes never *die.* They just smell that way.
    d.   Daniel Boone was born in a log *cabin* which he *himself* built.
    e.   *Most* family trees have at least *one* crop failure.

3. Read the story in this exercise three or four times. During the first reading, use as much variation as you wish. Then, read it again, gradually working toward a monotone, narrowing and compressing the range until you've eliminated the upward and downward inflections. When you arrive at a level, sustain *ah* at that level, and find the corresponding note on the piano. You're probably at or near your habitual pitch level.

    There was a villager whose business caused him to travel every day to a nearby seaport. As his neighbors rarely traveled, he was their newspaper. Each night he told them about some strange sight he had seen until finally the time came when he had exhausted all of the seaport's novelties. As he hated to return without a story, he made up one about a fish so large that it filled the entire harbor. His amazed but trusting listeners were so impressed by the story that they set out to see the fish. On the way they overtook their storyteller who, carried away by his own invention, was also hurrying to see the amazing sight.

4. Starting with the *ah* that you leveled off with in Exercise 3 (and be sure that you check this again with a pitch pipe or piano), sing *one* on the *ah* and then down the scale with *two, three, four, five* to the lowest note you can produce comfortably and with reasonably good quality.

    Repeat this exercise several times. It will be the basis of another exercise to help you locate your OPTIMUM PITCH LEVEL—the pitch level that's most desirable and useful.

Finding Your Optimum Pitch Level: Exercises

5. Repeat Exercise 4, singing down the scale to the lowest good note you can produce without scraping. This time sing *one* on that note, and then go back up the scale with *two, three, four, five*. Sustain the *five* for a few seconds. (Actually, you'll be prolonging the *i* sound.) With the help of a piano or a pitch pipe, determine what note you're sustaining. Using this level, say monotonously:

    The day is dark and cold and dreary.

    Repeat the sentence one tone higher and then one tone lower. It's in this general area that your optimum pitch level is located.

6. Hold your hands over your ears and hum up and down the scale several times. You'll notice that one tone has an increased intensity. It sounds richer and fuller. This particular tone should be very close to your *optimum* pitch level. Now, compare the results of this exercise with the results of Exercise 5.

7. Start again at your lowest comfortable pitch, this time singing *ah*. You don't have to cover your ears. Then move up and down the scale several times. Again you'll hear and feel that one particular note seems to be the strongest, richest and easiest to produce. It should be the same or almost the same tone you discovered in Exercise 6, and also at or very near your most efficient pitch level.

Repeat Exercises 3, 4, 5, and 6 until you're able to tell the difference, if any, between your habitual and your optimum pitch levels.

If you find a difference of approximately one or two tones between the two levels, the pitch level you're using is probably satisfactory.

If the difference is greater, you should try to make your optimum pitch level habitual.

A Word of Warning

A large majority of us don't have problems as far as optimum pitch is concerned.

Your habitual pitch is, in most cases, also your optimum pitch. If a competent authority tells you that your habitual pitch level is too high or too low, raising or lowering your pitch level a note or two won't result in vocal abuse or damage. Exercises 8–12 will help.

But don't try to lower your voice three or more notes without professional supervision. You'll hurt your voice.

> IF YOUR HABITUAL LEVEL IS SATISFACTORY, SKIP EXERCISES 8–12, AND JUMP TO THE SECTION ON *RANGE*.

Making Your Optimum Pitch Level Habitual

8. Once again, locate your optimum pitch. A piano or pitch pipe will be necessary. Sing *ah* on the optimum pitch and hold it for approximately six seconds.

9. Chant these sentences with deliberate monotony at your optimum pitch level. In other words, concentrate on how you sound as you read the lines rather than what you are reading.

    a. There is no they, only us.
    b. I tended to place my wife under a pedestal. [Woody Allen]
    c. You are no bigger than the things that annoy you.
    d. We had seen the light at the end of the tunnel, and it was out.
    e. When turkeys mate they think of swans.
    f. Never get into fights with ugly people because they have nothing to lose.

10. Chant these words at your optimum pitch level. Practice with maximum controlled relaxation.

dawn	lot	feet	bath
murmur	hope	boat	all
hush	men	match	tip
moth	mar	tar	mail

11. Repeat the columns of words in Exercise 10, pronouncing each word twice. The first time, deliberately use your old habitual level—the one you're now trying to modify. Check this with a pitch pipe or piano. The second time, read the words at your newer optimum level—the one you're now trying to make permanent. Be certain that it *is* your optimum level.

12. This exercise is the trickiest one in the chapter. Tape it if you can.
    Read each selection differently, according to this key:

MON-OLD-HAB = Chant the material *monotonously* at your *old, habitual* level.
MON-NEW-OPT = Chant the material *monotonously* at your *new, optimum* level.
VAR-NEW-OPT = Read the material with vocal *variation*—avoid the monotone. But stay within your *new, optimum* level.

a. MON-OLD-HAB: Most of us hate to see a poor loser—or a rich winner.
b. MON-NEW-OPT: In this business you either sink or you swim or you don't.
c. VAR-NEW-OPT: Never keep up with the Joneses. Drag them down to your level.
d. MON-OLD-HAB: He who has a sharp tongue soon cuts his own throat.
e. MON-NEW-OPT: The only way to stop smoking is to just stop—no ifs, ands or butts.
f. VAR-NEW-OPT: Most children are spoiled because the parents can't spank Grandma.
g. MON-OLD-HAB: A person with a bad name is already half-hanged.
h. MON-NEW-OPT: First your kids leave home one by one—then they return two by two.
i. VAR-NEW-OPT: We are all here for a brief spell, so get all the good laughs you can.
j. MON-NEW-OPT: When a man sits with a pretty woman for an hour, it seems like a minute. But let him sit on a hot stove for a minute, and it's longer than an hour. That's relativity. [Albert Einstein]
k. VAR-NEW-OPT: When Bach's wife died, he had to make funeral arrangements. But the poor man had been used to having everything done by his wife, so when his old servant asked him for money to buy black crepe, he said tearfully, with his head buried, "Ask my wife."
l. MON-NEW-OPT: We are students of words: we are shut up in schools and colleges for ten or fifteen years, and come out at last with a bag of wind, a memory of words, and we don't know a thing. [Emerson]
m. VAR-NEW-OPT:
One summer evening, a sentinel who stood leaning on his spear at the entrance to the Han Ku Pass—for this was many years before the building of the Great Wall—beheld a white-bearded traveler riding toward him, seated cross-legged upon the shoulders of a black ox.
Said the elderly stranger, when he drew near and halted: "I am an old man, and wish to die peacefully in the mountains which lie to the westward. Permit me, therefore, to depart."
But the sentinel threw himself to the ground and said, in awe: "Are you not that great philosopher?"
For he suspected the traveler to be none other than Lin Tang, who was known to be the holiest and wisest man in China.
"That may or may not be," replied the stranger, "but I am an old man, wishing to depart from China and die in peace."
At this, the sentinel realized that he was indeed in the presence of the great Lin Tang, who had for more than a hundred years, sat in the shadow of a plum tree, uttering words of such extreme simplicity that no man in the whole world was learned enough to understand their meaning.
So the sentinel threw himself in the ox's path and cried out: "I am a poor and ignorant man, but I have heard it said that wisdom is a thing of priceless worth. Spare me, I beg of you, before you depart from China, one word of your great wisdom, which may enrich my poverty or make it easier to bear."
Whereupon Lin Tang opened his mouth, and said gravely: "Wow."
[Quoted in *The Theater Book of the Year* (1946–1947) by George Jean Nathan]

Assignment 16: Pitch Level

Prepare nine to twelve lines of material. Mark it as the selections in Exercise 12 are marked.

MON-OLD-HAB: Read monotonously at habitual pitch level.

MON-NEW-OPT: Read monotonously at optimum pitch level.

VAR-NEW-OPT: Read with vocal variation at optimum pitch level.

Schedule two practice sessions. The first session, work with the material as you've marked it.

The second session, practice at the VAR-NEW-OPT level only. And, of course, use this level when you do your assignment in class.

The Suggested Checklist for this assignment, which is at the end of the chapter, may be useful to you as you practice your material.

RANGE

A major general in the front row of a speech communication class? Yes, I had the gentleman as a student in a class at the Pentagon. Why would a major general be in a basic speech course? In his little speech of self introduction, he confessed all.

> "I've been putting audiences to sleep for years. I didn't realize what a turkey I was until I saw myself on film the other day. I look and sound like a zombie. I should be selling embalming fluid. I thought a course like this might help me."

At the end of the course, we "shot" the general once again, and we ran the *before* and *after* films for the entire class. His improvement was astonishing.

If you have a chance, listen to Henry Kissinger, former Secretary of State. A painful drone. The drone typically reads or talks using a skimpy, shrivelled range of two to four tones. People with glimmer in their voices have a range of twelve to fourteen tones!

The next few exercises will help you remove the dust from the upper and lower extremes of your range. Or they'll show you how to use expressively and flexibly the range you already have.

13. Hum a tone that is easy and comfortable for you. From there, hum down the scale to your lowest safe tone. Don't scrape rock bottom. Then hum back up the scale to your highest decent tone, but don't strain at the top. You'll most likely discover that your range is about twelve tones and possibly more.

14. Do a vocal walk *up* the scale. Say the first word in each line on a comfortably low pitch, and pitch each succeeding word a half or whole tone higher.

    a. Sink or swim.
    b. Long tongue; short friendships.
    c. Little things affect little minds.
    d. That most knowing of persons—gossip.
    e. Cigarettes are killers that travel in packs.
    f. The Bible promises no loaves to the loafer.
    g. Many a bee has drowned in his own honey.
    h. It is better to wear out than to rust out.
    i. Did the devil really create the world when God wasn't looking?
    j. How awful to reflect that what people say of us may be true.
    k. It pays to keep your feet on the ground, but keep them moving.
    l. It seems sort of significant that we have two ears and only one mouth.
    m. Love is a battle, love is a war; above all, love is a growing up.
    n. A drunkard can't make both ends meet because he's much too busy making one end drink.
    o. Diet: a system of starving yourself to death just so that you can live a little longer.
    p. If ants are such busy little workers, how come they find time to go to all the picnics?
    q. A doctor is a person who tells you that if you don't cut something out, he will.

15. Repeat Exercise 14, but this time do your vocal walk *down* the scale. Say the first word on a comfortably high pitch, and pitch each succeeding word a half or whole tone lower.

INTONATION

As you talk, your voice moves from sound to sound with an almost continuous rise and fall in pitch. The overall pattern of pitch changes in phrases and sentences is described as *intonation, speech melody* or *pitch contour*.

Let's consider these aspects of intonation: *key, inflections,* and *steps*.

Key

KEY is the general pitch level—ranging anywhere from high to low—that is used at any given moment in talking or reading.

If you win your state's $2,000,000 lottery, you'll report your good news to the world in a *high key*. Even if you don't luck out and are simply saying or reading something that is light, humorous or cheerful, your key will be in the higher part of your range.

The zany trial scene from *Alice in Wonderland*, in which the Queen of Hearts shouts, "Sentence first. Verdict afterwards. Off with his head!" is most convincing in a high key.

Catch a few TV commercials (can they be avoided?), and you'll note that many of the performers do their stuff in a comparatively high key: "Now that you've just seen how fast and deadly Mother Poppins's bug-killer is, why don't you rush out immediately and buy a case or two for your home?"

On the negative side, the voices of people in a rage or scared spitless also often soar into the upper regions.

If you talk about a recent shopping trip, a vacation at Disneyland or a date, you'll probably use a *middle key*. Informal, casual and unemotional ideas or material work best in this middle range.

But if you tell somebody about the death of a friend, if you're feeling romantic under a full moon or if you're digging deeply into Nietzsche, you'll use a *low key*. Quiet, melancholy or profound ideas tend to seek out the lower depths.

General Douglas MacArthur's classic speech to Congress in 1951 had the entire nation dissolved in tears. In his closing sentences, he carefully shifted to a low key: "Old soldiers never die; they just fade away. I now close my military career . . . an old soldier who tried to do his duty as God gave him to see that duty. Good-bye."

16. Read these selections in a *high key*. But don't deliver them in a high monotone. Work for contrast, color and variation *within* that area.

    a. Know thyself. A Yale undergraduate left on his door a note for a friend on which was written, "Call me at 7 o'clock; it is absolutely necessary that I get up at seven. Make no mistake. Keep knocking until I answer." Under this he had written: "Try again at ten."

    b. I'm tired of all this nonsense about beauty being only skin-deep. That's deep enough. What do you want—an adorable liver? If you are a miracle of beauty, you can't help it. That's why you are so much applauded for it. [Farrah Fawcett]

    c. Love makes you feel special. It changes everyone for the better. It is the one commodity that multiplies when you give it away. The more you spread it around, the more you are able to hang on to it because it keeps coming back to you. Where love is concerned, it pays to be an absolute spendthrift. It cannot be bought or sold, so throw it away! Splash it all over! Empty your pockets! Shake the basket! Turn it upside down! Shower it on everyone—even those who don't deserve it! You may startle them into behaving in a way you never dreamed possible. Not only is it the great mystery of life, it is also the most powerful motivator known to mankind.

    d. I'll do the explaining, Sir! When the war began, like the dutiful wives we are, we tolerated you men and endured your actions in silence. Small wonder. You wouldn't let us say boo. We'd sit at home, and we'd hear that you men had done it again—mishandled another big issue with your staggering incompetence. Then, masking our worry with a nervous laugh, we'd ask you: "And did you manage to end the war in the assembly this morning?" And what did you say to us? "What's it to you? Shut up!" Now we women are going to set you right! Inside there we have four battalions—fully armed fighting women completely equipped for war. What did you expect? We're not slaves. We're freedom women, and when we're scorned, we're full of fury. Never underestimate the power of a woman! Into the fray! Smash them to bits! The day is ours! [Aristophanes, *Lysistrata*]

17. Read these selections in a *middle key*. Again, strive for flexibility and variety.

   a.   I'm cheerful. I'm not happy, but I'm cheerful. There's a big difference. A happy woman has no cares at all; a cheerful woman has cares and learns to ignore that. [Beverly Sills]

   b.   The Statue of Liberty: Made by an Italian, presented to the American people on behalf of the French government for the purpose of welcoming Irish immigrants to New York, which was founded by Dutch people who had stolen it from the Indians and in which today's largest ethnic group is Jewish.

   c.   When I was a boy of fourteen, my father was so ignorant I could hardly stand to have the old man around. But when I got to be twenty-one, I was amazed at how much he had learned in seven years. [Mark Twain]

   d.   The crowd cheered lustily as the team trotted on the field. Eleven mighty and determined men going forth to fight for the old alma mater, to give their all. With them came Charlie. Everybody knew Charlie. On the campus his bubbling personality had won him many friends. He turned and faced the fans. He grinned. There was confidence as well as determination in his grin. He assumed the pose the vast crowd had seen so often. With an assured tone in his voice he barked out, "Peanuts, popcorn, candy!"

18. Read these selections in a *low key,* but don't freeze your voice at one level. Let it rise and fall.

   a.   Today marks my final roll call with you. But I want you to know that when I cross the river, my last conscious thoughts will be of the Corps, and the Corps, and the Corps. I bid you farewell. [Douglas MacArthur]

   b.   The day is cold, and dark, and dreary,
        It rains, and the wind is never weary;
        The vine still clings to the mouldering wall,
        But at every gust the dead leaves fall,
        And the day is dark and dreary.

   c.   What is the most famous monument ever built in honor of love? The incomparable Taj Mahal—a shimmering, white jewel that seems to float over the hot Indian plain. It is a tomb, and it tells one of the greatest love stories of all time. A great shah, when he was only sixteen, fell in love with a highborn beauty and married her. She gave the shah many children. She ruled at his side as an equal. He adored her and brought her diamonds and flowers. In the tenth year of their marriage, once again she was with child, but this time something strange occurred. She confided that shortly before the baby was born, she heard it cry in her womb—an ill omen. A healthy baby girl was born, but the queen did not recover. As she lay dying, she whispered a final wish to her grief-stricken husband: "Build for me a monument so pure and perfect that anyone who comes to it will feel the great power of love." She paused and then added, ". . . and the even greater power of death."

   d.   . . . Yea, though I walk through the valley of the shadow of death, I will fear no evil; for thou art with me. Thy rod and thy staff they comfort me. Thou preparest a table before me in the presence of mine enemies; thou anointest my head with oil. My cup runneth over. Surely goodness and mercy shall follow me all the days of my life, and I shall dwell in the house of the Lord forever. [The Twenty-third Psalm]

19. Which key— *high, middle,* or *low*—is most appropriate for each of the following? Experiment by trying the selections in more than one key. Be as expressive as you can.

   a.   I am thy father's spirit, doomed for a certain time to walk the night.

   b.   If you have to kiss somebody at 7:00 A.M. in front of the camera, you'd better be friends. [Liza Minelli]

   c.   Marriage is the process of finding out what sort of husband your wife would have preferred.

   d.   If I reach for the stars, I might not touch them. But I won't come up with a handful of dirt.

   e.   Do you ever get the feeling that the only reason we have elections is to find out if the polls are right?

   f.   We are such stuff as dreams are made of and our little life is rounded with a sleep.

   g.   Oh, fie, miss, you must not kiss and tell.

   h.   Whatever befalls the earth befalls the sons of the earth. Man did not weave the web of life. He is merely a strand in it. Whatever he does to the web, he does to himself.

   i.   Is that your foot in your mouth or have your tonsils taken up jogging?

   j.   Why condemn the devil? He's using the same defense many of us are using: "I'm doing my own thing."

   k.   Life is a tale told by an idiot, full of sound and fury, and signifying nothing.

l.   Soused? He spent the night in his closet trying to get it to go to the tenth floor.
m.   Silently, one by one, in the meadows of heaven, blossomed the lovely stars, the forget-me-nots of angels.
n.   Hip, hip, hooray! Hip, hip hooray!
o.   The hardest thing any person can do is to fall down on the ice when it's slippery, and get up and praise the Lord.
p.   If at first you don't succeed—try, try again. Then quit. There's no use being a damn fool about it.

Inflection

Changing pitch within a single, uninterrupted sound is called an *inflection*.

A RISING INFLECTION is an upward gliding of the voice from a low to a high pitch.

Say:

The upward slide indicates questioning, hesitancy, curiosity, suspense, surprise, perplexity.

A FALLING INFLECTION is a downward gliding of the voice from a high to a low pitch.

Say:

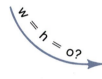

The downward slide denotes certainty, command, emphasis and finality.

A DOUBLE INFLECTION combines the upward and downward gliding of the voice.

Say:

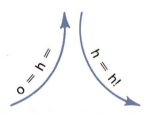

The double inflection signifies uncertainty, sarcasm, evasion, double or hidden meanings.

20. Read each of these words three times using a rising, a falling and then a double inflection. Exaggerate your inflections.

a. hey	d. well	g. please	j. maybe
b. ah	e. yes	h. good	k. don't
c. no	f. why	i. when	l. here

21. Experiment with the inflections and say *oh*, suggesting these meanings:

a. elation	e. sarcasm	i. indifference
b. fear	f. doubt	j. finality
c. pity	g. anger	k. curiosity
d. amazement	h. disgust	l. bashfulness

22. Try each of these words aloud, using a suitable inflection. The sentence in parentheses suggests a specific meaning for the word, but don't read the sentence aloud.

   a. So (We've caught you at last, you rascal!)
   b. So (What's it to you?)
   c. Stop (Here?)
   d. Stop (At once!)
   e. Please (Don't hurt the puppy.)
   f. Please (This is the last straw!)
   g. Why (I've never heard of such a thing.)
   h. Why (I'll tell you why.)
   i. Yes (I'm not so sure.)
   j. Yes (I'm positive.)
   k. Well (This is just what I expected.)
   l. Well (Have you made up your mind yet?)
   m. Ah (The poor thing.)
   n. Ah (I'm tired.)
   o. Mary (Who?)
   p. Mary (That's who.)
   q. Gosh (I dropped a button.)
   r. Gosh (I flunked three courses.)
   s. Wow (Isn't it a beauty?)
   t. Wow (I've had it!)
   u. Really (Did it actually happen?)
   v. Really (Don't ever speak to me again.)
   w. Help (I'm drowning!)
   x. Help (Why should I?)
   y. Jim (Is that you tiptoeing upstairs?)
   z. Jim (What do you mean by coming in at this hour?)

Steps

   A STEP is a pitch change between words or syllables. The voice leaps or springs from one pitch to another, either up or down. Only one tone is used per word.

23. Read each phrase twice, placing a slight pause between the two words: Use a higher pitch on the second word than on the first. Repeat, using a lower pitch on the second word than on the first.

   a. Don't stay.
   b. She did.
   c. Oh, no.
   d. How much?
   e. Who's there?
   f. Sign here.
   g. What time?
   h. Try that.
   i. Which one?
   j. All right.
   k. So what?
   l. You again.
   m. Try again.
   n. Why not?
   o. Not now.
   p. He's here.

24. In these sentences the position of the word indicates the location of the step and the relative size of the jump or skip. Read them in an exaggerated manner.

   a.
   ```
            you                              scream.
        say
             that
                again,
                     I'll
      If
   ```

b.
      be
To   or
      not   that
      to   is the
      be,
      question.

c. I
    won't   won't   tomorrow.
    answer   answer
    now,   I
    and

d.   now
    forever
    hold
Speak   your
    or   peace.

e.   I
    do   do
If   say   it
    it,   fast.

f.   mean?
    you
    what
    to understand
    supposed
    I
Am

g. Smile,
    that,
    when you say
    my friend!

h. I'm
    tired
    of
    telling
    you
    to
    get
    out.

i. Karen,   me?
    marry
    will you

j. Oh,   never
     Jim, you and I   get
                would   along!

---

k. Gee,
        it's spooky in here.

---

l.   told
          you   I?
              that   didn't
   I   would happen,

---

m. What   party,
      a   and
            darn,
               am
                 I
                  tired.

---

n. I   you
     don't
        think
           she   I think   pushed her.
           fell,

---

o. Well,
                    say
        what do you have to   for
      Erin,   yourself?

---

p.   that   not
  Don't try   again,   kidding!
              Jack,   I'm
             and

---

q. Care—   near—
      ful!   er.
        They're getting
                     Oops!
                        It's
                        too
                         late.

---

r.   you
               certainly
  I'm not ly—
          ing,
                     are!
        but

---

25. Look over these sentences and experiment with a pattern of keys, inflections and steps that fits the general meaning of the line. Then read the material aloud.

    a. Mark, I hate to do this. Here's your ring.
    b. I have never liked him, and I never will.
    c. When Jane comes home, we'll soon see who's boss around here.
    d. Strange—that I should run into her every place I go.
    e. John, darling, don't try to pull the wool over my eyes.
    f. Oh, so you think you know the answer, do you?
    g. I was afraid this would happen; I kept telling you it would.
    h. Rodney, is that lipstick on your shirt collar?
    i. Don't call us. Let us call you.
    j. Hey, did he get his comeuppance at last!
    k. Oh, Charles, a mink coat? It's just what I wanted.
    l. She said that about me?
    m. I'm tired, I'm sick, I'm disgusted, and I'm boiling mad.
    n. Well, what do you know about that?
    o. Helen, is that you? Why, Mabel, what are you doing here?
    p. It can't possibly flood here. Where's all that water coming from?
    q. All right, I'll go. Wait a second. Why are you so anxious for me to go?
    r. Judy? Didn't you know? She died more than three years ago.
    s. Who stole my billfold? Oh, here it is on the desk.
    t. He's such a wimp—how much money did you say he inherited?

STRESS AND EMPHASIS

Stress is the degree of prominence of a syllable within a word. The syllable is generally made louder and higher in pitch than neighboring syllables. You stress syllables because English is a subtle language, and by stressing syllables you increase intelligibility. There are obvious differences between <u>con</u>vict and con<u>vict</u>, between <u>pro</u>ject and pro<u>ject</u>.

26. Read aloud each word, making the underlined syllables louder than the other syllables in the same word:

<u>li</u> · brary	con · <u>clu</u> · sive	dis · <u>crim</u> · i · <u>na</u> · tion
re · <u>bel</u>	<u>ev</u> · i · dence	va · <u>ca</u> · tion · ist
<u>re</u> · bel	<u>prob</u> · a · bly	<u>Mis</u> · sis–<u>sipp</u> · i · an
<u>cav</u> · al · ry	<u>po</u> · di · um	re · pub · <u>li</u> · <u>ca</u> · tion
con · <u>cern</u>	neg · li · <u>gee</u>	prop · a · <u>gan</u> · da

Stress also refers to the degree of prominence of a word within a phrase or sentence. The word is often made louder and higher in pitch than adjacent words. You stress words to make meaning and feeling clear. Nouns and verbs, as well as their modifiers—adjectives and adverbs—often carry the meaning of a sentence. Such words are generally given more loudness than the less important articles, prepositions, conjunctions, and pronouns.

27. Read aloud these sentences, observing the differences in meanings as you stress the underlined words:

    a. <u>What</u> did you say to her?
    b. What <u>did</u> you say to her?
    c. What did <u>you</u> say to her?
    d. What did you <u>say</u> to her?
    e. What did you say to <u>her</u>?

Emphasis is the degree of prominence given to a phrase or thought grouping. An important phrase, or one containing a key idea, can be made louder and higher pitched than neighboring words. Sometimes it works if you speak softer and lower the pitch on the phrase you wish to emphasize.

Raise the pitch and turn up your volume on the underlined phrase as you try this one:

I forgot to call you. <u>I refuse to apologize.</u>

Repeat. This time lower the pitch and speak as softly as you can on the key phrase. Which one works better?

Just remember: the key, or idea, words that most truly reveal the meaning and thought of a passage are the nouns, verbs, adjectives, and adverbs. The shorter words—pronouns, prepositions, conjunctions, and helper verbs—are less frequently emphasized. You will find important exceptions to all of the foregoing, however.

28. Read each sentence in this exercise twice. The first time, emphasize the underlined sections. The second time, emphasize another section. Do you notice differences in meaning?

   a. <u>I'll give you the money tomorrow.</u> But not today.
   b. If you haven't got any socks, <u>you can't pull them up.</u>
   c. I told <u>you this would happen.</u> I knew it would happen.
   d. Professor Jones, from what <u>I</u> hear, is a terrible grader.
   e. When Jack hit Joe, <u>he lost control of the car,</u> and it rolled over.
   f. Experience: a comb <u>life gives you</u> after you lose your hair.
   g. Don't worry about <u>avoiding temptation.</u> As you grow older, it starts avoiding you.
   h. You can fool some of the people all of the time, and all of the people some of the time: <u>but you can't fool all of the people all of the time.</u>
   i. Marriage is a lot like the army; <u>everybody complains,</u> but you'd be surprised at the large number that reenlist.

29. Your best friend has just starred as Ophelia or Hamlet in a campus production of *Hamlet*. After the performance you go back stage and say to the person, "You were great! What a performance!" with these suggested meanings:

   a. Your friend was outstanding.
   b. Your friend was outstanding. The others in the cast were atrocious.
   c. Your friend was fair.
   d. Your friend was awful.
   e. Your friend was outstanding, and you didn't think he could do it.
   f. Your friend was a fine actor—several years ago.
   g. You slept through the entire performance and you're asking your friend how effective he or she was.

30. Read these sentences twice, the first time stressing the underlined word. The second time, stress a different word.

   a. But—on the contrary—it has given <u>me</u> faith.
   b. I haven't exactly decided <u>what</u> to do yet.
   c. Hell is what you make of what <u>might</u> have been.
   d. Not everyone who snores is <u>asleep.</u>
   e. <u>Hard</u> work never hurts people <u>who</u> don't do any.
   f. If you <u>itch</u> for success, keep on scratching.
   g. In spite of the cost of living, it's <u>still</u> popular.
   h. Speak well of your enemies. Remember, <u>you</u> made them.
   i. When it is not necessary to change, it is necessary <u>not</u> to change.
   j. <u>Half</u> the lies people tell aren't true.
   k. How to fold a diaper depends on the size of the baby <u>and</u> the diaper.
   l. When you have a choice and <u>don't</u> make it, that in itself is a choice.

Gimmicks

Anybody can say *I'm the happiest person in the world!* choosing the proper key, the right inflections, emphasis and the most effective steps. The sentence might be coldly correct, and yet the overall effect would still be mechanical, bland or false. Gimmicks are helpful, but they're not quite enough. If you're inhibited, all the gadgets and gewgaws in existence won't add one iota of color and flash to your voice.

31. As an interesting venture, read these one-liners twice. In your first reading, ignore the obvious emotional nature of the material. *Deliberately* give a flat and cold reading.
    In your second reading, respond with as much sincerity, vitality and animation as possible.

a.	I'm frightened.	l.	They're going to run me for president! Me? Me?
b.	Am I happy!	m.	I can't stand it another minute.
c.	She's dead! You're sure?	n.	You're too late—he just died.
d.	I hate him.	o.	This is the strangest thing that ever happened to me.
e.	I'm sad.	p.	That's disgusting.
f.	I'm suspicious of her.	q.	Go ahead! I dare you!
g.	My, how eerie it is.	r.	I'm getting sick and tired of your nagging.
h.	I guess I'm in love.	s.	I passed math? You must be kidding.
i.	Get out of here.	t.	Fasten your seat belts. We just ran out of fuel!
j.	Please don't leave me.	u.	Who could be knocking at the door at this hour of the night?
k.	You're the murderer!	v.	You won't believe this: I've just won the million-dollar lottery!

Assignment 17: Vocal Variation

The ideas suggested below have proven most effective in helping individuals whose reading and speaking tend to be somewhat dull and monotonous. They're also quite enjoyable, and the shy, reserved type of person will find any one of them conducive to "letting himself go."

The Suggested Checklist for this assignment, which can be found at the end of the chapter, may be useful to you as you practice your material.

Short, Short Story

Select narrative prose that contains conversation. A short, short story, or a paragraph or two taken from a short story, is suggested. Choose material that is exciting or dramatic. Analyze it carefully in terms of key, inflections, steps, and emphasis. In your performance before the class, however, concentrate on the story you're trying to tell and the ideas and emotions you're attempting to get across.

or

A Commercial

Many radio and TV commercials are irritating: dull material, schlock, endless repetition. A few of them, however, are effective as far as vocal variety is concerned. Not only are there some superior personalities out there in that vast wasteland of radio and TV, but often we're treated to the spectacle of genuine celebrities—everyone from Mark Harmon to Joan Rivers—delivering commercials. Some of their presentations are colorful and lively.

Using original material, preferably selling a product or service that is fictitious, prepare a brief commercial. Be a celebrity or just be yourself, but use your imagination!

or

A Fairy Tale

If you've ever been exposed to small, preschool-age children, you've discovered that a favorite phrase is "Tell us a story!" Delicate nuances and shadings may be too subtle for such a young audience, so the experienced storyteller generally uses a somewhat exaggerated melody pattern with considerable pitch variation.

Prepare a two- to three-minute fairy tale or children's story. Exaggerate when you present it—as though the age level of your audience is approximately three to five years.

> Whichever assignment you choose, be so familiar with your material that you don't have to read it word for word from your script. Tell your audience. Don't read to them. Inject as much spontaneity and animation as you can into your performance, and enjoy yourself while you're doing it.

RATE

Ever take a course in music appreciation?

You learned that a typical concerto has three movements which usually are to be performed Fast-Slow-Fast. But does this mean that when the composition is played, only three different tempos are used? Hardly. The general effect would be sheer boredom.

In the first section of his Piano Concerto No. 1, Tchaikovsky indicates forty-four different variations of tempo. In the second and third movements, twenty-eight tempo patterns are suggested. Thus, in listening to a thirty-six minute performance of the work, you'll hear about seventy-two different tempos, or approximately two contrasting rates of speed per minute.

Time and rate variations are as essential in reading and speaking as they are in music! Have you ever heard a speaker whose voice leaps upward, plunges downward, and never lingers on one pitch for more than two seconds? Yet in spite of all the acrobatics, he's still guilty of a certain tediousness.

Gene Shalit, the feisty movie critic on NBC's "Today" show, has remarkable pitch variance, but he also speaks at a speed that turns words into bullets. He averages about 190 words per minute and seldom alters it. This means that in five minutes, Shalit will have uttered, with almost no change of pace, 950 words. Fortunately, his articulation has snap and bite.

> *RATE includes the speed at which a person speaks, the length or duration of sounds, and the length and number of pauses.*

Measuring rate by counting the number of words read or spoken per minute (w.p.m.) isn't entirely accurate, because words vary in length. But it can give you some idea.

In terms of words per minute, Franklin Roosevelt clocked in at about 110 w.p.m. and John F. Kennedy at 180 w.p.m.

Martin Luther King opened his memorable "I have a dream. . ." speech at a pace of about 90 w.p.m., but finished at 150 w.p.m. Jimmy Carter, often described as a ponderous speaker—a drawler—averaged 160 w.p.m., and Ronald Reagan averages about ten more words per minute than Carter.

Speaking rates, of course, are almost always slower than reading rates.

120 to 140 w.p.m.

A speaking or reading rate of 120 to 140 w.p.m. can irk your listeners even more than the "faster-than-a-speeding-bullet" rate some hyperkinetic individuals use. It suggests that its user is ill, timorous or stupid. (Actors playing not-too-swift characters often speak at a tortoise-crawl.)

People can listen faster than you can talk, and if your rate is draggy or funereal, you'll soon lose their attention.

On the other hand, if your local Sesquipedalian Society invites you to give an after-dinner speech on "A Comparison of the Myoelastic-Aerodynamic and the Neurochronaxic Theories of Voice Production," you'd be wise to talk at 120–140 w.p.m. *Complex, technical, sad* or *profound* matter works well at this rate.

32. Even though you'll rarely have an occasion to read or speak in slow motion, get the feel of it. The selection below contains exactly 140 words. The number of words up to the diagonal lines is 120. A maximum and a minimum are established. Practice, timing yourself, until it takes you close to a minute to reach either terminal point.

All of you who live on after us, don't harden your hearts against us. If you pity wretches like us, maybe God will be merciful to you on Judgment Day. You see us here, five or six of us, strung up. As for the flesh we loved too well, it's already devoured and has rotted. And we, the bones, now turn to ashes and dust. Don't mock us or make us the butt of jokes. The rain has rinsed and washed us; the sun dried us and turned us black. Magpies and crows have pecked out our eyes and torn away our beards and our eyebrows. Never are we at rest. The winds keep swinging us—now here, now there. / /
Lord, keep us out of hell! There's nothing for us to do there! Friends, don't jeer! May God forgive us! [Villon, *Ballad of the Hanged*]

180 to 200 w.p.m.

A rate of 180 to 200 w.p.m. may exhaust your listeners. Burning up the road tells the world that you're highly nervous, unsure of yourself or emotionally rattled. Faster speaking isn't necessarily better speaking. And have you noticed? We tend to be suspicious of fast talkers; we pigeonhole them as slick operators, shady lawyers or politicians, or high-pressure used car salesmen.

A fast rate, however, is proper for some humorous material, elation, excitement, fear or anger. Even then—use it sparingly.

33. The selection will give you a general idea of this rate. It contains exactly 200 words. The diagonal lines are placed after the 180th word.

What is it, then? What do you want? What have you come for? What do you mean by this flightiness? Bursting in all of a sudden, like a cat having a fit! Well, what have you seen that's so surprising? What kind of an idea has gotten into your head? Really, you know, you act like a three-year-old child and not in the least like what one would expect from a girl of eighteen. I wonder when you'll get more sensible, and behave as a well brought-up young lady should and learn a few good manners? Oh, your head's always empty! You're copying the neighbor's girls. Why are you always trying to be like them? You've no business using them as models. You have other examples, young lady, right in front of you—your own mother. I repeat—your own mother! That's the model you ought to imitate! There, now you see—it was all because of you, you silly child, that our guest was on his knees in front of me—proposing—then you blunder in. / /
You come snooping around, just as though you'd gone completely out of your mind. Just for that, I refused him! [Gogol, *The Inspector General*]

140 to 180 w.p.m.

The most tolerable and useful all-purpose rate is 140 to 180 w.p.m. If you have to handle material that expresses sorrow, gravity, meditation or material that is technical—aim for the lower end of the range: 140 w.p.m.

If your material expresses happiness, humor, or, on occasion, wrath, target the upper end of the range: 180 w.p.m.

Purely conversational situations? 150 to 180 w.p.m. is excellent.

Have to deliver a speech? Our best public speakers find that 160 w.p.m. is a congenial and efficient average.

34. The selection contains 180 words; the diagonals are placed after the 140th word. Practice at the different rates until you feel natural and at ease.

Just how different are college students of today from students of the Middle Ages? Not much. They complained much more about food than we do. For a five-year period at the University of Paris, however, a lot of students discovered they could eat well and cheaply. Near the campus were the shops of a pieman and a barber. The pieman specialized in meat pies. Students could chip in and buy one and have a filling, delicious, inexpensive meal. The barber had the sharpest and fastest razor in Paris. So skilled was he that a client coming into his shop at the end of the day never felt the blade that shaped his beard until it slit his throat. The body was then dropped through a trap door into a cellar which connected with that of the pieman. / /
You've guessed the rest. But one day a neighborhood dog got into the baker's backyard and dug up human bones. He took them home; his owner was a constable. The two men were caught and burned alive at the stake.

35. Look over the selections below and decide on a general rate that fits the mood of the material. When you read aloud, however, be sure that you vary the rate: accelerate, decelerate, hold steady.

   a. One dark and stormy night, a ship struck a reef and sank. But one of the sailors clung desperately to a piece of wreckage and was finally cast up exhausted on an unknown beach. In the morning he struggled to his feet and, rubbing his salt-encrusted eyes, looked around to learn where he was. The only thing he saw that could have been made by man was a gallows. "Thank God!" he shouted. "Civilization!"

   b. A majority of gunslingers from the Wild West weren't too bright. A bad man named Wes Hardin was determined to shoot it out with Wild Bill Hickock. Hardin was extremely jealous of Wild Bill, because Bill was rated as number one gunman, but Hardin was only number two. Hardin heard that Wild Bill was in El Paso, so he rode there, went into a popular bar and was given the corner seat—in those days, the best seat in the house. He sat in the corner for three days, staring into the long mirror behind the bar so that he could instantly see anybody who came through the door. And on the fourth day, who should enter the bar with gun drawn? Wild Bill Hickock? No! The sheriff. And guess what Hardin did. He shot the mirror instead of the sheriff. The sheriff then shot Hardin. You can visit his grave in El Paso today.

   c. Tell General Howard I know what is in his heart. What he told me before, I have in my heart, I am tired of fighting. Our chiefs are killed. . . The old men are all dead. It is the young men who say yes or no. My brother, who led on the young men, is dead. It is cold and we have no blankets. The little children are freezing to death. My people, some of them, have run away to the hills, and have no blankets, no food. No one knows where they are—perhaps freezing to death. I want to have time to look for my children and see how many of them I can find. Maybe I shall find them among the dead. Hear me, my chiefs, I am tired. My heart is sick and sad. From where the sun now stands I will fight no more, forever. [Chief Joseph to the Nez Perce Indians]

   d. There is one contemporary artist who refuses to go along with all the wild and weird "modern" art—square-faced ladies with three ears and a nose sprouting from the middle of the forehead. Phil Ernst insists on realism. "Tell it like it is," is his motto. One day Ernst decided to paint a picture of his backyard and garden. There were eight rather large trees in the yard, but the artist decided that if he included all eight of them, it would clutter his painting, so he painted only seven. His wife came out to look at the completed work of art. "But Phil, darling!" she said. "Where's that missing tree? There are eight trees, but you painted only seven." And what did Phil do? Paint in the missing tree? NO! He took an axe and cut down the extra tree!

   e. Who were the greatest lovers of all time? Probably Cleopatra and Mark Antony. The queen of Egypt was the most talked about sexpot of ancient times, and Mark was lost in lust for her. It so happened that Cleo was an expert with poisons. Mark would never eat with her unless his own personal slave-taster was present. Cleo regarded this as an insult and decided to teach him a lesson. One day she took a flower from her hair and tossed it into Mark's wine cup and asked him to drink the wine as a symbol of his love. Mark's taster had already sipped the wine, so Mark raised the cup to his lips to drink. Quickly, Cleo grabbed the cup away from him. She ordered a man brought up from the palace dungeon, gave him the cup to drink, and he fell over—dead. Said Cleo to Mark: "I poisoned the petals of the flower. I only wanted to show you that in spite of your taster, if I really wanted to, I could kill you any time."

Assignment 18: Rate

If you're an excessively rapid or slow reader or talker, you may want additional practice in making yourself feel comfortable with a 140 to 180 w.p.m. range. Choose about two minutes of informal, colorful material, and place diagonal marks after word 140, word 180, word 280, and word 360. As you read, time yourself. Does your performance take approximately two minutes?

The Suggested Checklist for this assignment, which is at the end of the chapter, may be useful to you as you practice your material.

DURATION

DURATION refers to the length or amount of sound.

Words and syllables are squeezeboxes. Like accordions, they can be expanded or compressed. When do you squeeze and when do you stretch?

36. For demonstration purposes, read the following excerpts from two of the most popular poems in the English language:

    "Now, Dasher! now, Dancer! now, Prancer and Vixen!
    On, Comet! on, Cupid! on, Donder and Blitzen!
    To the top of the porch, to the top of the wall!
    Now dash away, dash away, dash away all!" [*A Visit From St. Nicholas,* Clement C. Moore]

    The curfew tolls the knell of parting day,
    The lowing herd winds slowly o'er the lea,
    The ploughman homeward plods his weary way,
    And leaves the world to darkness and to me. [*Elegy Written in a Country Churchyard,* Thomas Gray]

    As you read the Moore poem, you slashed and shortened most of the vowels and diphthongs. But with Gray's "Elegy," you instinctively lengthened and extended most of the vowels and diphthongs.

    In a real-life, nonpoetic situation, how would you shout this one? *Hey! The house is on fire! Quick, somebody, call for help!*

    You'd attack each word as though you were touching a hot stove. You wouldn't loiter long. For such brisk, riveting machine attacks, let's borrow the word staccato from musical terminology. A staccato treatment of words is relevant if you're trying to express extreme emotional states such as rage, fright, enthusiasm, and joy.

    Now pretend you're hypnotizing somebody and say: *Relax. Close your eyes. Go to sleep.*

    You gave it a legato treatment—the opposite of staccato. Legato describes a smooth, connected style. In speech, a more accurate term, as far as sound duration is concerned, is prolonged. Words are lengthened or drawn out.

    A prolonged treatment is what you want if you're dealing with calmness, reverence, awe, or deep grief.

    Now say: *I'm going shopping. Want to come along?*

    Staccato? No. *Prolonged?* Hardly.

    Regular? Yes. Let's use the word *regular* for matter-of-fact, offhand, routine conversation and speech.

37. These lines are marked S for Staccato, P for Prolonged and R for Regular. Read them accordingly, noting the contrasts.

    a. S: I can't stand it another minute!
    b. P: The sea is sad and calm tonight.
    c. R: May I see you later this evening?
    d. S: If I've told you once, I've told you a hundred times—no!
    e. P: Death—awful, cruel and weary—hung like a pall over the grim field of battle.
    f. R: Never slap a man who is chewing tobacco.
    g. S: Don't let them kill me, Your Honor! I'm innocent! I swear it!
    h. P: The silent forest stood there, cool and green and drowsy.
    i. R: The higher a monkey climbs, the more you can see of his behind.
    j. S: If that's the way you feel about it, all right.
    k. P: Even a small star shines in the darkness.
    l. R: The trouble with the rat race is that even if you win, you're still a rat.
    m. S: Look out! He's got a gun! Duck!
    n. P: I have never been so insulted!
    o. R: Oh, I wish I had that kind of money.
    p. S: Get out of here and don't ever come back.
    q. P: Get out of here and don't ever come back.
    r. R: Get out of here and don't ever come back.

38. Study each of these sentences and then give it the interpretation you think most apropos. Want to be ingenious? "Shift gears" within a line, going from a *prolonged* to a *staccato* or a *regular* reading.

   a. I'm sorry, but he died quite peacefully three hours ago.
   b. This is the last time you'll ever try anything like that, do you hear?
   c. Go ahead! Strike me if you dare!
   d. What would you do with a million dollars?
   e. The Shenandoah inched along, rippling quietly under the cool light of the slowly rising moon.
   f. Excited? Who's excited?
   g. What did you put in this drink? I'm getting so drowsy.
   h. Jill? It can't be you! You're supposed to be dead!
   i. I've never been so humiliated in my life! How dare you!
   j. I'm afraid the news is bad. Your family has been wiped out.
   k. Don't ever let me catch you in that place again!
   l. I wish you'd stop asking such stupid questions.
   m. She was such a decent person . . . quiet, patient, dignified . . . we couldn't have known that she was slowly dying.
   n. Give me three minutes to think it over and you'll have your answer.
   o. I've never heard of anything like this before. Have you?
   p. I guess it would be better if we didn't see each other again.
   q. That was the longest, dreariest bore I've ever sat through.
   r. I thought I told you to leave town, partner!

39. In these selections, you'll find that some phrases or lines sound best if you use *staccato* speech. Others work better if read with *prolonged* tones or tones of *regular* duration. Work for contrast and variety within each selection.

   a. Dear Ann Landers:
      I own a splendid golden retriever that can be mighty mean if provoked by another dog, but he is extremely gentle with people. "Champ" has one trait that worries me. While most dogs wag their tails back and forth, this animal wags his tail in a circle. I recently read that dogs with abnormal tail-wagging habits are apt to be gay. I know you have access to the best scientific minds in the country. Please check and let me know if "Champ" might just possibly be gay.

      (Signed) J. A. T. in Dallas, Texas

      Dear J. A. T.:
      I decided not to bother any of those fine scientific minds with this one because the answer couldn't possibly matter to anyone except another dog.
   b. No doubt I now grew very pale. But I talked more fluently and with a heightened voice. Yet the sound increased—and what could I do? It was a low, dull, quick sound—much such a sound as a watch makes when enveloped in cotton. I gasped for breath—and yet the officers heard it not. I talked more quickly, more vehemently, but the noise steadily increased. Oh God! What could I do? I foamed—I raved—I swore! I swung the chair upon which I had been sitting, and grated it upon the boards, but the noise arose overall and continually increased. It grew louder—louder—louder! And still the men chatted pleasantly, and smiled. Was it possible they heard not? Almighty God—no, no! They heard! They suspected! They knew! They were making a mockery of my horror! But anything was better than this agony! Anything was more tolerable than this derision! I could bear those hypocritical smiles no longer! I felt that I must scream or die! And now—again! Hark! Louder! Louder! Louder!

      "Villains!" I shrieked. "I admit the deed! Tear up the planks! Here, here! It is the beating of his hideous heart!" [Poe, "The Tell-Tale Heart"]
   c. Most of the world's experts agree that Leonardo da Vinci's *The Last Supper* is the greatest religious painting in existence. Did you know that a saltshaker is included in the painting? True enough. Judas knocked it over. Why? He's in a state of shock. Christ has found him out and just said, "One of you will betray me," and Judas reacts like a rattlesnake about to strike. "Twilight Zone" on TV had an interesting show based on Leonardo a few seasons ago. According to this story, Leonardo had completed the painting—except for Judas. He searched and searched, but couldn't find a face evil enough to paint

as Judas. Three years went by, and finally one day he found a man with an evil face. He asked the man if he would pose. The man said, "Certainly. After all, I posed for you before. Don't you remember me?" Leonardo said, "No." The man replied, "I've fallen on hard times, and I've been leading a terrible existence. But three years ago you used me to model for Christ!" It's an interesting story, but not true because Leonardo actually painted Christ last!

PHRASING AND PAUSES

Almost every actor from Lassie to Rambo wants to play *Hamlet*, one of the reasons being that it's the longest part—1,422 lines—in any one of Shakespeare's plays. The popular Hamlets of Richard Burton, Laurence Olivier, Richard Chamberlain, and Kevin Kline have been greeted with standing ovations, and some Hamlets with hisses and boos.

Hamlet's most universal moment is his famous meditation on death, the "To be or not to be. . ." soliloquy. Recordings of Burton, Olivier and others are available. If you have a chance to listen to any of them, you'll notice curious differences in the length and location of pauses.

A former student of mine played Horatio to the late Richard Burton's Hamlet. Burton delivered a different performance each night! On three consecutive evenings he gave completely dissimilar readings of the soliloquy:

To be   or not to be   that is the question.

To be or not to be   that is the question.

To be or not to be   that   is the question.

Which is the most effective? Probably none is better than the others. Taste alone, not rules, can decide. As long as clarity is preserved and the desired emphasis is achieved, a group of words can be phrased with the accompanying pauses in several different ways.

Nevertheless, something tells us that we might be annoyed at any of these readings:

To   be or not to   be that is the question.

To be or not   to be   that is the   question.

(With no pauses at all) Tobeornottobethatisthequestion.

The late Hubert Humphrey, 1968 presidential candidate, talked excessively fast with virtually no pauses. Former President Gerald Ford quipped: "Listening to Hubert is like trying to read *Playboy* with your wife turning the pages."

A PAUSE is a rest stop—a period of silence. A PHRASE is a group of related words expressing a thought or "sense" unit or an idea. Phrases are set off from each other with pauses.

WHY PAUSE?

To Take a Break and Take a Breath

You have to pause often enough so that you can replenish your breath supply and always keep a reserve amount in your lungs while speaking. Otherwise, you'll find yourself gasping for breath in the middle of a phrase, with the last two or three words of the phrase sounding like a series of strained grunts.

Then, of course, one occasionally hears this criticism of a speaker: "But he never stops to take a breath!" This individual gets wound up in his words and never runs down. Either fault, "gaspitis" or perpetual motion of the jaw, is apt to call attention to itself and detract from what is being said.

40.   As you read each section, pause briefly and breathe wherever you see a comma.

   a.   A B C D E F , G H I J K L
   b.   A B C D E F , G H I J K L , M N O P Q R
   c.   A B C D E F , G H I J K L , M N O P Q R , S T U V W X

Repeat, but this time don't breathe at the commas.

41. Read the following sentences. Pause wherever you see double vertical lines, but *breathe only when you have to.*

   a. If you think nobody cares if you're alive ‖ try missing a couple of car payments.
   b. Know what it is to be a child ‖ it is to turn pumpkins into coaches, mice into horses, and nothing into everything.
   c. The late Senator Margaret Chase Smith on politics ‖ Get elected. Get re-elected ‖ Don't get mad, get even.
   d. If you want the most out of life ‖ the thing is to be a gossiper by day and gossipee by night.
   e. I want nothing but bad losers ‖ Good losers get into the habit of losing ‖ You don't save a pitcher for tomorrow ‖ Tomorrow it may rain. [Billy Martin]
   f. The atomic bomb in the hands of a Francis of Assisi would be less harmful than a pistol in the hand of a thug ‖ what makes the bomb dangerous is not the energy it contains ‖ but the person who uses it.
   g. Give-and-take makes good friends ‖ To find a friend one must close one eye ‖ To keep a friend—two. Friendship is the only cement that will ever hold the world together ‖ Instead of loving your enemies, treat your friends a little better ‖ Don't use a hatchet to remove a fly from a friend's forehead ‖ Nine-tenths of the people were created so you would want to be with the other tenth ‖ A true friend will see you through when others will see that you are through ‖ When one friend washes another both become clean ‖ A friend that ain't in need is a friend indeed. [Pearl Bailey]

For Clarity

42. Read these twice. The first time, ignore the pause marks. The second time, pause where indicated.

   a. When Ann had eaten │ │ the dog ran away.
   b. Hank, her date │ │ said Bob │ │ was quite boring.
      Without the pauses, they're confusing. (Ann ate the dog? Who was boring—Hank or Bob?)

For Emphasis and Emotional Quality

43. Again read these twice, without pauses and with pauses. There's a vast difference.

   a. We shall fight on the beaches │ │ we shall fight on the landing grounds │ │ we shall fight in the fields and in the streets │ │ we shall fight in the hills │ │ we shall never surrender.
   b. How do you know love is gone │ │ If you said that you'd be there at seven, and you get there by nine, and he or she hasn't called the police yet │ │ it's gone. [Zsa Zsa Gabor]

44. Believe it or not, you can make sense out of the nonsense below—*if you pause in the right places.* You'll need to gulp some air while you're reading, but don't gasp for breath in the middle of a phrase.

   Esau Wood sawed wood. Esau Wood would saw wood. All the wood Esau Wood saw Esau Wood would saw. In other words, all the wood Esau saw Esau sought to saw. Oh, the wood Wood would saw! And oh, the wood-saw with which Wood would saw wood. But one day Wood's wood-saw would saw no wood, and thus the wood Wood sawed was not the wood Wood would saw if Wood's wood-saw would saw wood. Now, Wood would saw if Wood's wood-saw would saw wood, so Esau sought a saw that would saw wood. One day Esau saw a saw saw wood as no other wood-saw Wood saw would saw wood. In fact, of all the wood-saws Wood ever saw saw wood Wood never saw a wood-saw that would saw wood as the wood-saw Wood saw saw wood would saw wood, and I never saw a wood-saw that would saw as the wood-saw Wood saw would saw until I saw Esau saw wood with the wood-saw Wood saw saw wood. Now Wood saws wood with the wood-saw Wood saw saw wood.

The Pause that Refreshes

The pregnant pause—also known as the dramatic pause—is an understated way of bringing out meanings or emotional content. Ronald Reagan, Billy Graham, Jesse Jackson and Jane Fonda are clever in their use of this kind of pause.

   Polished conversationalists and public speakers understand the importance of the pregnant pause. So do actors. George C. Scott once said that not only is the pause the most precious thing in speech but it is the last fundamental the actor masters.

The most provocative thing about the dramatic pause, however, is not its frequency but its length. Solemn, profound, and complex subjects generally need longer pauses than lighthearted, unpretentious or familiar material.

45. A long pause *after* an idea or a phrase underscores what has just been said:

If God had wanted us to think with our wombs, why did he give us a brain? I don't mind living in a man's world as long as I can be a woman in it. God made man, and then said I can do better than that and made woman. I'm not radical. I'm just aware. | | I've come a long way, Baby!

46. A long pause *before* an important idea or a climactic key word heightens suspense:

Only one person could have killed her, and that person is | | you.

47. If you're trying to be funny or humorous, the punch or laugh line can often be pointed up and made funnier if it's preceded by a protracted pause. The late Laurel and Hardy were past masters of this kind of timing. Stan Laurel (the thin one) said on his deathbed, "Dying is hard, but not as hard as playing comedy."

Bill Cosby, Carol Burnett and Eddie Murphy are also particularly adept at accentuating their punch lines.

As a simple example of how to point up a line, try:

Rock Magazine recently took a poll to name the best-dressed rock star. | | Nobody won.

Caution: Punctuation is generally a guide for the eye rather than the ear. True, you sometimes pause where a writer has placed a comma or a dash, but not always. If you pause for every punctuation mark, you'll sound choppy and jerky. Pauses, in themselves, are *silent* punctuation marks.

48. In this material, | L | indicates a long pause, | M | a medium pause, and | S | a short pause. These are suggestions only. Obviously, *long, medium,* and *short* are comparative terms.

a. What is the most important thing in the world? | L | Love.
b. The public is wonderfully tolerant. It forgives everything | M | except genius.
c. Money doesn't always bring happiness. | S | People with ten million dollars are no happier than people with | S | nine million dollars. Money is like | S | manure | S | of very little use | L | except to spread. Money never made a fool of anybody | L | it only shows them up. Money doesn't make you happy | M | but it certainly quiets the nerves.
d. Sunday School | S | A place where they tell children about God for fifty-one weeks | L | then introduce them to Santa Claus.
e. If you watch a game, it's fun | S | If you play it, it's recreation | S | If you work at it | L | it's golf.
f. Gertrude Stein, poet, playwright and wit, lay dying. In her last moments she came out of her coma—a friend was nearby, weeping—and asked | M | "What is the answer?" She closed her eyes briefly; once again she came to, a smile on her lips and asked | L | "What is the question?"
g. Eating is self-punishment | L | Punish the food instead | M | Strangle a loaf of bread | S | Throw darts at a cheesecake | S | Chain a lamb chop to your bed | S | Beat up a cookie.
h. And there it lay | M | that moldy coffin | S | ugly and menacing in the bloodless moonlight. | S | We lurched forward | S | six pairs of trembling hands seized the grimy lid | S | ripped it open. | M | Something | S | somewhere shrieked. | M | Our eyes, hot and glazed, pierced the formless shadows inside the casket. | S | Again a godless scream | S | and then we knew | M | the evil box | S | was | L | empty.
i. Somewhere on this globe, every ten seconds | S | there is a woman giving birth to a child. | M | She must be found and stopped.
j. A billboard read | S | "You must pay for your sins!" | S | Somebody scrawled beneath it | M | "If you've already paid | L | please disregard this notice."
k. I have only one thing to say to you | L | You are a liar.
l. "Who is wise?" asks the wise man | S | and being wise he answers it himself. | M | "He is wise who knows that one is never too old | S | to learn something stupid."
m. From birth to 18 | S | a girl needs good parents. From 18 to 35 | S | she needs good looks. From 35 to 55 | S | she needs a good personality. From 55 on | L | she needs cash. [Linda Evans]

n. I don't like to break hearts. I don't really know these people and, gosh | S | it's a weird thing. You portray an image. And those people are into you so long, buying your records, waking up thinking about you and you're totally on their mind. | M | It's an awful thing. | L | I don't know how to handle it. [Michael Jackson]

o. There's still plenty of good old American know-how around. | M | Unfortunately | S | most of it's in Japan.

49. Study and analyze these selections for location and length of pauses. Mark according to your own judgment and then read.

a. I find TV very educational. The minute somebody turns it on, I go into the library and read a good book. [Woody Allen]

b. I don't worry about crime in the streets. It's the sidewalks I stay off of.

c. Why do celebrities always gripe about their lack of privacy? That's like a fighter coming out of the ring and saying, "There's somebody in there trying to hit me."

d. The biblical punishment for adultery was to be stoned in the marketplace. Nowadays, about half the population thinks that sounds like fun.

e. The U.S. congress seems to be divided into three categories: those who have gone out of their minds, those who are about to go out of their minds and those who have no minds to go out of.

f. Do you like "modern" art? I do. Even some of the crazy stuff which looks like doodlings by Jason, the psycho, in *Friday the Thirteenth, Part Ten*. I have some "modern" art at home. When I show it to friends, the comment I most often get is, "What does it mean?" My standard reply is, "What does a tree mean?" Do you want to know what "modern" art is all about? When my son Jeff was six, he had done something wrong and was being punished by being confined to the backyard for a day. He sat on the steps. It was a hot day, and Jeff felt sorry for himself because he had wanted to go swimming. He started talking to himself. I eavesdropped. Said he: "Am I a boy? Why aren't I a chair? What is a chair?" And that's what "modern" art is about.

g. The great box was in the same place. The lid was laid on it, not fastened down. I knew I must reach the body for the key, so I raised the lid, and then I saw something which filled my soul with horror. There lay the Count, but looking as if his youth had been half renewed, for the white hair was changed to iron-gray. The mouth was redder than ever. On the lips were gouts of blood, which trickled from the corners of the mouth and ran over the chin and neck. Even the deep, burning eyes were set in bloated flesh. It seemed as if the whole awful creature was simply gorged with blood. I felt all over the body, but no sign could I find of the key. Then I stopped and looked at the Count. There was a mocking smile on that ghastly face. A terrible desire came upon me to rid the world of this monster. I seized a shovel. I lifted it high. I struck downward at the hateful face. But as I did so the head turned. The eyes fell full upon me, with all their blazing horror. The sight seemed to paralyze me. The shovel fell from my hand. The last glimpse I had was of that hideous face, blood-stained and fixed with an evil grin which would have held its own in the bottom level of hell. [Stoker, *Dracula*]

h. **Milgrig and the Tree Wilfs**
(Something like Hans Christian Andersen)
Once upon a time there was a little girl named Milgrig, believe it or not. She lived in the middle of a deep, dark forest with her three ugly sisters and their husbands, who were charcoal burners. Every night the three ugly sisters used to take little Milgrig and pull out a strand of her golden hair, so that by the time she was thirteen years old, she looked something awful. And after the three sisters had pulled out her hair, their three husbands (I forgot to tell you that the three husbands were even uglier than the three sisters and much nastier) would stick pins into little Milgrig until she looked like a war map.
One night, when little Milgrig was so full of pins that she couldn't see straight, a fairy prince came riding up to the door of the charcoal burners' hut and asked if he had lost the way.
"How should I know?" replied the oldest sister, who was uglier than all the rest. "What was your way?"
"My way was to the king's castle," replied the prince, "and I must get there before midnight, for my father is torturing my mother with red-hot irons."

"Your father sounds like a good egg," replied the oldest husband, who was uglier than all the rest. "We must ask him down some night."

The prince, however, did not think that this was very funny and asked if little Milgrig might not be allowed to show him the way to the castle.

The ugly husbands and sisters, thinking that Milgrig would not know the way and would get the prince lost in the forest, agreed heartily to this suggestion, and the pins were pulled out of Milgrig to make it possible for her to walk.

"Good luck and a happy landing!" they all called out after the two young people as they set forth on their perilous journey.

But the prince was no fool, and knew his way through the forest as well as you or I do (better, I'll wager), and he took little Milgrig to the palace just as fast as his palfrey would carry him.

She wasn't particularly crazy about going, but a prince is a prince, and she knew enough to keep her mouth shut.

When they reached the palace and the prince found that his father had already killed his mother, he turned to little Milgrig and said: "Now you are the ruler."

At this, little Milgrig was very pleased and immediately dispatched messengers to the charcoal burners' hut, where the three ugly sisters and three still-uglier brothers-in-law were burned alive in a slow fire. Little Milgrig and the prince, happy in this termination to their little affair, lived happily ever after. [Robert Benchley. Reprinted by permission of Harper & Row, Publishers, Inc.]

Assignment 19: Duration, Phrasing, and Pauses

Prepare fifteen to twenty lines of material. A brief cutting from a short story or a play would be ideal. Try to choose material that contains several contrasting moods.

Analyze your selection. What kind of treatment works best with certain words, phrases or lines? *Staccato? Prolonged? Regular?*

Mark your selections into appropriate phrases and pauses of various length.

The Suggested Checklist for this assignment, which is at the end of the chapter, may be useful to you as you practice.

When you present your selection to the class, work for as much spontaneity as you can. The techniques you use shouldn't call attention to themselves.

PUTTING IT ALL TOGETHER

"Take care of the sense," Lewis Carroll wrote, "and the sounds will take care of themselves."

As you work with the selections below, blend and weave together the various elements that have to do with vocal expressiveness. Don't get hung up on devices! What is the general effect you're trying to achieve? Search for meaning and intelligibility. Search for various feelings and moods. Above all, search for freshness and spontaneity.

50. Use all the vocal versatility you can muster. Be original.

   a. **COUNTESS:** Oh, I wish she hadn't brought up the Alps, Lucy. It always reminds me of that nasty moment I had the day Gustav made me climb to the top of one of them. Anyhow, there we were. And suddenly it struck me that Gustav had pushed me. I slid halfway down the mountain before I realized that Gustav didn't love me any more. But love takes care of its own, Lucy. I slid right into the arms of my fourth husband, the count. [Boothe, *The Women*]

   b. **SID:** You're right, Lily!—right not to forgive me! I'm no good and never will be! I'm a no-good drunken bum! You shouldn't even wipe your feet on me! I'm a dirty rotten drunk!—no good to myself or anybody else! If I had any guts, I'd kill myself, and good riddance!—but I haven't—I'm yellow, too—a yellow, drunken bum! [O'Neill, *Ah, Wilderness!*]

c. **SALLY:** Two days ago. Just after we left here. He saw us in the street . . . Mother and me, I mean—and our eyes met—his and mine, I mean—and he sort of followed me. To a tea shop, where he sat and gazed at me. And back to the hotel. And at the restaurant. He had the table next to us, and he kept sort of hitching his foot around my chair. And he passed me a note in the fruit basket. Only Mother got it by mistake. But it was in German. I told her it was from a movie agent. And I went over and talked to him, and he was! Then we met later. He's quite marvelous, Chris. He's got a long, black beard. Well, not really long. I've never been kissed by a beard before. I thought it would be awful. But it isn't. It's quite exciting. Only he doesn't speak much German. He's a Yugoslavian. That's why I don't know much about the picture. But I'm sure it will be all right. He'll write in something. And now I've got to run. [Van Druten, *I Am a Camera*]

d. **PAUL:** Corie, there is one thing I learned in court. Be careful when you're tired and angry. You might say something you will soon regret. I-am-now-tired-and-angry . . . And I will now say something I will soon regret . . . Okay, Corie, maybe you're right. Maybe we have nothing in common. Maybe we rushed into this marriage a little too fast. Maybe love isn't enough. Maybe two people should have to take more than a blood test. Maybe they should be checked for common sense, understanding and emotional maturity. [Simon, *Barefoot in the Park*]

e. **FANNY:** Do you mean that? You're not just trying to be polite? Nick, I'm a good friend of yours. And in a dumb way I'm kinda smart. So I'm going to tell you what you ought to do. You ought to marry me. You don't have to, I'm all yours anyway. But the kind of wife I'd be, you wouldn't *believe!* Look at my past record—no errors, no strikeouts, nothing! That means—no bad habits! I'd be learning the part fresh—*your* way! Besides that, I'm lucky! And I'd be lucky for you! What could be better for a gambler than a lucky wife?! [Lennart, *Funny Girl*]

f. **ARTHUR:** I went to London as squire to my cousin, Sir Kay. The morning of the tournament, Kay discovered that he'd left his sword at home and gave me a shilling to ride back and fetch it. On my way through London, I passed a square and saw there a sword rising from a stone. Not thinking very quickly, I thought it was a war memorial. The square was deserted, so I decided to save myself a journey and borrow it. I tried to pull it out. I failed. I tried again. I failed again. Then I closed my eyes and with all my force tried one last time. Lo, it moved in my hand! Then slowly it slid out of the stone. I heard a great roar. When I opened my eyes, the square was filled with people shouting: "Long live the King! Long live the King!" Then I looked at the sword and saw the blade gleaming with letters of gold. [Lerner and Loewe, *Camelot*]

g. **BIRDIE:** I've never had a headache in my life. You know it as well as I do. I never had a headache. That's a lie they tell for me. I drink. All by myself, in my own room, by myself, I drink. You know what? In twenty-two years I haven't had a whole day of happiness. Oh, a little like today with you all. But never a single, whole day. And in twenty years you'll be just like me. They'll do the same things to you. [Hellman, *The Little Foxes*]

h. **ANDRE:** Oh, where has all my past life gone to? The time when I was young and clever, when I used to have great dreams. Why do we all become so dull and commonplace and uninteresting almost before we've begun to live? Why do we get lazy, useless, unhappy? People in this town do nothing but eat, drink, and sleep. Then they die, and some more take their places, and they eat, drink, and sleep too. And they indulge in their stupid gossip and vodka and gambling. The wives deceive their husbands, and the husbands lie to their wives, and they pretend they don't see anything and don't hear anything. It's all so stupid! [Chekhov, *The Three Sisters*]

i. **ROSE:** But she says I can't make her an actress like she wants to be. The boys walk because they think the act's finished. They think we're nothing without her. Well, she's nothing without me! I'm her mother and I made her! And I can make you now! And I will, baby, I swear I will! I am going to make you a star! I'm going to build a whole new act—all around you! It's going to be better than anything we ever did before! Better than anything we even dreamed! The old act was getting stale and tired! But the new one? Look at the new star, Herbie! She's going to be beautiful! She is beautiful! Finished?! We're just beginning and there's no stopping us this time! [Laurents, *Gypsy*]

j.   **HORACE:** I'm sick of you, sick of this house, sick of my life here. I'm sick of your brothers and their dirty tricks to make a dime. There must be better ways of getting rich than cheating poor people on a pound of bacon. Why should I give you the money? You wreck the town, you and your brothers, you wreck the town and live on it. Not me. Maybe it's easy for the dying to be honest. But it's not my fault I'm dying. I'll do no more harm now. I've done enough. I'll die my own way. And I'll do it without making the world any worse. I leave that to you. [Hellman, *The Little Foxes*]

k.   **CRYSTAL:** Now get this straight, Mrs. Haines. I like what I've got and I'm going to keep it. You handed me your husband on a silver platter. But I'm not returning the compliment. I can't be stampeded by gossip. What you believe and what Stephen believes will cut no ice in a divorce court. You need proof and you haven't got it. When Mr. Winston comes to his senses, he'll apologize. And Stephen will have no choice, but to accept—my explanations. Now, that's that! Good night! [Boothe, *The Women*]

l.   **CYRANO:** My nose is very large? Young man, you might say many other things, changing your tone. For example—Aggressively: "Sir, if I had such a nose, I'd cut it off!" Friendly: "You'd have to drink from a tall goblet or your nose would dip into it." Descriptive: " 'Tis a crag . . . a peak . . . a peninsula!" Graciously: "Are you so fond of birds that you offer them this roosting place to rest their little feet?" Quarrelsome: "When you smoke a pipe and the smoke comes out of your nose, doesn't some neighbor shout 'Your chimney is on fire'?" Warning: "Be careful, or its weight will drag down your head and stretch you prostrate on the ground." Tenderly: "Have a small umbrella made to hold over it, lest its color fade in the sun." Dramatic: "It's the Red Sea when it bleeds!" Countrified: "That's a nose that is a nose! A giant turnip or a baby melon!" My friend, that is what you'd have said if you had had some learning or some wit. But wit you never had a bit of. As for letters, you have only the four that spell out "fool"! [Rostand, *Cyrano de Bergerac*]

m.   **JULIE:** You don't think I can stand the sight of blood, is that it? Oh, how I'd love to see your brains on that chopping block. I'd love to see the whole of your sex swimming in a sea of blood. The way I feel I could drink out of your skull. I could eat your heart roasted whole! You think I'm weak! My father will come home—find his money stolen! He'll send for the sheriff—and I'll tell him everything. Then there'll be peace and quiet . . . forever. [Strindberg, *Miss Julie*]

n.   **CORBACCIO:** I . . . hee, hee . . . like to look at dying men. I've seen so many and I enjoy each one more. I'm eighty-two. I've buried brothers, sisters, friends, enemies, but I'm still alive . . . hee, hee . . . I'll outlive 'em all. I've known many of them in the cradle, and seen 'em grow up and all at once they lie there—blue, cold, and dead . . . hee, hee. And now this one, too! He lived a merry life . . . young, could have been my son—and he's come to die already, hee, hee! I want to take a look at him. Here, stand up, carcass, face an old man. You're younger—you have better legs. Stand up . . . hee, hee! Often you've mocked poor old Corbaccio for being miserly . . . hee, hee . . . who's mocking now, you windbag, you glutton! He'll outlive you all, will old Corbaccio! [Jonson, *Volpone*]

o.   **MURIEL:** You did too! You're lying and you know it! You did too! And there I was right at that time lying in bed and not able to sleep, wondering how I was ever going to see you again and crying my eyes out, while you—I hate you! I wish you were dead! I'm going home this moment! I never want to lay eyes on you again! And this time I mean it! [O'Neill, *Ah, Wilderness!*]

p.   **DION:** Look at you! You, a man with one foot in the grave, sitting there and kissing that lovely girl! Don't you like to kiss your own wife? How do you intend to explain this to her? You'll lie to her, won't you? You'll tell her it's only fatherly kissing, I suppose. Ha! And all that money you have? You stole it from your wife, didn't you? I'll be damned if I'm going to keep my mouth shut about this. I'm going straight to your wife and tell her that you're going to strip her bare unless she stops you—and stops you right now! [Plautus, *The Comedy of Asses*]

q.   **RACHEL:** I remember feeling this way when I was a little girl. I would wake up at night, terrified of the dark. I'd think that sometimes my bed was on the ceiling, and the whole house was upside down. And if I didn't hang onto the mattress, I might fall outward to the stars. I wanted to run to my father, and have him tell me I was safe, that everything was all right. But I was always more frightened of him than I was of falling. It's the same way now. [Lawrence and Lee, *Inherit the Wind*]

r. **MARTHA:** Pushed around. We're being pushed around by crazy people. That's an awful thing. And we're standing here—we're standing here taking it. Try to understand this: you're not playing with paper dolls. We're human beings, see? It's our lives you're fooling with. Our lives. That's serious business for us. Can you understand that? [Hellman, *The Children's Hour*]

s. **DON JUAN:** Aha! And where did this one come from? Did you ever see anything more delightful? Turn just a little, please. What a charming figure! Look up a little. What a pretty little face. Open your eyes wide. Aren't they beautiful? Now a glimpse of your teeth. Delicious! And what inviting lips! And a girl like you is marrying a scrubby peasant? Never! You weren't born to live in the middle of a hellhole. I've been sent here to prevent you from marrying that dolt. To get to the point. I love you with all my heart. Say the word and I'll take you away and show you the kind of life you deserve. Is my proposal rather sudden? It's your fault. You're much too beautiful. You have made me fall as deeply in love with you in a quarter of an hour as in six months with anyone else. [Molière, *Don Juan*]

t. **DONNA ELVIRA:** For a man who is used to this sort of thing, you're certainly not very convincing, are you? I'm almost sorry to see you so embarrassed. And now the lies will start again, won't they? Why don't you swear that your feelings for me are the same as ever? Why don't you swear that you love me more than anything else in this world—'til death do us part? Oh, I'm amazed at my own stupidity! I knew what you were doing. Common sense told me you were guilty. But my simple little mind was busy inventing excuses for you. Did a day pass that you weren't with some other woman? No! You're going to be punished for what you've done to me, Don Juan. If God Himself has no terrors for you, then let me warn you. Beware the fury of a scorned woman! [Molière, *Don Juan*]

u. **DR. PANGLOSS:** Well, it's true—they hanged me. They were supposed to burn me, but just as they were ready to roast me, along came a cloudburst. They couldn't start a fire, so for lack of anything better to do, they hanged me. Know what happened? They bungled it. The executioner was superb at burning people alive, but he didn't know beans about hanging. The rope was wet and didn't tighten properly. It got caught on a knot. I was still breathing, but they didn't know I was alive. So along came this surgeon who took me home to dissect me. He made an incision in my belly—all the way up to my shoulders. I yelled so loudly that the poor man thought he was dissecting the devil. He was terrified and he ran away so fast that he fell all the way down the stairs. With the last strength I had, I screamed, "I'm alive! Have mercy! Help me!" He recovered his courage, returned and sewed me up, and in two weeks I was up and about. [Voltaire, *Candide*]

v. **PRUDENCE:** Oh, I've always known it would turn out like this! I felt it in my bones. I knew something marvelous was going to happen the day you came here. And what's more, I can always tell a married man from a bachelor. And I knew that you were dying to get married. How did I know? Last night I dreamt that I was at your funeral. When you dream about a funeral, it's always a sure sign of a wedding. And I knew from the first that you were a farmer, too. Oh, I know all about feeding chickens and laying eggs and milking cows and all that sort of thing. I adore, absolutely adore farmers! . . . What did you just say? You're not a bachelor? You're not a farmer? Well, I knew the day you came here you were nothing but a liar! [Ritchie, *Fashion*]

w. **ORGON:** You were a miserable pauper, and I saved you from starvation. I housed you, I treated you like a brother. I gave you almost everything I own. But, just hold on, my friend, not so fast! A little more caution on your part! So you thought you'd fool me? You tried to act like a saint! You're not cut out to be a saint, and you got tired of your little act sooner than you thought you would, didn't you? Trying to marry my daughter, and worse, trying to seduce my wife—right under my nose. I've been suspicious for a long time, and I knew I would catch you in the act. And you've given me all the evidence I need. It's enough! And I don't need any more talk from you. Spare me your lies, and get out of here! [Molière, *Tartuffe*]

x. **DORINE:** If you ask me, both of you are insane. Stop this nonsense, now! You do want to marry each other, don't you? Mariane, surely you don't want to marry the quack—that imposter—your father has picked out for you? So stop fussing and be quiet. You two are like all other lovers—you're crazy. Your father's a tyrant, and he has a plan we've got to stop. He's acting like a dunce. You'd better humor the old fossil. Pretend to give in to him. Tell him you'll marry the man he wants you to marry. Then keep postponing the wedding day. That way you'll gain time, and time will turn the trick. Your father is the most superstitious man I've ever known. He believes in omens and dreams. The day before your wedding, tell him that you had a dream the night before about a hearse and a funeral or that you broke a mirror or that a black cat crossed your path. He'll call off the wedding! But if everything else fails, no man can force you to marry him unless you take his ring and say "I do." That's the scheme. Now get going! There's no time to chat. Come on, now! Walk! [Molière, *Tartuffe*]

y.   **VOLPONE:** Ah, Mosca, you clever puppy, what a fool you are, how little you have learned of me! Do you really think you have to let the ducats fly in order to have everything? No, you fool! Let them rest quietly, side by side. Then, people will come of their own accord to offer you everything. Get this through your head: The magic of gold is so great that its smell alone can make men drunk. They only need to sniff it, and they come creeping here on their bellies; they only need to smell it, and they fall into your hands like moths in a flame. I do nothing but say I am rich—they bow their backs in reverence. Then I make a pretense at mortal illness. Ah, then the water drips off their tongues, and they begin to dance for my money. Ah, how they love me: Friend Volpone! Best beloved friend! How they flatter me! How they serve me! How they rub against my shins and wag their tails! I'd like to trample the life out of these cobras, these vipers, but they dance to the tune of my pipe. They bring presents! Who, I ask you, does a more thriving business here in Venice and has a juicier sport to boot? [Jonson, *Volpone*]

z.   **MARTHA:** My husband—dead? That dear man! Not really dead? Oh, help me—I may faint! Wait! Do you have the evidence I need? I want a death certificate. I want to know where, when, and how that miserable creature died. What did he say on his death bed? Didn't he send anything to me? A few gold coins, perhaps? A ring or two? He deserted my bed and board three years ago. But that dear, sweet man . . . I forgive him. Oh, I'll be a widow for a year—well, maybe not a whole year—then I'll look around for another man. It won't be easy finding one like him. No woman on the face of this earth had a sweeter fool than mine. If only he hadn't roamed around so much. He was never home. And he couldn't resist that foreign wine, not to mention those foreign women. And those damnable dice! He had a passion for rolling them. Why, that wretch! To rob his children and his wife! May his soul rot in hell! [Goethe, *Faust*]

aa. **YSABEAU:** You have gold for your wine and for your friends—the worst rats and cats in Paris. A swarm of thieves. Sewer scum! Pimps! Hired assassins! But I, Master Bad Rat. I wear the same dress you stole for me three months ago. We can't even stay in Paris. There's a price on your head. Jailbird! You have that gallows' look. Do you ever think of our future, Francois? We live as long as other men have gold you can plunder. You want me to share a life time of filching . . . pilfering? Really, I grow tired of you! [Mayer, *Villon*]

bb. **JUDGE BRACK:** There is something else, Hedda—something rather ugly. The gun he carried—he was here this morning, wasn't he? I saw the gun Eilert had with him, and I recognized it. It was yours! Well, Hedda, think of the scandal! The scandal of which you're so terrified! Naturally you'd have to appear in court—both you and Madame Diana. She'd have to explain how the thing happened. Did he threaten to shoot her, and did the gun go off then—or did she grab the gun, shoot him, and then put it back in his pocket? You'll have to answer that question. Why did you give Eilert the gun? And what conclusion will people draw from the fact that your former lover either killed himself or was murdered in a house of prostitution? [Ibsen, *Hedda Gabler*]

Assignment 20: Putting It All Together

For this assignment, do one of these three choices:

1. Choose two to three minutes of material which requires several contrasting moods or emotional qualities. Interviews with individuals prominent in sports, the arts, politics, and other fields can be found in newspapers and most weekly magazines. These are often excellent sources for colorful, lively, and up-to-date material. You might enjoy quoting from one or more of these interviews.

2. Restudy one or two of the selections from Exercise 50. Practice the material thoroughly and when you present it before the class, read it with as much vocal variety as possible.

3. Select a two- to four-minute scene from a play involving two characters. Choose a climactic moment in the play, one which is intensely dramatic, suspenseful, or funny. *Rehearse with your partner.* Delineate as sharply as you can the characters you select.

The Suggested Checklist for this assignment may be useful to you as you practice your material.

1. What causes vocal monotony?
   Personality characteristics: lazy, frigid, indifferent or introverted individuals—also those plagued by stage-fright—sometimes tend to be monotonous.
   Dull, technical, repetitious subject matter: The speaker may simply have to try harder to communicate with listeners. If the material isn't animated, the speaker *must* be.
   Bad listening habits; poor health or partial hearing loss.

2. Pitch is the highness or lowness of tone or sound. It is determined by age, sex, and general emotional attitudes as well as by length, thickness, mass, and degree of tension of the vocal folds.

3. The optimum (natural) pitch level is your most desirable and efficient pitch level.

4. The habitual (average or customary) pitch level is the one that you use most often. It isn't always the same as the optimum pitch level. If the habitual level is more than two tones higher or lower than the optimum level, an adjustment should be made.

5. The overall rise and fall of the voice or the melody of pitch changes is known as intonation.

6. A pitch level, ranging from high to low, used at any given moment in speaking is known as key. A low key often fits material that is quiet, thoughtful or sad. Excitement, rage, joy, and humor are compatible with a high key. A middle key is used in routine conversation.

7. A pitch change within a single, uninterrupted vocal sound is an inflection. A rising inflection indicates questioning, doubt, incompleteness of thought. A falling inflection indicates certainty or completeness of thought. A double inflection registers uncertainty, hidden meanings, and complexity of thought.

8. A step is a pitch change between words or syllables. It is more emphatic than an inflection.

9. Rate is the fastness or slowness of speech. A general speaking rate of 140 to 180 words per minute (w.p.m.) will accommodate most speaking situations.

10. Duration is the length or amount of sounds.
    Staccato: vowels and diphthongs are cut short. Often used for expressing extreme emotional states.
    Prolonged: vowels and diphthongs are stretched. Particularly suited for less extreme emotions—peacefulness, awe, reverence, sadness.
    Regular: vowels and diphthongs are not attacked briskly, cut short, or lengthened. Appropriate for casual, matter-of-fact conversation and speaking.

11. A pause is an empty space, a period of silence. A phrase is a thought unit. Phrases are set off from each other with pauses.

12. Phrasing is used to underscore the exact meaning of a thought, to prevent confusion between adjacent phrases and for emotional effect.

13. Pauses also help achieve emphasis, clarity, and emotional quality. A pause is often a natural place to take a breath.

Suggested Checklist for Assignments 16–20

As you practice, you may want to work with this checklist. Listen carefully to yourself. If it is feasible, record your assignment, or get a classmate or friend to listen to you as you present the material. Eventually, your goal will be to have a check mark in the **Yes** column for each category. (Optional: Perhaps your instructor will want to use the checklist to evaluate you during your classroom presentation(s).)

	Yes	No

Pitch

Uses most desirable, serviceable pitch level.

Uses effective pitch range.

Keys (general pitch levels) appropriate to content and mood of material.

Inflections appropriately varied to suit emotional demands of material.

Steps used effectively to give greater (or lesser) prominence to words and phrases.

Rate

Avoids—

excessively rapid rate.

excessively slow rate.

Rate of reading/speaking appropriate to material.

Overall rate varied effectively.

Appropriate use of staccato, prolonged, and regular durations.

Pauses and phrases—

appropriate to emotional quality of material.

used effectively to achieve emphasis, clarity, and intelligibility.

Responds to emotional requirements of material.

Achieves spontaneity: does not call undue attention to techniques used.

Additional comments or suggestions:

Assignment 21: Spontaneity

The final oral assignment may be devoted to a final examination performance. Prepare a minimum of three to four minutes of interesting and varied material. In your presentation to the class, some of your material may be read, but at least half of it should be told from memory and not read. An anecdote or a short, short story are almost always suitable. (Particularly good choices are stories that consist of personal experiences: funny, frightening, or embarrassing moments.)

Please *don't* memorize verbatim the material you choose for this section of your performance. Work, instead, for *conversational spontaneity*.

As you practice your selection, rather than concentrating primarily on a certain aspect, fault, or problem of voice, try to think of the many phases of voice and speech you have dealt with in this course as being integrated and blended together.

Demonstrate to your classmates and instructor to the best of your ability the *general* improvement you have made.

The Final Oral Performance chart in Appendix B is included largely as a matter of convenience for your instructor in evaluating specifically, if he or she so desires, various elements of voice and speech.

APPENDIX

PRONUNCIATION AND VOCABULARY

WOULD YOU BELIEVE THAT

. . . The longest word in the Random House Dictionary (forty-five letters) is *pneumonoultramicroscopicsilicovolcanoconiosis* (lung disease)?
How do you pronounce it? Simple.
no͞o´ mə no͞ ul´ trə mī´ krə skop´ ik sil´ ə ko͞´ vol ka͞´ no͞ ko͞´ ne͞ o͞´ sis

or

`nu mə no ʌltrə mɑɪ krə skɑp ɪk `sɪl ə ko vɑl ke no ko ni`o sɪs

. . . A pangram (you won't find the word in most dictionaries) is a short sentence that uses every letter of the alphabet at least once? An example is *Pack my box with five dozen liquor jugs.*

. . . There are a few words and phrases which are spelled the same frontwards and backwards? *mom, pop; Madam, I'm Adam; Red rum, sir, is murder.*

. . . The English language contains about 750,000 words? Only about sixty to seventy of those words are employed in half of all daily conversation.

STANDARD PRONUNCIATION

When Joe tried to swim ACROSST the lake, he DROWNDED.
Is something wrong with the capitalized words? Errors in articulation? Errors in pronunciation?
Technically speaking, these aren't articulatory mistakes. The sounds might be clearly and distinctly produced, and articulation, of course, refers to sharpness and crispness of speech.
Something more than articulation is involved: It's pronunciation.

Pronunciation includes the correct production of sounds, but it also includes saying them in the right order (and without omitting any of them or adding extra ones), and with the appropriate stress on syllables in words.

In this section the word *standard* is used to indicate that the listed pronunciation is frequently used by educated and cultured people. The term *nonstandard* indicates that the listed pronunciation is used less frequently by educated and cultured individuals.
How should we pronounce *advertisement?*

ad ver TISE ment   or   ad VER tise ment?

Both are *standard.*

How should we pronounce *preferable?*

PREF er able   or   pre FER able?

The first is *standard*.

How should we pronounce *cache* (hiding place)?

CATCH   or   CASH?

The second is *standard*.

Now and then we become involved in arguments about pronunciation. Somebody will say, "Let's look it up in the dictionary." If we know how to use a dictionary and don't regard it as divinely inspired, this is an excellent suggestion.

Editors of good dictionaries are quite specific in stating that their volumes simply attempt to describe and record what people say. They don't try to dictate, command, or prescribe rules of conduct. They're aware that our language isn't embalmed or frozen in time and space. English is a dynamic language—forever developing and changing. It is, in short, a gutsy language.

There are about 750,000 words in the English language, and no dictionary can possibly keep up with the latest trends, changes, or fads in words. For example, most of the hippie jargon of the 1960s and early 1970s has disappeared in the 1980s.

Current teen talk (teenspeak) has its own vocabulary. Would you care to translate?

He: *I flailed it. Now I'm popped. Squash that full-on party Saturday. My rents are harsh.*
She: *Chill out!*
(He: I flunked the test. Now I'm in trouble. Forget that big party on Saturday. My parents are strict.
She: Take it easy!)

Will this odd talk make much sense to anyone in the 1990s? Highly doubtful.

Now that a few of us are sailing around in outer space and quite a few of us are playing around with computers, would anybody care to guess how many new words we've added to our language within the past twenty years? And the SDI (Star Wars) program, when and if it's activated, could add 10,000 more *new* words to the English language, according to one space scientist.

To keep up, publishers would have to put out a new dictionary every year. Nor can a dictionary always take into account all the regional variations or modifications in pronunciation.

Professional radio and TV announcers who handle commercials frequently pronounce *caramel* as *CAR-a-mel* (the first *a* sound is like the *a* in *act*) or as ['kærəml'] according to the International Phonetic Alphabet (IPA). Yet one often hears, especially in the Midwest, *CAR-mel* (the first syllable rhymes with *tar*) or, in IPA symbols, ['kɑrml]. Both pronunciations of *caramel* are standard and are widely used by educated people.

Walter Cronkite, for many years an outstanding newscaster, once received considerable mail from irate listeners taking him to task for his mispronunciation of *February*. He had omitted the first *r* and said *Feb-yoo-ary*.

Cronkite has an interesting defense: "I say *Feb-yoo-ary* [with only one *r*] and to hell with it." (It's only fair to note, however, that later in the same newscast Cronkite pronounced *library* with both *r* sounds, not omitting the first *r* as so many of us do in unguarded conversation.)

If you decided to isolate the word *February,* however, and to build a case on its pronunciation, you might possibly—at that moment—say *Feb-roo-ary* (with the two *r* sounds) and completely convince yourself that you'd been saying it that way all along. And you'd probably be wrong!

The pronunciations listed in a dictionary tend to be formal. Words are considered in isolation. In connected and rapid speech and especially in informal situations, pronunciations of words are influenced by other words that precede or follow them.

Is there really a standard pronunciation? No. There is, however, a standard of pronunciation. It's this: *pronunciation that is standard does not attract undue attention to itself.*

If it does, the speaker is either guilty of affectation or of "putting on airs," or the speaker is trying out a pronunciation in an unfavorable environment.

In affected speech the speaker is noticeably artificial in certain pronunciations. This person attempts to attract notice with a manner of speaking that he or she considers to be elegant or genteel. A professor of clothing design in a Midwestern college opened every class meeting with "Good *aw*fternoon, cl*aw*ss"—the *aw* being pronounced as "awe." Needless to say, this same teacher spent much time lecturing about *fawshion,* bypassing *fashion* entirely. Student reaction? Totally negative.

Standard pronunciation, like good articulation, is always desirable. If someone occasionally mispronounces a word, the person won't be labelled as a barbarian or automatically consigned to purgatory. But consistent and frequent mispronunciations definitely stamp an individual as careless, somewhat crude, lacking in culture, refinement, and know-how.

How may your pronunciation be improved?

- **Be a good listener.** Listen carefully to the speech around you, and especially to the speech of educated and cultured individuals. As often as opportunity permits, listen to recordings of your own speech. Compare your pronunciation with that of established, successful speakers and leaders in your own general region.

- **Have access to a good dictionary,** and learn how to use it properly.

ABOUT DICTIONARIES

Some dictionaries rate an A+. A few rate an F.

When is a Webster not a Webster? The name "Webster" is no longer copyrighted, and it now appears on reliable dictionaries, as well as on a few unreliable ones.

If you're about to buy a paperback dictionary, check out a few of them before you part with your money. For example, just how much information do you want from a dictionary? "If you think all dictionaries are the same," as the ad says, "look up a few words that you already understand."

Ask your instructor, librarian, or bookstore salesperson for recommendations.

Even a good dictionary will not be of much help, however, unless you know how to use it. Study the guides and explanatory notes that almost all dictionaries include in their introductory sections.

In all honesty, many of these guides look about as simple as the control panel of a 747.

As far as this course is concerned, however, you will need to know two things: (1) how to define and use a word correctly in a sentence, and (2) how to pronounce the word.

Here are a few shortcuts and, I hope, simplified suggestions.

DEFINITIONS

Many words, of course, have more than one meaning.

One dictionary lists forty-nine definitions for such a simple word as *top,* for example (on *top* of Old Smokey; sleep like a *top;* over the *top;* blow your *top*).

Where does all this put you? Once again, *check the guide* at the front of the dictionary you buy or borrow. In the meantime, here is some simple information about handling definitions.

Dictionaries generally list definitions in one of two ways.

- *The earliest known meaning of a word is placed first.* More recent or current meanings of the word follow. In other words, the order of definitions is historical.

    caboose: 1. a ship's galley. 2. the last car on a freight train mainly for the use of the train crew.

- This format is used by *Webster's Ninth New Collegiate Dictionary* and *Webster's New World Dictionary.*

- *The most common definition with the most basic and central meaning is placed first.* Less common meanings and older definitions follow.

    caboose: 1. the last car on a freight train; used chiefly by the crew. 2. a ship's kitchen; an outdoor oven.

- This format is used by the *Random House Dictionary,* the *American Heritage Dictionary,* and *Funk and Wagnall's Dictionary.*

Having a problem using an unfamiliar word in a sentence? Check the unabridged dictionaries—those two-ton tomes in your library. (An unabridged dictionary isn't condensed or shortened. It may contain 500,000 or more entries. Your abridged paperback, or even hardback, dictionary is condensed. It generally contains 150,000 to 200,000 entries.) The unabridged dictionaries give you many examples of how to use difficult words in phrases or sentences.

PRONUNCIATION

In this book I have provided you with standard pronunciations of 300 different words. But suppose you want to do a little snooping yourself. What do you do when you look up a word and find not one, but two, varying pronunciations?

In most dictionaries both of the pronunciations are regarded as standard. In some cases, however, the first pronunciation shown is considered to be the one most frequently used. But let me emphasize that *the second choice is also widely used by educated speakers.*

There's one small fly in the ointment. No doubt, by now you've noticed that your knowledge of the International Phonetic Alphabet [ˌɪntəˈnæʃənl̩ foˈnɛtɪk ˈælfə ˌbɛt] will not necessarily help you determine a standard pronunciation of a word.

For example, look up the word *chic* (stylish, elegant) in the *Random House Dictionary.* Its first pronunciation is given as

shēk

This bears little resemblance to the phonetic transcription

[ʃik]

As a matter of fact, a majority of popular dictionaries do not use the IPA.* They use dictionary symbols—dik′ shə ner′ ēsimˋbəlz. This means that a mark, a sign, or a symbol may be attached to a certain letter to designate one of several sounds for which the letter might stand. This system is also known as the Diacritical Marking System (DMS).

Are dictionary symbols easier to master than phonetic symbols? This is a matter of endless controversy, and it seems to me that it's six of one and half dozen of another. Dictionary symbols, however, are certainly not as precise as phonetic symbols. With the IPA, you have a one-to-one relationship between the symbol and the sound itself.

Dictionary symbols are neither uniform nor consistent. Look up the word *abdomen* in four popular dictionaries, and this is what you'll find:

ab′ də mən	ăb′ də mən
\ˋab-də-mən	AB.duh.mun

In spite of the discrepancies among the dictionary symbols, you should be reasonably familiar with at least one system. Whatever your choice of career, and regardless if your personal library contains six books or six thousand, a dictionary will probably be one of them. A dictionary for most people is an inescapable fact of life.

A brief introduction to dictionary symbols will help you better use and understand most dictionaries. The system presented here (table A.1) is derived largely from the *Random House Dictionary, American Heritage Dictionary* and *Webster's New World Dictionary,* which are three superior and widely used dictionaries. There have been a few minor simplifications and changes. In each case, the IPA symbol is also listed. The comparison is interesting.

In most dictionaries, the principal accent of a word is indicated by a heavy mark (′) that is placed after the syllable that receives the greater stress. The secondary accent is indicated by a lighter mark (′) after a syllable.

In IPA transcription, the mark (ˋ) above the line and before a syllable indicates that this syllable receives the greater stress. The mark (ˌ) below the line and before a syllable indicates that this syllable receives a lesser or weaker stress.

The following three words are transcribed with dictionary symbols and phonetic symbols:

	Dictionary Symbols	Phonetic Symbols
Mississippi	mis′i sip′ē	[ˌmɪsəˋsɪpɪ]
interpretation	in tûr′ pri tā′ shən	[ɪnˌtɝprɪˋteʃən]
desperado	des′ pə rä′ dō	[ˌdɛspəˋrado]

*A Pronouncing Dictionary of American English by John S. Kenyon and Thomas A. Knott uses phonetic symbols exclusively. No definitions. This dictionary has become the bible of many speech authorities. Even the Gospels, however, have been revised recently. The Kenyon and Knott work is more than a third of a century old and desperately in need of updating. It is, nevertheless, still a valuable dictionary.

Table A.1   Comparison of Dictionary and Phonetic Symbols

Dictionary Symbols	Key Word	Phonetic Symbols	Key Word
Consonants			
1. b	bib (bib)	[b]	bɪb
2. ch	church (chûrch)	[tʃ]	tʃɝtʃ
3. d	dud (dud)	[d]	dʌd
4. f	fife (fīf)	[f]	faɪf
5. g	gag (gag)	[g]	gæg
6. h	hope (hōp)	[h]	hop
7. hw	while (hwīl)	[hw]	hwaɪl
8. j	jig (jig)	[dʒ]	dʒɪg
9. k	cake (kāk)	[k]	kek
10. l	lull (lul)	[l]	lʌl
11. m	mate (māt)	[m]	met
12. n	nun (nun)	[n]	nʌn
13. ŋ/ng	ring (riŋ)	[ŋ]	rɪŋ
14. p	pipe (pīp)	[p]	paɪp
15. r	rip (rip)	[r]	rɪp
16. s	sass (sas)	[s]	sæs
17. sh	shall (shal)	[ʃ]	ʃæl
18. t	tot (tot)	[t]	tɑt
19. th (voiceless)	thin (thin)	[θ]	θɪn
20. t̸h̸ (voiced)	t̸h̸en (then)	[ð]	ðɛn
21. v	vat (vat)	[v]	væt
22. w	won (wun)	[w]	wʌn
23. y	yell (yel)	[j]	jɛl
24. z	zip (zip)	[z]	zɪp
25. zh	azure (azh′ər)	[ʒ]	ˋæʒɚ

(Continued on next page)

Dictionary Symbols	Key Word	Phonetic Symbols	Key Word
Vowels and Diphthongs			
1. a	at (at)	[æ]	æt
2. ā	way (wā)	[e]	we
3. â	hare (hâr)	[ɛ, æ]	hɛr, hær
4. ä	calm (käm)	[ɑ]	kɑm
5. e	let (let)	[ɛ]	lɛt
6. ē	eat (ēt)	[i]	it
7. ê	dear (dêr, dēr)	[i]	dir
8. i	is (iz)	[ɪ]	ɪz
9. ī	ice (īs)	[ɑɪ]	ɑɪs
10. o	odd (od)	[ɑ]	ɑd
11. ō	ode (ōd)	[o]	od
12. ô	dawn (dôn)	[ɔ]	dɔn
13. oi	oil (oil)	[ɔɪ]	ɔɪl
14. o͞o	too (to͞o)	[u]	tu
15. o͝o	book (book)	[ʊ]	bʊk
16. ou	cow (kou)	[ɑʊ]	kɑʊ
17. u	cup (kup)	[ʌ]	kʌp
18. û	burn (bûrn)	[ɝ]	bɝn
19. ə	about (əbout′)	[ə]	ə`bɑʊt
	violent (vī′ələnt)		`vɑɪələnt
	sanity (san′ətē)		`sænətɪ
	comply (kəmplī′)		kəm`plɑɪ
	rumpus (rum′pəs)		`rʌmpəs
	little (lit′əl)		`lɪtl̩
	pardon (pär′dən)		`pɑrdn̩
	tire (tīər)		tɑɪr

PRONUNCIATION AND VOCABULARY LISTS

The word lists, which follow this section, contain words that are quite commonly mispronounced. Most of the mispronunciations result from one or more reasons.

In the following examples dictionary pronunciations are unbracketed—unbrak´ ətəd—and phonetic transcriptions are bracketed [ˈbrækətəd]:

■ Substitution of One Sound for Another Sound

Chef is not pronounced the way it looks. It is often mispronounced with the substitution of a *ch* sound for the correct *sh*.

Nonstandard:	chef	[tʃɛf]
Standard:	shef	[ʃɛf]

■ Omission of a Sound

Arctic is often mispronounced because the third sound is omitted.

Nonstandard:	är′tik	[ˈartɪk]
Standard:	ärk′tik	[ˈarktɪk]

■ Addition of a Sound

Escape is often mispronounced with the insertion of an extra sound.

Nonstandard:	ekskāp′	[ɛksˋkep]
Standard:	əskāp′	[əˋskep]

■ Misplaced Stress

Abyss is often mispronounced with the stress incorrectly placed on the first syllable.

Nonstandard:	ab′əs	[ˋæbəs]
Standard:	əbis′	[əˋbɪs]

■ Reversal of Two Sounds

Larynx is commonly mispronounced because the *yn* is reversed to *ny*.

Nonstandard:	lar′niks	[ˋlærnɪks]
Standard:	lar′iŋks	[ˋlærɪŋks]

Sometimes, of course, persons may pronounce a certain word correctly, but use it incorrectly in their speech. For example, *guile* (trickery, deception) is pronounced correctly by most people: gīl. However, many of these same people do not always correctly use the word *guile* as a noun. Instead, they use *guile* as an adjective.

Incorrect:	Henry VIII was a guile ruler.
Correct:	Henry VIII was a ruler who practiced guile.

Obviously, then, pronunciation and usage cannot be completely divorced from each other. An expressive and flexible vocabulary, not to mention correct pronunciation, is the mark of an educated and refined person.

Practice the words in the lists that follow. Consult a reputable dictionary for definitions. Use the words in spoken as well as written English.

Please Note: Some words have more than one standard pronunciation. In the word lists, however, only one is given. Dictionary symbols and phonetic symbols in separate columns indicate each standard pronunciation.

LIST A

The words in the following list are most frequently mispronounced because **one sound is substituted for another.** Practice the list until you have mastered it.

Words	Dictionary Symbols	Phonetic Symbols
1. ad infinitum	ad in′ fə nī′ təm	ˈæd͵ɪnfəˈnaɪtəm
2. agile	aj′ əl	ˈædʒəl
3. alma mater	äl′mə mä′tər	ˈɑlmə ˈmatɚ
4. amphetamine	am fet′ ə mēn	æmˈfɛtəˌmin
5. androgynous	an droj′ ə nəs	ænˈdradʒənəs
6. anesthetist	ə nes′ thə tist	əˈnɛsθətɪst
7. aphrodisiac	af′ rə diź iak	æfrəˈdɪzɪ æk
8. architect	är′ kə tekt	ˈɑrkəˌtɛkt
9. aria	är′ i ə	ˈɑrɪə
10. attaché	at′ ə shā′	͵ætəˈʃe
11. avant-garde	ə vänt′ gärd′	əˈvantˈgard
12. Beethoven	bā′ tō vən	ˈbetovən
13. beige	bāzh	beʒ
14. bestial	bes′ chəl	ˈbɛstʃəl
15. blasé	blä zā′	blaˈze
16. blatant	blāt′ nt	ˈbletn̩t
17. bona fide	bō′nə fīd′	ˈbonə ˈfaɪd
18. brevity	brev′ə ti	ˈbrɛvəti
19. cache	kash	kæʃ
20. catharsis	kə thär′ səs	kə ˈθɑrsəs
21. censure	sen′ shər	ˈsɛnʃɚ
22. chameleon	kə mēl′ yən	kə ˈmiljən
23. charade	shə rād′	ʃəˈred
24. charisma	kə riz′ mə	kə ˈrɪz mə
25. charlatan	shär′ lə tən	ˈʃarlətn̩
26. chasm	kaz′ əm	ˈkæzəm
27. chauvinism	shō′ və niz′ əm	ˈʃovənˌɪzəm
28. chef	shef	ʃɛf
29. chic	shēk	ʃik
30. Chopin	shō′ pan	ˈʃopæn
31. chutzpah	kho͝ot′ spə	ˈkhʊtspə
32. coiffure	kwä fyo͝or′	kwa ˈfjur

Words	Dictionary Symbols	Phonetic Symbols
33. coma	kō′ mə	ˈkomə
34. comely	kum′ li	ˈkʌmli
35. complacent	kəm plā′ sənt	kəm ˈplesn̩t
36. congratulate	kən grach′ ə lāt	kənˈgrætʃə͵ let
37. conjecture	kən jek′ chər	kənˈdʒɛktʃɚ
38. connoisseur	kon′ ə sûr′	kanəˈsɝ
39. copious	kō′ pi əs	ˈkopɪəs
40. crux	kruks	krʌks
41. cuisine	kwi zēn′	kwɪˈzin
42. data	dā′ tə	ˈdetə
43. deaf	def	dɛf
44. debauched	di bôcht′	dɪˈbɔtʃt
45. deluxe	də lŏoks′	dəˈluks
46. demise	di mīz′	dɪˈmaɪz
47. détente	dā tänt′	deˈtɑnt
48. diary	dī′ ə rē	ˈdaɪəri
49. discretion	di skresh′ ən	dɪˈskrɛʃən
50. disheveled	di shev′ əld	dɪˈʃɛvl̩d
51. docile	dos′ əl	ˈdasl̩
52. echelon	esh′ ə lon′	ˈɛʃə͵lan
53. elite	i lēt′	iˈlit
54. ensemble	än säm′ bəl	ɑn ˈsɑmbl̩
55. entrée	än′ trā	ˈɑntre
56. et cetera	et set′ ər ə	ɛt ˈsɛtərə
57. euphoria	yŏo fôr′ i ə	juˈfɔriə
58. exorcise	ek′ sôr sīz	ˈɛksɔr͵saɪz
59. facade	fə säd′	fəˈsad
60. facetious	fə sē′ shəs	fəˈsiʃəs
61. faux pas	fō pä′	ˈfo ˈpɑ
62. filet mignon	fi lā′ min yon′	fɪ ˈle mɪn ˈjɔn
63. fungi	fun′ jī	ˈfʌndʒaɪ
64. futile	fyŏot′l	ˈfjutl̩
65. garrulous	gar′ə ləs	ˈgærələs
66. geisha	gā′ shə	ˈgeʃə
67. genuine	jen′yŏo ən	ˈdʒɛnjuən

Words	Dictionary Symbols	Phonetic Symbols
68. gesture	jes′ chər	ˋdʒɛstʃɚ
69. giblet	jib′ lət	ˋdʒɪblət
70. gigantic	jīgan′ tik	dʒaɪ ˋgæntɪk
71. gist	jist	dʒɪst
72. guarantee	gar ən tē′	ˌgærən ˋti
73. habituate	hə bich′ oͅo āt	hə ˋbɪtʃuͅ ˌet
74. handkerchief	haŋ′ kər chif	ˋhæŋkɚtʃɪf
75. harbinger	här′ bən jər	ˋharbəndʒɚ
76. hearth	härth	harθ
77. height	hīt	haɪt
78. heinous	hā′ nəs	ˋhenəs
79. hirsute	hûr′ so͢ot	ˋh ɝ sut
80. homage	hom′ ij	ˋhamɪdʒ
81. homicide	hom′ ə sīd	ˋhamə ˌsaɪd
82. hostage	hos′ tij	ˋhastɪdʒ
83. indict	in dīt′	ɪn ˋdaɪt
84. inflammable	in flam′ ə bəl	ɪn ˋflæməbl̩
85. Italian	i tal′ yən	ɪ ˋtæljən
86. italics	i tal′ iks	ɪ ˋtælɪks
87. kitsch	kich	kɪtʃ
88. laconic	lə kon′ ik	lə ˋkanɪk
89. laissez-faire	les′ ā fâr′	ˌlɛse ˋfɛr
90. latent	lāt′ nt	ˋletn̩t
91. lingerie	län′zhə rā′	ˋlanʒə ˌre
92. longevity	lon jev′ ə ti	lanˋdʒɛvəti
93. macho	mä ′chō	ˋmatʃo
94. malignant	mə lig′ nənt	mə ˋlɪgnənt
95. malinger	mə liŋ′ gər	mə ˋlɪŋgɚ
96. martial	mär′shəl	ˋmarʃəl
97. masochist	mas′ ə kist	ˋmæsə ˌkɪst
98. massage	mə säzh′	mə ˋsaʒ
99. memento	mə men′ tō	mə ˋmɛnto
100. microscopic	mī′ krə skop′ ik	ˌmaɪkrə ˋskapɪk
101. Mozart	mō′ tsärt	ˋmotsart
102. negligee	neg′ lə zhā′	ˌnɛglə ˋʒe

Words	Dictionary Symbols	Phonetic Symbols
103. niche	nich	nɪtʃ
104. obesity	ō bē′ sə ti	oˈbisətɪ
105. ogle	ō′ gəl	ˈogl̩
106. orgy	ôr′ji	ˈɔrdʒɪ
107. pantomime	pan′ tə mīm	ˈpæntəˌmaɪm
108. pathos	pā′ thos	ˈpeθas
109. persona non grata	pər sō′ nə non grät′ ə	pɚ ˈsonə nan ˈgratə
110. pique	pēk	pik
111. pitcher	pich′ ər	ˈpɪtʃɚ
112. placard	plak′ ärd	ˈplækard
113. placid	plas′ əd	ˈplæsəd
114. plagiarism	plā′ jə riz əm	ˈpledʒəˌrɪzəm
115. poignant	poin′ yənt	ˈpɔɪnjənt
116. portentous	pôr ten′ təs	por ˈtɛntəs
117. posthumous	pos′ chə məs	ˈpastʃəməs
118. precocious	pri kō′ shəs	prɪ ˈkoʃəs
119. pretentious	pri ten′ shəs	prɪ ˈtɛnʃəs
120. prima donna	prē′ mə don′ə	primə ˈdanə
121. pronunciation	prə nun′si ā′ shən	prə nʌnsɪ ˈeʃən
122. propitiate	prə pish′ i āt	prə ˈpɪʃɪ et
123. psychosis	sī kō′ sis	saɪ ˈkosɪs
124. puberty	pyoo′ bər ti	ˈpjubɚtɪ
125. pugilist	pyoo′ jə list	ˈpjudʒəˌlɪst
126. recalcitrant	ri kal′ si trənt	rɪˈkælsɪtrənt
127. regalia	ri gāl′ yə	rɪ ˈgeljə
128. regime	rə zhēm′	rə ˈʒim
129. renege	ri nig′	rɪ ˈnɪg
130. robot	rō′ bət	ˈrobət
131. rudiment	roo′ də mənt	ˈrudəmənt
132. ruthless	rooth′ ləs	ˈruθləs
133. sadist	sād′ ist	ˈsedɪst
134. sagacious	sə gā′ shəs	sə ˈgeʃəs
135. salient	sāl′ yənt	ˈseljənt
136. savory	sā′ və ri	ˈsevərɪ
137. schizophrenia	skit′ sə frē′ ni ə	skɪtsə ˈfrinɪə

Words	Dictionary Symbols	Phonetic Symbols
138. slovenly	sluv′ ən li	ˋslʌvənlɪ
139. strength	streŋkth	strɛŋkθ
140. suave	swäv	swɑv
141. suite	swēt	swit
142. surrogate	sûr′ ə gāt	ˋsɝəˌget
143. taciturn	tas′ ə tûrn	ˋtæsəˌtɚn
144. Tchaikovsky	chī kôf′ski	tʃaɪˋkɔfskɪ
145. titular	tich′ ə lər	ˋtɪtʃələ˞
146. unscathed	un skāᵗʰd′	ʌn ˋskeðd
147. vagrant	vā′grənt	ˋvegrənt
148. verbatim	vər bā′təm	vɚˋbetəm
149. vicarious	vī kâr i əs	vaɪˋkɛrɪəs
150. virile	vir′ əl	ˋvɪrəl
151. visa	vē′zə	ˋvizə
152. Wagner (composer)	väg′ nər	ˋvɑgnɚ
153. zoology	zō ol′ ə ji	zoˋalədʒɪ

LIST B

The words in this list are most frequently mispronounced because **one or more sounds have been omitted.** Practice the list until you have mastered it.

Words	Dictionary Symbols	Phonetic Symbols
1. accelerate	ak sel′ ə rāt	æk ˋsɛləˌret
2. accessory	ak ses′ ə ri	æk ˋsɛsərɪ
3. Arctic	ärk′ tik	ˋɑrktɪk
4. asphyxiate	as fik′ si āt	æs ˋfɪksɪet
5. banquet	baŋ′ kwit	ˋbæŋkwɪt
6. berserk	bər sûrk′	bɚˋsɝk
7. Caribbean	kar′ə bē′ ən	ˌkærəˋbiən
8. champion	cham′ pi ən	ˋtʃæmpɪən
9. correct	kə rekt′	kə ˋrɛkt

Words	Dictionary Symbols	Phonetic Symbols
10. couldn't	kŏŏd′ nt	ˋkʊdnt
11. environment	en vī′ rən mənt	ɛn ˋvaɪrənmənt
12. February	feb′ rŏŏ er i	ˋfɛbru ɛrɪ
13. figure	fig′ yər	ˋfɪgjɚ
14. forte (music)	fôr′ tā	ˋforte
15. hierarchy	hī′ ə rär ki	ˋhaɪər arkɪ
16. idiosyncrasy	id′ i ə sin′ krə si	ɪdɪə ˋsɪn krə sɪ
17. length	leŋkth	lɛŋkθ
18. library	lī′ brer i	ˋlaɪ brɛrɪ
19. meticulous	mə tik′ yə ləs	mə ˋtɪkjələs
20. naïve	nä ēv′	naˋiv
21. particularly	pər tik′ yə lər li	pɚ ˋtɪkjələˑlɪ
22. picture	pik′ chər	ˋpɪktʃɚ
23. poem	pō′ əm	ˋpoəm
24. probably	prob′ ə bli	ˋprabəblɪ
25. quiet	kwī′ ət	ˋkwaɪət
26. quixotic	kwik sot′ ik	kwɪks ˋatɪk
27. recognize	rek′ əg nīz	ˋrɛkəg ˌnaɪz
28. repertoire	ˈrep′ ər twär	ˋrɛpɚ ˌtwɑr
29. sanguine	saŋ′ gwin	ˋsæŋ gwɪn
30. scrupulous	skrŏŏ′ pyə ləs	ˋskrupjələs
31. surprise	sər prīz′	sɚˋpraɪz
32. temperature	tem′ pər ə chər	ˋtɛmpɚˑətʃɚ
33. twenty	twen′ ti	ˋtwɛntɪ
34. ubiquitous	yŏŏ bik′ wə təs	juˋbɪkwətəs
35. vice versa	vī′ sə vûr′sə	ˋvaɪsə ˋvɝˑsə
36. wouldn't	wŏŏd′nt	ˋwʊdn̩t

LIST C

The words in this list are most frequently mispronounced because **one or more sounds have been added.** Practice the list until you have mastered it.

Words	Dictionary Symbols	Phonetic Symbols
1. accompanist	ə kum′ pə nist	əˈkʌmpənɪst
2. across	ə kros′	əˈkrɔs
3. ambidextrous	am′ bə dek′ strəs	ˌæmbəˈdɛkstrəs
4. anonymous	ə non′ ə məs	əˈnɑnəməs
5. athlete	ath′ lēt	ˈæθlit
6. athletics	ath let′ iks	æθˈlɛtɪks
7. attacked	ə takt′	əˈtækt
8. business	biz′ nis	ˈbɪznɪs
9. clique	klēk	klik
10. column	kol′ əm	ˈkɑləm
11. corps	kôr	kor
12. disastrous	di zas′ trəs	dɪzˈæstrəs
13. drowned	dround	draʊnd
14. escape	ə skāp′	əˈskep
15. extraordinary	ek strôr′ də neri	ɛkˈstrɔrdn ɛrɪ
16. forte (strong point)	fôrt	fort
17. gaffe	gaf	gæf
18. grievous	grē′ vəs	ˈgrivəs
19. heir	âr	ɛr
20. hors d'oeuvres	ôr dûrvz′	ɔr ˈdɝvz
21. hurricane	hûr′ ə kān	ˈhɝə ˌken
22. Illinois	il ə noi′	ˌɪləˈnɔɪ
23. momentous	mō men′ təs	moˈmɛntəs
24. monstrous	mon′ strəs	ˈmɑnstrəs
25. nuclear	nōō′ kli ər	ˈnuklɪɚ
26. often	of′ ən	ˈɔfən
27. once	wuns	wʌns
28. pedantic	pə dan′ tik	pəˈdæntɪk
29. psalm	säm	sɑm
30. righteous	rī′ chəs	ˈraɪtʃəs
31. schism	siz′ əm	ˈsɪzəm
32. scintillate	sin′ t'l āt	ˈsɪntl̩ et

Words	Dictionary Symbols	Phonetic Symbols
33. scion	sī′ ən	ˈsɑɪən
34. statistics	stə tis′ tiks	stəˈtɪstɪks
36. sword	sôrd	sord
37. tremendous	tri men′ dəs	trɪˈmɛndəs

LIST D

The words in this list are frequently mispronounced because of **misplaced syllable stress** (also described as placing the accent on the wrong syllable). Practice the list until you have mastered it.

Words	Dictionary Symbols	Phonetic Symbols
1. abdomen	ab′də mən	ˈæbdəmən
2. aberrant	ab er′ ənt	aˈbɛrənt
3. admirable	ad′mər ə bəl	ˈædmərəbl̩
4. affluent	af′lŏŏ ənt	ˈæfluənt
5. alias	ā′ li əs	ˈeliəs
6. alienate	āl′ yə nāt	ˈeljənˌet
7. altruism	al′ trŏŏ iz əm	ˈæltruˌɪzəm
8. ambiguous	am big′ yŏŏ əs	æmˈbɪgjuəs
9. amicable	am′ ə kə bəl	ˈæməkəbl̩
10. auspices	ô′ spi siz	ˈɔspɪsɪz
11. autopsy	ô′ top si	ˈɔtɑpsɪ
12. barbarous	bär′ bər əs	ˈbarbərəs
13. bravado	brə vä′ dō	brəˈvado
14. cannabis	kan′ ə bəs	ˈkænəbəs
15. caricature	kar′ə kə chər	ˈkærəkətʃɚ
16. casualty	kazh′ ŏŏ əl ti	ˈkæʒuəltɪ
17. chagrin	shə grin′	ʃəˈgrɪn
18. clandestine	klan des′ tin	klænˈdɛstɪn
19. cliché	klē shā′	kliˈʃe
20. defense (football)	dē′ fens	ˈdifɛns
21. defense (military)	də fens′	dəˈfɛns
22. deluge	del′ yōōj	ˈdɛljudʒ
23. Detroit	di troit′	diˈtrɔɪt

Words	Dictionary Symbols	Phonetic Symbols
24. epitome	i pit′ə mē	ɪ ˈpɪtəmɪ
25. facile	fas′ əl	ˈfæsl̩
26. finance	fə nans′	fəˈnæns
27. formidable	fôr′ mə də bəl	ˈfɔrmədabl̩
28. gamut	gam′ ət	ˈgæmət
29. guitar	gi tär′	gɪ ˈtɑr
30. hallucinogen	hə loō′ sə nə jən	həˈlusənədʒən
31. horizon	hə rī′ zən	həˈrɑɪzn̩
32. ignominious	ig′ nə min′ i əs	ɪgnəˈmɪnɪəs
33. impious	im′ pi əs	ˈɪmpɪəs
34. impotence	im′ pə təns	ˈɪmpətəns
35. incomparable	in kom′ pər ə bəl	ɪn ˈkɑmpərəbl̩
36. infamous	in′ fə məs	ˈɪnfəməs
37. inquiry	in kwīr′i	ɪnˈkwɑɪrɪ
38. irreparable	i rep′ ər ə bəl	ɪˈrɛpərəbl̩
39. libido	li bē′ dō	lɪ ˈbido
40. magnanimous	mag nan′ ə məs	mægˈnænəməs
41. maintenance	mān′ tə nəns	ˈmentənəns
42. maniacal	mə nī′ ə kəl	məˈnɑɪəkl̩
43. medieval	mē′ di ē′ vəl	midɪˈivl̩
44. mischievous	mis′chə vəs	ˈmɪstʃəvəs
45. omnipotent	om nip′ ə tənt	ɑmˈnɪpətənt
46. periphery	pə rif′ ə ri	pəˈrɪfərɪ
47. perseverance	pûr′ sə vir′ əns	ˌpɝsəˈvɪrəns
48. phlegmatic	fleg mat′ ik	flɛgˈmætɪk
49. placebo	plə sē′ bō	pləˈsibo
50. police	pə lēs′	pəˈlis
51. preferable	pref′ ər ə bəl	ˈprɛfɚəbl̩
52. prelude	prel′ yoōd	ˈprɛljud
53. renaissance	ren′ə säns	ˌrɛnəˈsɑns
54. respite	res′ pit	ˈrɛspɪt
55. risqué	ris kā′	rɪsˈke
56. superfluous	soō pûr′ floō əs	suˈpɝfluəs
57. theater	thē′ ə tər	ˈθiətɚ
58. vehement	vē′ ə mənt	ˈviəmənt

LIST E

The words in this list are frequently mispronounced because **two or more sounds have been reversed.** Practice the list until you have mastered it.

Words	Dictionary Symbols	Phonetic Symbols
1. cavalry	kav′ əl ri	ˋkævḷ rɪ
2. dais	dā′ əs	ˋdeəs
3. entrepreneur	an′trə prə nûr′	ˌɑntrəprəˋnɝ
4. equanimity	ē′ kwə nim′ ə ti	ikwə ˋnɪmətɪ
5. graffiti	grə fē′ ti	grə ˋfitɪ
6. hundred	hun′ drəd	ˋhʌndrəd
7. introduction	in′ trə duk′ shən	ˌɪntrəˋdʌkʃən
8. irrelevant	i rel′ ə vənt	ɪ ˋrɛləvənt
9. larynx	lar′ iŋks	ˋlærɪŋks
10. perspiration	pûr′ spə rā′ shən	ˌpɝspəˋreʃən
11. prescription	pri skrip′ shon	priˋskrɪpʃən
12. prestige	pre stēzh′	prɛsˋtiʒ
13. prodigy	prod′ ə ji	ˋprɑdədʒɪ
14. professor	prə fes′ ər	prəˋfɛsɚ
15. solemnity	sə lem′ nə ti	sə ˋlɛmnətɪ
16. voluminous	və loo′ mə nəs	vəˋlumənəs

PRONUNCIATION LISTS

The 300 words you have studied in six categories are now listed again, not according to category, but simply alphabetized and divided into six lists.

Transcribe each word with dictionary symbols, or transcribe the words phonetically, using the IPA. Then, construct sentences using the words correctly. As far as possible, try to incorporate the words into your vocabulary. Use them in conversation, writing or both as soon as you can. It's been said: *Use a word three times and it's yours.*

Use the lists for oral reviews or written assignments. "Doing" one list approximately every second or third week during the term is generally most convenient, and your instructor will recommend a specific time schedule.

NOTE: For those who prefer shorter lists, the 150 MOST frequently mispronounced words are marked with asterisks.

Pronunciation List 1

*1. abdomen

*2. aberrant

*3. accelerate

 4. accessory

*5. accompanist

*6. across

 7. ad infinitum

*8. admirable

 9. affluent

*10. agile

11. alias

12. alienate

*13. alma mater

14. altruism

15. ambidextrous

16. ambiguous

*17. amicable

*18. amphetamine

*19. androgynous

20. anesthetist

*21. anonymous

22. aphrodisiac

23. architect

*24. Arctic

25. aria

*26. asphyxiate

*27. athlete

*28. athletics

29. attaché

*30. attacked

31. auspices

*32. autopsy

33. avant-garde

34. banquet

*35. barbarous

36. Beethoven

37. beige

*38. berserk

*39. bestial

40. blasé

*41. blatant

*42. bona fide

43. bravado

44. brevity

45. business

*46. cache

*47. cannabis

48. Caribbean

49. caricature

50. casualty

Pronunciation List 2

  1. catharsis

 *2. cavalry

 *3. censure

  4. chagrin

 *5. chameleon

 *6. champion

  7. charade

  8. charisma

  9. charlatan

*10. chasm

 11. chauvinism

*12. chef

*13. chic

*14. Chopin

 15. chutzpah

*16. clandestine

 17. cliché

*18. clique

 19. coiffure

*20. column

*21. coma

*22. comely

 23. complacent

 24. congratulate

25. conjecture

*26. connoisseur

27. copious

28. corps

*29. correct

*30. couldn't

*31. crux

*32. cuisine

*33. dais

34. data

35. deaf

*36. debauched

37. defense (football)

38. defense (military)

*39. deluge

*40. deluxe

41. demise

42. détente

43. Detroit

44. diary

45. disastrous

46. discretion

*47. disheveled

*48. docile

*49. drowned

50. echelon

Pronunciation List 3

*1. elite

 2. ensemble

 3. entrée

 4. entrepreneur

*5. environment

 6. epitome

 7. equanimity

*8. escape

*9. et cetera

10. euphoria

11. exorcise

*12. extraordinary

13. facade

14. facetious

*15. facile

*16. faux pas

*17. February

*18. figure

19. filet mignon

20. finance

*21. formidable

22. forte (music)

23. forte (strong point)

*24. fungi

25. futile

26. gaffe

*27. gamut

*28. garrulous

*29. geisha

*30. genuine

*31. gesture

32. giblet

*33. gigantic

*34. gist

35. graffiti

*36. grievous

37. guarantee

38. guitar

39. habituate

*40. hallucinogen

41. handkerchief

42. harbinger

43. hearth

*44. height

*45. heinous

*46. heir

47. hierarchy

*48. hirsute

49. homage

*50. homicide

Pronunciation List 4

*1. horizon

*2. hors d'oeuvres

3. hostage

*4. hundred

5. hurricane

6. idiosyncrasy

*7. ignominious

8. Illinois

*9. impious

*10. impotence

*11. incomparable

12. indict

*13. infamous

14. inflammable

*15. inquiry

16. introduction

*17. irrelevant

*18. irreparable

19. Italian

20. italics

21. kitsch

22. laconic

23. laissez-faire

*24. larynx

*25. latent

*26. length

*27. libido

*28. library

29. lingerie

*30. longevity

31. macho

*32. magnanimous

*33. maintenance

34. malignant

35. malinger

36. maniacal

37. martial

*38. masochist

39. massage

*40. medieval

*41. memento

42. meticulous

43. microscopic

*44. mischievous

45. momentous

46. monstrous

47. Mozart

48. naïve

49. negligee

*50. niche

Pronunciation List 5

*1. nuclear

2. obesity

*3. often

*4. ogle

*5. omnipotent

6. once

*7. orgy

8. pantomime

9. particularly

*10. pathos

11. pedantic

12. periphery

*13. perseverance

*14. persona non grata

*15. perspiration

16. phlegmatic

*17. picture

*18. pique

*19. pitcher

20. placard

*21. placebo

22. placid

23. plagiarism

24. poem

*25. poignant

*26. police

*27. portentous

28. posthumous

29. precocious

*30. preferable

31. prelude

*32. prescription

33. prestige

34. pretentious

35. prima donna

*36. probably

37. prodigy

*38. professor

39. pronunciation

*40. propitiate

41. psalm

42. psychosis

43. puberty

*44. pugilist

45. quiet

*46. quixotic

47. recalcitrant

*48. recognize

49. regalia

*50. regime

Pronunciation List 6

1. renaissance

*2. renege

3. repertoire

*4. respite

5. righteous

6. risqué

7. robot

8. rudiment

*9. ruthless

*10. sadist

11. sagacious

*12. salient

13. sanguine

14. savory

*15. schism

16. schizophrenia

17. scintillate

*18. scion

19. scrupulous

20. slovenly

21. solemnity

*22. statistics

*23. strength

*24. suave

25. subtle

26. suite

*27. superfluous

*28. surprise

29. surrogate

30. sword

*31. taciturn

*32. Tchaikovsky

33. temperature

*34. theater

*35. titular

*36. tremendous

*37. twenty

38. ubiquitous

*39. unscathed

*40. vagrant

*41. vehement

42. verbatim

43. vicarious

*44. vice versa

*45. virile

46. visa

*47. voluminous

48. Wagner

*49. wouldn't

50. zoology

Practice List 1

Consonants are emphasized in the following. Transcribe the words in phonetic or dictionary symbols.

1. pie

2. been

3. hip

4. rub

5. tan

6. hot

7. den

8. hide

9. call

10. pick

11. get

12. mug

13. fight

14. life

15. vase

16. love

17. thin

18. both

19. them

20. bathe

21. ice

22. zest

23. is

24. cash

25. shun

Practice List 2

Consonants are emphasized in the following. Transcribe the words in phonetic or dictionary symbols.

1. crush

2. vision

3. rouge

4. hail

5. awry

6. chop

7. lurch

8. just

9. huge

10. my

11. exit

12. excel

13. sin

14. ring

15. dancing

16. which

17. whale

18. well

19. choir

20. yell

21. union

22. rope

23. fire

24. linger

25. pal

Practice List 3

Vowels and diphthongs are emphasized in the following. Transcribe the words in phonetic or dictionary symbols.

1. beet

2. bit

3. ale

4. bed

5. and

6. palm

7. all

8. tea

9. pail

10. raw

11. farm

12. bad

13. tin

14. fell

15. goat

16. look

17. phone

18. put

19. Ida

20. spoon

21. bin

22. duck

23. ahead

24. tube

25. psalm

Practice List 4

Vowels and diphthongs are emphasized in the following. Transcribe the words in phonetic or dictionary symbols.

1. mayor

2. bird

3. urgent

4. perform

5. eye

6. bout

7. toil

8. side

9. coy

10. louse

11. cow

12. cruel

13. gone

14. petty

15. two

16. yore

17. cough

18. gabby

19. hawk

20. wow

21. urn

22. poem

23. off

24. cute

25. loss

Practice Material 5

The following material contains all of the sounds in the English language. Transcribe into phonetic or dictionary symbols.

1. If it is to be, it's up to me.

2. A harp is a piano after taxes.

3. Since I gave up hope, I feel much better.

4. Playboy: a plowboy with a Rolls-Royce.

5. Whose bread I eat, his song I sing.

6. Liar: one who tells an unpleasant truth.

7. I'm just a bug on the windshield of life.

8. What's one person's poison is another's pleasure.

9. To eat is human; to digest, divine.

10. It is not death; it is dying that alarms me.

11. To feel fit as a fiddle, you must tone down your middle.

12. One shabby camel carries the burdens of many donkeys.

13. When you play, play hard. When you work, don't play at all.

14.   It's hard to be so smart that the next minute can't fool you.

15.   I don't smoke, dip or chew, and I don't kiss the folks who do.

Practice Material 6

The following selection is printed in phonetic symbols. Write it out in orthographic spelling.

wʌn de ðə bɛr mɛt ðə faks hu kem ˈslɪŋkɪŋ əˈlɔŋ wɪθ ə strɪŋ ʌv fɪʃ hi hæd ˈstolən

ʍɛr dɪd ju gɛt ðoz æskt ðə bɛr

O aɪv bɛn aʊt ˈfɪʃɪŋ ænd kɔt ðɛm sɛd ðə faks

so ðə bɛr hæd ə maɪnd tə lɝn tə fɪʃ tu ænd bæd ðə faks tɛl hɪm haʊ hi wʌz tə sɛt əˈbaʊt ɪt

O ɪts ən ˈizi kræft fɔr ju ˈænsɚd ðə faks ænd sun lɝnd juv ˈonlɪ gat tə go əˈpan ðə aɪs kʌt ə hol ænd stɪk jur tel daʊn ˈɪntu ɪt ju mʌst hold ɪt ðɛr æz lɔŋ æz ju kæn jur nat tə maɪnd ɪf jur tel stɪŋz ə lɪtl̩ ðæts ʍɛn ðə fɪʃ baɪt ðə ˈlɔŋgɚ ju hold ɪt ðɛr ðə mor fɪʃ jul gɛt ænd ðɛn ɔl æt wʌns aʊt wɪθ ɪt ænd wɪθ ə krɔs pʊl ˈsaɪdwez ænd wɪθ ə strɔŋ pʊl tu

jes ðə bɛr dɪd æz ðə faks hæd sɛd ænd hɛld hɪz tel ə lɔŋ lɔŋ taɪm ɪn ðə hol tɪl ɪt wʌz fæst ˈfrozən ɪn ðɛn hi pʊld ɪt aʊt wɪθ ə ʃarp pʊl ænd ɪt snæpt ʃɔrt ɔf

ðæts ʍaɪ ðə bɛr goz əˈbaʊt wɪθ ə ˈstʌmpɪ tel tə ðɪs ˈvɛrɪ de

Practice Material 7

The following selection is printed in dictionary symbols. Write it out in orthographic spelling.

ə trav'ələr with ə dong'ki and ə hôrs, h$\overline{oo}$ kar'id mûr'chəndīz frum toun tə toun, wəz in thə hab'ət əv let'ing thə dong'ki kar'i ôl əv thə lōd.

wun hot dā ðə dong'ki wəz fē'ling kwīt wēk and sik, and shē begd thə hôrs tə kar'i sum əv thə lōd. "fôr," shē sed, "if ī hav tə kar'i ôl əv it tədā', ī am gō'ing tə kəlaps' fôr go͝od, but if y$\overline{oo}$ wil help mē kar'i pärt əv it, ī wil s$\overline{oo}$n get wel əgen' and then īl bē ā'bəl tə kar'i ôl."

but thə hôrs wəz ver'i proud and stub'ərn and sed that hē did'ənt wish tə bē both'ərd with thə kəm-plān'ingz əv ə mēr dong'ki. thə dong'ki jogd on in sī' ləns, but s$\overline{oo}$n, hwut with thə hev'i lōd, shē fel doun and dīd.

hwen this hap'ənd, thə mas'tər fas'ənd thə hōl lōd on thə hôrs and mād him kar'i thə de͝d dong'ki bəsīdz' az fär az thə nekst tan'əri.

thə môr'əl əv thə fā'bəl iz ob'viəs: ən unwil'ing pärt'nər iz hiz ōn und$\overline{oo}$'ing.

APPENDIX

VOICE AND SPEECH ANALYSIS CHARTS

Your Name _____   Your Subject's Name _____

Class or Section _____   Subject's Occupation _____

Date _____

Analysis Chart 1

1 = Excellent   **2** = Good   **3** = Fair   **4** = Passable   **5** = Poor

Overall Effectiveness:

Quality   1   2   3   4   5

Was the voice pleasant to listen to?

Comments: (If you check **Yes,** elaborate briefly. If you check **No,** give reasons. Follow this procedure below also.)

Articulation   1   2   3   4   5

Was the speech clear, distinct, and easy to understand?

Comments:

Loudness   1   2   3   4   5

Was the voice easily heard?

Comments:

Expressiveness   1   2   3   4   5

Was the voice varied and flexible?

Comments:

Unobtrusiveness and Appropriateness   1   2   3   4   5

Did the voice, speech, and pronunciation seem to be natural, unaffected, and generally
acceptable?

Comments:

Analysis Chart 2

1 = Excellent   **2** = Good   **3** = Fair   **4** = Passable   **5** = Poor

Overall Effectiveness:

Quality

Was the voice pleasant to listen to?

Comments: (If you check **Yes,** elaborate briefly. If you check **No,** give reasons. Follow this procedure below also.)

1   2   3   4   5

Articulation

Was the speech clear, distinct, and easy to understand?

Comments:

1   2   3   4   5

Loudness

Was the voice easily heard?

Comments:

1   2   3   4   5

Expressiveness

Was the voice varied and flexible?

Comments:

1   2   3   4   5

Unobtrusiveness and Appropriateness

Did the voice, speech, and pronunciation seem to be natural, unaffected, and generally acceptable?

Comments:

1   2   3   4   5

Your Name _____   Your Subject's Name _____

Class or Section _____   Subject's Occupation _____

Date _____

Analysis Chart 3

1 = Excellent   **2** = Good   **3** = Fair   **4** = Passable   **5** = Poor

Overall Effectiveness:

Quality
1   2   3   4   5

Was the voice pleasant to listen to?

Comments: (If you check **Yes,** elaborate briefly. If you check **No,** give reasons. Follow this procedure below also.)

Articulation
1   2   3   4   5

Was the speech clear, distinct, and easy to understand?

Comments:

Loudness
1   2   3   4   5

Was the voice easily heard?

Comments:

Expressiveness
1   2   3   4   5

Was the voice varied and flexible?

Comments:

Unobtrusiveness and Appropriateness
1   2   3   4   5

Did the voice, speech, and pronunciation seem to be natural, unaffected, and generally acceptable?

Comments:

Name _____

Class or Section _____

Date _____

Analysis Chart 4

Quality

Overall Effectiveness

1   2   3   4   5

(Check applicable terms)

Breathy _____   Nasal _____

Glottal shock _____   Denasal _____

Strident _____   Throaty _____

Harsh _____   Hoarse _____

Vocal Fry _____

Articulation

1   2   3   4   5

General inaccuracy _____

Sounds omitted or dropped _____

Sounds substituted _____

Sounds added _____

Loudness

1   2   3   4   5

Too loud _____   Unvaried _____

Too soft _____   Lacks emphasis _____

Expressiveness

Overall Effectiveness

1   2   3   4   5

(Check applicable terms)

Pitch

Too high _____

Too low _____

Monotonous _____

Patterned _____

Rate

Too fast _____   Hesitant _____

Too slow _____   Jerky _____

Monotonous _____   Poor phrasing _____

Patterned _____   Lack of pauses _____

Unobtrusiveness and Appropriateness

1   2   3   4   5

Arty (overly precise articulation) _____

Affected pronunciation _____

Mispronunciation _____

Regional dialect _____

Foreign dialect _____

Overall Effectiveness

1   2   3   4   5

What is your best vocal attribute? _____

In which aspects of voice and speech do you need to make the most improvement? _____

Name _____

Class or Section _____

Date _____

Analysis Chart 5

	Overall Effectiveness		Overall Effectiveness

Quality   Overall Effectiveness   1 2 3 4 5

(Check applicable terms)

Breathy _____   Nasal _____

Glottal shock _____   Denasal _____

Strident _____   Throaty _____

Harsh _____   Hoarse _____

Vocal Fry _____

Articulation   1 2 3 4 5

General inaccuracy _____

Sounds omitted or dropped _____

Sounds substituted _____

Sounds added _____

Loudness   1 2 3 4 5

Too loud _____   Unvaried _____

Too soft _____   Lacks emphasis _____

Expressiveness   Overall Effectiveness   1 2 3 4 5

(Check applicable terms)

Pitch

Too high _____

Too low _____

Monotonous _____

Patterned _____

Rate

Too fast _____   Hesitant _____

Too slow _____   Jerky _____

Monotonous _____   Poor phrasing _____

Patterned _____   Lack of pauses _____

Unobtrusiveness and Appropriateness   1 2 3 4 5

Arty (overly precise articulation) _____

Affected pronunciation _____

Mispronunciation _____

Regional dialect _____

Foreign dialect _____

Overall Effectiveness

1 2 3 4 5

What is your best vocal attribute? _____

In which aspects of voice and speech do you need to make the most improvement? _____

Name _____

Class or Section _____

Date _____

Analysis Chart 6

Quality   Overall Effectiveness   1   2   3   4   5

(Check applicable terms)

Breathy _____	Nasal _____
Glottal shock _____	Denasal _____
Strident _____	Throaty _____
Harsh _____	Hoarse _____
Vocal Fry _____	

Articulation   1   2   3   4   5

General inaccuracy _____

Sounds omitted or dropped _____

Sounds substituted _____

Sounds added _____

Loudness   1   2   3   4   5

Too loud _____	Unvaried _____
Too soft _____	Lacks emphasis _____

Expressiveness   Overall Effectiveness   1   2   3   4   5

(Check applicable terms)

Pitch

Too high _____

Too low _____

Monotonous _____

Patterned _____

Rate

Too fast _____	Hesitant _____
Too slow _____	Jerky _____
Monotonous _____	Poor phrasing _____
Patterned _____	Lack of pauses _____

Unobtrusiveness and Appropriateness   1   2   3   4   5

Arty (overly precise articulation) _____

Affected pronunciation _____

Mispronunciation _____

Regional dialect _____

Foreign dialect _____

Overall Effectiveness

1   2   3   4   5

What is your best vocal attribute? _____

In which aspects of voice and speech do you need to make the most improvement? _____

Name _____

Class or Section _____

Date _____

VOICE QUALITY ANALYSIS CHART

Present material orally before the class or listen to a recording of your voice. If you listen to a recording, you may use the one you recorded at the beginning of the course, or you may make a new one. With the aid of your instructor and classmates, analyze your voice quality as candidly as possible. Use this chart as a guide.

Overall effectiveness

            1   2   3   4   5

If my voice quality needs improvement, the following term(s) most accurately describes the sound of my voice:

Breathy _____   Nasal _____

Glottal shock _____   Denasal _____

Strident _____   Throaty _____

Harsh _____   Hoarse _____

Vocal Fry _____

If my quality is unpleasant, it may be due to

Excessive tension _____   Inefficient breathing habits _____

Inadequate loudness _____   Improper pitch level _____

Lazy lips, jaw, and tongue _____   Tongue humping _____

Rigid jaw _____   Excessive relaxation of soft palate _____

Burying chin in neck _____

Do you think you possess personality traits that might contribute to undesirable voice quality? If so, what are they? (Be frank.)

Note any problems of health or hearing that might have a direct bearing on the quality of your voice.

Suggestions for improvement:

ARTICULATION ANALYSIS CHART

Present material orally before the class or listen to a recording of your voice. If you listen to a recording, you may use the one you recorded at the beginning of the course, or you may make a new one. With the aid of your instructor and classmates, analyze your articulation as candidly as possible. Use this chart as a guide.

Overall effectiveness:

         1   **2**   **3**   **4**   **5**

In general, my speech is

Clear, distinct, and accurate _____

Sluggish and indistinct _____

Overly precise _____

If my articulation is unsatisfactory, it may be due to

Sluggish tongue activity _____

Immobile lips _____

Inaccuracy of tongue position and movement _____

Rigid jaw _____

Inactive velum _____

Specific errors:

Sounds omitted in words (list examples and circle the sounds you dropped):

Sounds substituted in words such as _____

Sounds added in words such as _____

Sounds distorted in words such as _____

Sounds inadequate in words such as _____

Mispronunciation:
Foreign dialect:

Regional dialect:

Do you think you possess personality traits that might contribute to problems of articulation? If so, what are they? (Be frank.)

Note any problems of health or hearing that might have a direct bearing on your articulation:

Suggestions for improvement:

Name _____

Class or Section _____

Date _____

LOUDNESS ANALYSIS CHART

Present material orally before the class. With the aid of your instructor and classmates, analyze your loudness as candidly as possible. Use this chart as a guide.

Overall effectiveness:

                    1   2   3   4   5

In general, my voice is

Easily heard _____   Difficult to hear _____

If my loudness needs improvement, the following term or phrase most accurately describes my problem:

Too loud _____   Lacks emphasis and contrast _____

Too soft _____   Patterned _____

Unvaried _____

If my loudness is unsatisfactory, one or more of the following factors may be responsible:

Inadequate openness of mouth _____   Unsatisfactory voice quality _____

Improper pitch level _____   Sluggish articulation _____

Excessive muscular
  constrictions of throat _____   Insufficient
  energy and animation _____

Improper control
  of breath pressure _____   Too rapid rate of speaking _____

Do you think you possess personality traits that might contribute to problems of loudness? If so, what are they? (Be frank.)

Note any problems of health or hearing that might have a direct bearing on your loudness:

Suggestions for improvement:

VOICE EXPRESSIVENESS ANALYSIS CHART

Present material orally before the class or listen to a recording of your voice. If you listen to a recording, you may use the one you recorded at the beginning of the course, or you may make a new one. With the aid of your instructor and classmates, analyze your expressiveness as candidly as possible. Use this chart as a guide.

Overall effectiveness:

1   2   3   4   5

In general, my voice is

Varied and flexible _____   Unvaried and monotonous _____

If my vocal expressiveness needs improvement, the following terms or phrases most accurately describe my problem:

Pitch   **Rate**

Too high _____   Too fast _____   Hesitant _____

Too low _____   Too slow _____   Jerky _____

Monotonous _____   Monotonous _____   Poor phrasing _____

Patterned _____   Patterned _____   Lack of pauses _____

Excessive variation _____

_____

Personality factors are important in determining vocal variety. What traits do you think you possess that might be responsible for problems of expressiveness? (Be frank.)

Note any problems of health or hearing that might have a direct bearing on your vocal expressiveness:

Suggestions for improvement:

Name _____

Class or Section _____

Date _____

Final Oral Performance

Quality

Satisfactory improvement _____

Needs further improvement _____

Specific comments: _____

Articulation

Satisfactory improvement _____

Needs further improvement _____

Specific comments: _____

Loudness

Satisfactory improvement _____

Needs further improvement _____

Specific comments: _____

Expressiveness Pitch

Satisfactory improvement _____

Needs further improvement _____

Specific comments: _____

Rate

Satisfactory improvement _____

Needs further improvement _____

Specific comments: _____

Unobtrusiveness and Appropriateness

Satisfactory improvement _____

Needs further improvement _____

Specific comments: _____

Overall Effectiveness

1   2   3   4   5

In what aspect of voice and speech have you made the greatest improvement?

In what aspect of voice and speech do you most need to continue working for additional improvement?

GLOSSARY

Pronunciation is given for less familiar words. In each case the pronunciation is first written in dictionary symbols. The bracketed pronunciation that follows is written in phonetic symbols.

abdominal breathing ab däm′ ə nəl [æb´dɑm ə nḷ] A type of breathing that is regulated by controlled movements of the abdominal muscles. Most of the expansion-contraction activities occur in the abdominal area.

Adam's apple *See* thyroid cartilage.

accent The stress, or the degree of prominence, given to a syllable in a word or to a word in a phrase or sentence. The stressed syllable or word is made louder and is generally higher in pitch than adjacent syllables or words.

affricate af′ rə kit [´æfrə kɪt] A single consonant sound that results from a plosive and a fricative closely and rapidly blended. The underlined sounds are affricates: child, logic, jack.

alveolar ridge al vē′ ə lər [æl´vi ə lɚ] The gum ridge or the tissues behind the upper front teeth. The alveolar ridge is used in the underlined sounds: Tom, seem, raise, awl.

articulation Movements of the lips, the jaw, the tongue, and the velum (soft palate) to form, separate, and join speech sounds.

articulators The organs of speech used to produce speech sounds. The most important are the lips, the front teeth, the jaw, the tongue, and the velum.

arytenoid cartilage ar′ ə tē′ noid kärt′ lij [ˌærəˈti nɔɪdˈkɑrt lɪdʒ] A pair of small, pyramid-shaped, and movable cartilages to which the vocal folds are attached. They have to do with the opening and closing of the vocal folds.

assimilation Occurs when a sound in a word is changed or modified as the result of the influence or overlapping of neighboring sounds (for example: "Jeat?" for "Did you eat?")

assimilation nasality The tendency for the production of a vowel to be influenced by a preceding or following nasal consonant [m n ŋ] Example: Say "man" and "rap," and notice that the vowel in the first word has more nasality than the same vowel in the second word.

back vowels Vowel sounds produced when the back portion of the tongue is most active. The underlined sounds are back vowels: cool, look, obey, all, calm.

bilabial bi lā′ bi əl [bɑɪ´le bɪəl] Sounds produced by using the two lips. The underlined sounds are bilabials: pie, bit, Mac, won.

breathiness An excessive loss of breath while talking—as if the speaker were sighing or half-whispering. A fuzzy, feather-edged sound results.

cartilage kärt′ lij [´kɑrtḷɪdʒ] A firm but flexible tissue related to bone. Gristle.

central (middle) vowels Vowel sounds produced when the middle portion of the tongue is most active. The underlined sounds are central vowels: dirt, never, idea, but.

clavicular breathing klə vik′ yə lər [klə ´vɪk jə lɚ] A type of breathing in which most of the movement consists of raising and lowering the collarbones (clavicles) while inhaling and exhaling.

clusters Two or more consonants side-by-side in the same syllable, with no vowel between them. The underlined sounds are clusters: drink, streak, cram, groan, trout, thrill.

consonant A sound that can be made either by stopping the breath, making it explode, or making it buzz or hum. There are about twenty-five consonants in American English. The underlined sounds represent a few of them: up, lie, raw, on, the, woe, buy, aggie.

cricoid cartilage krī′ koid [´krɑɪ kɔɪd] The signet-ring-shaped cartilage in the lower and back portion of the larynx. It forms a base, or foundation, for the rest of the larynx.

decibel des′ ə bel [´dɛs ə ˌbɛl] A unit that expresses the relative intensity of sounds or sound waves.

denasality dē′ nā zal′ ə tē [ˌdine ´zælə ti] Negative or inadequate nasality resulting in a voice that sounds as if the speaker has a stuffed-up nose. "Mining" becomes "bidig"; "thing" becomes "thig"; "hand" becomes "had."

diacritical marking system (DMS) *See* dictionary symbol.

dialect A form of a language differing from other varieties of the same language. A dialect is used by a group of speakers who are set apart, geographically or socially, from others who speak the language.

diaphragm dī′ ə fram [´dɑɪə fræm] A tough, double-domed muscle that separates the chest and abdominal cavities. It is the main muscle of breathing.

diction Refers to accuracy and clarity of speech. For all practical purposes, the word has the same meaning as *articulation* or *enunciation*. (In another sense it means the choice of words in speaking and the accuracy with which they are used.)

dictionary symbol The Diacritical Marking System or the DMS mark or symbol accompanying a letter, as in ēt (cat), ôr (or), käm (calm), o͝o (took), which indicates the pronunciation of the letter's sound.

diphthong dif′ thông [ˋdɪf θɔŋ] A rapid blending together of two vowel sounds within the same syllable. The first vowel element receives greater stress than the second vowel element. The underlined sounds are diphthongs: f<u>i</u>ve, j<u>oi</u>n, s<u>ou</u>th.

drone A speaker whose words or sentences are continually pitched at, or very near, one sound level. A dull, monotonous speaker.

duration The length or amount of sound: how long a sound is held.

eastern dialect A form of American English, which differs from other varieties of the same language and which is heard primarily in the Eastern United States.

emphasis The degree of prominence given to a syllable, a word, or a phrase.

enunciation i nun′ sē ā′ shən [ɪ ˌnʌn si ˋeʃə n] Accuracy and clarity of speech.

exhalation The expelling of air from the lungs.

extrinsic muscles ek strin′ sik [ɛk ˋstrɪn sɪk] Those muscles that are concerned with movements of the larynx as a whole, as in swallowing.

frequency The number of vibrations per second of a sound.

fricative frik′ ə tiv [ˋfrɪk ə tɪv] A frictionlike sound produced when the outgoing breath stream is partially obstructed. The underlined sounds are fricatives: <u>s</u>it, <u>z</u>ap, <u>f</u>in, <u>v</u>im, <u>th</u>in, <u>th</u>us, <u>sh</u>y, rou<u>g</u>e, <u>h</u>ot.

front vowels Vowel sounds produced when the front portion of the tongue is most active. The underlined sounds are front vowels: b<u>e</u>, <u>i</u>t, r<u>a</u>te, b<u>e</u>g, <u>a</u>sk.

fundamental pitch A tone produced by the overall vibration of the vocal folds, which is recognized as the basic pitch of the tone.

general American dialect A form of American English, which differs from other varieties of the same language and which is heard primarily in the Midwest (as far south as the Mason-Dixon line), in the West, and in parts of the Southwest.

glide A consonant sound in which the articulators move or glide from one position to another. The underlined sounds are glides: <u>w</u>in, <u>l</u>ake, <u>r</u>ope, <u>y</u>et.

glottal shock glät′l [ˋglɑtl] A raspy little bark or a sharp click or pop on vowel sounds, which may result from extremely tense vocal folds.

glottis glät′ əs [ˋglɑt əs] The space or opening between the vocal folds.

habitual pitch level həbich′oo əl [hə ˋbɪtʃʊəl] The pitch level most frequently used by an individual. The pitch may rise or fall, but the person's speech most often returns to this level.

hard palate pal′ it [ˋpælɪt] The dome-shaped, bony roof of the mouth.

harsh A rough, raspy, gravelly, and possibly low-pitched voice quality, which may result from abnormal vibrations of the vocal folds or excessive tensions within the larynx.

hoarse A harsh, raw, and strained voice quality that may also be somewhat breathy. It sounds as though the speaker has a sore throat.

hyoid bone hī′ oid [ˋhɑ ɪɔɪd] A horseshoe-shaped, free-floating bone of the neck. The larynx is extended from this bone; the muscles of the jaw and tongue are attached to it.

hypertension Excessive or extreme tension.

inflection in flek′ shən [ɪn ˋflɛk ʃən] A pitch change that occurs within a single, uninterrupted, vocal tone or sound. An inflection may be described as rising, falling, or circumflex (a combination of rising and falling).

inhalation The drawing of breath into the lungs.

International Phonetic Alphabet (IPA) An alphabet that uses a special set of symbols to represent the sounds of language. Each symbol represents one sound. The underlined sounds in the following words are shown with their IPA equivalents: <u>th</u>e = ð; e<u>gg</u> = ɛ; ic<u>er</u> = ɚ; si<u>ng</u>= ŋ; su<u>ch</u> = tʃ; c<u>a</u>t = æ; <u>u</u>p = ʌ.

intonation in′ tə nā′ shən [ˌɪntə ˋne ʃən] The overall pattern or melody of pitch changes in phrases or sentences.

intrinsic muscles in trin′ sik [ɪn ˋtrɪn sɪk] Relatively tiny muscles attached entirely to various points within the larynx itself. They are directly concerned with the process of making speech sounds.

key The general pitch level—ranging anywhere from high to low—that is used at any given moment in talking or reading.

labial lā′ biəl [ˋle biəl] Pertaining to the lips.

labiodental lā′ biō den′ t′l [ˋlebiō ˋden tl̩] Consonant sounds that are produced by placing the lower lip against the upper teeth. The underlined sounds are labiodentals: <u>f</u>og, <u>v</u>at.

larynx lar′ ingks [ˋlærɪŋks] The voice box. The structure for producing voice. It includes the vocal bands, and it is the uppermost part of the trachea.

lingua-alveolar ling′ gwə əl vē′ ə lər [ˋlɪŋ wə æl ˋvi ə lər] Sounds that are produced with the tongue touching or near the gum ridge. The underlined sounds are lingua-alveolars: <u>h</u>it, <u>d</u>o, li<u>p</u>, <u>s</u>o, ja<u>zz</u>, <u>n</u>ick.

linguadental Sounds that are produced by placing the tip of the tongue against the upper front teeth. The underlined sounds are linguadentals: <u>th</u>in, <u>th</u>ey.

linguapalatal ling′ gwə pal′ ət′l [ˋlɪŋgwə ˋpælət l̩] Sounds that are produced with the tip or the blade of the tongue on or near the hard palate. The underlined sounds are linguapalatals: <u>sh</u>all, plea<u>s</u>ure, <u>y</u>et, <u>r</u>ock.

lingua-avelar ling′ gwə vē′ lər [ˋlɪŋ gwə ˋvi lər] Sounds that are produced by raising the back portion of the tongue against the soft palate or velum. The underlined sounds are linguavelars: <u>k</u>ill, <u>g</u>et, si<u>ng</u>.

loudness The power or intensity (sound level) of the vocal tone. Volume. Projection.

nasal Pertaining to the nose.

nasal consonants Consonants produced as the oral cavity is blocked off at some point, the velum is relaxed and lowered, and the breath stream is directed through the nose. The underlined sounds are nasals: hi<u>m</u>, <u>n</u>ot, ri<u>ng</u>.

nasality A nasal twang, as if talking through the n<u>o</u>se. The voice has a foghorn (and sometimes a whiny) sound.

optimum pitch level äp′ tə məm [ˋɑp tə məm] The most desirable and serviceable level of pitch for the individual speaker. It is the level at which a person can produce the best vocal quality and the loudest voice with the least effort.

oral cavity The mouth.

overtones Tones produced as the vocal folds vibrate in small parts or segments. Overtones are higher in pitch than the fundamental tone. *See also* fundamental pitch.

pause A period of silence. Pauses are used for expression (to achieve clarity, emphasis, meaning, contrast, and variety) and for taking breath.

pharynx far′ ingks [`færɪŋks] The throat.

phonation fō nā′ shən [fo `neʃən] Vocal tones or sounds produced by the vibration of the vocal folds as breath is forced between them.

phoneme fō′ nēm [`fo nim] The basic sound unit or sound family; a group of closely related sounds. The *t* sounds in t̲ip and pit̲ are not exactly alike, but are recognizable as member sounds of the phoneme *t*.

phonetic symbols *See* International Phonetic Alphabet (IPA).

phrase A group of words expressing a thought unit or an idea. A phrase need not be a complete sentence.

pitch The highness or lowness of a tone or a sound.

pitch pattern A fixed melody pattern of speech used over and over again.

plosive plō′ siv [`plo sɪv] A consonant sound made by blocking the outgoing airstream. The tongue is dropped or the lips opened suddenly, and the built-up air is released in a little explosion. The underlined sounds are plosives: p̲op̲, b̲ib̲, fit̲, hid̲, lak̲e, rug̲.

projection Controlled energy that gives impact, precision, and intelligibility to spoken sounds. Similar to *loudness, strength,* and *volume.*

pronunciation The correct production of word sounds in the right order without omissions or additions, and with appropriate stress on syllables.

quality The texture of a sound or a tone that distinguishes it from other tones having the same pitch, duration, and loudness.

rate The number of words spoken per minute: the fastness or slowness of speaking, which includes the quantity or duration of sounds and the lengths and number of pauses.

resonance rez′ ə nəns [`rɛz ə nəns] The process by which sounds produced at the vocal folds are amplified, modified, and enriched by the cavities of the head and chest.

resonators The main human resonators: the cavities of the mouth, throat, nose, and larynx (voice box).

respiration res′ pə rā′ shən [ˌres pə `reʃən] The inhalation and exhalation of air.

soft palate The velum: a soft, flexible, and muscular flap of tissue attached to the hard palate and located in the rearmost portion of the roof of the mouth.

southern dialect A form of American English that differs from other varieties of the same language and that is heard primarily in the states of the Old South. It is used as far west as Arkansas and in parts of Texas.

step An abrupt pitch change between words or syllables. A step is also known as a shift or a jump.

stress The degree of prominence given a syllable within a word or a word within a phrase or a sentence. The stressed syllable or word is made louder and is often higher in pitch than its neighbors.

strident strad′nt [`straɪd n̩t] A voice quality that is offensively metallic, tense, hard, and strained. It is often relatively high-pitched.

thorax thôr′ aks [`θɔr æks] The chest.

throaty A voice quality that is hollow, muffled, and dullish—voice-from-the-tomb quality, which is often relatively low-pitched.

thyroid cartilage thī′ roid [`θaɪ rɔɪd] The Adam's apple. The large, butterfly-shaped cartilage that rests upon the cricoid.

timbre tam′ bər [`tæmbɚ] The characteristic tone color or texture of a voice, regardless of pitch or loudness. Quality.

trachea trā′ kiə [`tre kɪə] The windpipe.

velum vē′ ləm [`vi ləm] *See* soft palate.

vocal folds Two small, tough bands of connective tissue located in the larynx. Voice is produced when the folds are set into vibration by the airstream from the lungs. Also known as vocal bands, vocal cords, or vocal lips.

vocal (glottal) fry A noisy, growling, or "bacon-frying" voice quality that closely resembles harshness. It usually occurs when the pitch of the voice is dropped at the end of a sentence.

voiced consonant A consonant on which the vocal folds vibrate. The underlined sounds are voiced: t̲he, d̲ip, a̲zure, o̲r, w̲ay, hi̲s, v̲ideo.

voiceless consonant A consonant on which the vocal folds do not vibrate. The underlined sounds are voiceless: t̲hick, p̲al, s̲hould, c̲at, c̲hin, s̲ill.

vowel A relatively open and continuous sound that is sonorous and free of friction noises. In normal utterance (nonwhispered speech) all vowels are voiced. They result from vocal tone created by the vibration of the vocal folds. There are about fifteen vowels in American English. The underlined sounds represent a few of them: b̲e, e̲nd, h̲a̲d, c̲u̲rl, c̲u̲p, fo̲o̲l, to̲o̲k, o̲ld, c̲a̲lm.

CREDITS

Line Art Credits

Chapter 5

Fig. 5.2: From Bloodstein, Oliver, *Speech Pathology: An Introduction.* © 1979, Houghton Mifflin Company.

Illustrator Credits

Chapter 2

Figs. 2.1, 2.2, 2.3, 2.4, 2.5, 2.6: Marcia Mayer

Text Credits

Chapter 1

p. Arnold E. Aronson. From *Clinical Voice Disorders.* Copyright 1985. Used by permission of the author.

Chapter 6

p. 155 Stephen E. Lucas. From *The Art of Public Speaking* by Stephen E. Lucas. Copyright 1983. Reprinted by permission of Random House, Inc.

Chapter 7

p. 182 Ann Landers. Reprinted by permission. © New America Syndicate./ p. 186 "Milgrig and the Tree Wilfs" (pp. 153–154) from *The Benchley Roundup* by Robert Benchley. Copyright 1932 by Robert Benchley. Reprinted by permission of Harper & Row, Publishers, Inc./ pp. 187 and 189 Clare Boothe. From *The Women.* Copyright 1938. Reprinted by permission of Random House, Inc./ pp. 187 and 189 Eugene O'Neill. From *Ah, Wilderness!* in *The Later Plays of Eugene O'Neill.* Reprinted by permission of Random House, Inc./ p. 188 John Van Druten. From *I Am a Camera.* Copyright 1952. Reprinted by permission of Random House, Inc./ p. 188 Neil Simon. From *Barefoot in the Park.* Copyright 1964. Reprinted by permission of Random House, Inc./ p. 188 Isobel Lennart and Bob Merrill. From *Funny Girl.* Copyright 1965. Reprinted by permission of Random House, Inc./ p. 188 Alan Lerner. From *Camelot.* Copyright 1960. Reprinted by permission of Random House, Inc./ pp. 188, 189, and 190 Lillian Hellman. From *The Children's Hour* and *The Little Foxes* in *Six Plays by Lillian Hellman.* Reprinted by permission of Random House, Inc./ p. 188 From *Gypsy.* © Copyright 1959, 1960 by Arthur Laurents, Gypsy Rose Lee, and Stephen Sondheim./ p. 189 Jerome Lawrence and Robert Edwin Lee. From *Inherit the Wind.* Copyright 1969. Reprinted by permission of Random House, Inc.

INDEX

53   100